STATICS

AND INTRODUCTION TO
STRENGTH OF MATERIALS

Steve M. Slaby
PRINCETON UNIVERSITY

and

Herbert I. Tyson
BRONX COMMUNITY COLLEGE OF
THE CITY UNIVERSITY OF NEW YORK

PROJECTIVE GRAPHICS—TECHNICAL
DESIGN AND ANALYSIS SERIES

STATICS

AND INTRODUCTION TO
STRENGTH OF MATERIALS

HARCOURT, BRACE & WORLD, Inc.

New York | Chicago | San Francisco | Atlanta

Library of Congress Catalog Card Number: 69-11482

Printed in the United States of America

Drawings by Bertrick Associate Artists, Inc.

PHOTO CREDITS:

figures 8.1, 8.10	From *An Introduction to Physical Metallurgy* by S. H. Avner, Copyright© 1964 by McGraw-Hill, Inc.
figures 8.2, 8.4a, 8.4b, 8.7	Courtesy of Tinius Olsen Testing Machine Company
figure 8.3	Courtesy of Wiedmann Division, The Warner & Swasey Company
figure 8.8	Courtesy of Detroit Testing Machine Company
figure 8.9	Courtesy of Wilson Instrument Division, American Chain & Cable Company, Inc.
figure 8.11	Courtesy of United States Steel Corporation
cover: *(left)*	Adelaide De Menil, Photo Researchers
(center)	Gita Lenz, DPI
(right)	F. B. Grunzweig, Photo Researchers

PREFACE

This book provides a thorough grounding in the branch of mechanics known as statics. It also includes basic topics in the study of strength of materials. The authors' combined teaching experiences —one in a university and the other in a community college—have converged in a design to meet the needs of students and instructors in technical institutes, community colleges, engineering schools, and universities. It is our conviction that a solid background in statics is an irreducible requisite to a student's understanding of any field of technology. The approach to statics is one of wide and concurrent utilization of both mathematical and graphical analyses.

In statics, the student must learn to grasp the physical realities of a problem and then bridge the gap between the physical or real model and the mathematical or symbolic model. To help the student do this, statements of basic principles have generally been presented mathematically and have then been followed by a graphical analysis. This double-barreled approach—graphical reinforcement of mathematical analysis and mathematical reinforcement of graphical analysis—gives the student an insight into the basic concepts and problem-solving techniques of this branch of mechanics.

Although most students show an affinity for one method of problem solving in preference to another, the dual approach used here provides many avenues of comprehension and fosters assimilation of both major methods of problem solving. For those with limited mathematical backgrounds, greater emphasis can be placed on the graphical techniques. In dealing with real problems, the engineer and the technician must learn to think not only in terms of mathematical symbols but also in terms of spatial relations. Graphics as presented here aids the mathematically inclined student to grasp a basic form of space thinking.

Because the authors feel that it is beneficial to develop a logical approach to problem solving and that repeated exposure to problem-solving techniques builds a student's confidence, a great number of detailed examples, problems, and diagrams are included. No attempt has been made to develop sophisticated solutions to the problems; rather, an emphasis has been placed on step-by-step solutions to problems of basic statics principles, of elements of strength of materials, and of applications of both.

The organization of the material gives the instructor flexibility in selection of topics and reflects concern with curricular content. Part One, Statics, can be used alone for a basic statics course. It can also be combined with Part Two, Introduction to Strength of Materials, as a general introduction to or preparation for a sequential course in strength of materials. Part Three, Supplementary Topics, is included to broaden the scope of the book, to present a number of topics currently in vogue, to offer optional material for inquisitive students, and to introduce "case studies" of statics application.

We express our appreciation to Thomas Davinroy for contributing statics problems to the book and also to Robert W. Bosma for contributing statics problems and case studies. Our deepest appreciation is extended to Mrs. Suzanne Fisher and Mrs. Susan Hirschberg for doing a careful job in typing the manuscript.

STEVE M. SLABY
HERBERT I. TYSON

NOTE TO THE STUDENT

One third of all jobs that will exist in engineering technology in the remaining years of this century are unknown today. A survey by the National Science Foundation indicates that in all major American industries demand for engineers and engineering technicians will outstrip the supply of qualified candidates. This does not guarantee positions for graduates of the technology programs of today, but it emphasizes the importance of thorough training in basic science as a solid background for developing a continuing capability to bridge the gap between today's advancing education and tomorrow's changing careers. College graduates with a thorough understanding of mathematics, physics, and applied mechanics, including statics and strength of materials, will be prepared for post-graduate training and for specialized on-the-job training programs.

The American Society for Engineering Education defines the engineering technician as follows:

> An engineering technician is one whose education and experience qualify him to work in the field of engineering technology. He differs from the craftsman in his knowledge of scientific and engineering theory and methods and from an engineer in his more specialized background and in his use of technical skills in support of engineering activities.

All students should note "knowledge of scientific and engineering theory."

It is hoped that this book as an introduction to statics and strength of materials will provide a solid foundation in basic theory and problem-solving techniques on which new knowledge can be built.

CONTENTS

Part Three — SUPPLEMENTARY TOPICS

Part One

STATICS

One
FUNDAMENTAL CONCEPTS

1.1 Introduction

Mechanics, the branch of physics that deals with motion and the action of forces on material bodies, is divided into two major subjects, statics and dynamics. Dynamics deals with the motion of bodies and the forces that create or change this motion. Statics, a major topic in this book, is the science of equilibrium, or balance, of force systems at rest.

For more than two thousand years, philosophers and scholars have studied equilibrium and motion, seeking basic laws that describe motion and explain its causes. In the fourth century B.C., a Greek philosopher recorded his interest in both the equilibrium related to forces on a lever and displacements in straight-line motion. The principles of the lever, the pulley, and buoyancy were discovered in the third century B.C. by Archimedes, a Greek mathematician and inventor generally credited with inventing an ancient water-raising device later called the Archimedean screw. This primitive device is still used for irrigation in the Nile Valley.

In the fifteenth century, after 1700 years during which no study in mechanics was recorded, Leonardo da Vinci noted the concept of statical moments in equilibrium. Considered one of the greatest artists and experimental scientists of the Italian Renaissance, Leonardo, inventor, architect, and civil and military engineer, compiled thousands of pages of notes, but produced few tangible engineering achievements.

During the latter part of the seventeenth century and the early part of the eighteenth, Isaac Newton, the great English mathematician, systematized the principles of mechanics into formal statements or laws. Other mathematicians—including D'Alembert, Lagrange, and Hamilton—later expressed Newton's laws in different ways, but they never suggested that these laws were invalid. But at the dawn of the twentieth, Albert Einstein, with his theory of relativity challenged Newton's laws on a very special condition: that they are not valid at speeds approaching the speed of light. Most engineering applications, however, are concerned with speeds considerably less than that of light, and Newton's laws remain the basis of engineering science and technology.

1.2 The Concept of a Force

Force is the *effect* of one body on another that tends to change the state of motion of the bodies. To understand what is meant by force, we can utilize our everyday experience, the physical force of "push" and "pull." We can also illustrate force by a weight hanging by a cable from a support (see Fig. 1.1). Gravity due to the earth's attraction tends to pull the weight down, and the cable from which the weight hangs tends to pull the weight up. The cable is in direct contact with the weight, and therefore its supporting or pulling effect is called a *contact force*. The earth, which is not in contact with the weight, exerts *noncontact forces* of gravitational attraction on the weight (another example of noncontact attraction forces is electromagnetic forces).

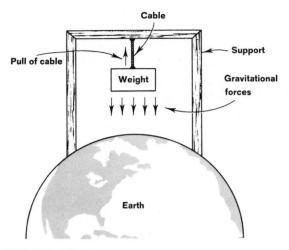

FIGURE 1.1

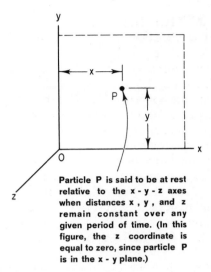

Particle **P** is said to be at rest relative to the **x - y - z** axes when distances **x**, **y**, and **z** remain constant over any given period of time. (In this figure, the **z** coordinate is equal to zero, since particle **P** is in the **x - y** plane.)

FIGURE 1.3

To define a more specific concept of force, we use the physical notion of a *particle*, a small solid sphere whose diameter approaches zero. This infinitesimal sphere (or particle) is an idealized physical concept of the smallest possible body having mass (mass being defined as the quotient of the weight divided by the acceleration of gravity). A particle is said to be at rest if its location relative to some frame of reference remains constant over any given period of time (see Figs. 1.2 and 1.3). A particle at rest will remain at rest, unless it is acted upon by some *external effect*.

Let us assume that a particle P is suspended, at rest, in space (see Fig. 1.3). Let us also assume that a particle Q is moving relative to the same frame of reference in which we have assumed a state of

rest for particle P (see Fig. 1.4). If particle Q comes into contact with particle P, it will cause particle P to change its position relative to the given frame of reference. In other words, particle Q will cause particle P to move. The external effect that particle Q has on particle P is defined as force (see Fig. 1.5).

Particle **Q** is assumed to move along a straight-line path. Note that relative to the frame of reference, which is the **x - y** axes, the **x** and **y** distances of **Q** change during a time lapse, indicating that **Q** is not in a state of rest.

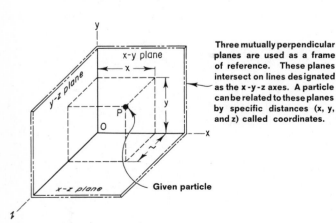

Three mutually perpendicular planes are used as a frame of reference. These planes intersect on lines designated as the **x - y - z** axes. A particle can be related to these planes by specific distances (x, y, and z) called coordinates.

FIGURE 1.2

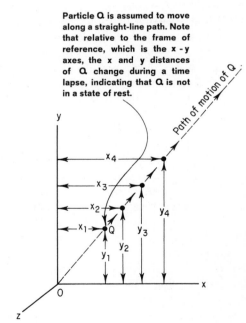

FIGURE 1.4

1.3 The Concept of a Vector

To describe a force completely in a physical way, let us refer to Fig. 1.5, the diagram that was used to illustrate the concept of force. Note that particle Q moved along a specific *line* having a certain direction in space and struck particle P at a specific *point* in space, producing an external effect at that point. The intensity of this external effect must have a specific *magnitude* in every instance that it is produced. From this physical description, we see that certain basic factors must be specified in order to define any force completely. These factors are as follows:

1. A force must have *magnitude*, which is a measure of the intensity of the force. In the engineering system, the magnitude of a force is usually measured in pounds.

2. A force must have a *point of application*, which in this case is the point of contact between particle P and particle Q.

3. A force must have a *line of action*, which in this example is designated by the path of motion of particle Q.

4. A force must have a *sense*, which shows the direction in which the force is acting.

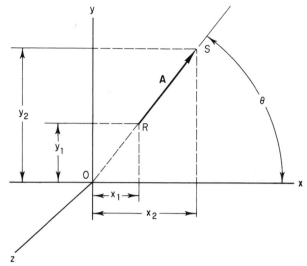

FIGURE 1.6

These four factors define a force graphically, and this graphical concept is called a *vector*. By means of a line in a specific position with respect to a frame of reference, drawn to a given length, and having an arrowhead at one end to indicate sense, we can graphically express the physical model of a force (see Fig. 1.6). We can say that a force is a vector quantity having a specific point of application. In general, then, a force may be represented by a vector that has a magnitude, a point of application, and a sense or direction.

In this book, vectors will be denoted by boldface letters, such as $\mathbf{A}$, $\mathbf{i}$, $\mathbf{j}$, or $\mathbf{k}$, or by italic letters and numbers with short arrows above them, such as $\overrightarrow{RS}$, $\overrightarrow{F_1}$, or $\overrightarrow{0\text{–}1}$. The magnitude of vectors will be represented by the distance between the tail of the arrow, represented by a point such as R in Fig. 1.6, and the tip of the arrow, represented by a point such as S. This *magnitude* will be denoted symbolically by italic capital letters and numbers, as follows, indicating an absolute value: $|\overrightarrow{A}|$, $|\overrightarrow{F_1}|$, $|\overrightarrow{RS},|$ or A, F_1, and RS. This system of notation will be varied throughout the book within the definition indicated above to allow flexibility in the notation and to accustom the student to the various types of notation used in different textbooks. Forces *not* drawn to a vector scale or not noted as vectors will be denoted by italic letters alone. The magnitude of such forces, when given, will be indicated by numbers (for example, 50 lb).

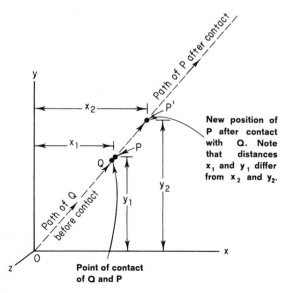

FIGURE 1.5

Vector $\overrightarrow{RS}$ in Fig. 1.6 may be denoted by **A**, which represents the length of the line segment *RS*, as well as its line of action and sense. If the magnitude of **A** is 10 lb, and a vector scale of 1 in. = 10 lb is adopted, the distance between *R* and *S* should be 1 in. Vector **A** has a direction related to the *x*-*y*-*z* axes by the coordinates (x_1, y_1) and (x_2, y_2). Since it is in the *x*-*y* plane, the *z* coordinates in this case are zero. Also, the vector can be related to the axes by the angle θ it makes with the *x* axis. The sense of vector **A** is indicated by the arrow.

1.4 Scalar Quantities

A vector quantity has magnitude, direction, and sense and can be represented by a line segment having these characteristics. A scalar quantity, on the other hand, has *only* magnitude and can be represented by a line segment that has a specific length only, and no specific direction or sense. Scalars can also be represented by numbers. Some examples of scalar quantities are: temperature (given in degrees), length (given in feet, inches, etc.), and speed (given in miles per hour, feet per second, etc.).

1.5 Force Systems

As shown in Sec. 1.3, force is an external effect that can be represented as a vector quantity. Let us now consider a number of forces acting on a particle. If any group of forces, whatever their nature, acts on a particle or a body, we define this group of

forces as a *force system*. For example, when a jet airplane flies, the basic forces acting on the wings of the airplane are the gravity forces downward; the lifting force due to the airfoil, or the cross-sectional shape, of the wing; the thrust of the jet engines that produce the forward motion of the wing and fuselage; and forces resisting forward motion in the form of frictional resistance of the air passing around the fuselage and the wing surface. This group of forces comprises a force system (see Fig. 1.7).

The general types of force systems we will discuss in this book may be categorized and briefly defined as follows:

1. *Coplanar force systems.* Lines of action of the forces lie in one plane.

2. *Noncoplanar force systems.* Lines of action of the forces do not lie in one plane.

3. *Concurrent force systems.* Lines of action of the forces meet at one point. (These forces may be either coplanar or noncoplanar.)

4. *Nonconcurrent force systems.* Lines of action of the forces do not meet at one point. (These forces may be either coplanar or non-coplanar, or they may be parallel.)

1.6 Equilibrium of a Force System

With force and force systems thus defined, we can apply these concepts through the use of the vector concept.

As stated at the beginning of this chapter, in statics we consider force systems that are *balanced*,

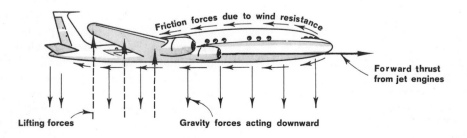

FIGURE 1.7

that is, force systems that do *not* cause motion when they are applied to bodies at rest. Thus, if we have a given body in a state of rest, and a given force system is applied to this body, we are interested in knowing whether or not the body will remain in a state of rest after the force system has been applied. If the body moves from its original position, a statically unstable or unbalanced force system is acting on the body. To put the body back into a state of rest, it is necessary to determine the additional force system that must be applied to the given body. On the other hand, if the body remains at rest when the initial force system is applied, the total force system acting on the body is balanced or is in a *state of equilibrium*.

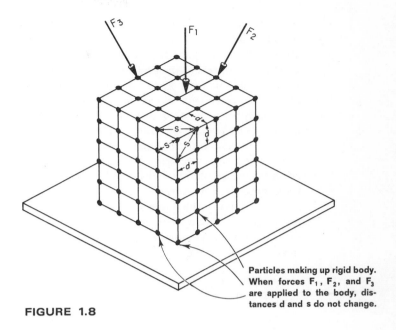

Particles making up rigid body. When forces F_1, F_2, and F_3 are applied to the body, distances d and s do not change.

FIGURE 1.8

1.7 The Rigid Body and Point Application of a Force

In statics, we assume that the body on which any force system acts is a *rigid body*. Further, we assume that a force can be applied at a *point*.

A rigid body is a body that is made up of many individual particles whose distances from each other are fixed and do not change when a force or force system is applied to the body (see Fig. 1.8). Therefore, in considering the static equilibrium of a body, we say that *the body does not deform under applied forces.*[1]

The second assumption we make is that individual forces can physically be applied to a body, with finite dimensions, at one point. Actually, this assumption is not valid: a point can be mathematically defined as a geometric element that has no dimensions. In reality, when a force is applied to a body, it acts over a small area of contact on the surface of the body. However, for static-equilibrium studies, we assume that the force can make point contact with the body.

1.8 Resultant and Equilibrant of a Force System

In order to determine whether or not a force system is in equilibrium, we must know the *total effect* a given force system has on a point or a rigid body. This total effect of a force system is called the *resultant* of the force system, and can be represented by a vector. The resultant is the simplest form of any force system (see Fig. 1.9).

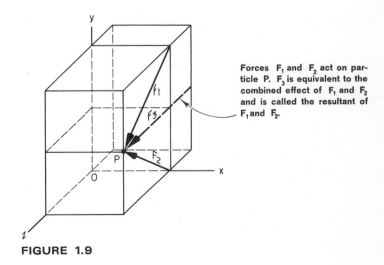

Forces F_1 and F_2 act on particle P. F_3 is equivalent to the combined effect of F_1 and F_2 and is called the resultant of F_1 and F_2.

FIGURE 1.9

---

[1] This is a simplifying assumption. Physically, the application of forces on any body does cause a deformation of the body, which indicates that the distances between the particles do change under applied loads. The study of the internal resisting forces due to external loads is dealt with in strength of materials, which is covered in the second part of this book.

If a force system is in equilibrium, the resultant of the force system is zero. If a *balanced force system* acts on a rigid body at rest, it has no effect on the state of rest of the body, indicating that the resultant of this force system must be zero. If an *unbalanced force system* acts on a rigid body that is initially in a state of rest, it will change the position or the state of equilibrium of the body. When it is desired to keep the body in its original state of rest, it is necessary to *counterbalance* the effect of the resultant of the applied unbalanced force system with another force equal in magnitude and having the same line of action as the resultant, but having a sense opposite to that of the resultant. This counterbalancing force is called the *equilibrant* of the force system (see Fig. 1.10).

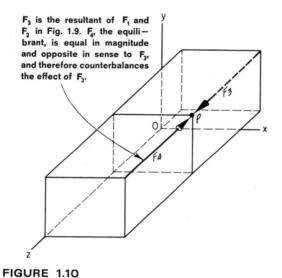

F_3 is the resultant of F_1 and F_2 in Fig. 1.9. F_4, the equili— brant, is equal in magnitude and opposite in sense to F_3, and therefore counterbalances the effect of F_3.

FIGURE 1.10

1.9 Composition and Resolution of Forces and Force Systems

The *composition* of a force system is the *adding up* of the individual forces in the system in order to determine the *total effect* of the force system. In other words, the composition of a force system is defined as the determination of the resultant of the force system. When we speak of adding forces to determine a resultant, we speak in terms of *vector addition* (this is discussed in Chapter 2.)

The *resolution* of a force is the process of dividing a given force into other forces called *components* whose total effect is *equivalent* to the given force. Any force can be considered a resultant of at least two other component forces; and, therefore, any given force can be resolved into two other forces, or, for that matter, into any number of other component forces, whose total effect will be equivalent to the original force.

When a force is resolved into two components that are perpendicular to each other, the components are called *rectangular* components and usually are related to the *x-y* coordinate directions.[2]

1.10 Moment of a Force

Up to this point, we have considered force systems which, when applied to a rigid body at rest, would cause a *translational motion* of the body if the force systems were unbalanced. By a translational motion we mean that the body would move in a straight line along the line of action of the resultant of the applied force system. To place the body in equilibrium, we would need only one counterbalancing force or equilibrant. Other force systems, however, require more than one equilibrant force to maintain equilibrium. One such system is a force system that causes *rotation* as well as translation of a rigid body (see Fig. 1.11).[3] With the rotational effect, we encounter another concept, the *moment* of a force. In order for the body in Fig. 1.11 to be in a state of equilibrium, two counterbalancing forces are required, and these two counterbalancing forces cannot be combined to form a single counterbalancing resultant, since their lines of action do not intersect.[4] The

---

[2] If a force has *x*, *y*, and *z* coordinates, it usually is resolved into three components.

[3] Forces F_1 and F_2 in Fig. 1.11 form a force system that creates a tendency for the body to twist or rotate as if it were acted upon by a couple. A couple has the characteristic of having a *torque* effect only, and causes a body in space to rotate about its center of gravity. The concept of couples is discussed in detail later in this book.

[4] Figure 1.9 shows that F_1 and F_2 intersect at point *P*; therefore, the resultant of F_1 and F_2 must act through point *P*. The equilibrant is F_4, applied at *P* to counterbalance this resultant force (see Fig. 1.10).

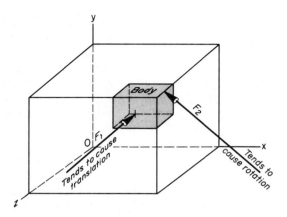

FIGURE 1.11

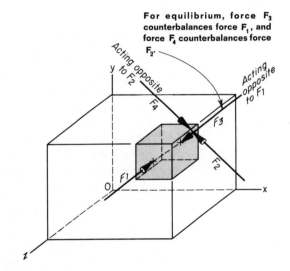

FIGURE 1.12

two nonintersecting forces are resisting a rotational, or *torque* effect, caused by the two given applied forces, which is defined as the *moment of the force system* (see Fig. 1.12).

Let us consider the moment of a single force. In Fig. 1.13 is shown a tangential force F that is applied to a disk at a point P in the plane of the disk. The disk is restrained so that it can have only rotational motion about the axis Ax when the force F is applied. The rotational or torque effect caused by force F has a magnitude equal to the magnitude of force F multiplied by the perpendicular distance from the point of application of

the force to the center of rotation of the disk (the *moment arm*, in this case the distance OP). Thus, the magnitude of the moment of a force is the product of two quantities, distance in feet (ft) or inches (in.) and force in pounds (lb). Therefore, the magnitude of the moment of force F can be expressed in pound-feet (lb-ft). If $F = 10$ lb and $OP = 1.5$ ft, then the moment of the force F about the point O will have a magnitude of 15 lb-ft.

The moment of a force can be represented by a vector. (At this point, we shall show that the concept of moment is a vector quantity; later in the book, we shall work with this concept in more detail.) It can be seen from the discussion above that a force can have a moment, about a point, that tends to cause a rotation in a definite direction, either clockwise or counterclockwise, depending upon the sense of the force, and that this rotational effect or moment has a magnitude. From this description, we see that a moment possesses the specifications of a vector.

The vector $\vec{M}$ in Fig. 1.14 *graphically* represents the moment of force $\vec{F}$ about point O. Its magnitude is equal to $|\vec{F}| \times |\overrightarrow{OP}|$, its direction is *perpendicular to the plane of rotation of force F* at point O, and its sense depends on whether there is clockwise or counterclockwise rotation. Here it must be emphasized that force $\vec{F}$ only causes rotation about point O and that vector $\vec{M}$ is a *graphical representation* of this moment of force $\vec{F}$. This graphical representation does *not* imply that

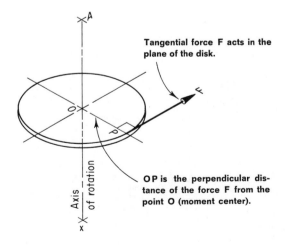

FIGURE 1.13

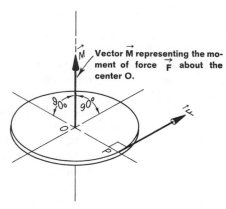

Vector **M** representing the moment of force **F** about the center O.

FIGURE 1.14

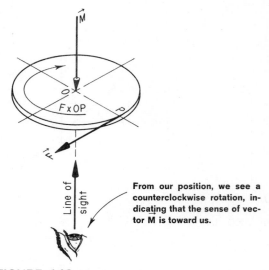

From our position, we see a counterclockwise rotation, indicating that the sense of vector M is toward us.

FIGURE 1.16

there is motion in the direction (represented by the arrowhead) of vector M. In this definition, we are concerned with the rotational effect only.

To define the sense of a moment vector, we shall use the following convention: if we consider our observation point as a frame of reference from which we can see rotation and we observe a *clockwise* rotation of a force about a point, the sense of the moment vector will be *away* from us, as indicated by the arrowhead in Fig. 1.15. If, from the same position, we observe a *counterclockwise* rotation (due to an opposite sense of force $\vec{F}$), the

sense of the moment vector $\vec{M}$ will be *toward* us, as indicated by the arrowhead in Fig. 1.16.

It is important in both of the above cases to keep in mind the *position* from which we observe the rotation. For example, if in Fig. 1.15 we changed our position and looked at the disk from a position above the disk, the rotation would be counterclockwise relative to us, and the sense of the moment vector $\vec{M}$ would be heading toward us (see Fig. 1.17).

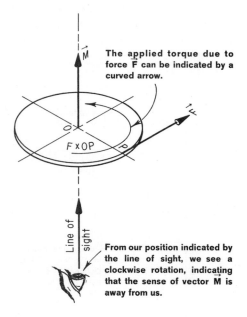

The applied torque due to force **F** can be indicated by a curved arrow.

From our position indicated by the line of sight, we see a clockwise rotation, indicating that the sense of vector **M** is away from us.

FIGURE 1.15

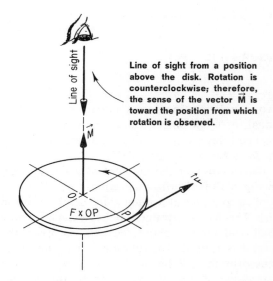

Line of sight from a position above the disk. Rotation is counterclockwise; therefore, the sense of the vector **M** is toward the position from which rotation is observed.

FIGURE 1.17

The sense of a moment can also be determined in the following way. If we turn a standard right-handed screw in a *clockwise* direction, the screw will *advance* into the material into which it is being screwed. This advance caused by a clockwise torque defines the sense of the moment vector. If this same screw is turned in a *counterclockwise* direction, the screw will *withdraw* from the material it has been screwed into. This withdrawal due to a counterclockwise torque defines a sense opposite to that of the first case (see Fig. 1.18).

The "right-hand rule" can also be used to determine the sense or direction of the moment vector. If the fingers of the right hand curl in the direction of the torque or rotation, the thumb will indicate the direction of the moment vector.

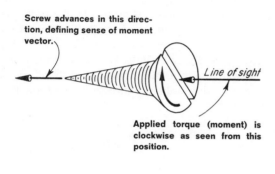

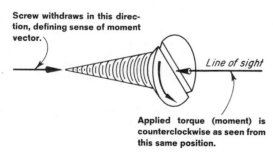

FIGURE 1.18

1.11 Free-Body Diagram

Another important concept used extensively in the study of statics is the *free-body diagram.* Let us consider a body in equilibrium on which a number of loads or forces act, such as a simple beam loaded with several vertical loads and supported

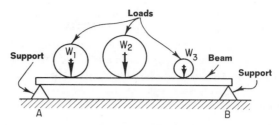

(a) Structure Diagram

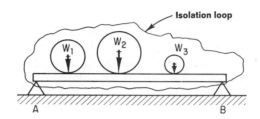

(b) Structure Diagram Showing Isolated Section

FIGURE 1.19

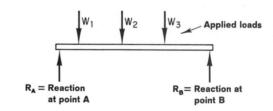

FIGURE 1.20
Free-body Diagram

at two points, as shown in Fig. 1.19a.[5] (The picture of the actual physical loading and support of a beam or any structure is called a *structural diagram.*)

Analyzing the given condition, we see that the beam is acted on by an *external force system* that includes the given loads on the beam and the forces at the supporting points (*A* and *B*), which keep the beam in *static equilibrium.* If we *isolate* the loaded beam from its supporting points and represent the *external* force system acting on the beam by arrows, the isolated picture of the beam we obtain is called a *free-body diagram* (see Fig. 1.20). In

---

[5] A beam is defined as a bar or a structural member that carries transverse loads, i.e., loads acting in an axial or longitudinal plane of the bar.

effect, we have "frozen" the picture of the *external force system* acting on the given beam so that we can apply *statical analysis* to this force system and thus determine the magnitude and direction of the forces in the system. Note that we "froze" the part of the physical system that was circled by a loop (Fig. 1.19b). In this case, we "froze" the entire *loaded* beam; generally, the isolation loop can be applied to an entire structure or any section of a structure.

A free-body diagram represents a structure or a part of a structure upon which an external force system acts. In drawing the free-body diagram, we reduce the structural members to straight lines and all the forces acting on the structure to lines with arrows. In the above example, the directions, senses, and magnitudes of the applied forces (loads) are known. The forces at the points of support, which are known as *reactions* (the beam presses down on these supports, and the supports react against this pressure to maintain equilibrium), have directions and senses that we know, but we do not know the magnitudes of these reactions for equilibrium conditions. There are

cases where the senses of the reactions cannot be determined by inspection. Therefore, in analyzing such a structure, we assume a positive sense for the reactions (*upward* forces being *positive* and *downward* forces *negative*), and if, in our final solution, we get a negative answer, we conclude that the actual sense is opposite to that of our assumed sense.

Various surfaces and structural elements have unique reactions, which are illustrated below. If you become familiar with these reactions, you will find it easy to sketch accurate free-body diagrams.

Frictionless or perfectly smooth surfaces (an idealization)

The reaction of a perfectly smooth surface (Fig. 1.21) is *one force*, that acts perpendicular (*normal*) to the surface, regardless of the angle at which a load is applied to the surface (see Figs. 1.21c and 1.21d). A perfectly smooth surface cannot resist sidewise or longitudinal motion, and therefore, it prevents motion only in a direction perpendicular to the surface itself.

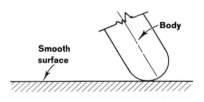

(a) Structure Diagram

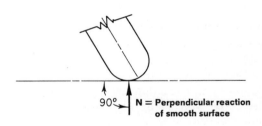

(b) Free-body Diagram of (a)

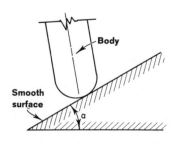

(c) Structure Diagram

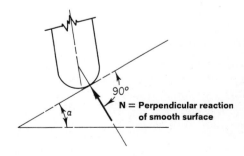

(d) Free-body Diagram of (c)

FIGURE 1.21

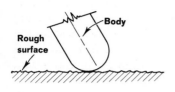

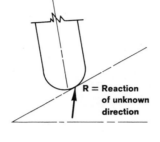

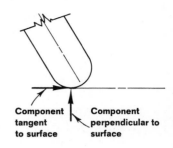

(a) Structure Diagram

(b) Free-body Diagram I of (a)

(c) Free-body Diagram II of (a)

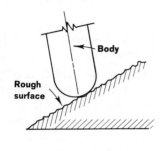

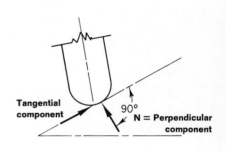

(d) Structure Diagram

(e) Free-body Diagram I of (d)

(f) Free-body Diagram II of (d)

FIGURE 1.22

Rough surface (friction present)

The reaction of a rough surface (Fig. 1.22) can be considered as *one force* having an *unknown direction*. There is no way to physically determine the direction of this reaction, and therefore, the reactive force is given by *two components* having *known directions*: one *tangent* and one *perpendicular* to the surface on which the body rests. Thus, a rough surface can resist motion in a direction that is *parallel* (tangential) to and *perpendicular* to the given surface.

Flexible cable, string, rope, or wire

A flexible cable, string, rope, or wire (Fig. 1.23) has a *single* reaction to an applied load.[6] The reaction is assumed to act along the *longitudinal axis* of the cable, string, rope, or wire and is effective only under *tensile* or pulling loads. These

flexible structural elements cannot resist compressive loads or torque-producing loads.

Short strut, link, or bar

A short strut, link, or bar (Fig. 1.24) has *one reaction*, which is assumed to act along its *longitudinal axis*. This type of support can resist both *tensile* and *compressive* loads. Figures 1.24a and 1.24c illustrate loading that produces tension (or pulling effect) in the bars. Figure 1.24e shows loading that produces compression in the bars.

Rollers

A roller (or group of rollers, Fig. 1.25) has *one reaction*, which acts perpendicular to the surface on which it rests or rolls. Since a roller on a smooth surface cannot resist sidewise motion, its reaction must be perpendicular to the supporting surface. The reaction of a group of rollers is transmitted through the roller carriage to the pin, as shown in Figs. 1.25d and 1.25f.

[6] By definition, a flexible body offers no resistance to bending.

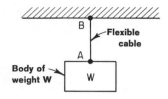

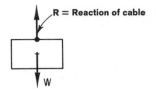

(a) Structure Diagram

(b) Free-body Diagram of (a)

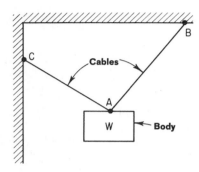

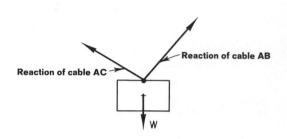

(c) Structure Diagram

(d) Free-body Diagram of (c)

FIGURE 1.23

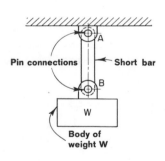

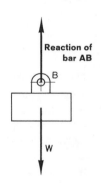

(a) Structure Diagram

(b) Free-body Diagram of (a)

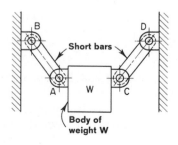

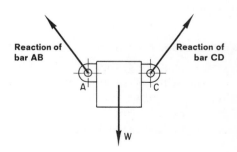

(c) Structure Diagram

(d) Free-body Diagram of (c)

FIGURE 1.24(a)–(d)

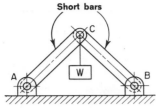

(e) Structure Diagram

(f) Free-body Diagram of (e)

FIGURE 1.24(e), (f)

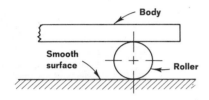

(a) Structure Diagram

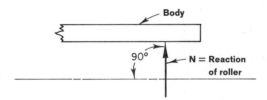

(b) Free-body Diagram of (a)

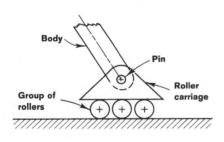

(c) Structure Diagram

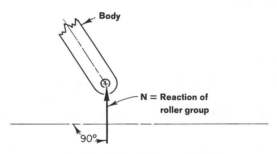

(d) Free-body Diagram of (c)

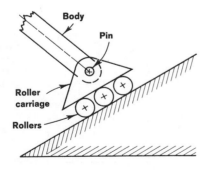

(e) Structure Diagram

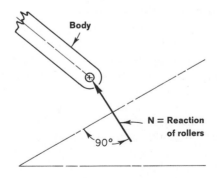

(f) Free-body Diagram of (e)

FIGURE 1.25

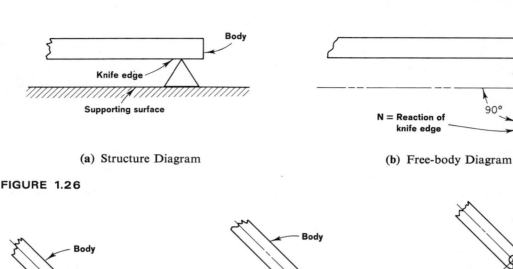

(a) Structure Diagram   **(b)** Free-body Diagram

FIGURE 1.26

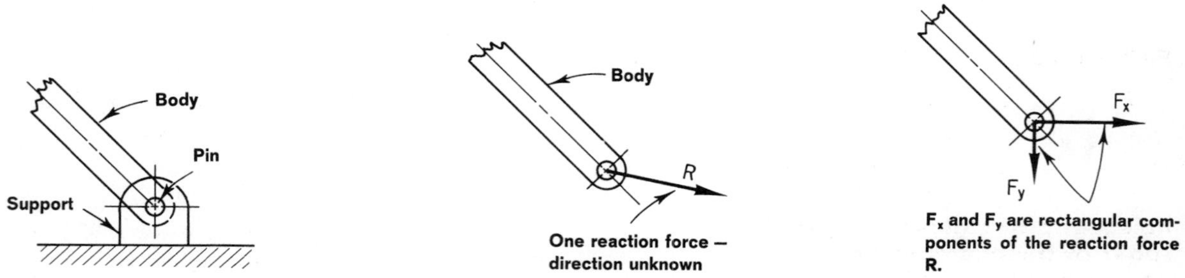

(a) Structure Diagram   **(b)** Free-body Diagram I   **(c)** Free-body Diagram II

FIGURE 1.27

Knife edge

The reaction of a knife edge (Fig. 1.26) is *one force* having a direction *perpendicular* to the surface on which it is supported. It does not resist sidewise motion.

Smooth pin (frictionless pin or hinge—an idealization)

Since a pin can resist motion in all directions (sidewise, as well as vertical), it is not always possible to physically determine the direction of the reaction force of a pin (see Fig. 1.27). Therefore, the directions of the *rectangular components* of this reaction force are used in setting up free-body diagrams involving pins (see Fig. 1.27).

If we analyze the reaction of a pin to an applied load, we see that the pin actually resists motion through a force *system* that is distributed over the *area of contact* of the pin and the member to which it is attached. Figure 1.28 shows a body, assumed to be in equilibrium, on which two forces F_1 and F_2 act. The body is held in a state of equilibrium

by a smooth pin connection. The pin resists the effect of F_1 and F_2 by a distributed force system that acts radially from the center of the pin to the contacting surfaces of the pin, the body, and the support. The *resultant* of this radially distributed force system acts through the center of the pin and is equal to R.

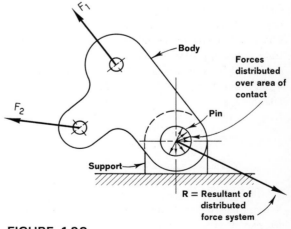

FIGURE 1.28

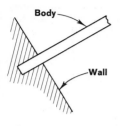

(a) Structure Diagram

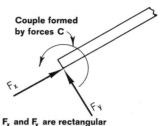

(b) Free-body Diagram I

(c) Free-body Diagram II

FIGURE 1.29

Fixed-end or rigid-end support (post or beam embedded in a concrete, solid wall)

Figure 1.29 shows a body embedded in a wall; any nonaxial forces applied to this body will tend to cause a *rotational* effect on the body, as well as a *translational* effect, since the applied forces will have a moment relative to the fixed end of the body. Up to this point, we have discussed reactions of various structural elements that prevent translatory motion only.

Resisting the translational effect is a reactive force of unknown direction; resisting the rotational effect is a force system of *two parallel forces*. The reactive force of unknown direction is the resultant of a complicated force system that can be resolved into rectangular components. The force system preventing rotation is also a complex one, and its resultant is a *couple*. A couple is defined as two *parallel* forces that are equal in magnitude, but opposite in sense. Thus, as shall be discussed further in Chapter 3, a couple has only a *rotational* effect and does not have a translational effect.

1.12   Summary and Examples

When drawing or sketching the free-body diagram for any statics problem, it is important to show all the external forces (of known and unknown magnitudes) acting on the body, or structure, or any part of it chosen to be the free body. The omission of any of the external forces of a force system would invalidate any solution to a statics problem.

The free-body diagram must be used extensively and as a rule is the *first step* in the analysis of any problem involving static equilibrium. Always make a neat sketch of all free-body diagrams; note carefully the magnitudes, directions, and senses of all known forces in a system; properly label by letters and arrows all unknown forces, indicating their directions and assumed senses.

Following are several examples of free-body diagrams, for all of which equilibrium conditions are assumed. Analyze each diagram carefully until you truly understand the various factors that must be considered when sketching free-body diagrams.

EXAMPLE 1.1 _____

Given: A structure diagram showing a ladder resting on a floor and against a wall and carrying a load *W*, as shown in Fig. 1.30a. Assume that the ladder is weightless and the floor and wall are frictionless.

Find: Sketch free-body diagrams showing:
A. The external forces acting on the given ladder to maintain a condition of static equilibrium.

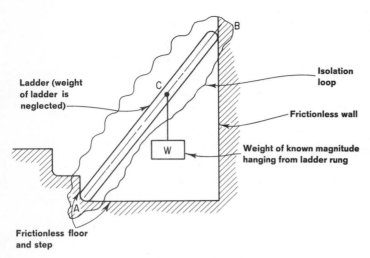

Ladder (weight of ladder is neglected)

Isolation loop

Frictionless wall

Weight of known magnitude hanging from ladder rung

W

Frictionless floor and step

(a) Structure Diagram

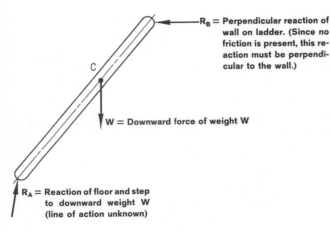

R_B = Perpendicular reaction of wall on ladder. (Since no friction is present, this reaction must be perpendicular to the wall.)

W = Downward force of weight W

R_A = Reaction of floor and step to downward weight W (line of action unknown)

(b) Free-body Diagram I

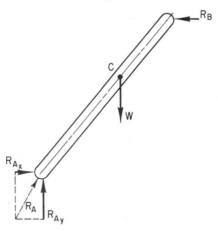

R_B

W

R_{A_x}

R_A

R_{A_y}

(c) Free-body Diagram II

FIGURE 1.30

B. The horizontal and vertical components (x and y directions, respectively) of the external forces acting on the given ladder.

Solution

R_B and R_A are two unknown quantities that can be directly solved for by graphical analysis. In Fig. 1.30b, the direction of the force exerted by weight W and the reaction R_B are known, and the direction of R_A is unknown.

If R_A is resolved into rectangular components R_{A_x} and R_{A_y}, then all unknowns may be found by mathematical analysis. The computed values of components R_{A_x} and R_{A_y} may be added vectorially to obtain the magnitude and direction of R_A (see Fig. 1.30c).

In many types of force systems, we can determine the actual magnitudes, senses, and lines of action of the unknown external forces acting on a body through *direct* graphical analysis. In others, it is necessary to use mathematical analysis. In using mathematical analysis, it is often expedient to resolve unknown forces into their x and y components before beginning the mathematical computation. This resolution of unknown forces into components is indicated in the free-body diagram (see Fig. 1.30c).

In this book we use both graphical and mathematical analysis to solve statics problems. Graphical analysis emphasizes the physical significance of statics problems and also acts as a check on the results obtained through mathematical analysis. Mathematical analysis, on the other hand, makes it possible to express and manipulate physical conditions related to statics in a generalized manner and can be used as a check on the results obtained through graphical analysis. The two approaches are complementary, and their utilization will give the student a deeper insight into statics and strength of materials.

EXAMPLE 1.2 ————————

Given: A structure diagram showing a ladder having a weight P resting on a rough floor and wall (friction *is* a factor) and carrying a load W, as shown in Fig. 1.31a.

Find: Sketch free-body diagrams showing:
A. The external forces acting on the given

ladder to maintain a condition of static equilibrium.

B. The horizontal and vertical components (*x* and *y* directions, respectively) of the external forces acting on the given ladder.

Solution

Knowing the coefficient of friction between the ladder and the wall and between the ladder and the floor, we can solve graphically (how will be discussed later in the book), even though the directions of the reactions R_A and R_B are unknown (see Fig. 1.31b).

In order to solve this example through mathematical analysis, we must resolve R_A and R_B into their rectangular components (see Fig. 1.31c).

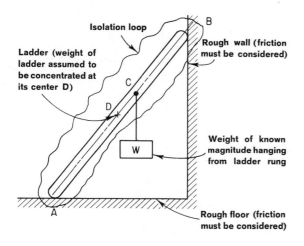

(a) Structure Diagram

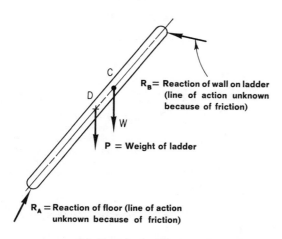

(b) Free-body Diagram I

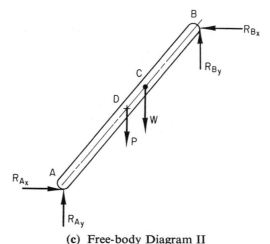

(c) Free-body Diagram II

FIGURE 1.31

EXAMPLE 1.3 _____

Given: A structure diagram showing a weightless bar *AB* carrying a weight *W*. The bar is pin connected to a stationary support at point *A* and to a roller support at point *B*. All pin connections are smooth (frictionless). (See Fig. 1.32a.)

Find: Sketch free-body diagrams showing:
A. The external forces acting on the given bar to maintain a condition of static equilibrium.
B. The horizontal and vertical components of the external forces acting on the given bar.

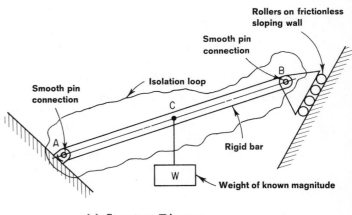

(a) Structure Diagram

FIGURE 1.32(a)

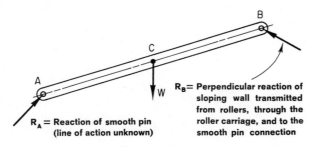

(b) Free-body Diagram for Graphical Solution

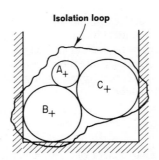

(a) Structure Diagram

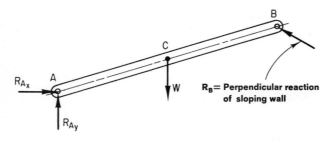

(c) Free-body Diagram for Mathematical Solution

FIGURE 1.32(b), (c)

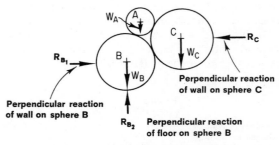

(b) Free-body Diagram Showing Forces that Maintain Equilibrium of the Entire System of the Three Spheres

Solution

The solutions to parts A and B are given, respectively, in Figs. 1.32b and 1.32c.

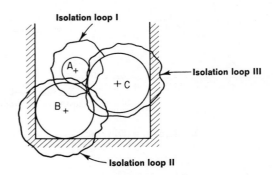

(c) Structure Diagram

EXAMPLE 1.4 _____

Given: A structure diagram of three spheres, *A*, *B*, and *C*, each having a different weight and being supported by two walls and a floor, as shown in Fig. 1.33a. The spheres, the walls, and the floor are all frictionless.

Find: Sketch free-body diagrams showing:
  A. The external forces that maintain equilibrium of the *entire* system of three spheres.
  B. The external forces acting on sphere A.
  C. The external forces acting on sphere B.
  D. The external forces acting on sphere C.

Solution

The solutions are shown in Figs. 1.33b, 1.33c, 1.33d, 1.33e, and 1.33f.

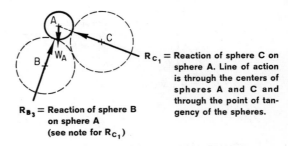

(d) Free-body Diagram for Sphere A

FIGURE 1.33(a)–(d)

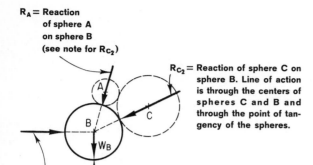

R_A = Reaction of sphere A on sphere B (see note for R_{C_2})

R_{C_2} = Reaction of sphere C on sphere B. Line of action is through the centers of spheres C and B and through the point of tangency of the spheres.

W_B

R_{B_2} = Perpendicular reaction of floor

R_{B_1} = Perpendicular reaction of wall

(e) Free-body Diagram for Sphere B

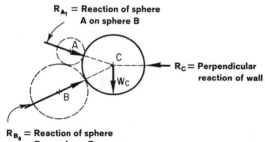

R_{A_1} = Reaction of sphere A on sphere B

R_C = Perpendicular reaction of wall

W_C

R_{B_4} = Reaction of sphere B on sphere C

(f) Free-body Diagram for Sphere C

FIGURE 1.33(e), (f)

EXAMPLE 1.5 ─────────────

Given: A structure diagram of three pulleys, A, B, and E, supported by rigid bars and a cable as shown in Fig. 1.34a. A weight W_1 is attached to one end of a cable that passes over the pulleys. At the other end of the cable a weight W_2 rests on a rough inclined surface.

Find: Sketch free-body diagrams showing:
  A. The entire system as a whole.
  B. Weight W_1.
  C. Pulley A.
  D. Pulley B.
  E. Pulley E.
  F. Bar BC.
  G. Bar BD.
  H. Bar EF.
  I. Bar EG.
  J. Weight W_2.

Solution

In this example, we assume that the pulleys are weightless and frictionless, that the rigid bars are weightless, and that the cable connecting weights W_1 and W_2 through the pulley system is perfectly flexible. In Fig. 1.34a, points C, D, F, and G are smooth pin connections. Pulleys A, B, and E are held in place by smooth pins.

With the foregoing assumptions, a model of the force system that maintains the mechanical system in

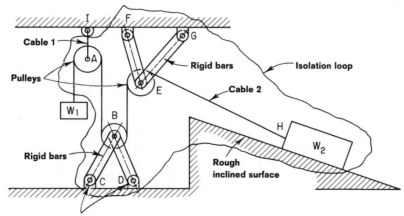

Cable 1

Pulleys

W_1

Rigid bars

Typical smooth pin connections

Rigid bars

Isolation loop

Cable 2

Rough inclined surface

W_2

(a) Structure Diagram

FIGURE 1.34(a)

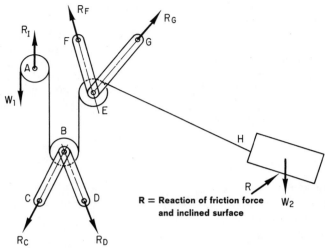

(b) Free-body Diagram I

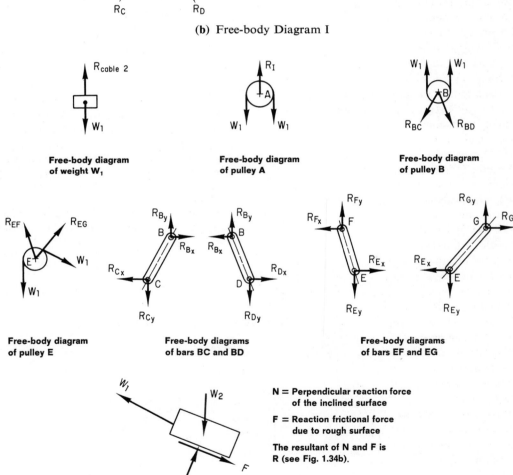

(c) Free-body Diagrams II

FIGURE 1.34(b), (c)

equilibrium may then be created through the free-body diagrams.

The isolation loop in Fig. 1.34a isolates the *entire mechanical system* from its supports. A free-body diagram of this system then shows all of the reactions that maintain the *entire system* in equilibrium (see Fig. 1.34b).

In order to be able to determine the magnitudes and directions of all the reactions in the given mechanical system, we isolate the various components of the system so that each can be statically analyzed. The individual free-body diagrams are shown in Fig. 1.34c. (Trace the isolation loops [not shown] on the structure diagram for each component.)

PROBLEMS

Problems for solution are presented at the end of each chapter. Develop a methodical approach to the solution of these problems, using the examples in the book as guides until you develop an ability for a more independent approach. The problems should be set up on cross-section paper, which facilitates sketching and making scale diagrams of the given loaded structures and force systems; also, it helps keep calculations neat and orderly.

The starting point in graphical analysis and solution is usually a structure diagram (or a force system) laid out to a convenient space scale (which is noted on the layout). The next general step is to apply the proper principles of statics through graphical-vectorial relationships to the isolated force system and then to determine numerical values by careful scalar measurements.

Because of limitations on the page size, the dimensions of the figures do not always agree with the scales indicated in the illustrations. You should remember, however, that you must always choose a convenient scale when using graphical analysis.

In mathematical analysis and solution, (a) the given information is defined by the structure diagram, (b) a free-body diagram is sketched representing the given and assumed forces in the isolated force configuration, (c) the appropriate principles of statics are applied, and (d) appropriate mathematical techniques are used to arrive at a numerical solution to a problem.

Numerical results obtained by graphical and mathematical analyses are bound to involve discrepancies because much of the given data is based on physical dimensions (actual physical geometry of a structure and actual locations of forces in a given force system) that cannot be determined without error. The errors that enter into the results are due, in part, to imperfect measuring instruments and to imperfect use and reading of

these instruments. The degree of accuracy therefore depends upon the quality of the measuring instruments and the skill with which these instruments are used. Keep this in mind when you compare results obtained by the various approaches presented in this book.

Further, the matter of "significant figures" in numerical answers arises. The usual procedure here is to not carry out an answer to more significant figures than there are in the given data, since the answer cannot be more accurate than the data upon which it is based. In this book, some liberty has been taken in the use of significant figures in the answers in order to compare the relative accuracy of graphical and mathematical analyses.

1.1 Given: A structure diagram of a block (in equilibrium) of weight W resting on a frictionless surface. An inclined force F_1 and a horizontal force F_2 act on the block. (See Fig. 1.35.)

Find: Neatly sketch the free-body diagram of the block, showing all applied and supporting forces.

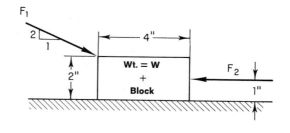

FIGURE 1.35

1.2 Given: A structure diagram of a cylindrical roller (in equilibrium) of weight W resting on an inclined, frictionless surface and prevented from rolling down the inclined surface by a rope attached to the axle of the roller. (See Fig. 1.36.)

Find: Neatly sketch the free-body diagram of the roller, showing all applied and supporting forces.

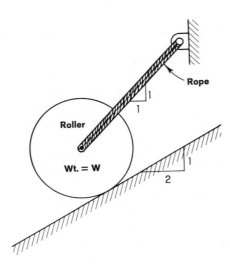

FIGURE 1.36

1.3 Given: A post (in equilibrium) embedded in concrete, acted upon by an inclined force *P* (Fig. 1.37). (Assume post to be weightless.)

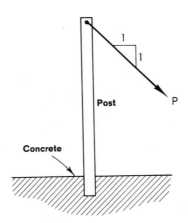

FIGURE 1.37

Find: Neatly sketch the free-body diagram of the post, showing all applied and supporting forces. (*Note:* Applied inclined force *P* has a torque effect on the post that must be counterbalanced by the concrete to maintain static equilibrium.)

1.4 Given: A weightless link *AB* (in equilibrium) with a frictionless joint (pin) at its lower end *A* and with its upper end *B* resting on a frictionless wall. A horizontal force *F* acts on the link. (See Fig. 1.38.)

Find: Neatly sketch the free-body diagram of the given link, showing all applied and supporting forces.

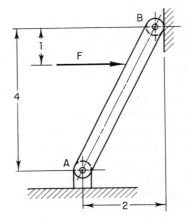

FIGURE 1.38

1.5 Given: Two weightless links *AB* and *BC* (in equilibrium) pinned together at *B* and at support points *A* and *C* with frictionless pins. A horizontal force *F* acts on link *AB*. (See Fig. 1.39.)

Find: Neatly sketch the free-body diagrams of the following, showing the *resultant* force that acts at any point, rather than its components:
A. The entire structure.
B. The link *AB* alone.
C. The link *BC* alone.

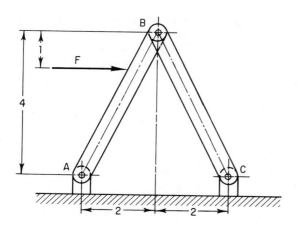

FIGURE 1.39

1.6 Given: A structure (in equilibrium) made up of three weightless links, *AB*, *BC*, and *DE*, pinned with frictionless pins at joints *A*, *B*, *D*, and *E* and supported by a roller attached with a frictionless pin at point *C*. A horizontal force *F* acts on link *AB*. (See Fig. 1.40.)

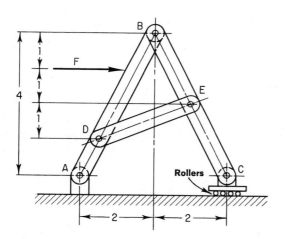

FIGURE 1.40

Find: A. Neatly sketch the free-body diagrams of the following, showing the *resultant* force that acts at any point, rather than its components:
(1) The entire structure.
(2) The link *DE* alone.

(3) The link *BC* alone.
(4) The link *AB* alone.
B. Identify the force systems acting in (1), (2), (3), and (4).

1.7 Given: A structure diagram of a beam supported by a knife edge at the right end, with its left end embedded in a wall. The beam is loaded to the right of the knife edge with a weight *W*. (See Fig. 1.41.)

Find: Neatly sketch the free-body diagram of the beam, showing all applied and supporting forces.

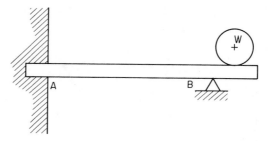

FIGURE 1.41

1.8 Given: A structure diagram of a frame made up of two struts and supported from a wall with frictionless pin connec-

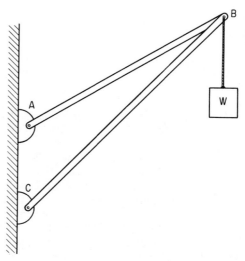

FIGURE 1.42

tions. The two struts are pin connected and support a load *W*. (See
Fig. 1.42.)

Find: Neatly sketch a free-body diagram
of the following:
A. The entire structure.
B. The individual members (struts)
of the structure.

1.9 Given: A weight *W* hanging from a rigid
ring by a flexible cable. The ring is
supported in space by two flexible
and inextensible cables: one attached
to the ceiling and the other fixed to
a wall. (See Fig. 1.43.)

Find: Neatly sketch the free-body diagram
of the ring.

Find: Neatly sketch the free-body dia-
grams of the following:
A. The entire structure.
B. The pulley alone.

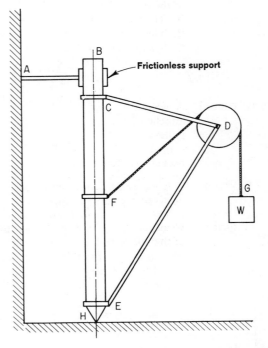

FIGURE 1.44

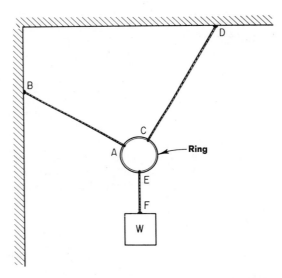

FIGURE 1.43

1.10 Given: A weight *W* supported by a flexible
cable (passing over a frictionless pul-
ley) with its end fixed to a vertical
pole (Fig. 1.44). The pulley is supported by two struts that are also
attached to the vertical pole by
frictionless sleeves. The bottom of
the vertical pole is a point that rests
on a rough rigid floor, while the upper
part of the pole is supported by a
frictionless sleeve attached to a wall
with a strut.

1.11 Given: Weight W_2 supported at one end of
a flexible cable that passes over a
frictionless pulley and is fixed in a

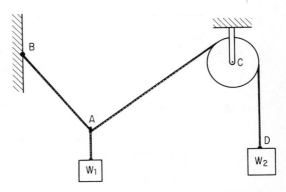

FIGURE 1.45

wall (Fig. 1.45). The pulley is supported by a strut embedded in a rigid ceiling. A weight W_1 is suspended by a cable from the cable supporting W_2.

Find: Neatly sketch the free-body diagrams of the following:
A. The structure as a whole.
B. The weight W_1 alone.
C. The pulley alone.

1.12 Given: A weight W supported by a cable attached to a system of frictionless pulleys, flexible cables, and struts (Fig. 1.46). The struts are pin connected and attached to and supported by a wall, the upper attachment being a pin connection, the lower support a roller support.

Find: Neatly sketch the free-body diagrams of the following:

A. The entire structure.
B. The horizontal strut and the middle pulley attached.
C. The middle pulley alone.
D. The sloping strut and the upper pulley attached.
E. The upper pulley alone.
F. The lower pulley alone.

1.13 Given: Weights W_1 and W_2 supported by a series of flexible cables and frictionless pulleys (Fig. 1.47). The upper, middle, and lower pulleys are attached to the ceiling and to each other with flexible cables.

Find: Neatly sketch the free-body diagrams of the following:
A. The entire structure.
B. The lower pulley alone.
C. The lower-middle pulley alone.
D. The upper-middle pulley alone.
E. The upper pulley alone.

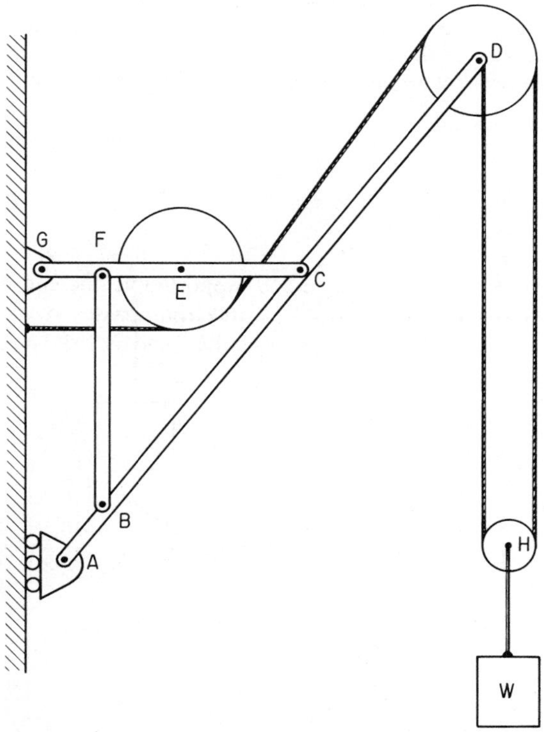

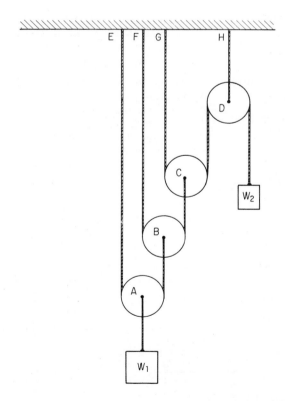

FIGURE 1.46

FIGURE 1.47

1.14 Given: A vertical post having two cross bars embedded in a rigid floor (Fig. 1.48). The ends of the upper cross bar support two weights of W_1 each, and the ends of the lower cross bar support two weights of W_2 each. The cross bars are rigidly attached to the post.

Find: Neatly sketch the free-body diagram of the following:
A. The entire structure.
B. The upper cross bar alone.
C. The lower cross bar alone.

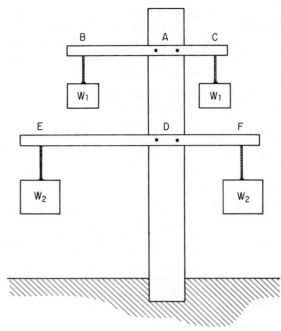

FIGURE 1.48

1.15 Given: A system of three horizontal beams and vertical struts, pin connected and supported on knife edges (the structure is called Roberval's balance, Fig. 1.49). A weight W_1 rests on the center beam, while a weight W_2 hangs from the right end of the upper beam. The center beam is supported on the right by a strut, while its left end rests on a knife support.

Find: Neatly sketch the free-body diagrams of the following:
A. The entire structure.
B. The lower beam alone.
C. The middle beam alone.
D. The upper beam alone.

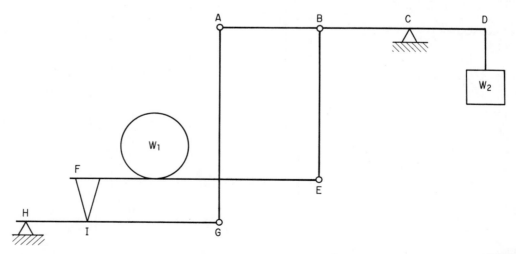

FIGURE 1.49

1.16 Given: Three weights W_1, W_2, and W_3, as shown in Fig. 1.50. Weight W_3 is supported at one end of a flexible cable that passes over two frictionless pulleys (supported by struts embedded in a rigid floor). The other end of the cable is attached to W_1, which rests on a rough inclined surface. Weight W_2 is attached to the cable (between the two pulleys) connecting W_3 and W_1.

Find: Neatly sketch the free-body diagrams of the following:
A. The entire structure.
B. The left pulley alone.
C. The right pulley alone.

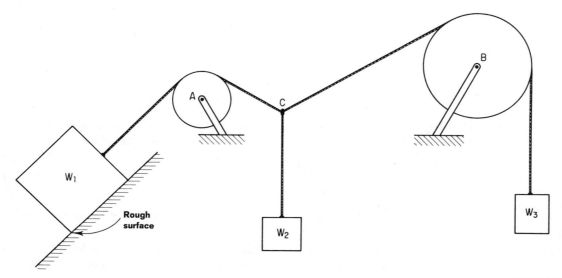

FIGURE 1.50

Two
BASIC LAWS OF STATICS

2.1 Parallelogram Law and Triangle Law

To determine the actual magnitude, line of action, and sense of a given force system, we can apply a law of statics that permits us to add forces represented by vectors. This law can be summarized as follows.

Two forces acting on a body at one point can be combined into a single force called the *resultant*. The forces are combined geometrically by means of a parallelogram whose sides are parallel to the lines of action of the given forces and whose lengths represent the magnitudes (to a proper scale) of the given forces. The *diagonal* of this parallelogram graphically represents the *resultant* of the given forces.

Figure 2.1a shows two forces F_1 and F_2 acting on a body at point A. This type of figure, which shows the actual lines of action of the given forces, their senses, and their point of application is called a *space diagram*, or *structure diagram*. Figure 2.1b, which shows the addition of the vectors in the given force system, is called a *vector diagram*.

If, as in Fig. 2.1b, we represent F_1 as a vector $\vec{F_1}$ having a length AB and F_2 as a vector $\vec{F_2}$ having a length AD and then construct a parallelogram as described above, the diagonal (AC) will represent the resultant $\vec{R}$ of the two given forces, and the length of AC will give the magnitude of the resultant. The resultant has thus been determined by *vector* addition of the given forces through the medium of a graphical construction.

The parallelogram law can be expressed by a general *vector equation*, as follows:

(1) $\vec{F_1} + \vec{F_2} = \vec{R} =$

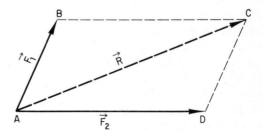

This equation represents the *addition of vectors*. Always visualize the basic concept of the *paral-*

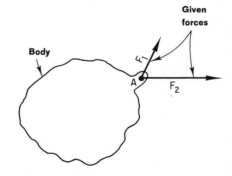

(a) Space Diagram

(b) Vector Diagram

FIGURE 2.1

30

lelogram law when reading or writing vector equations that represent the addition or subtraction of vectors.[1]

Since the opposite sides of a parallelogram are equal and parallel, we see that, through the parallelogram law, two vectors can be added in two ways: $\vec{F}_1 + \vec{F}_2 = \vec{R}$ or $\vec{F}_2 + \vec{F}_1 = \vec{R}$. In other words, vector addition is independent of the order in which the vectors are combined; that is, vector addition is *commutative* (see Fig. 2.2).

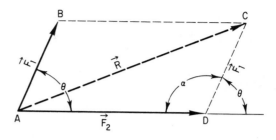

FIGURE 2.3

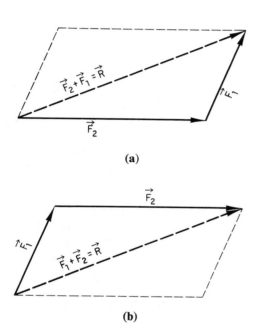

(a)

(b)

FIGURE 2.2

Note from Fig. 2.2 that we actually use one half of the parallelogram divided by the diagonal AC to perform the operation of vector addition. Since this is a triangular half, we arrive at the concept called the *triangle law* of vector addition; both triangles are the same, so either can be used to perform vector addition.

The parallelogram law or the triangle law can also be used to resolve a force into two components. In Fig. 2.2, for example, the components of $\vec{R}$ are $\vec{F}_1$ and $\vec{F}_2$. To determine the resultant of two forces analytically, we can apply a combina-

tion of geometry, algebra, and trigonometry. (Later in the book, an analytical method known as *vector notation* will be presented.) If the angle θ between two given concurrent forces $\vec{F}_1$ and $\vec{F}_2$ is known, we can use the law of cosines to determine the magnitude of $\vec{R}$ (see Fig. 2.3).

Applying the law of cosines to triangle ADC, and keeping in mind that we are now dealing with scalar quantities where lengths $\overline{AD}$ (and $\overline{BC}$) and $\overline{AB}$ (and $\overline{CD}$), as well as $\overline{AC}$, represent magnitudes of $\vec{F}_2$, $\vec{F}_1$, and $\vec{R}$, respectively, we write:

$$(2) \qquad \overline{AC}^2 = \overline{AB}^2 + \overline{AD}^2 - 2(\overline{AB})(\overline{AD}) \cos \alpha$$

where α is the supplementary angle of the given angle θ. To write the equation in terms of θ, we proceed as follows: since $\alpha = 180° - \theta$, we may write, from the standard trigonometric formula

$$\cos(180° - B) = -\cos B,$$

$$\cos \alpha = \cos(180° - \theta) = -\cos \theta$$

Substituting $-\cos \theta$ for $\cos \alpha$ in equation (2), we get

$$(3) \qquad \overline{AC}^2 = \overline{AB}^2 + \overline{AD}^2 + 2(\overline{AB})(\overline{AD}) \cos \theta$$

Solving for AC, we get

$$(4) \qquad \overline{AC} = \sqrt{\overline{AB}^2 + \overline{AD}^2 + 2(\overline{AB})(\overline{AD}) \cos \theta}$$
$$= \text{the magnitude of the resultant } \vec{R}$$

When we wrote previously the vector equation $\vec{R} = \vec{F}_1 + \vec{F}_2$, we were expressing the magnitude of $\vec{R}$ as a scalar value obtained by the parallelogram law through equation (3). Each time a vector equation is written or read, it must be remembered that the graphical or geometrical addition of vectors is being expressed through the parallelogram law. It is important to note that the mathematical statement dealing with the parallelo-

---

[1] A detailed discussion of vector equations is presented in the "Supplementary Topics."

gram law is *not* a proof of the law—it is merely a description. Actually, there is no rigorous mathematical proof of the graphical parallelogram law. It is verified experimentally and is accepted as a geometrical fact.

2.2 Equilibrium Law

If two concurrent forces are in equilibrium, their vector sum, or resultant, must equal zero. *Therefore, in order for two concurrent forces to be in equilibrium, they must be equal in magnitude, opposite in sense, and collinear in action* (see Figs. 1.10 and 2.4). Figure 2.4 shows how this law evolves from the parallelogram law. In this figure, the given concurrent forces F_1 and F_2 are assumed to be of equal magnitude.

The equilibrium law can be applied to more than two concurrent forces. Consider a concurrent force system involving three coplanar forces (forces that lie in one plane). In order for this

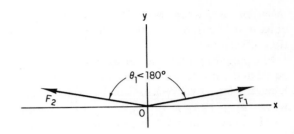

(c) Space Diagram

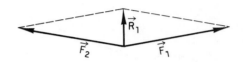

(d) Parallelogram of Forces. $\vec{F_1} + \vec{F_2} = \vec{R_1}$, and since R_1 has a magnitude greater than zero, the given force system is not in equilibrium. Note that as the angle between $\vec{F_1}$ and $\vec{F_2}$ increases, the resultant force decreases.

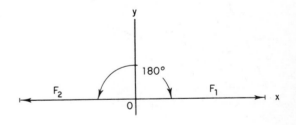

(e) Space Diagram

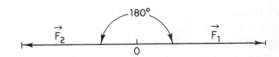

(f) Parallelogram of Forces. The parallelogram becomes a straight line, and the diagonal reaches the limiting value of zero. Since $\vec{F_1} = \vec{F_2}$ in magnitude, we can write a general vector equation for equilibrium: $\vec{F_1} + (-\vec{F_2}) = 0$. (The minus sign indicates that the *sense* of $\vec{F_2}$ is opposite to that of $\vec{F_1}$.)

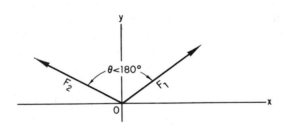

(a) Space Diagram

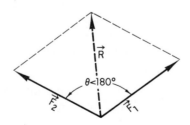

(b) Parallelogram of Forces. $\vec{F_1} + \vec{F_2} = \vec{R}$, and since $\vec{R}$ has a magnitude greater than zero, the given force system is not in equilibrium.

FIGURE 2.4

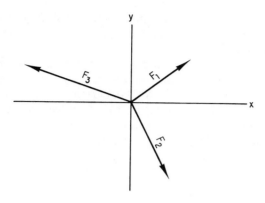

(a) Space Diagram

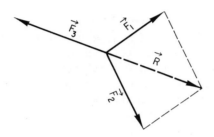

(b) Parallelogram of Forces. The resultant $\vec{R}$ of $\vec{F}_1$ and $\vec{F}_2$ is determined by the parallelogram law. It is equal and opposite to $\vec{F}_3$, indicating that the given force system is in static equilibrium. $\vec{F}_3$ in this case can be considered the equilibrant.

FIGURE 2.5

force system to be in equilibrium, the resultant of any two forces of the system must be equal in magnitude to, opposite in sense to, and collinear in action with the remaining third force (see Fig. 2.5). If, in Fig. 2.5b, forces $\vec{F}_1$ and $\vec{F}_3$ were added vectorially, their resultant would be equal in magnitude and opposite in sense to $\vec{F}_2$, indicating equilibrium with $\vec{F}_2$, the equilibrant. Similarly, vector addition of $\vec{F}_2 + \vec{F}_3$ would show that $\vec{F}_1$ is the equilibrant. In such a force system, all the forces are equilibrating forces.

We can see from Fig. 2.5 that in writing a general mathematical description of a given force system that we have analyzed graphically, we get the following general equations:

Vector addition of forces F_1 and F_2:

$$\vec{F}_1 + \vec{F}_2 = \vec{R}$$

Vector addition of forces F_3 and R:

$$\vec{F}_3 + \vec{R} = 0$$

(since for equilibrium of the force system $\vec{R}$ must equal $-\vec{F}_3$ and be collinear in action with and opposite in sense to $\vec{F}_3$, as indicated by the minus sign).

We can determine if this same concurrent, coplanar force system consisting of three forces is in equilibrium by a *consecutive* vector addition, as illustrated by the triangle law of vector addition (see Fig. 2.6). The diagram in which vectors are added consecutively is also called a *vector diagram* (compare Fig. 2.1b).

The consecutive addition of vectors illustrating the equilibrium law can be analyzed graphically by constructing the vectors in the vector diagram parallel to the lines of action of the forces in the space diagram, and by connecting these vectors to

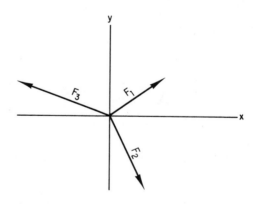

(a) Space Diagram

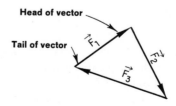

(b) Vector Diagram. Vectors are parallel to the forces in the space diagram.

FIGURE 2.6

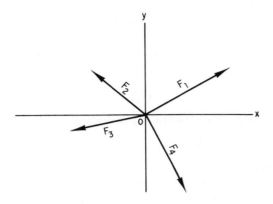

(a) Space Diagram

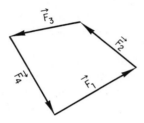

(b) Vector Diagram I. Vectors are added consecutively in numerical order: $\vec{F_1} + \vec{F_2} + \vec{F_3} + \vec{F_4}$.

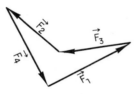

(c) Vector Diagram II. Vectors are added consecutively: $\vec{F_4} + \vec{F_1} + \vec{F_3} + \vec{F_2}$. Both vector diagrams (b) and (c) are closed polygons, indicating that the given force system has no resultant force and is therefore in equilibrium.

FIGURE 2.7

each other such that the *head* of the first vector is connected to the *tail* of the next vector, continuing this addition until the last vector of the system is included. If the head of the *last* vector meets the *tail* of the *first* vector, the given force system does *not* have a resultant force (or the resultant force has zero magnitude); in a concurrent force system, this result would indicate a condition of static

equilibrium (see Fig. 2.6). Thus, whenever equilibrium exists, the vector diagram will be a *closed polygon*.

The consecutive addition of force vectors can be used to determine the resultant of any system having any number of concurrent forces. The order in which the vectors are added has no effect on the result, since the resultant force of a given system represents the *total effect* of the given system (see Fig. 2.7).

2.3 Superposition and the Transmissibility of a Force

Law of superposition

When a force system is in equilibrium, the resultant of the system is zero. If such a force system is added to, applied to, or subtracted from another force system acting on a rigid body, it will have *no effect* whatsoever on the body or the initial system acting on the body (see Fig. 2.8).

Principle of the transmissibility of a force

A force on a rigid body may be applied anywhere along *its line of action* without changing its effect on the body.

This principle can be illustrated by the application of a special case of the law of superposition (see Fig. 2.9).

2.4 Law of Action and Reaction

Newton's third law of motion states, in general, that to every active force there is an equal and opposite force. Applied to conditions of static equilibrium, this law can be restated as follows: to every *applied* force there must be an equal and opposite *reaction* force for equilibrium to exist.

In Chapter 1, we discussed free-body diagrams that involved applied forces (active forces) and reaction forces from supports. Review the various figures in that chapter to see how the law of action and reaction is applied in the study of statics.

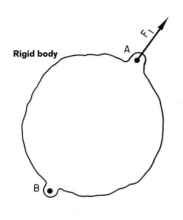

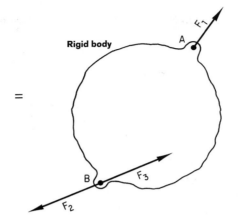

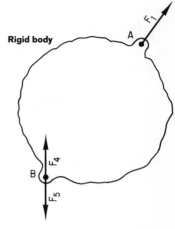

(a) Given force F_1 is applied to a rigid body at point A.

(b) Forces F_2 and F_3 are in equilibrium, and are applied to the rigid body at point B. Since their resultant is zero, the body is not affected by these forces.

(c) Forces F_2 and F_3 have been subtracted from point B, and forces F_4 and F_5, which are in equilibrium, have been added. The original condition of the body does not change with the application of this second balanced force system.

FIGURE 2.8

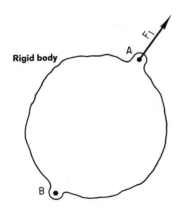

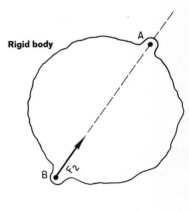

(a) Given force F_1 is applied to a rigid body at point A.

(b) A balanced force system composed of forces F_2 and F_3 is applied at point B. Forces F_1, F_2, and F_3 have equal magnitudes and the same line of action. Since F_1 and F_3 are equal and opposite collinear forces, they are balanced and can be subtracted from the body without changing the effect of F_2.

(c) Since F_1 and F_3 were subtracted in (b), this leaves only F_2, which is equal in magnitude to and has the same sense and line of action as the original force F_1; therefore, its effect on the body is the same as the effect of F_1.

FIGURE 2.9

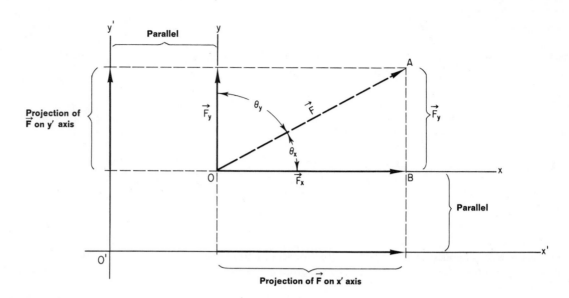

FIGURE 2.10

2.5 Principle of Components or Projections

Since a given force can be resolved into two components, we can say that the given force is the resultant of these two components. If we resolve a given force into components that are perpendicular to each other and *parallel* to the rectangular coordinate axes, we call these components *rectangular components* (see Fig. 2.10).

We write the vector equation denoting the addition of components $\vec{F}_x$ and $\vec{F}_y$ to get the resultant vector $\vec{F}$ as follows:

$$\vec{F}_x + \vec{F}_y = \vec{F}$$

To determine the magnitudes of $\vec{F}_x$ and $\vec{F}_y$, we can apply trigonometric analysis, using the angles θ_x and θ_y that the given force F makes with the x and y axes, respectively, as follows:

$$\left.\begin{array}{ll} \cos\theta_x = \dfrac{F_x}{F} & \text{therefore, } F_x = F\cos\theta_x \\[2mm] \cos\theta_y = \dfrac{F_y}{F} & \text{therefore, } F_y = F\cos\theta_y \end{array}\right\}\begin{array}{l}\text{scalar}\\\text{quantities}\end{array}$$

From the expressions for F_x and F_y, we see that the rectangular components $\vec{F}_x$ and $\vec{F}_y$ are actually the *projections* of the given force $\vec{F}$ on the x and y

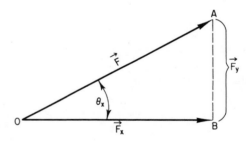

FIGURE 2.11

axes. If we apply the Pythagorean theorem to the right triangle OAB formed by $\vec{F}_x$ and $\vec{F}_y$, we can determine an expression for the magnitude of $\vec{F}$ (see Fig. 2.11):

$$(5) \qquad F = \sqrt{F_x{}^2 + F_y{}^2}$$

Writing expressions for the rectangular components, or projections, of the force $\vec{F}$ on the x and y axes in terms of the angle θ_x only, we arrive at this same expression for the magnitude of $\vec{F}$ in the following manner:

$$\left.\begin{array}{ll} \cos\theta_x = \dfrac{F_x}{F} & \text{therefore, } F_x = F\cos\theta_x \\[2mm] \sin\theta_x = \dfrac{F_y}{F} & \text{therefore, } F_y = F\sin\theta_x \end{array}\right\}\begin{array}{l}\text{scalar}\\\text{quantities}\end{array}$$

Squaring and adding both sides of the expressions for F_x and F_y, we get

(6)
$$F_x{}^2 + F_y{}^2 = F^2 \cos^2 \theta_x + F^2 \sin^2 \theta_x$$
$$= F^2(\cos^2 \theta_x + \sin^2 \theta_x)$$

Since $\cos^2 \theta_x + \sin^2 \theta_x = 1$ from trigonometry, $F_x{}^2 + F_y{}^2 = F^2$. Solving for F, we get

$$F = \sqrt{F_x{}^2 + F_y{}^2}$$

Since we have shown that the components of a force can be considered projections of the force onto an axis system, the concept can be generalized by the following statement, which is called *the principle of components or projections*: the projections of the *resultant* of a force system on a given axis system is equal to the *algebraic* sum of the projections of the individual forces in the given force system onto the same axes.

Consider a system of two concurrent forces $\vec{F}_1$ and $\vec{F}_2$ that have a resultant $\vec{R}$. For convenience, we place the point of application of these forces at the origin O of the x and y axes (Fig. 2.12). Considering the components $\vec{R}_x$ and $\vec{R}_y$ of the resultant $\vec{R}$ of the given force system, we see that the magnitude of $\vec{R}$ is defined by

(7)
$$R = \sqrt{R_x{}^2 + R_y{}^2}$$

Also, the angle the resultant $\vec{R}$ makes with the x axis can be defined as follows:

(8)
$$\sin \theta_x = \frac{R_y}{R}$$

(9)
$$\cos \theta_x = \frac{R_x}{R}$$

(10)
$$\tan \theta = \frac{R_y}{R_x}$$

From the principle of components, we see that the projections of $\vec{R}$ on the x and y axes are $\vec{R}_x$ and $\vec{R}_y$, and therefore, the resultant can be expressed in two ways:

$$\vec{R} = \vec{R}_x + \vec{R}_y \qquad \text{and} \qquad \vec{R} = \vec{F}_1 + \vec{F}_2$$

The projections of the force $\vec{F}_1$ on the given axis system are $\vec{F}_{1_x}$ and $\vec{F}_{1_y}$. Therefore,

$$\vec{F}_1 = \vec{F}_{1_x} + \vec{F}_{1_y} \qquad \text{[vector equation]}$$

The projections of the force $\vec{F}_2$ on the given axis system are $\vec{F}_{2_x}$ and $\vec{F}_{2_y}$. Therefore,

$$\vec{F}_2 = \vec{F}_{2_x} + \vec{F}_{2_y}$$

Equating the components of the resultant and the two given forces in vector form, we get

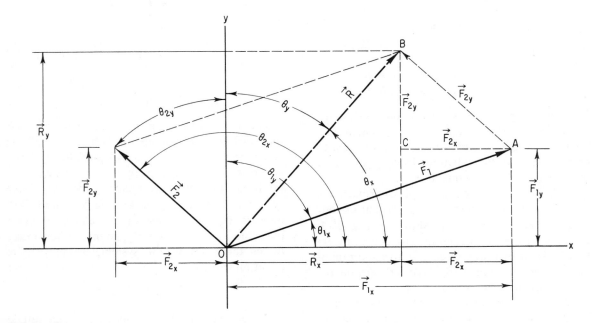

FIGURE 2.12

(11) $\underbrace{\vec{R}_x + \vec{R}_y}_{\vec{R}} = \underbrace{[\vec{F}_{1_x} + \vec{F}_{1_y}]}_{\vec{F}_1} + \underbrace{[-\vec{F}_{2_x} + \vec{F}_{2_y}]}_{\vec{F}_2}$

where $\vec{F}_{2_x}$ is negative, since it acts in the direction opposite to the positive x axis.

Graphically,

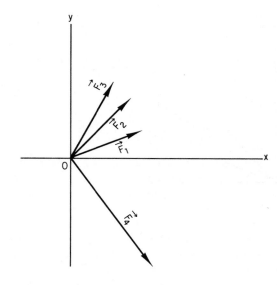

FIGURE 2.13

Analytically, the magnitudes of the projections of $\vec{R}$, $\vec{F}_1$, and $\vec{F}_2$ can be expressed in terms of the angles they make with the x and y axes:

Projections of $\vec{R}$, $\vec{F}_1$, and $\vec{F}_2$ on the x axis

$$\vec{R}_x = R \cos \theta_x$$
$$\vec{F}_{1_x} = F_1 \cos \theta_{1_x}$$
$$\vec{F}_{2_x} = F_2 \cos \theta_{2_x}$$

Projections of $\vec{R}$, $\vec{F}_1$, and $\vec{F}_2$ on the y axis

$$\vec{R}_y = R \cos \theta_y$$
$$\vec{F}_{1_y} = F_1 \cos \theta_{1_y}$$
$$\vec{F}_{2_y} = F_2 \cos \theta_{2_y}$$

Therefore,

$$R \cos \theta_x = F_1 \cos \theta_{1_x} + F_2 \cos \theta_{2_x}$$
$$R \cos \theta_y = F_1 \cos \theta_{1_y} + F_2 \cos \theta_{2_y}$$

Thus, as the principle of projections states, the projections of the resultant of a force system on a given axis system is equal to the algebraic sum of the projections of the individual forces in the given force system onto the same axes.

To illustrate further the principle of projections, let us consider a concurrent force system of four forces $\vec{F}_1$, $\vec{F}_2$, $\vec{F}_3$, and $\vec{F}_4$, as shown in Fig. 2.13. By applying the parallelogram law consecutively (Fig. 2.14), or by using the consecutive addition of the force vectors (Fig. 2.15), we can determine the resultant of the given force system.

Using Fig. 2.15 for convenience, we can apply the principle of projections to derive general mathematical expressions that describe the graphi-

cal addition of the given forces. Writing expressions for the projections of the given forces on the x and y axes, respectively, and summing (algebraically) all the projections on the x axis and the y axis, we write

(12) $\underbrace{[\vec{F}_{1_x} + \vec{F}_{2_x} + \vec{F}_{3_x} + \vec{F}_{4_x}]}_{\sum \vec{F}_x}$

$$+ \underbrace{[\vec{F}_{1_y} + \vec{F}_{2_y} + \vec{F}_{3_y} + \vec{F}_{4_y}]}_{\sum \vec{F}_y}$$

$$= \vec{R}_x + \vec{R}_y = \vec{R}$$

The above expression in vector form says that the algebraic sum of all the projections of the given force system on the x axis plus the algebraic sum of all the projections on the y axis is equal to the projections of the resultant of the given force system on the same axes. Letting $\sum \vec{F}_x$ and $\sum \vec{F}_y$ indicate the *algebraic sum* of all the projections on the x and y axes, respectively, no matter how many forces there are in the system, we may write equation (12) as

$$\sum \vec{F}_x + \sum \vec{F}_y = \vec{R}$$

Referring to Fig. 2.15, we see that the magnitude of the resultant can now be defined as follows:

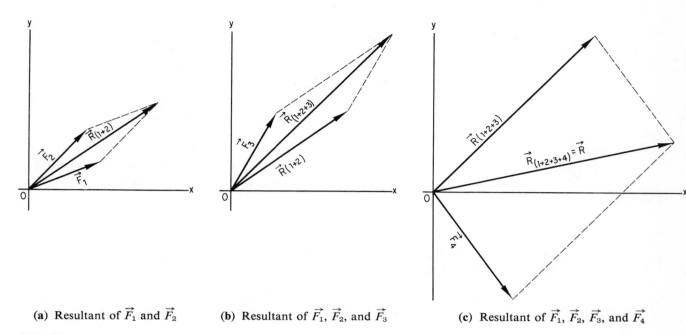

(a) Resultant of $\vec{F_1}$ and $\vec{F_2}$ **(b)** Resultant of $\vec{F_1}$, $\vec{F_2}$, and $\vec{F_3}$ **(c)** Resultant of $\vec{F_1}$, $\vec{F_2}$, $\vec{F_3}$, and $\vec{F_4}$

FIGURE 2.14
Consecutive Application of the Parallelogram Law

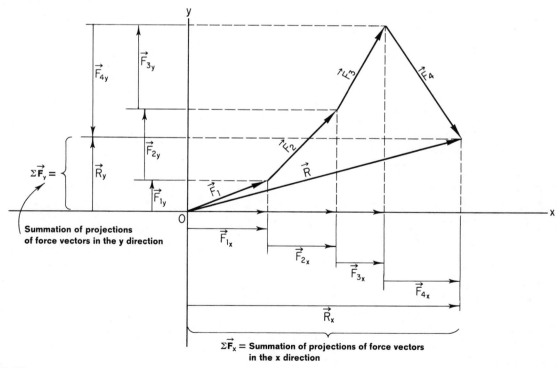

FIGURE 2.15
Consecutive Addition of Vectors

$$R^2 = (\textstyle\sum F_x)^2 + (\textstyle\sum F_y)^2$$

Therefore,

$$(13) \qquad R = \sqrt{(\textstyle\sum F_x)^2 + (\textstyle\sum F_y)^2}$$

Also,

$$(14) \qquad \tan \theta_x = \frac{\sum F_y}{\sum F_x}$$

Equations (13) and (14) are more general forms of equations (7) and (10).

2.6 Principle of Moments; Varignon's Theorem

Since a force can be resolved into two components, it seems logical that the moment of the given force about any given axis will be equal to the algebraic sum of the moments of the individual components of the given force about the same axis of rotation. This is the basic premise of *Varignon's theorem*.

Consider a force $\vec{R}$ having components $\vec{F_1}$ and $\vec{F_2}$, as shown in Fig. 2.16. Point P is any point in the plane of the given force system about which moments are taken. Distances $PI = a$, $PA = b$, and $PJ = c$ are the moment arms for the forces $\vec{R}, \vec{F_1}$, and $\vec{F_2}$, respectively, about the point P. The y axis has conveniently been passed through the point P. The moment of $\vec{R}$ about P is equal to the moment of $\vec{F_1}$ about P plus the moment of $\vec{F_2}$ about P or, in equation form,

$$(15) \qquad \vec{R} \times a = \vec{F_1} \times b + \vec{F_2} \times c$$

This is Varignon's theorem. This analysis can be applied to any number of forces in computing the moment of $\vec{R}$, the resultant force.

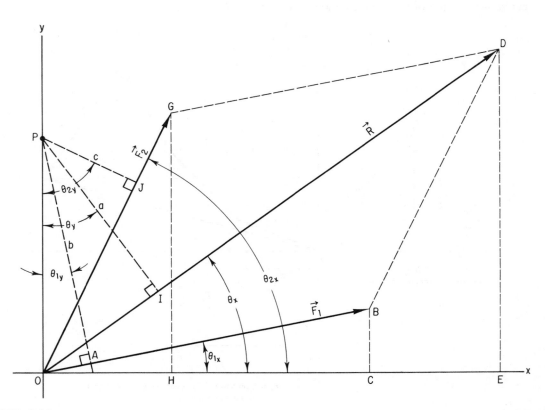

FIGURE 2.16

2.1 Given: The magnitudes and directions of a force $\vec{F}$ and a component $\vec{F_1}$ (Fig. 2.17).

Find: Using graphical analysis, resolve the force $\vec{F}$ into two components, one being the given component $\vec{F_1}$.

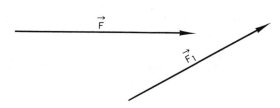

FIGURE 2.17

Find: Using graphical analysis, resolve force $\vec{F}$ into two forces $\vec{F_1}$ and $\vec{F_2}$ where the magnitude of $\vec{F_1}$ is less than the magnitude of $\vec{F_2}$ and the magnitude of $\vec{F_2}$ is less than the magnitude of $\vec{F}$.

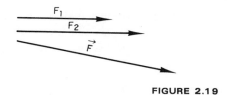

FIGURE 2.19

2.2 Given: The magnitude and direction of a force $\vec{F}$, a component F_1 having a known *magnitude only*, and a second component F_2 having a known *direction only* (Fig. 2.18).

Find: Using graphical analysis, resolve force $\vec{F}$ into the two components $\vec{F_1}$ and $\vec{F_2}$.

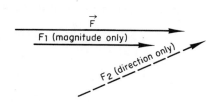

FIGURE 2.18

2.3 Given: The magnitude and direction of a force $\vec{F}$, and the magnitudes *only* of two other forces $\vec{F_1}$ and $\vec{F_2}$ (Fig. 2.19).

2.4 Given: A force system composed of forces $\vec{F_1}, \vec{F_2}, \vec{F_3}, \ldots, \vec{F_n}$ (Fig. 2.20).

Find:
A. Graphically show by the successive application of the parallelogram law that the system can be added by the polygon "law."
B. Graphically show that the resultant determined for the given system is independent of the order in which the forces in the given system are added.

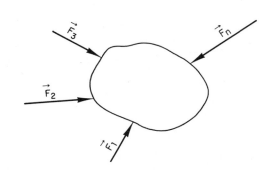

FIGURE 2.20

41

2.5 Given: The magnitudes and directions of force vectors $\vec{F}_1$ and $\vec{F}_2$ (Fig. 2.21).

     Find: A. Their sum, by graphical analysis.
               B. Their difference, by graphical analysis.

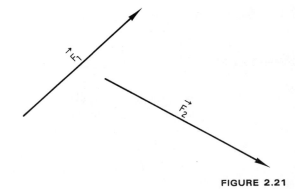

FIGURE 2.21

2.6 Given: The magnitudes and directions of force vectors $\vec{F}_1$, $\vec{F}_2$, $\vec{F}_3$, and $\vec{F}_4$ (Fig. 2.22).

     Find: Using graphical analysis, find
          A. The summation of $\vec{F}_1 + \vec{F}_2 + \vec{F}_3 + \vec{F}_4$.   C. The summation of $\vec{F}_1 - (\vec{F}_2 + \vec{F}_3) + \vec{F}_4$.
          B. The summation of $\vec{F}_1 + \vec{F}_2 - (\vec{F}_3 + \vec{F}_4)$.   D. The summation of $-\vec{F}_1 + (\vec{F}_2 + \vec{F}_3) - \vec{F}_4$.

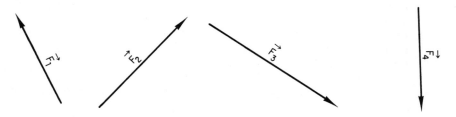

FIGURE 2.22

2.7 Given: The force system composed of $\vec{F}_1$, $\vec{F}_2$, $\vec{F}_3$, and $\vec{F}_4$, with known magnitudes and directions (Fig. 2.23).

     Find: A. Determine by graphical analysis whether or not the given force system is in equilibrium (no translation).
          B. If the given system is not in equilibrium, determine the magnitude and direction of the resultant force.

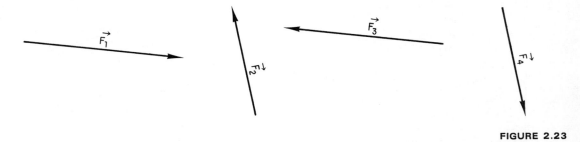

FIGURE 2.23

2.8 Given: The force system composed of $\vec{F}_1$, $\vec{F}_2$, $\vec{F}_3$, $\vec{F}_4$, and $\vec{F}_5$, with known magnitudes and directions (Fig. 2.24).

Find: A. Determine by graphical analysis whether or not the given force system is in equilibrium (no translation).
         B. If the given system is not in equilibrium, determine the magnitude and direction of the resultant force.

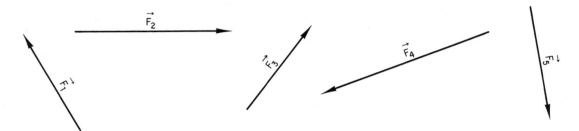

FIGURE 2.24

2.9 Given: A force system composed of forces $F_1 = 120$ lb, $F_2 = 140$ lb, $F_3 = 100$ lb, and $F_n = 160$ lb. The angle that each force makes with the horizontal is shown in Fig. 2.25.

Find: A. Using mathematical analysis, determine the resultant force of the given force system, and prove the law of projections.
         B. Using graphical analysis, determine the resultant force of the given force system, and prove the law of projections.
         C. Compare the results of the two methods used above.

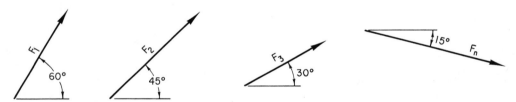

FIGURE 2.25

2.10 Given: The force system composed of $\vec{F}_1$, $\vec{F}_2$, $\vec{F}_3$, and $\vec{F}_4$, with known magnitudes and directions (Fig. 2.26).

Find: A. Determine by graphical analysis whether or not the given force system is in equilibrium (no translation).
         B. If the given system is not in equilibrium, determine the magnitude and direction of the resultant force.

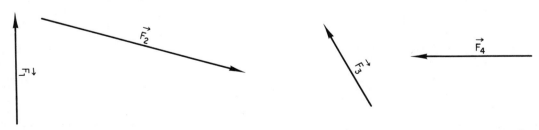

FIGURE 2.26

2.11 Given: A force system consisting of forces $\vec{F}_1, \vec{F}_2, \vec{F}_3, \ldots, \vec{F}_n$ (Fig. 2.27).

Find: By means of the polygon law, show graphically that the sum of the components of the individual forces in the given system is equal to the components of the resultant of the force system.

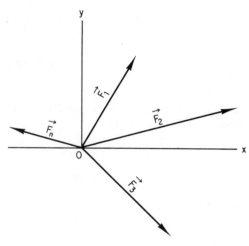

FIGURE 2.27

2.12 Given: Three concurrent forces $F_1 = 100$ lb, $F_2 = 300$ lb, and $F_3 = 100$ lb (Fig. 2.28).

Find: A. Using the method of projections, determine

(1) The resultant force R of the given force system.
(2) The angle the line of action of the resultant R makes with the x axis.

B. Check your answers using graphical analysis.

2.13 Given: Three concurrent forces, $F_1 = 750$ lb and $F_2 = 1000$ lb making angles α and θ, respectively, with the x axis, and $F_3 = 1250$ lb acting vertically downward (Fig. 2.29).

Find: A. Using the method of projections, determine

(1) The resultant force $\vec{R}$ of the given force system.
(2) The angle the line of action of the resultant force $\vec{R}$ makes with the x axis.

B. Check your answer using graphical analysis.

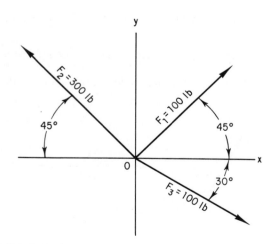

FIGURE 2.28

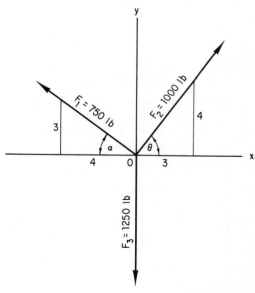

FIGURE 2.29

2.14 Given: Two parallel forces $F_1 = 1000$ lb and $F_2 = 1000$ lb (Fig. 2.30).

Find: A. The resultant force of the given system.
  B. The resultant moment of the given force system (use Varignon's theorem).
  C. Whether or not the given force system is in static equilibrium.

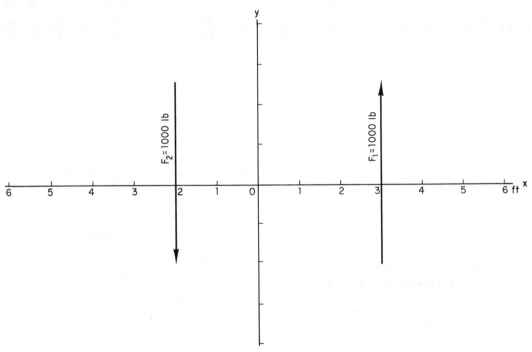

FIGURE 2.30

2.15 Given: Forces $F_1 = 160$ lb and $F_2 = 200$ lb, with directions as shown in Fig. 2.31.

Find: A. Prove that the moment of the resultant of forces F_1 and F_2 about point O is equal to the sum of the moments of F_1 and F_2 about the same point O.

  B. Prove that the moment of the resultant of forces F_1 and F_2 about point O is equal to the sum of the moments of the x and y components of the resultant about the same point O.

  C. Prove that the moment of the resultant of the forces F_1 and F_2 is equal to the sum of the moments of its components about any other point, such as A.

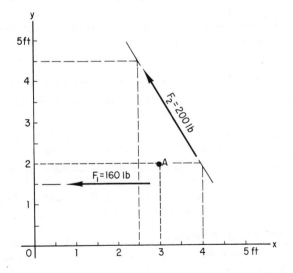

FIGURE 2.31

Three
COPLANAR FORCE SYSTEMS AND STATICS OF SIMPLE STRUCTURES

3.1 Introduction

A coplanar force system is one in which all of the *lines of action* of the forces lie in one plane (see Fig. 3.1).

3.2 Resultant of Coplanar, Collinear Force Systems

A *collinear* force system consists of two forces having the *same* line of action. The senses of the forces can be in the same or opposite directions (see Fig. 3.2).

The resultant of a collinear force system can be determined by the algebraic addition of the forces in the system. Since the forces have lines of action that lie on one line, the magnitude of the resultant is easily determined.

EXAMPLE 3.1 _____

The resultant of a collinear force system of two forces.

Given: Two forces $F_1 = 50$ lb and $F_2 = 125$ lb acting at point A, as shown in Fig. 3.3.

Find: A. The magnitude of the resultant of the given system by graphical analysis.
B. The magnitude of the resultant by mathematical analysis.

Graphical Analysis

1. Establish positive and negative directions for the given forces (see Fig. 3.4). Consider force $\vec{F_1}$, which has a sense to the right ($\xrightarrow{+}$), as positive and force $\vec{F_2}$,

which has a sense to the left ($\xleftarrow{-}$), as negative.
2. Graphically add forces $\vec{F_1}$ and $\vec{F_2}$ by consecutively laying out the forces to a vector scale, as shown in the vector diagram in Fig. 3.4.

Mathematical (Algebraic) Analysis

1. Establish positive and negative directions for the given forces, as above.
2. Algebraically add the scalar quantities (numbers) that represent the magnitudes of F_1 and F_2.

$$\vec{R} = (\vec{F_1}) + (-\vec{F_2}) \quad \text{[vector equation]}$$
$$R = F_1 - F_2 \quad \text{[scalar equation]}$$
$$= 50 \text{ lb} - 125 \text{ lb}$$
$$= -75 \text{ lb}$$

where the minus sign indicates that the resultant has a sense to the left ($\xleftarrow{75\,\text{lb}}$).

EXAMPLE 3.2 _____

The resultant of a collinear force system of three forces.

Given: Forces $F_1 = 25$ lb, $F_2 = 150$ lb, and $F_3 = 80$ lb acting through point A, as shown in Fig. 3.5.

Find: A. The magnitude of the resultant of the given system by graphical analysis.
B. The magnitude of the resultant by mathematical analysis.

Graphical Analysis

1. Establish positive ($\xrightarrow{+}$) and negative ($\xleftarrow{-}$) directions for the given forces.
2. Graphically add forces $\vec{F_1}$, $\vec{F_2}$, and $\vec{F_3}$ by consecutively laying out the forces to a vector scale, as shown in the vector diagram in Fig. 3.6.

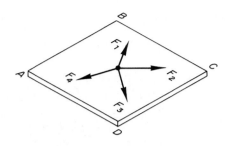

(a) Coplanar, concurrent forces F_1, F_2, F_3, and F_4 lie in plane *ABCD*.

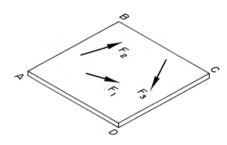

(b) Coplanar, nonconcurrent, nonparallel forces F_1, F_2, and F_3 lie in plane *ABCD*.

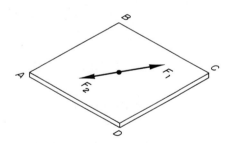

(c) Collinear forces F_1 and F_2 lie in plane *ABCD*.

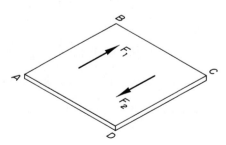

(d) Parallel forces F_1 and F_2 lie in plane *ABCD*.

FIGURE 3.1

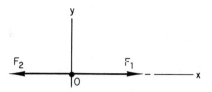

(a) F_1 and F_2 have opposite senses.

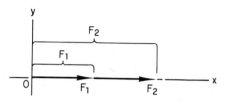

(b) F_1 and F_2 have the same sense.

FIGURE 3.2

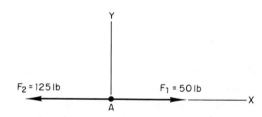

FIGURE 3.3

Space Diagram

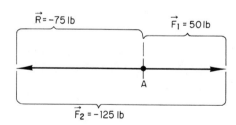

FIGURE 3.4

Vector Diagram
Vector Scale: 1 in. = 50 lb[1]

---

[1] Because of limitations on the page size, the dimensions of the figures do not always agree with the scales indicated in the illustrations. You should remember, however, that you must always choose a convenient scale when using graphical analysis.

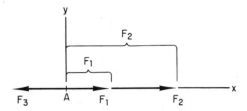

FIGURE 3.5

Space Diagram

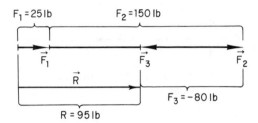

FIGURE 3.6

Vector Diagram
Vector Scale: 1 in. = 50 lb

Mathematical Analysis

1. Assume positive and negative directions for the forces, as above.

2. Algebraically add the scalar quantities that represent the magnitudes of F_1, F_2, and F_3.

$$\vec{R} = \vec{F}_1 + \vec{F}_2 + (-\vec{F}_3) \qquad \text{[vector equation]}$$
$$R = F_1 + F_2 - F_3 \qquad \text{[scalar equation]}$$
$$= 25 \text{ lb} + 150 \text{ lb} - 80 \text{ lb}$$
$$= +95 \text{ lb}$$

where the plus sign indicates that the resultant has a sense to the right ($\xrightarrow{95\,\text{lb}}$).

3.3 Resultant of Coplanar, Concurrent Force Systems

The resultant of a concurrent force system has a line of action that passes through the point of concurrency of the given forces. The magnitude of this resultant is determined by the application of the parallelogram law (or triangle law) or by the principle of projections.

EXAMPLE 3.3

The resultant of a coplanar, concurrent force system of two forces.

Given: Forces $F_1 = 100$ lb and $F_2 = 80$ lb, as shown in Fig. 3.7a.

Find: A. The magnitude and direction (relative to the x axis) of the resultant force of the given system by graphical analysis.
B. The magnitude and direction of the resultant force by mathematical analysis.

Graphical Analysis

1. Graphically add forces $\vec{F}_1$ and $\vec{F}_2$ by drawing the forces to a vector scale and adding them consecutively by the triangle law (Fig. 3.7b). Length OA represents $\vec{F}_1$ to the established vector scale, and length AC represents the vector length of $\vec{F}_2$.

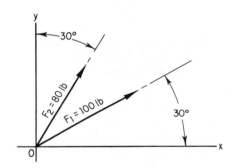

(a) Space Diagram

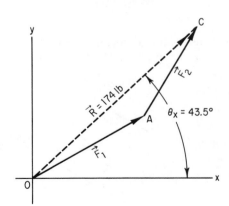

(b) Vector Diagram
Vector Scale: 1 in. = 50 lb

FIGURE 3.7

2. Measure length OC (the vector length of the resultant of the given system) to the established vector scale to determine the magnitude of the resultant. $R = 174$ lb.

3. The angle that the resultant $\vec{R}$ makes with the given x-y axes can be measured directly with a protractor. $\theta_x = 43.5°$.

Mathematical (Direct Trigonometric) Analysis

1. Complete the parallelogram $OACB$, as shown in Fig. 3.8. (For mathematical analysis, this parallelogram does not have to be drawn to scale.)

2. The angle θ between forces $\vec{F_1}$ and $\vec{F_2}$ is

$$90° - (30° + 30°) = 30°$$

3. Applying the law of cosines, as indicated on page 313, we can write

$$R = \sqrt{F_1{}^2 + F_2{}^2 - 2F_1F_2 \cos(180° - \theta)}$$

Since $\cos(180° - \theta) = \cos(180° - 30°) = \cos 150° = -\cos 30°$, we can substitute for F_1, F_2, and $-\cos 30°$ to get

$$\begin{aligned} R &= \sqrt{100^2 + 80^2 + 2(100)(80) \cos 30°} \\ &= \sqrt{10,000 + 6400 + 16,000(\sqrt{3}/2)} \\ &= \sqrt{30,250} \\ &= 174 \text{ lb} \end{aligned}$$

4. We determine the angle θ_x that the resultant $\vec{R}$ makes with the x axis by applying the *law of sines* to the triangle OAC (see Fig. 3.8). From Fig. 3.9, we see that the angle between sides OA and AC is $180° - 30° = 150°$. Then, if α is the angle between the resultant $\vec{R}$ and $\vec{F_1}$, according to the law of sines we can write[2]

$$\begin{aligned} \frac{\sin \alpha}{AC} &= \frac{\sin 150°}{OC} \\ \therefore \sin \alpha &= \frac{AC \sin 150°}{OC} \\ &= \frac{F_2 \sin 150°}{R} \\ &= \frac{(80 \text{ lb})(0.500)}{174 \text{ lb}} \\ &= 0.230 \\ \therefore \alpha &= 13.3° \end{aligned}$$

Therefore, $\theta_x = 30° + \alpha = 30° + 13.3°$ or

$$\theta = 43.3°$$

---

[2] The calculations in the examples in this book have been performed on the slide rule and therefore reflect "slide-rule accuracy."

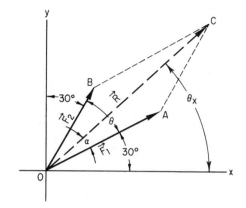

FIGURE 3.8

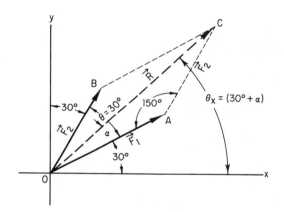

FIGURE 3.9

Mathematical Analysis Using the Principle of Projections

1. Find the projections of forces $\vec{F_1}$ and $\vec{F_2}$ on the x and y axes (Fig. 3.10).

$$\begin{aligned} R_x &= \sum F_x = F_{1_x} + F_{2_x} \\ &= OA \cos 30° + OB \cos 60° \\ &= (100 \text{ lb})\left(\frac{\sqrt{3}}{2}\right) + (80 \text{ lb})\left(\frac{1}{2}\right) \\ &= (86.6 + 40.0) \text{ lb} \\ &= 126.6 \text{ lb} \end{aligned}$$

$$\begin{aligned} R_y &= \sum F_y = F_{1_y} + F_{2_y} \\ &= OA \cos 60° + OB \cos 30° \\ &= (100 \text{ lb})\left(\frac{1}{2}\right) + (80 \text{ lb})\left(\frac{\sqrt{3}}{2}\right) \\ &= (50.0 + 69.2) \text{ lb} \\ &= 119.2 \text{ lb} \end{aligned}$$

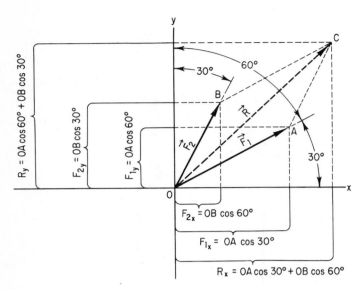

FIGURE 3.10

EXAMPLE 3.4

The resultant of a coplanar, concurrent force system of four forces.

Given: Forces $F_1 = 80$ lb, $F_2 = 50$ lb, $F_3 = 100$ lb, and $F_4 = 120$ lb, as shown in Fig. 3.12a.

Find: The magnitude and direction (relative to the x axis) of the resultant of the given force system, using graphical and mathematical analysis.

Graphical Analysis

1. Choose a vector scale (1 in. = 50 lb), and connect the vectors representing the forces $\vec{F_1}$, $\vec{F_2}$, $\vec{F_3}$, and $\vec{F_4}$ in consecutive order and parallel to the lines of action of the forces in the space diagram (Fig. 3.12b).

2. The *closing vector* represents the resultant $\vec{R}$ of the given system. Note that the sense of $\vec{R}$ is from the

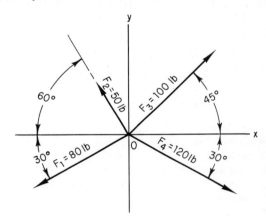

(a) Space Diagram

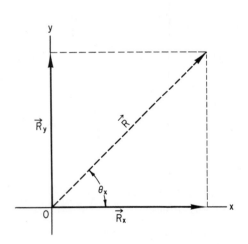

FIGURE 3.11

2. Determine the magnitude of R (see Fig. 3.11).

$$R^2 = R_x{}^2 + R_y{}^2$$
$$\therefore R = \sqrt{R_x{}^2 + R_y{}^2} = \sqrt{126.6^2 + 119.2^2}$$
$$= \sqrt{16,000 + 14,200} = \sqrt{30,200}$$
$$= 174.3 \text{ lb}$$

Determine θ_x. From Fig. 3.11,

$$\tan \theta_x = \frac{R_y}{R_x} = \frac{119.2}{126.6} = 0.940$$
$$\therefore \theta_x = 43.3°$$

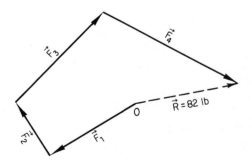

(b) Vector Diagram
Vector Scale: 1 in. = 50 lb

FIGURE 3.12

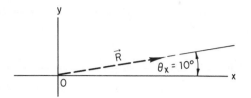

FIGURE 3.13

tail of $\vec{F_1}$ to the head of the last vector drawn in the vector diagram. Measure $\vec{R}$, and convert inches to pounds by the vector scale: $R = 82$ lb.

3. Transfer the direction and sense of $\vec{R}$ to the coordinate axis system used for the given forces (see Fig. 3.13). Measure the angle the resultant makes with the x axis: $\theta_x = 10°$.

Mathematical Analysis
Using the Principle of Projections

1. Find the algebraic sum of the projections of the given forces on the x and y axes (Fig. 3.14), as expressed by the following vector equations:

$$\vec{R}_x = \Sigma \vec{F}_x = \vec{F}_{1_x} + \vec{F}_{2_x} + \vec{F}_{3_x} + \vec{F}_{4_x}$$
$$\vec{R}_y = \Sigma \vec{F}_y = \vec{F}_{1_y} + \vec{F}_{2_y} + \vec{F}_{3_y} + \vec{F}_{4_y}$$

The magnitudes of $\vec{R}_x$ and $\vec{R}_y$ are determined by the following scalar equations:

$$R_x = -F_1 \cos 30° - F_2 \cos 60°$$
$$+ F_3 \cos 45° + F_4 \cos 30°$$
$$= (-80 \text{ lb})\left(\frac{\sqrt{3}}{2}\right) + (-50 \text{ lb})\left(\frac{1}{2}\right)$$
$$+ (100 \text{ lb})\left(\frac{1}{\sqrt{2}}\right) + (120 \text{ lb})\left(\frac{\sqrt{3}}{2}\right)$$
$$= -69.2 \text{ lb} - 25.0 \text{ lb} + 70.7 \text{ lb} + 104.0 \text{ lb}$$
$$= 80.5 \text{ lb}$$

$$R_y = -F_1 \cos 60° + F_2 \cos 30°$$
$$+ F_3 \cos 45° - F_4 \cos 60°$$
$$= (-80 \text{ lb})\left(\frac{1}{2}\right) + (50 \text{ lb})\left(\frac{\sqrt{3}}{2}\right)$$
$$+ (100 \text{ lb})\left(\frac{1}{\sqrt{2}}\right) + (-120 \text{ lb})\left(\frac{1}{2}\right)$$
$$= -40 \text{ lb} + 43.3 \text{ lb} + 70.7 \text{ lb} - 60 \text{ lb}$$
$$= 14 \text{ lb}$$

2. Determine the magnitude of the resultant $\vec{R}$ (see Fig. 3.15).

$$R = \sqrt{R_x{}^2 + R_y{}^2}$$
$$= \sqrt{80.5^2 + 14^2} = \sqrt{6480 + 196}$$
$$= \sqrt{6676}$$
$$= 81.7 \text{ lb}$$

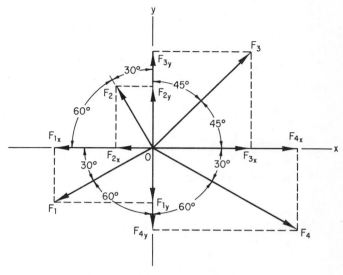

FIGURE 3.14

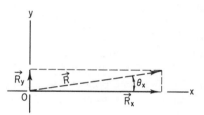

FIGURE 3.15

3. Determine θ_x, the angle that the resultant $\vec{R}$ makes with the x axis (see Fig. 3.15).

$$\tan \theta_x = \frac{R_y}{R_x} = \frac{14 \text{ lb}}{80.5 \text{ lb}} = 0.174$$
$$\therefore \theta_x = 9.88°$$

3.4 Resultant of Coplanar, Nonconcurrent Force Systems

A coplanar, nonconcurrent force system is one in which the lines of action of the forces in the system all lie in one plane and *do not* intersect at one point (see Fig. 3.16).

The resultant of such a force system may consist of a *resultant force* or a *resultant moment*. The *magnitude* of the resultant force can be readily

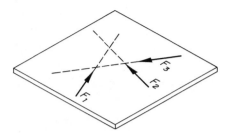

FIGURE 3.16

Forces F_1, F_2, and F_3 *do not* intersect at one point.

determined through graphical or mathematical analysis. In graphical analysis, the magnitude of the resultant force is determined by drawing, to scale, a vector diagram. The actual *position* of the resultant force (relative to the forces in the given system) can be located by graphical analysis through the use of the *funicular* and *ray polygons*, also known as the *string polygons* or *equilibrium polygons*. The ray polygon represents the *components* of the given forces in the vector diagram, while the funicular polygon represents the *lines of action* of these components, which *replace* the lines of action of the *forces* in the *given* system (see Example 3.5).

The mathematical equivalent of the vector-ray-funicular-polygon analysis makes use of the prin-

ciple of projections and Varignon's theorem (see Example 3.5).

EXAMPLE 3.5 ————————————

The resultant of a coplanar, nonconcurrent force system of three nonparallel forces.

Given: Forces $F_1 = 80$ lb, $F_2 = 60$ lb, and $F_3 = 100$ lb, as shown in Fig. 3.17a.

Find: The magnitude of the resultant of the given system and its location relative to the given forces and coordinate axis system.

Graphical Analysis

1. Construct the vector diagram, as shown in Fig. 3.17b: ($\vec{R} = \vec{F_1} + \vec{F_2} + \vec{F_3}$).
2. Measure the length of the vector representing $\vec{R}$ to the vector scale used: $R = 166$ lb.
3. By protractor measurement (see Fig. 3.17b), $\theta_x = 79°$.
4. Since a force can be resolved into *any two* concurrent components, we can derive a method by which the location of the resultant can be determined relative to the given force system. But first we must adopt a notation system (Bow's notation) that facilitates the identification of vectors and lines that is used in statics and structural analysis.

A *number* is assigned to each *space* on either side of the line of action of each force in the system, as given in a space diagram (see Fig. 3.17c). Since each

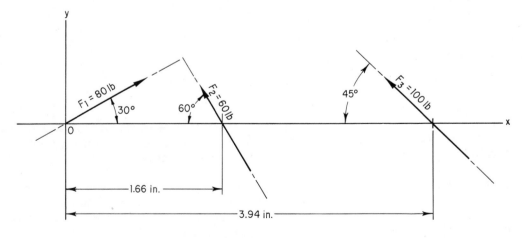

(a) Space Diagram
Space Scale: 1 in. = 1 in.

FIGURE 3.17(a)

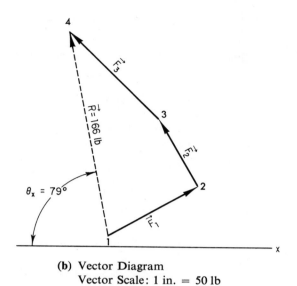

(b) Vector Diagram
Vector Scale: 1 in. = 50 lb

(c) Space Diagram with Bow's Notation (No Scale)

FIGURE 3.17(b), (c)

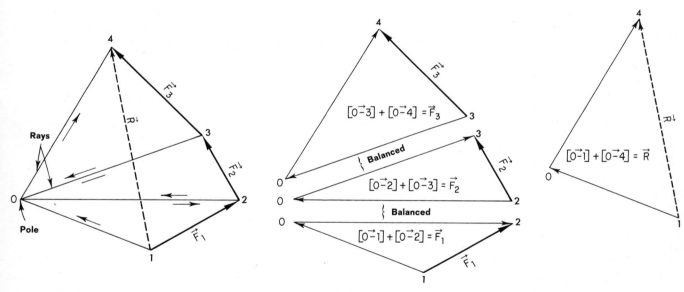

(a) Vector Diagram with Ray Diagram
Vector Scale: 1 in. = 50 lb

(b) In this figure, the vector diagram with the rays from point 0 has been separated into individual diagrams.

FIGURE 3.18

force is now between two numbers, the vectors representing these forces are identified by these numbers. For example, the vector representing $\vec{F_1}$ is denoted as a line (to a vector scale) starting at 1 and ending at 2. The vector representing $\vec{F_2}$ starts at 2

and ends at 3, and the vector for $\vec{F_3}$ starts at 3 and ends at 4. The line [1–4] represents the length of the resultant $\vec{R}$ (see Fig. 3.17b).

Derivation of the funicular polygon

1. Choose any point 0 (called a *pole*) in the vicinity of the vector diagram (see Fig. 3.18a).

2. Construct lines (called *rays*) from point 0 to the head and tail of each vector in the vector diagram. (This diagram is referred to as a *ray diagram*. See Fig. 3.18a.)

3. The rays ($\overrightarrow{[0-1]}$, $\overrightarrow{[0-2]}$, $\overrightarrow{[0-3]}$, and $\overrightarrow{[0-4]}$) emanating from point 0 can be considered components of the forces $\vec{F}_1$, $\vec{F}_2$, and $\vec{F}_3$ and the resultant $\vec{R}$. That is, rays $\overrightarrow{[0-1]}$ and $\overrightarrow{[0-2]}$ are the components of $\vec{F}_1$, $\overrightarrow{[0-2]}$ and $\overrightarrow{[0-3]}$ are the components of $\vec{F}_2$, $\overrightarrow{[0-3]}$ and $\overrightarrow{[0-4]}$ are the components of $\vec{F}_3$, and $\overrightarrow{[0-1]}$ and $\overrightarrow{[0-4]}$ are the components of the resultant $\vec{R}$. (See Fig. 3.18b.)

NOTE: Component $\overrightarrow{[0-2]}$ is in one case a component of $\vec{F}_1$ and has a definite sense that fulfills its role as a component of $\vec{F}_1$. On the other hand, $\overrightarrow{[0-2]}$ is also a component of $\vec{F}_2$, and in this case,

its sense must be opposite to that which it has as a component of $\vec{F}_1$. Since the two equal and opposite collinear forces balance each other, they *cancel* one another.

$$\overrightarrow{[0-1]} - \overrightarrow{[0-2]} = \text{zero}$$

(See Fig. 1.10.) From this it can be seen that $\overrightarrow{[0-3]}$ is a component of $\vec{F}_2$ and $\vec{F}_3$ and is also canceled. The only two components that are not balanced are the components $\overrightarrow{[0-1]}$ and $\overrightarrow{[0-4]}$, which are the components of the resultant $\vec{R}$ (as well as of $\vec{F}_1$ and $\vec{F}_3$). Therefore, through the application of the concept of components of a force, we have defined two components of the resultant of a given force system.

-------------------- **EXAMPLE 3.5 (cont.)**

If, in the space diagram (Fig. 3.17c), the *lines of action* of the forces in the given system are replaced by the *lines of action* of the components (as deter-

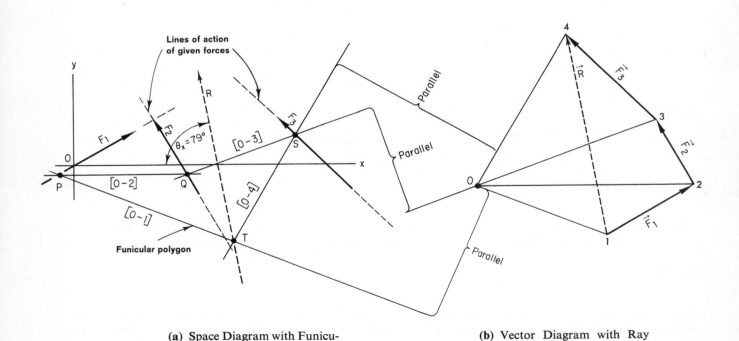

(a) Space Diagram with Funicular Polygon

(b) Vector Diagram with Ray Polygon

FIGURE 3.19

mined in the ray diagram) of the forces in this system, then the given force system is represented in space by an *equivalent* force system (see Fig. 3.19).

This equivalent force system of components (funicular polygon) may be developed as follows:

a. From *any point P* on the line of action of force F_1 in the space diagram, construct a line parallel to the line of action of component [0–1] in the ray diagram.

b. From this same point P, construct another line parallel to the line of action of component [0–2] in the ray diagram. Both [0–1] and [0–2] must be drawn from the same point P on the line of action of F_1, since they are both components of F_1 (see Fig. 3.20).

c. Extend the line of action of [0–2] until it intersects the line of action of F_2 (at point Q in this case). Since [0–2] is a component of F_2, it must intersect the line of action of F_2 (the other component of F_2 is [0–3]).

d. From point Q, draw a line parallel to the line of action of component [0–3] in the ray diagram (see Figs. 3.19 and 3.21).

e. Extend the line of action of [0–3] until it intersects the line of action of F_3 (at point S in this case). Since [0–3] is a component of F_3, it must

intersect the line of action of F_3 (the other component is [0–4]).

f. From point S, draw a line parallel to the line of action of [0–4] in the ray diagram (see Figs. 3.19–3.22).

g. We see from Fig. 3.19 that the components [0–2] and [0–3] are balanced, whereas [0–1] and [0–4], which are the components of the resultant R, are *unbalanced*. Extend the lines of action of [0–1] and [0–4] until they intersect at point T. Through this point the line of action of the resultant must pass (see Figs. 3.19 and 3.23).

h. Through point T, construct a line parallel to the line of action of the resultant $\vec{R}$ in the ray diagram. This is the required location ($a_x = 2.24$ in.) of the resultant of the given force system. (See Fig. 3.24 for a complete solution.)

Varignon's theorem is inherent in this analysis, as can be shown by locating the resultant of the given nonconcurrent, coplanar force system by graphical analysis. By taking moments about any assumed point in the plane of the forces, we see that the moment of the resultant R is equal to the algebraic sum of the moments of the individual forces about the same point in the given system. (See Fig. 3.25.)

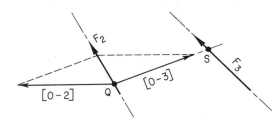

FIGURE 3.20

F_1 is the resultant of [0–1] and [0–2], as defined in Fig. 3.18. In this diagram, the forces and the components are not laid off to a vector scale, since we are only interested in the *directions* of the lines of action of the components.

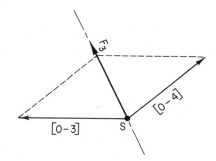

FIGURE 3.22

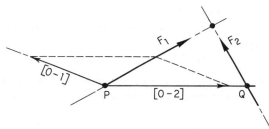

FIGURE 3.21

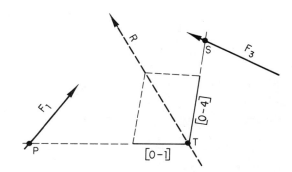

FIGURE 3.23

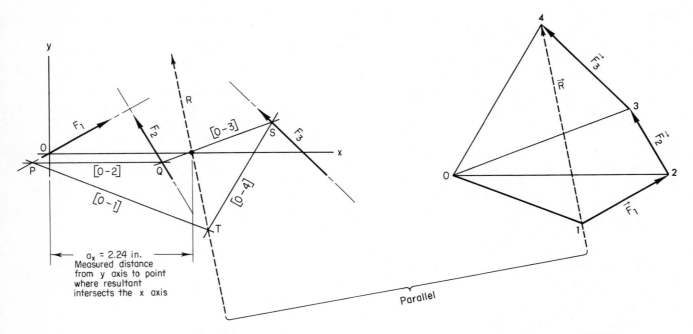

(a) Space Diagram with Funicular Polygon

(b) Vector Diagram with Ray
Polygon

FIGURE 3.24

Using W as a moment center and the measured distances a, b, c, and d as moment arms of the respective forces R, F_1, F_2, and F_3, we see that

$$Ra = -F_1b + F_2c + F_3d$$

where counterclockwise rotation is assumed to be positive. Substituting the values for distances a, b, c, and d, as shown above, we get

$$(166\ \text{lb})(1.39\ \text{in.}) = (-80\ \text{lb})(1.22\ \text{in.})$$
$$+ (60\ \text{lb})(1.00\ \text{in.}) + (100\ \text{lb})(2.68\ \text{in.})$$

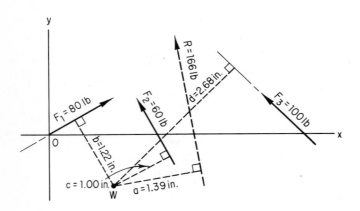

FIGURE 3.25

230.7 lb-in. = −97.5 lb-in.
$$+ 60.0\ \text{lb-in.} + 268.0\ \text{lb-in.}$$

Therefore,

$$230.7\ \text{lb-in.} \approx 230.5\ \text{lb-in.}$$

The discrepancy is due to the absence of absolute precision in measuring the distances and to the use of the slide rule.

**Mathematical Analysis Using
the Principle of Projections and
Varignon's Theorem**

1. Find the algebraic sum of the projections of the given forces $\vec{F}_1$, $\vec{F}_2$, and $\vec{F}_3$ on the x and y axes (Fig. 3.26), as represented by the following vector equations:

$$\vec{R}_x = \sum \vec{F}_x = \vec{F}_{1_x} - \vec{F}_{2_x} - \vec{F}_{3_x}$$
$$\vec{R}_y = \sum \vec{F}_y = \vec{F}_{1_y} + \vec{F}_{2_y} + \vec{F}_{3_y}$$
$$R_x = F_1 \cos 30° - F_2 \cos 60° - F_3 \cos 45°$$
$$= (80\ \text{lb})\left(\frac{\sqrt{3}}{2}\right) - (60\ \text{lb})\left(\frac{1}{2}\right) - (100\ \text{lb})\left(\frac{1}{\sqrt{2}}\right)$$
$$= 69.2\ \text{lb} - 30\ \text{lb} - 70.7\ \text{lb}$$
$$= -31.5\ \text{lb}$$

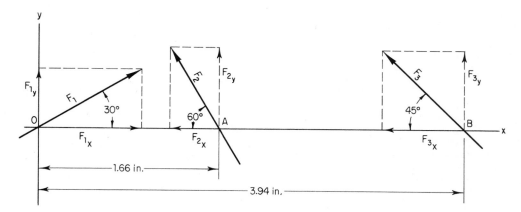

FIGURE 3.26

$$R_y = F_1 \cos 60° + F_2 \cos 30° + F_3 \cos 45°$$

$$= (80 \text{ lb})\left(\frac{1}{2}\right) + (60 \text{ lb})\left(\frac{\sqrt{3}}{2}\right) + (100 \text{ lb})\left(\frac{1}{\sqrt{2}}\right)$$

$$= 40 \text{ lb} + 51.9 \text{ lb} + 70.7 \text{ lb}$$

$$= 162.6 \text{ lb}$$

2. Determine the magnitude of $\vec{R}$ and the angle θ_x (see Fig. 3.27).[3]

$$R = \sqrt{R_x{}^2 + R_y{}^2}$$

$$= \sqrt{(-31.5)^2 + 162.6^2}$$

$$= \sqrt{990 + 26,400}$$

$$= \sqrt{27,390}$$

$$= 166 \text{ lb}$$

$$\tan \theta_x = \frac{R_y}{R_x} = \frac{162.6}{31.5} = 5.16$$

$$\therefore \ \theta_x = 79°$$

3. Locate the point where the line of action of the resultant intersects the x axis. Since the given forces are related to the x-y coordinate axes the resultant R is located relative to these axes. (See distance a_x in Fig. 3.27.)

To determine the distance a_x take moments of the x and y components of the given forces about the origin O. To facilitate this operation resolve each given force into its x and y components at the points

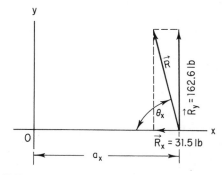

FIGURE 3.27

where the line of action of each force intersects the x axis (at origin O and points A and B as indicated in Fig. 3.26). These points are easily located by the units on the x axis. A is 1.66 in., and B is 3.94 in. from the origin O.

Y components:

$$F_{1y} = F_1 \cos 60° = 80 \text{ lb}(\tfrac{1}{2}) = 40 \text{ lb}$$

(Since the line of action of F_{1y} passes through the origin O, it has no moment relative to O)

$$F_{2y} = F_2 \cos 30° = 60 \text{ lb} \left(\frac{\sqrt{3}}{2}\right) = 51.9 \text{ lb}$$

$$F_{3y} = F_3 \cos 45° = 100 \text{ lb} \left(\frac{1}{\sqrt{2}}\right) = 70.7 \text{ lb}$$

X components:

Since all lines of action of the x components of the given forces pass through the origin O, they have *no moments* relative to O. Therefore it is not necessary to determine the scalar values of these components.

---

[3] Since the x and y axes were chosen so that the lines of action of the forces in the given system either passed through the origin O or ran to the right of it, the line of action of the resultant intersects the x axis to the right of the origin. Figure 3.27 shows an approximate location of the resultant $\vec{R}$ based on the values determined for $\vec{R}_x$ and $\vec{R}_y$ (having negative and positive senses, respectively).

The algebraic sum of the moments of the y components about the origin O (using counterclockwise rotation as positive) is

$$\sum M_0 = 1.66 \text{ in. } (F_{2y}) + 3.94 \text{ in. } (F_{3y})$$
$$= 1.66 \text{ in. } (51.9 \text{ lb}) + 3.94 \text{ in. } (70.7 \text{ lb})$$
$$= 86.2 \text{ lb-in.} + 278 \text{ lb-in.}$$
$$= 364.2 \text{ lb-in.}$$

We can now determine the point where the line of action of the resultant R intersects the x axis by finding where $\sum F_y$ (the y component R_y of the resultant) intersects the x axis. Referring to Fig. 3.27, we can write the following relationship, which expresses Varignon's theorem:

$$\sum M_0 = a_x R_y$$

Solving for a_x, we obtain

$$a_x = \frac{\sum M_0}{R_y}$$

Substituting values determined for $\sum M_0$ and R_y,

$$a_x = \frac{364.2 \text{ lb-in.}}{162.6 \text{ lb}}$$
$$= 2.24 \text{ in.}$$

(See Fig. 3.24 for solution by graphical analysis.)

3.5 Resultant of Coplanar, Parallel Force Systems

The coplanar, parallel force system is a special case of a nonconcurrent force system: the lines of action of the forces in such a system lie in one plane, are parallel to each other, and therefore do not intersect (see Fig. 3.28).

As shown in Fig. 3.29, there are three basic types of parallel force systems:

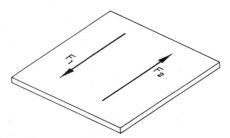

FIGURE 3.28

F_1 and F_2 are parallel and are therefore not concurrent.

1. The resultant is a single force.

2. The resultant is a couple (moment).

3. The resultant is equal to zero (no resultant force and no resultant moment).

The three different types of parallel force systems will be illustrated by examples, using graphical and mathematical analysis in each case.

EXAMPLE 3.6 _____

The coplanar, parallel force system in which the resultant is a single force.

Given: Four coplanar, parallel forces $F_1 = 50$ lb, $F_2 = 100$ lb, $F_3 = 150$ lb, and $F_4 = 200$ lb (see Fig. 3.30a).

Find: The resultant of the given force system and its location relative to the given forces.

Graphical Analysis

1. Determine whether or not a resultant force exists in the given system by adding graphically the force vectors representing $\vec{F_1}$, $\vec{F_2}$, $\vec{F_3}$, and $\vec{F_4}$. Lay off vector $[\overrightarrow{1-2}]$ representing $\vec{F_1}$, add vector $[\overrightarrow{2-3}]$ representing $\vec{F_2}$, add vector $[\overrightarrow{3-4}]$ representing $\vec{F_3}$, and lastly, add vector $[\overrightarrow{4-5}]$ representing $\vec{F_4}$.

2. We see from Fig. 3.30b that the given force system has a resultant force as represented by the vector $[1-5]$. Measure the vector to the vector scale indicated. We find that $\vec{R} = 100$ lb. (NOTE: The sense of the resultant is the same as the sense of the last vector $[\overrightarrow{4-5}]$ in the vector diagram.)

3. Construct the ray diagram by choosing any point O as a pole (see Fig. 3.31). From Fig. 3.31a, we see that

$[\overrightarrow{0-1}]$ and $[\overrightarrow{0-2}]$ are components of $\vec{F_1}$
$[\overrightarrow{0-2}]$ and $[\overrightarrow{0-3}]$ are components of $\vec{F_2}$
$[\overrightarrow{0-3}]$ and $[\overrightarrow{0-4}]$ are components of $\vec{F_3}$
$[\overrightarrow{0-4}]$ and $[\overrightarrow{0-5}]$ are components of $\vec{F_4}$

Canceling the "balanced" components $[\overrightarrow{0-2}]$, $[\overrightarrow{0-3}]$, and $[\overrightarrow{0-4}]$ leaves the "unbalanced" components $[\overrightarrow{0-1}]$ and $[\overrightarrow{0-5}]$, which are the components of the resultant force.

4. Construct the funicular (string) polygon of Fig. 3.31b. Starting at an assumed point A on the line of action of force F_1, construct the "strings" representing the lines of action of the components $[\overrightarrow{0-1}]$ and $[\overrightarrow{0-2}]$ of $\vec{F_1}$, etc.

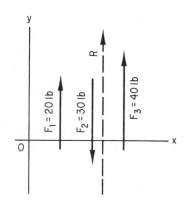

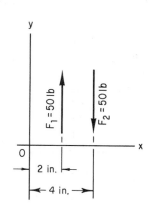

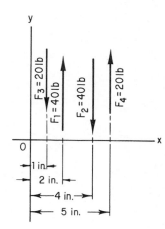

(a) The resultant is a single force, $\sum F_y = R$.

(b) The resultant is a couple, $\sum F_y = 0$ (but a moment is involved).

(c) There is no resultant force and no resultant moment, $\sum F_y = 0$ and $\sum M_O = 0$.

FIGURE 3.29

5. Point P, the point of intersection of the lines of action of the unbalanced components $\overrightarrow{[0\text{-}1]}$ and $\overrightarrow{[0\text{-}5]}$ in the funicular polygon, is the point through which the resultant of the given force system passes. The resultant has a direction *parallel* to the given forces. This locates the resultant relative to the forces in the given system.

Mathematical Analysis

1. Determine the algebraic sum of the given forces (see Fig. 3.32):

$$\sum \vec{F}_y = \vec{R} = -\vec{F}_1 + \vec{F}_2 - \vec{F}_3 + \vec{F}_4$$
$$\therefore \ R = -50 \text{ lb} + 100 \text{ lb} - 150 \text{ lb} + 200 \text{ lb}$$
$$= 100 \text{ lb}$$

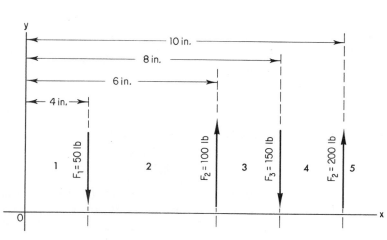

(a) Space Diagram
Space Scale: $\frac{1}{2}$ in. = 1 in.

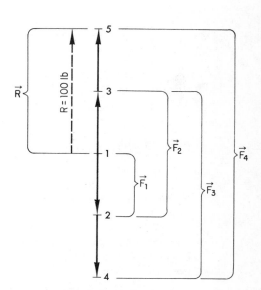

(b) Vector Diagram
Vector Scale: 1 in. = 50 lb

FIGURE 3.30

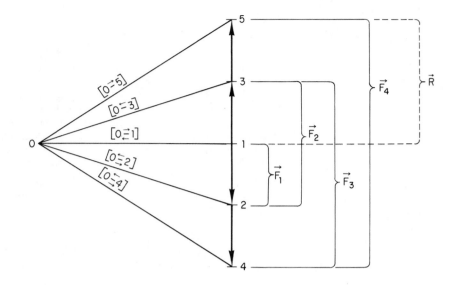

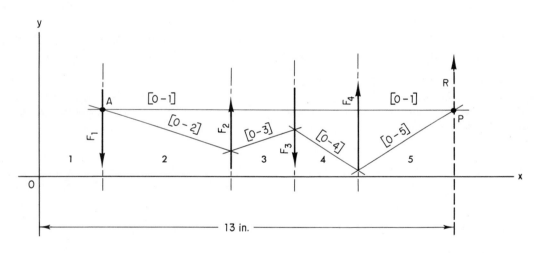

(b) Funicular Polygon

FIGURE 3.31

2. Determine the location of the resultant by applying Varignon's theorem:

$$\sum \vec{M}_O = a\vec{R}$$

Taking moments of the individual forces about the origin O and letting counterclockwise motion be positive, we write

$$-2F_1 + 6F_2 - 8F_3 + 10F_4 = aR$$
$$-(2 \text{ in.})(50 \text{ lb}) + (6 \text{ in.})(100 \text{ lb})$$
$$-(8 \text{ in.})(150 \text{ lb}) + (10 \text{ in.})(200 \text{ lb}) = a(100 \text{ lb})$$
$$(-100 + 600 - 1200 + 2000) \text{ in.-lb} = 100a \text{ lb}$$

Solving for a,

$$a = \frac{1300 \text{ in.-lb}}{100 \text{ lb}} = 13 \text{ in.}$$

Therefore, the line of action of the resultant $\vec{R}$ is located 13 in. to the right of the origin.

Next we consider a parallel force system that is a couple. A couple, as previously defined, consists

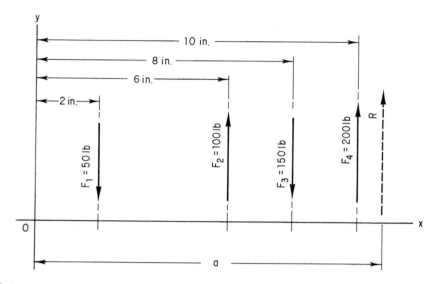

FIGURE 3.32

of two *parallel forces* that are *equal in magnitude* and *opposite in sense*. Let us analyze a couple formed by two parallel, equal, and opposite forces F_1 in the *x-y* plane as shown in Fig. 3.33. (Since the two forces F_1 are parallel, it is convenient to place the *y* ordinate parallel to these forces.) Algebraically adding the *x* and *y* projections of the two forces F_1 we get

$$\sum F_x = 0$$

and

$$\sum F_y = -F_{1_y} + F_{1_y}$$
$$= 0$$

Thus, these two forces have *no single resultant force*. However, if we take moments of these forces about any point in the plane of the couple (*x-y*

plane), we find that the algebraic sum of these moments *is not* zero. Further, if we sum the moments of these forces about several different points in the *x-y* plane, we find that the moment of a couple is always equal to the product of the *arm* of the couple and the *magnitude* of one of the forces in the couple, no matter where the center is about which moments are taken.

Referring to Fig. 3.34, we see that by taking the algebraic sum of the moments of both forces F_1 about the origin *O* we can write (assuming counterclockwise rotation of *individual* forces to be positive).

$$\sum M_O = -F_1b + F_1c$$

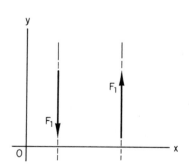

FIGURE 3.33

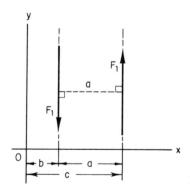

FIGURE 3.34

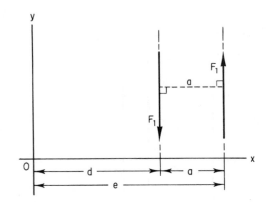

FIGURE 3.35

where the center of moments is taken in the plane of the couple. (What would be the result of assuming a moment center *between* the forces F_1?)

1. As shown in Figs. 3.33 and 3.36a,
   a. it has a *rotational* effect only
   b. its resultant is a *torque* or moment that cannot be reduced to any simpler form
   c. it cannot be replaced by a single force
   d. it acts in a plane, since the lines of action of the forces creating the couple are parallel—and parallel lines define a plane.

Since $c = a + b$ we can make the substitution and write

$$\sum M_O = -F_1 b + F_1(a + b)$$
$$= -F_1 b + F_1 a + F_1 b$$
$$= F_1 a$$
$$\therefore \ M_{F_1} = F_1 a$$

Keeping this same couple in the *x-y* plane but moving it farther away from the origin *O* (see Fig. 3.35), and proceeding as in step 1, we find that $M_{F_1} = F_1 a$ again. This will be true no matter

2. As shown in Figs. 3.34, 3.35, and 3.37,
   a. it can be moved anywhere in its plane of action or parallel to its plane of action without changing its effect on the body
   b. it has an *arm* which is the *perpendicular* distance between the lines of action of the parallel forces creating the couple.

3. As shown in Figs. 3.34, 3.35, and 3.37, its *moment* is defined by the product of the perpendicular distance (arm) between the lines of action of the parallel forces and the magnitude of one of the forces in the couple; this moment can be specified as a vector quantity (see page 8–11).

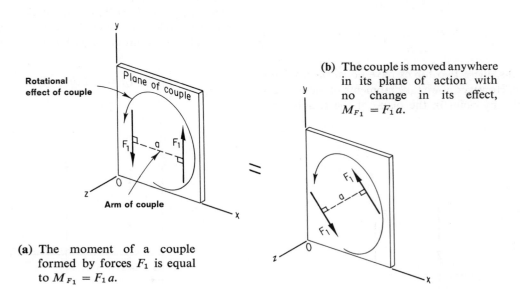

Rotational effect of couple

Arm of couple

(b) The couple is moved anywhere in its plane of action with no change in its effect, $M_{F_1} = F_1 a$.

(a) The moment of a couple formed by forces F_1 is equal to $M_{F_1} = F_1 a$.

FIGURE 3.36(a), (b)

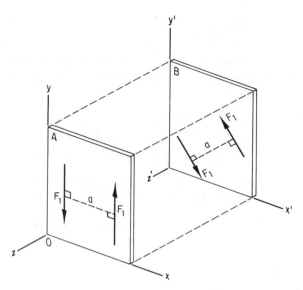

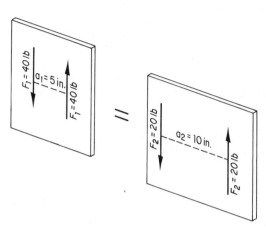

(c) The couple moved in its plane of action and parallel to its plane of action (from the x-y plane to the $x'y'$ plane) with no change in its effect.

(d) Equivalent Couples:

$$M_{F_1} = a_1 F_1 = 5(40) = 200 \text{ lb-in.};$$
$$M_{F_2} = a_2 F_2 = 10(20) = 200 \text{ lb-in.}$$

FIGURE 3.36(c), (d)

4. As shown in Fig. 3.36d, two couples are *equivalent* if their moments are equal and their rotational directions are the same. This means that the forces making up the respective couples need not have the same magnitudes; the perpendicular distance between the forces in each of the equivalent couples is such that their products with the magnitudes of the respective forces are *equal*.

In Chapter 1, *moment* was shown to be a vector quantity. Since a couple has a moment as a *resultant*, this moment can be added and subtracted vectorially with moments of other couples. The vector representing the moment of a couple has a direction *perpendicular* to the plane of the couple; its sense is established by clockwise or counterclockwise rotation of the couple by applying the right-hand rule. (See Fig. 3.37.) Curl the fingers of the right hand in the direction of the moment, and the right thumb will point in the direction of the *moment vector*.

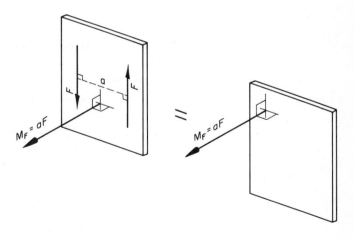

FIGURE 3.37

The vector representing the moment of the couple formed by forces F acts perpendicular to the plane of action of the couple. The foot of this vector can be located *anywhere* in the plane of the couple, since a couple may be moved anywhere in its plane of action without changing its effect.

Sign convention for moment vectors

The senses of moment vectors are defined as positive or negative, relative to the positive and negative directions of the *x-y-z* coordinate axes. Referring to Figs. 3.38, 3.39, and 3.40, we see the following.

A positive sense in the x direction results when a couple has a rotation (related to the *y* and *z* axes) that goes from

$$\left.\begin{matrix} +y \text{ axis to } +z \text{ axis} \\ +z \text{ axis to } -y \text{ axis} \end{matrix}\right\} \quad \text{See Fig. 3.38a.}$$

$$\left.\begin{matrix} -y \text{ axis to } -z \text{ axis} \\ -z \text{ axis to } +y \text{ axis} \end{matrix}\right\} \quad \text{See Fig. 3.38a.}$$

A negative sense in the x direction results when a couple has a rotation (relative to the *y* and *z* axes) that goes from

$$\left.\begin{matrix} +y \text{ axis to } -z \text{ axis} \\ -z \text{ axis to } -y \text{ axis} \\ -y \text{ axis to } +z \text{ axis} \\ +z \text{ axis to } +y \text{ axis} \end{matrix}\right\} \quad \text{See Fig. 3.38b.}$$

A positive sense in the y direction results when a couple has a rotation (related to the *x* and *z* axes) that goes from

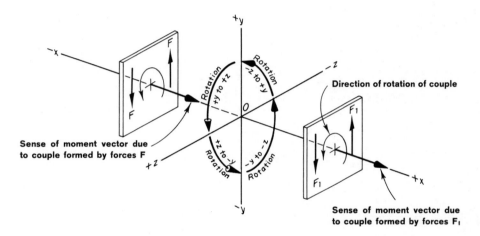

(a) Positive Sense in the *x* Direction

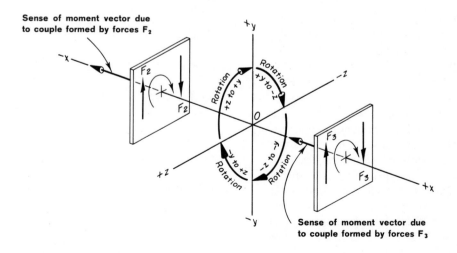

(b) Negative Sense in the *x* Direction

FIGURE 3.38

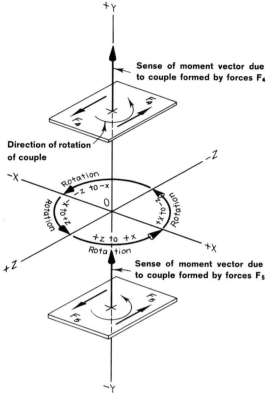

(a) Positive Sense in the *y* Direction

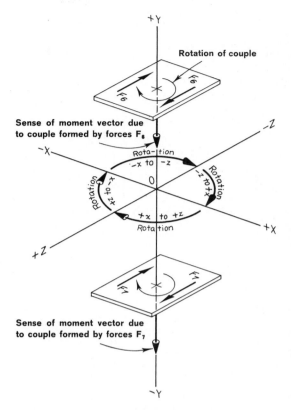

(b) Negative Sense in the *y* Direction

FIGURE 3.39

$$
\left.\begin{array}{l}
+x \text{ axis to } -z \text{ axis} \\
-z \text{ axis to } -x \text{ axis} \\
-x \text{ axis to } +z \text{ axis} \\
+z \text{ axis to } +x \text{ axis}
\end{array}\right\} \quad \text{See Fig. 3.39a.}
$$

A negative sense in the y direction results when a couple has a rotation (related to the *x* and *z* axes) that goes from

$$
\left.\begin{array}{l}
+x \text{ axis to } +z \text{ axis} \\
+z \text{ axis to } -x \text{ axis} \\
-x \text{ axis to } -z \text{ axis} \\
-z \text{ axis to } +x \text{ axis}
\end{array}\right\} \quad \text{See Fig. 3.39b.}
$$

A positive sense in the z direction results when a couple has a rotation (related to the *x* and *y* axes) that goes from

$$
\left.\begin{array}{l}
+x \text{ axis to } +y \text{ axis} \\
+y \text{ axis to } -x \text{ axis} \\
-x \text{ axis to } -y \text{ axis} \\
-y \text{ axis to } +x \text{ axis}
\end{array}\right\} \quad \text{See Fig. 3.40a.}
$$

A negative sense in the z direction results when a couple has a rotation (related to the *x* and *y* axes) that goes from

$$
\left.\begin{array}{l}
+y \text{ axis to } +x \text{ axis} \\
+x \text{ axis to } -y \text{ axis} \\
-y \text{ axis to } -x \text{ axis} \\
-x \text{ axis to } +y \text{ axis}
\end{array}\right\} \quad \text{See Fig. 3.40b.}
$$

EXAMPLE 3.7 _____

The coplanar, parallel force system in which the resultant is a couple.

Given: Forces $F_1 = 25$ lb, $F_2 = 75$ lb, $F_3 = 150$ lb, and $F_4 = 50$ lb located in the *x-y* plane (see Fig. 3.41).

Find: The resultant of the given force system.

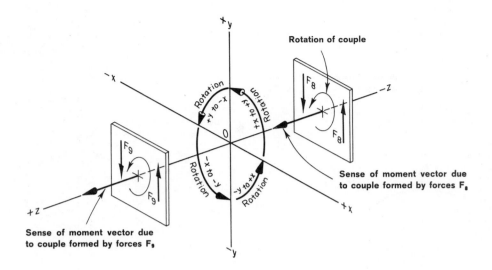

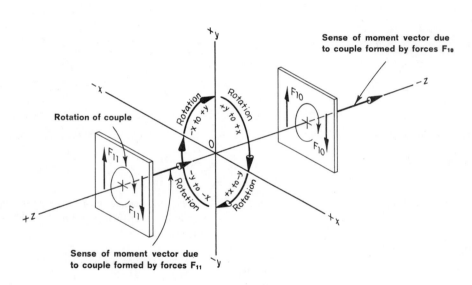

(**b**) Negative Sense in the *z* Direction

FIGURE 3.40

Graphical Analysis

1. Determine whether or not a *single resultant force* exists for the given force system by adding graphically the force vectors representing $\vec{F_1}$, $\vec{F_2}$, $\vec{F_3}$, and $\vec{F_4}$ (see Fig. 3.42a). From the vector diagram (Fig. 3.42a), we see that the given force system has no single resultant force.

2. Choosing any point 0 as a pole next to the vector diagram, construct the ray polygon. The following is evident:

$[\overrightarrow{0\text{--}1}]$ and $[\overrightarrow{0\text{--}2}]$ are components of $\vec{F_1}$
$[\overrightarrow{0\text{--}2}]$ and $[\overrightarrow{0\text{--}3}]$ are components of $\vec{F_2}$
$[\overrightarrow{0\text{--}3}]$ and $[\overrightarrow{0\text{--}4}]$ are components of $\vec{F_3}$
$[\overrightarrow{0\text{--}4}]$ and $[\overrightarrow{0\text{--}5}]$ are components of $\vec{F_4}$

Canceling the balanced components $[\overrightarrow{0\text{--}1}]$, $[\overrightarrow{0\text{--}2}]$, $[\overrightarrow{0\text{--}3}]$, and $[\overrightarrow{0\text{--}4}]$, we see that all the components are balanced, including $[\overrightarrow{0\text{--}5}]$ with $[\overrightarrow{0\text{--}1}]$, as the case must be, since there is no single resultant force in this system.

3. Construct the funicular polygon, as shown in Fig. 3.42b, starting at any assumed point A on the line of action of force F_1. Note that *strings* [0–1] and [0–5] *do not intersect and are parallel, which indicates that there is a resultant couple.*

4. Measure the length of vector $\overrightarrow{[0\text{–}1]}$ or $\overrightarrow{[0\text{–}5]}$ (which are equal in magnitude but opposite in sense) to the vector scale in the vector diagram (Fig. 3.42a), and measure the *perpendicular distance a* between strings [0–1] and [0–5] in the funicular polygon (Fig. 3.42b). The magnitude of the moment of the resultant couple is

$$M_R = ([0\text{–}1])(a)$$
$$= (140 \text{ lb})(1.07 \text{ in.}) = 150 \text{ lb-in.}$$

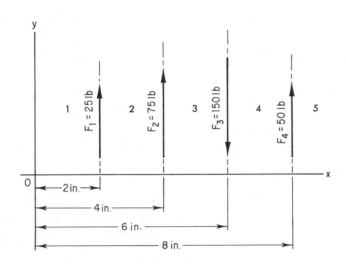

FIGURE 3.41

Space Diagram
Space Scale: $\frac{1}{2}$ in. = 1 in.

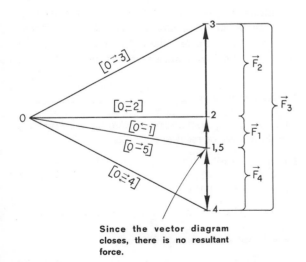

(a) Vector Diagram with Ray Polygon
Vector Scale: 1 in. = 50 lb

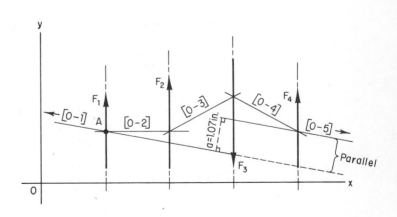

(b) Funicular Polygon

FIGURE 3.42

5. Determine the sense of the moment vector by considering the two senses of $\overrightarrow{[0-1]}$ and $\overrightarrow{[0-5]}$ in the vector diagram. Using these respective senses, which determine the direction of rotation of the resultant couple (from $+y$ to $+x$), we see that the sense of the *moment vector* is in the $-z$ direction (see Fig. 3.43).

Mathematical Analysis

1. Determine the algebraic sum of the given forces $\overrightarrow{F_1}$, $\overrightarrow{F_2}$, $\overrightarrow{F_3}$, and $\overrightarrow{F_4}$.

$$\sum \overrightarrow{F_y} = \overrightarrow{F_1} + \overrightarrow{F_2} - \overrightarrow{F_3} + \overrightarrow{F_4}$$
$$\sum |\overrightarrow{F_y}| = 25 \text{ lb} + 75 \text{ lb} - 150 \text{ lb} + 50 \text{ lb}$$
$$\therefore \ \sum \overrightarrow{F_y} = 0$$

(indicating no single resultant force).

2. Determine the algebraic sum of the moments of the individual forces, using the origin O as a center and assuming counterclockwise rotation of individual forces to be positive. (Refer to Fig. 3.41.)

$$\sum M_O = 2F_1 + 4F_2 - 6F_3 + 8F_4$$
$$= (2 \text{ in.})(25 \text{ lb}) + (4 \text{ in.})(75 \text{ lb})$$
$$- (6 \text{ in.})(150 \text{ lb}) + (8 \text{ in.})(50 \text{ lb})$$
$$= 50 \text{ lb-in.} + 300 \text{ lb-in.}$$
$$- 900 \text{ lb-in.} + 400 \text{ lb-in.}$$
$$\therefore \ \sum M_O = -150 \text{ lb-in.}$$
$$= M_R$$

Since the given forces are in the x-y plane, the minus sign indicates that the moment of the resultant couple has a clockwise rotation (according to the sign convention). Therefore, the vector representing

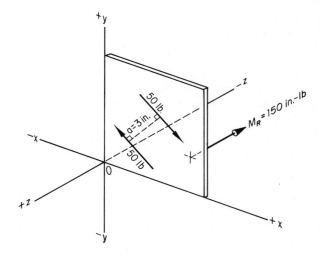

FIGURE 3.44

the moment of the resultant couple has a sense in the $-z$ direction, as shown in Figs. 3.43 and 3.44.

The magnitude of the parallel forces of the resultant couple and the perpendicular distance a between these forces can have any values, as long as their product is equal to $M_R = -150$ lb-in. (See Figs. 3.44 and 3.36.)

Finally, let us consider a parallel force system that has *no single resultant force* and *no resultant moment*; that is, a parallel force system that satisfies the *conditions necessary for static equilibrium*.

EXAMPLE 3.8

The coplanar, parallel force system having no single resultant force or resultant couple.

Given: Parallel forces $F_1 = 30$ lb, $F_2 = 60$ lb, $F_3 = 40$ lb, $F_4 = 90$ lb, and $F_5 = 20$ lb (Fig. 3.45).

Find: The resultant of the given force system.

Graphical Analysis

1. Determine whether a resultant force exists by graphical addition of the vectors representing the forces in the given system (see Fig. 3.45). From the vector diagram, we see that the given force system has no single resultant force (Fig. 3.46a).

2. Choose any point O as a pole next to the vector

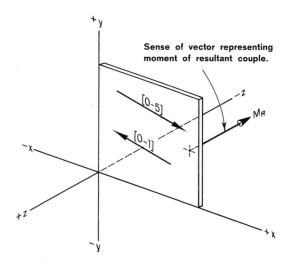

FIGURE 3.43

diagram, and construct the ray polygon (see Fig. 3.46a).

[$\overrightarrow{0\text{-}1}$] and [$\overrightarrow{0\text{-}2}$] are components of $\vec{F_1}$
[$\overrightarrow{0\text{-}2}$] and [$\overrightarrow{0\text{-}3}$] are components of $\vec{F_2}$
[$\overrightarrow{0\text{-}3}$] and [$\overrightarrow{0\text{-}4}$] are components of $\vec{F_3}$
[$\overrightarrow{0\text{-}4}$] and [$\overrightarrow{0\text{-}5}$] are components of $\vec{F_4}$
[$\overrightarrow{0\text{-}5}$] and [$\overrightarrow{0\text{-}6}$] are components of $\vec{F_5}$

Since [$\overrightarrow{0\text{-}1}$] and [$\overrightarrow{0\text{-}6}$] are equal in magnitude, opposite in sense, and *collinear* in action, they *cancel*, as do all the other components.

If we construct the funicular polygon, as shown in Fig. 3.46b, we see that strings [0–1] and [0–6] are also collinear; thus, there is no perpendicular distance *a* between them by which to establish a moment value (assuming components [$\overrightarrow{0\text{-}1}$] and [$\overrightarrow{0\text{-}6}$] are not "balanced" components). Since the resultant force is zero ($\sum F = 0$) and the summation of the moments of the individual forces also is zero ($\sum M_O = 0$, as indicated by the funicular polygon), the given system must be in a state of static equilibrium.

Mathematical Analysis

1. Determine the algebraic sum of the given forces (see Fig. 3.45):

$$\sum \vec{F_y} = -\vec{F_1} + \vec{F_2} + \vec{F_3} - \vec{F_4} + \vec{F_5}$$
$$= -30\text{ lb} + 60\text{ lb} + 40\text{ lb} - 90\text{ lb} + 20\text{ lb}$$
$$\therefore \sum F_y = 0$$

Also
$$\sum F_x = 0$$

Since the *x* axis is perpendicular to the lines of action of the given forces, these forces have no projections on this axis.

2. Determine the algebraic sum of the moments of the individual forces $\vec{F_1}$, $\vec{F_2}$, $\vec{F_3}$, $\vec{F_4}$, and $\vec{F_5}$, using the origin *O* as a moment center and assuming counterclockwise rotation of individual forces to be positive.

$$\sum M_O = -2F_1 + 5F_2 + 8F_3 - 10F_4 + 17F_5$$
$$= (-2\text{ in.})(30\text{ lb}) + (5\text{ in.})(60\text{ lb})$$
$$+ (8\text{ in.})(40\text{ lb}) - (10\text{ in.})(90\text{ lb})$$
$$+ (17\text{ in.})(20\text{ lb})$$
$$= -60\text{ lb-in.} + 300\text{ lb-in.} + 320\text{ lb-in.}$$
$$- 900\text{ lb-in.} + 340\text{ lb-in.}$$
$$\therefore \sum M_O = 0$$

Since $\sum F_y = 0$, $\sum F_x = 0$, and $\sum M_O = 0$, the given system has *no single resultant force and no resultant moment* and is therefore in *static equilibrium*.

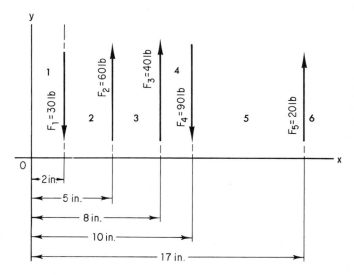

FIGURE 3.45

Space Diagram
Space Scale: $\frac{1}{4}$ in. = 1 in.

3.6 Resultant of Coplanar Systems of Couples

Coplanar systems of couples may be added vectorially, either graphically or mathematically, to determine a resultant couple (if one exists).

EXAMPLE 3.9 _____

The resultant of a coplanar system of couples.

Given: Three couples, each formed by two equal and opposite forces of $F_1 = 30$ lb, $F_2 = 40$ lb, and $F_3 = 20$ lb, respectively. The couples all are in the *y-z* plane, as shown in Fig. 3.47, and have arms $a_1 = 4$ in., $a_2 = 5$ in., and $a_3 = 3$ in., respectively.

Find: The resultant couple of the given system.

Graphical Analysis

1. Determine the magnitudes of the moments of each couple by multiplying the moment arm by one force in each couple:

$$M_1 = a_1F_1 = (4\text{ in.})(30\text{ lb}) = 120\text{ lb-in.}$$
$$M_2 = a_2F_2 = (5\text{ in.})(40\text{ lb}) = 200\text{ lb-in.}$$
$$M_3 = a_3F_3 = (3\text{ in.})(20\text{ lb}) = -60\text{ lb-in.}$$

gram, as shown in Fig. 3.48b. To perform the addition graphically, we look at the *x-z* plane in a direction *perpendicular* to it, so that the *y-z* plane now appears as an *edge* (see Fig. 3.48). The vectors representing the moments of each given couple now are seen as true length lines and can be added as a collinear system of vectors. The resultant couple vector has a magnitude of 260 lb-in. (as measured in

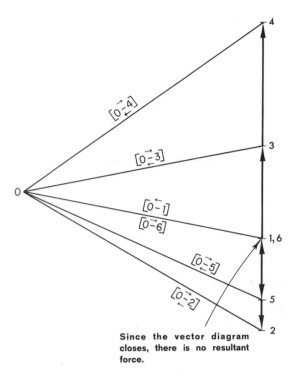

Since the vector diagram closes, there is no resultant force.

(a) Vector Diagram with Ray Polygon
Vector Scale: 1 in. = 30 lb

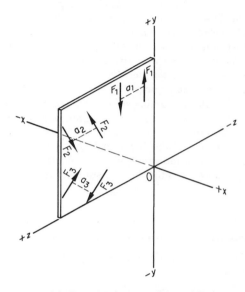

(a) Space Diagram (Pictorial)

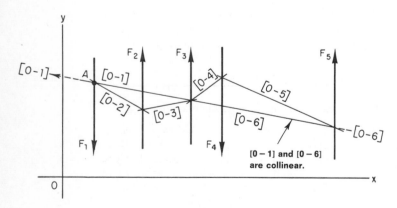

(b) Funicular Polygon

FIGURE 3.46

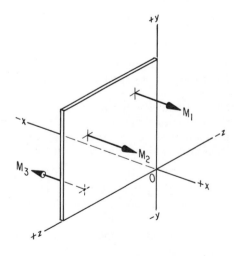

(b) Space Diagram (Pictorial)
Moments of Couples
Shown as Vectors

FIGURE 3.47(a), (b)

2. Since the given couples can be moved anywhere in the *y-z* plane and/or parallel to their planes of action, the vectors representing the moments of the given couples can all be moved to one point and added vectorially. Add the moments M_1, M_2, and M_3 as *vectors* to a moment scale in a moment vector dia-

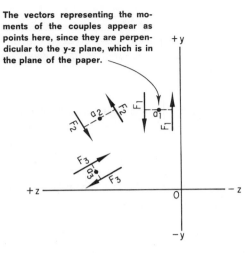

The vectors representing the moments of the couples appear as points here, since they are perpendicular to the y-z plane, which is in the plane of the paper.

(c) Space Diagram

FIGURE 3.47(c)

the moment vector diagram) and a sense in the $+x$ direction. This vector can be resolved into its component parallel forces by assuming any distance a between the forces and solving for their magnitude (see Fig. 3.48a):

$$M_R = a_R F_R$$

$$\therefore \; F_R = \frac{M_R}{a_R}$$

Assume $a_R = 5$ in. Then

$$F_R = \frac{260 \text{ lb-in.}}{5 \text{ in.}}$$
$$= 52 \text{ lb}$$

Mathematical Analysis

1. Determine the magnitude of the moment of each given couple and the senses and signs of these moments, as in the graphical approach.

$$M_1 = 120 \text{ lb-in.}$$
$$M_2 = 200 \text{ lb-in.}$$
$$M_3 = -60 \text{ lb-in.}$$

2. Algebraically add these vector quantities:

$$\vec{M_R} = \vec{M_1} + \vec{M_2} - \vec{M_3}$$
$$\therefore \; M_R = +120 \text{ lb-in.} + 200 \text{ lb-in.} - 60 \text{ lb-in.}$$
$$= 260 \text{ lb-in.}$$

3. The rest of the analysis is the same as that presented in step 2 in the graphical analysis.

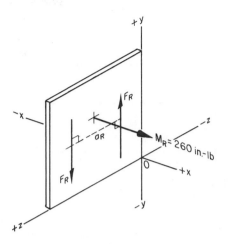

(a) Diagram of Resultant Moment Vector

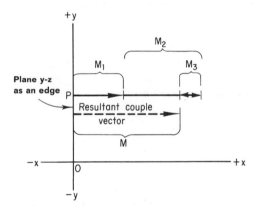

(b) Moment Vector Diagram
   Moment Scale: 1 in. = 200 lb-in.

FIGURE 3.48

3.7 Equilibrium of Collinear Force Systems

A collinear force system is in a state of static equilibrium when the algebraic sum of the forces (the resultant) in the system is equal to zero (see Fig. 2.4e). When a collinear force system is analyzed, one of the coordinate axes, to which the system may be related, can be placed *parallel* to the forces in the system. Thus, the projections of these forces appear *only* on the axis that is parallel

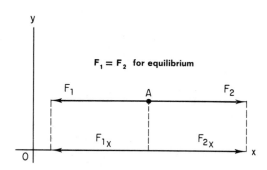

FIGURE 3.49

to them (see Fig. 3.49). Consequently, a summation of forces in the parallel-axis direction is sufficient to determine whether or not a state of static equilibrium exists (see Fig. 3.50b). This summation is expressed mathematically by one independent equation and, for equilibrium, is

$$\sum F_x = 0$$

Similarly, if the y axis is parallel to a given collinear force system, the single independent equation expressing equilibrium is

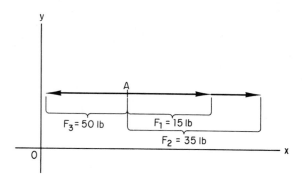

(a) Space Diagram

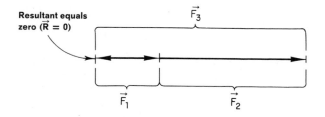

(b) Vector Diagram
Vector Scale: 1 in. = 10 lb

FIGURE 3.50

$$\sum F_y = 0$$

If the z axis is parallel to a given collinear system, the single independent equation expressing equilibrium is

$$\sum F_z = 0$$

It is important to note that these three equations are alike; that is, they all say the same thing in the same way. Only *one* of them is necessary to define equilibrium for a collinear force system; the one that would be used in a particular situation is the one that is related to the axis that is parallel to the forces in the given system.

EXAMPLE 3.10 _____

The equilibrium of a collinear force system by algebraic summation of forces.

Given: Collinear forces $F_1 = 15$ lb, $F_2 = 35$ lb, and $F_3 = 50$ lb whose lines of action pass through point A (see Fig. 3.50a).

Find: Whether or not the given force system is in equilibrium.

Graphical Analysis

1. Lay out the given forces to a vector scale and graphically add the vectors representing these forces (Fig. 3.50b).
2. The vector diagram "closes." Therefore, there is no resultant force, and the vector diagram shows that $\sum \vec{F}_x = 0$.

Mathematical Analysis

1. Algebraically add the given forces:

$$\sum \vec{F}_x = \vec{F}_1 + \vec{F}_2 - \vec{F}_3$$
$$= +15\text{ lb} + 35\text{ lb} - 50\text{ lb}$$
$$\therefore \sum F_x = 0$$

The condition of equilibrium of a collinear force system can also be expressed by an *independent moment equation*. If such a system is in equilibrium, the *algebraic sum of the moments* of the individual forces in the system will be equal to zero:

$$\sum M_O = 0$$

EXAMPLE 3.11 _____

The equilibrium of a collinear force system by algebraic summation of moments.

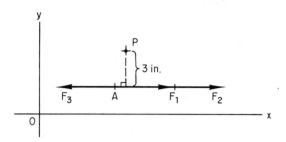

FIGURE 3.51

Space Diagram

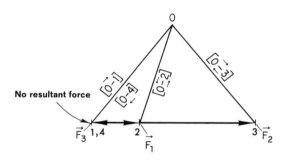

(a) Vector Diagram with Ray Polygon
Vector Scale: 1 in. = 10 lb

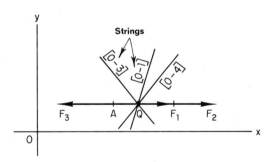

(b) Funicular Polygon

FIGURE 3.52

Given: Collinear forces $F_1 = 15$ lb, $F_2 = 35$ lb, and $F_3 = 50$ lb (see Fig. 3.50a).

Find: Whether or not the given force system is in equilibrium.

Mathematical Analysis

1. Take moments of each force in the given system about an assumed point P (in Fig. 3.51, point P is assumed to be a perpendicular distance of 3 in. from the lines of action of the given forces):

$$\sum M_P = 3F_1 + 3F_2 - 3F_3$$
$$= (3 \text{ in.})(15 \text{ lb}) + (3 \text{ in.})(35 \text{ lb}) - (3 \text{ in.})(50 \text{ lb})$$
$$= 45 \text{ lb-in.} + 105 \text{ lb-in.} - 150 \text{ lb-in.}$$
$$= 0$$

and the system is therefore in equilibrium.

Graphical Analysis

1. Draw the vector diagram showing the graphical addition of the force vectors representing F_1, F_2, and F_3 (see Fig. 3.52a). Since this diagram closes, there is no resultant force.

2. Assume a point 0 as a pole, and construct the ray polygon, as in Fig. 3.52a.

3. Construct the funicular polygon (see Fig. 3.52b) starting at an assumed point Q on the line of action of F_1. From this funicular polygon, we see that all the strings [0–1], [0–2], [0–3], and [0–4] intersect at the point Q. This indicates that *no resultant moment* exists for the given system; but it also indicates that the funicular polygon (being an expression of Varignon's theorem) did *not* add any new information in our determination of equilibrium conditions for the given system beyond that given by the vector diagram. Therefore, we conclude that only *one equation* is necessary to define static equilibrium for a *collinear force system*. This *single equation* can be either a summation of forces equation ($\sum F_x = 0$) or a summation of moments equation ($\sum M_O = 0$). Since only *one independent equation* is available, we can solve for only one unknown quantity.[4]

3.8 Equilibrium of Coplanar, Concurrent Force Systems

A coplanar, concurrent force system is in a state of static equilibrium when the algebraic sum (resultant) of its forces is equal to zero or when the algebraic sum of the moments of the individual forces about any point is equal to zero. Graphically, this means that the vector diagram and the funicular polygon of the force system would close ($\sum F = 0$ and $\sum M = 0$). (See Figs. 2.6, 2.7, and 3.54a.)

---

[4] If $\sum F_x = 0$ is taken as the independent equation, then $\sum M_O = 0$ is a *dependent* equation, and vice versa.

According to the principle of projections, the sum of the projections of the individual forces of a coplanar, concurrent force system in static equilibrium on two coordinate axes is equal to *zero*, and this summation is expressed mathematically by *two independent* force summation equations: $\sum F_x = 0$ and $\sum F_y = 0$. *Two independent equations* are necessary since the forces in a coplanar, concurrent force system, which are not parallel to the assumed coordinate axes, require *two projections* (or rectangular components) to be completely specified (see Fig. 2.10).

The moment equation expressing the condition of static equilibrium of a coplanar, concurrent force system, about any assumed point P in the plane of the forces is $\sum M_P = 0$. This equation is *not independent* when related to $\sum F_x = 0$ and $\sum F_y = 0$ together, since a coplanar, concurrent force system in equilibrium can be reduced to a collinear force system by combining all the forces in the system, *except one*, into one resultant force. This resultant force must be equal in magnitude, opposite in sense, and collinear in action to the force that was not included in determining the resultant of the other forces in the system (see Fig. 2.5). Then, the reasoning developed in Example 3.11 in Sec. 3.7 can be applied relative to moments.

Basically only *two independent equations* are available for determining the static equilibrium conditions of a given coplanar, concurrent force system. Therefore, we can solve for only two unknowns.

In many static equilibrium problems, it is useful to apply the moment equilibrium equation ($\sum M_P = 0$); however, since it is a dependent equation, *it cannot be used with both of the force summation equations*. On the other hand, it can be used with *one* of the force summation equations, in which case it becomes an independent equation, since it gives information that would have been given by one of the other force summation equations. Therefore, we have available the following *pairs* of equations:[5]

---

[5] By careful choice of the location of coordinate axes, it is possible to solve many problems involving coplanar structures in static equilibrium by using all three equations in proper pair combinations (see Example 3.17).

$$\sum F_x = 0 \quad \text{and} \quad \sum F_y = 0$$

or

$$\sum F_x = 0 \quad \text{and} \quad \sum M_P = 0$$

or

$$\sum F_y = 0 \quad \text{and} \quad \sum M_P = 0$$

EXAMPLE 3.12

The equilibrium of a coplanar, concurrent force system involving one unknown.

Given: Coplanar, concurrent forces $F_1 = 70$ lb and $F_2 = 100$ lb at angles $\theta_{1_x} = 30°$ and $\theta_{2_x} = 45°$, respectively (see Fig. 3.53).

Find: The magnitude, sense, and direction (θ_{3_x}) of the force F_3 required to establish static equilibrium in the given force system.

Graphical Analysis

1. Graphically determine the resultant of forces F_1 and F_2 by drawing the forces to a vector scale and adding them consecutively by the triangle law. (See Fig. 3.54a for the vector diagram; Bow's notation has been used to identify the vectors.)

2. Measure vector $[\overrightarrow{1-3}]$ to the vector scale; the magnitude of $\vec{F}_1 + \vec{F}_2$ equals 136.5 lb.

3. Since the equilibrant $\vec{F}_3$ (represented by vector $[\overrightarrow{3-1}]$ in Fig. 3.54b) must be equal in magnitude, opposite in sense, and collinear in action to the resultant $\vec{R}$ of $\vec{F}_1$ and $\vec{F}_2$ (represented by vector $[\overrightarrow{1-3}]$ in Fig. 3.54a), all that is necessary to determine the *sense* of this equilibrant is to *reverse* the sense of the resultant $\vec{R}$.

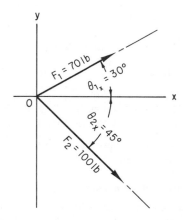

FIGURE 3.53

Space Diagram

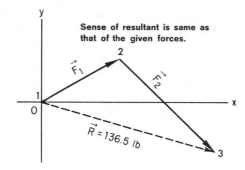

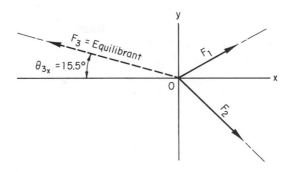

FIGURE 3.55

Space Diagram

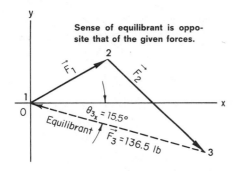

(a) Vector Diagram Showing Resultant
Vector Scale: 1 in. = 50 lb

(b) Vector Diagram Showing Equilibrant
Vector Scale: 1 in. = 50 lb

FIGURE 3.54

In reversing the sense of the resultant of $\vec{F}_1$ and $\vec{F}_2$, we have established a *closed vector polygon* (diagram) in which the senses of the vectors follow in consecutive order, defining a state of static equilibrium ($\sum F_x = 0$ and $\sum F_y = 0$).

4. From point O (origin) in the space diagram, draw a line parallel to vector $\overrightarrow{[3\text{–}1]}$ in the vector diagram (Fig. 3.54b), and indicate the sense of $\overrightarrow{[3\text{–}1]}$, which is the sense of the equilibrant $\vec{F}_3$.

5. Measure the angle that $\vec{F}_3$ makes with the x axis ($\theta_{3_x} = 15.5°$), which defines the direction of $\vec{F}_3$ relative to the given force system (see Fig. 3.55).

Mathematical Analysis

1. Determine the resultant of the given force system by applying the principle of projections (see Fig. 3.56a). For equilibrium,

$$\sum F_x = 0 \quad \text{and} \quad \sum F_y = 0$$
$$\therefore \ \sum F_x = F_1 \cos 30° + F_2 \cos 45°$$
$$= (70 \text{ lb})\left(\frac{\sqrt{3}}{2}\right) + (100 \text{ lb})\left(\frac{1}{\sqrt{2}}\right)$$
$$= 60.6 \text{ lb} + 70.7 \text{ lb}$$
$$= 131.3 \text{ lb}$$

and

$$\therefore \ \sum F_y = F_1 \cos 60° - F_2 \cos 45°$$
$$= (70 \text{ lb})\left(\frac{1}{2}\right) - (100 \text{ lb})\left(\frac{1}{\sqrt{2}}\right)$$
$$= 35 \text{ lb} - 70.7 \text{ lb}$$
$$= -35.7 \text{ lb}$$

2. The magnitude of the resultant R is (see Fig. 3.56b):

$$R^2 = \sum F_x{}^2 + \sum F_y{}^2$$
$$= 131.3^2 + (-35.7)^2$$
$$= 17{,}240 + 1275$$
$$= 18{,}515$$
$$\therefore \ R = \sqrt{18{,}515}$$
$$= 136.1 \text{ lb}$$

3. The angle that R makes with the x axis may be determined as follows:

$$\tan \theta_{R_x} = \frac{\sum F_y}{\sum F_x}$$
$$= \frac{35.7 \text{ lb}}{131.3 \text{ lb}}$$
$$= 0.272$$
$$\therefore \ \theta_{R_x} = -15.34°$$

where the minus sign indicates that the angle is measured *below* the x axis (see Fig. 3.56c).

4. Since $\vec{F}_3$ (equilibrant) is equal to $-\vec{R}$ (minus sign indicates opposite sense) and $\theta_{3_x} = -\theta_{R_x}$, the speci-

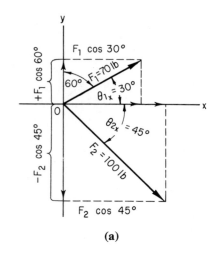

(a)

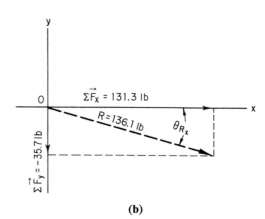

(b)

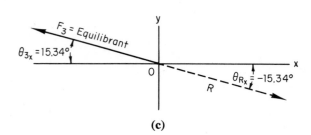

(c)

FIGURE 3.56

fications of the required equilibrant are complete, as shown in Fig. 3.56c.

EXAMPLE 3.13 _____

The equilibrium of a coplanar, concurrent force system of two unknowns.

Given: A coplanar, concurrent force system in _equilibrium_ consisting of forces $F_1 = 120$ lb, $F_2 = 100$ lb, $F_3 = 70$ lb, $F_4 = 110$ lb, $F_5 = 80$ lb, $F_6 = ?$, and $F_7 = ?$ The directions, magnitudes, and senses of forces F_1, F_2, F_3, F_4, and F_5 are known; only the directions of forces F_6 and F_7 are known (see Fig. 3.57a).

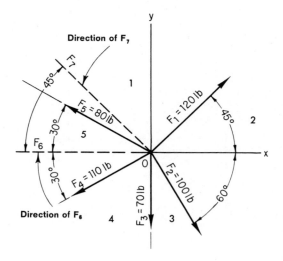

(a) Space Diagram

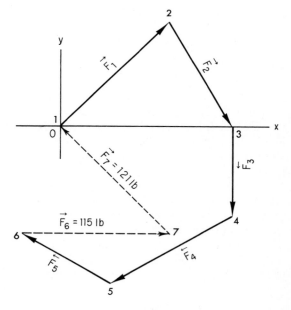

(b) Vector Diagram
      Vector Scale: 1 in. = 50 lb

FIGURE 3.57

Find: The magnitudes and senses of forces F_6 and F_7.

Graphical Analysis

1. Draw the vector diagram, starting with the known forces F_1, F_2, F_3, F_4, and F_5 represented by vectors $[1\text{–}\vec{2}]$, $[2\text{–}\vec{3}]$, $[3\text{–}\vec{4}]$, $[4\text{–}\vec{5}]$, and $[5\text{–}\vec{6}]$, respectively (see Fig. 3.57b).
2. Since the entire system of forces is in equilibrium, the vectors representing forces F_6 and F_7 must close the vector polygon. Therefore, from point 6 in the vector diagram, construct a line parallel to the line of action of F_6 (in the space diagram), and from point 1, construct a line parallel to the line of action of F_7 (in the space diagram). These two lines intersect at point 7 (in the vector diagram), which now defines the lengths $[6\text{–}\vec{7}]$ and $[7\text{–}\vec{1}]$, which are the vectors representing the forces F_6 and F_7.
3. Measuring vectors $[6\text{–}\vec{7}]$ and $[7\text{–}\vec{1}]$ to the vector scale, we find

$$F_6 = 115 \text{ lb} \quad \text{and} \quad F_7 = 121 \text{ lb}$$

4. To define a state of static equilibrium, the senses of all the vectors in the vector diagram must follow each other in consecutive order. Transfer the senses of the vectors representing F_6 and F_7 to the space diagram (see Fig. 3.58b).

Mathematical Analysis

1. Assume that the senses of F_6 and F_7 head away from the origin 0 (see Fig. 3.58a).
2. Determine the algebraic sum of the given forces on the x and y axes by applying the principle of projections. (Note that F_3 has no projection on the x axis, since its line of action is perpendicular to that axis; F_6 has no projection on the y axis, since its line of action is perpendicular to the y axis.)

a. For equilibrium, $\sum F_x = 0$

$$\therefore \ F_1 \cos 45° + F_2 \cos 60° - F_4 \cos 30°$$
$$- F_5 \cos 30° - F_6 - F_7 \cos 45° = 0$$

$$(120 \text{ lb})\left(\frac{1}{\sqrt{2}}\right) + (100 \text{ lb})\left(\frac{1}{2}\right) - (110 \text{ lb})\left(\frac{\sqrt{3}}{2}\right)$$
$$- (80 \text{ lb})\left(\frac{\sqrt{3}}{2}\right) - F_6 - F_7\left(\frac{1}{\sqrt{2}}\right) = 0$$

$$84.9 \text{ lb} + 50 \text{ lb} - 95.3 \text{ lb} - 69.3 \text{ lb}$$
$$- F_6 - 0.707F_7 = 0$$

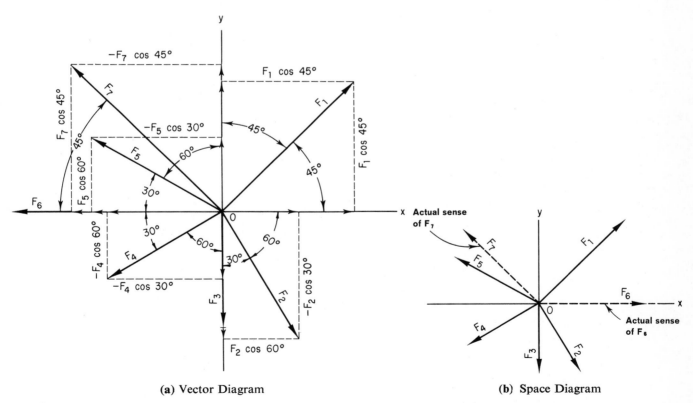

(a) Vector Diagram   **(b) Space Diagram**

FIGURE 3.58

Adding and transposing, we get

$$F_6 + 0.707F_7 = -29.7 \text{ lb}$$

an equation with two unknowns. To solve for the two unknowns, we need another *independent equation*. $\sum F_y = 0$ of the given force system will provide us with the second independent equation.

b. For equilibrium, $\sum F_y = 0$

$$\therefore F_1 \cos 45° - F_2 \cos 30° - F_3$$
$$- F_4 \cos 60° + F_5 \cos 60° + F_7 \cos 45° = 0$$

$$(120 \text{ lb})\left(\frac{1}{\sqrt{2}}\right) - (100 \text{ lb})\left(\frac{\sqrt{3}}{2}\right) - (70 \text{ lb})$$
$$- (110 \text{ lb})\left(\frac{1}{2}\right) + (80 \text{ lb})\left(\frac{1}{2}\right) + (F_7)\left(\frac{1}{\sqrt{2}}\right) = 0$$

$$84.9 \text{ lb} - 86.6 \text{ lb} - 70 \text{ lb} - 55 \text{ lb}$$
$$+ 40 \text{ lb} + 0.707F_7 = 0$$

Adding and transposing, we get

$$0.707F_7 = 86.7 \text{ lb}$$

or

$$F_7 = \frac{86.7}{0.707} \text{ lb} = 122.6 \text{ lb}$$

where the positive sign indicates that our assumed sense for F_7 is correct.

3. Substituting F_7 in the equation for $\sum F_x = 0$, we find F_6:

$$F_6 + 0.707F_7 = -29.9 \text{ lb}$$
$$\therefore F_6 = -29.9 \text{ lb} - 0.707F_7$$
$$= -29.9 \text{ lb} - (0.707)(122.6 \text{ lb})$$
$$= -29.9 \text{ lb} - 86.7 \text{ lb}$$
$$= -116.6 \text{ lb}$$

The minus sign indicates that our assumed sense for F_6 is opposite to the actual sense. Therefore, we change the assumed sense to the actual sense in the space diagram (see Fig. 3.58b).

EXAMPLE 3.14 _____

The equilibrium of a coplanar, concurrent force system of two unknowns.

Given: A coplanar, concurrent force system, in equilibrium, of forces $F_1 = 120$ lb, $F_2 = 150$ lb, $F_3 = 200$ lb, $F_4 = 110$ lb, and $F_5 = 75$ lb. The *senses and directions* of forces F_4 and F_5 are unknown (see Fig. 3.59a).

Find: The senses and directions of forces F_4 and F_5 necessary to satisfy equilibrium conditions.

Graphical Analysis

1. Determine the equilibrant of forces F_1, F_2, and F_3 by graphical addition of the vectors representing these forces ($[\overrightarrow{1-2}]$, $[\overrightarrow{2-3}]$, and $[\overrightarrow{3-4}]$, respectively).

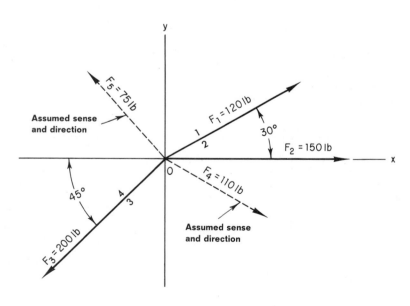

(a) Space Diagram

FIGURE 3.59(a)

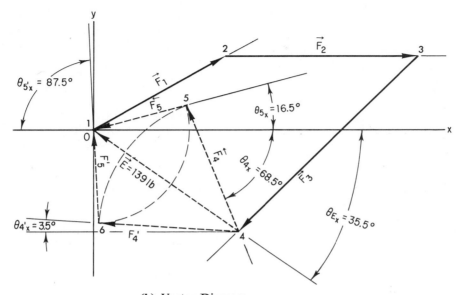

(b) Vector Diagram
Vector Scale: 1 in. = 50 lb

FIGURE 3.59(b)

The equilibrant is represented by vector $[\overrightarrow{4-1}]$ whose magnitude $E = 139$ lb is measured in the vector diagram. (See Fig. 3.59b.)

2. From the end of vector $[\overrightarrow{3-4}]$ in Fig. 3.59b, swing an arc having a radius equal to the vector length of F_4.

3. From the tail of vector $[\overrightarrow{1-2}]$ in Fig. 3.59b, swing an arc having a radius equal to the vector length of F_5.

4. The points of intersection of the arcs (5 and 6) determine the *directions* of vectors $[\overrightarrow{4-5}]$ and $[\overrightarrow{5-1}]$, which represent the forces F_4 and F_5, respectively. Note that two directions for each force are possible in this solution.

5. Since $\overrightarrow{F_4}$ and $\overrightarrow{F_5}$ can be considered components of the equilibrant E, their senses are readily determined by inspection.

6. Measure the angles each force makes with the x axis:

$$\left.\begin{array}{l} \theta_{4_x} = 68.5° \\ \theta_{5_x} = 16.5° \end{array}\right\} \quad \text{first solution}$$

$$\left.\begin{array}{l} \theta_{4'_x} = 3.5° \\ \theta_{5'_x} = 87.5° \end{array}\right\} \quad \text{second solution}$$

$$\theta_{E_x} = 35.5°$$

Mathematical Analysis

1. Determine the resultant of forces F_1, F_2, and F_3, using the principle of projections (see Fig. 3.59a).

$$\sum F_x = F_1 \cos 30° + F_2 - F_3 \cos 45°$$
$$= (120 \text{ lb})\left(\frac{\sqrt{3}}{2}\right) + 150 \text{ lb} - (200 \text{ lb})\left(\frac{1}{\sqrt{2}}\right)$$
$$= 104 \text{ lb} + 150 \text{ lb} - 141 \text{ lb}$$
$$= 113 \text{ lb}$$

$$\sum F_y = F_1 \cos 60° - F_3 \cos 45°$$
$$= (120 \text{ lb})\left(\frac{1}{2}\right) - (200 \text{ lb})\left(\frac{1}{\sqrt{2}}\right)$$
$$= 60 \text{ lb} - 141 \text{ lb}$$
$$= -81 \text{ lb}$$

$$R = \sqrt{(\sum F_x)^2 + (\sum F_y)^2}$$
$$= \sqrt{113^2 + (-81)^2}$$
$$= \sqrt{12,770 + 6560}$$
$$= \sqrt{19,330}$$
$$= 139.0 \text{ lb}$$

2. Since the equilibrant is equal in magnitude, collinear in action, and opposite in sense to the resultant, we can change the signs of $\sum F_x$ and $\sum F_y$ so that they become the rectangular components of the equilibrant. Now determine the angle (θ_{E_x}) that the equilibrant makes with the x axis (see Fig. 3.60c).

$$\tan \theta_{E_x} = \frac{-(\sum F_y)}{+(\sum F_x)} = \frac{+81}{-113}$$
$$= 0.717$$
$$\therefore \ \theta_{E_x} = 35.6°$$

3. The forces $F_4 = 110$ lb and $F_5 = 75$ lb having unknown directions and senses can now be con-

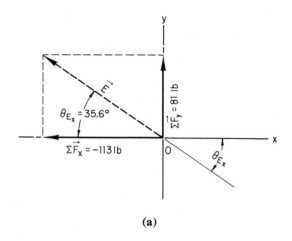

(a)

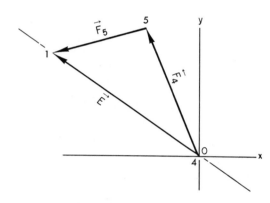

(b) $\vec{F_4}$ and $\vec{F_5}$ as Components of Equilibrant $\vec{E}$.

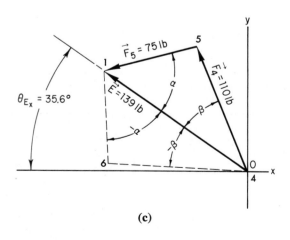

(c)

FIGURE 3.60

sidered *components* of the equilibrant E, since their vector sum must equal E if conditions of equilibrium are to be satisfied in the given force system (see Fig. 3.60b).

4. Considering the triangle of forces (4–5–1) as shown in Fig. 3.60c, we can define the angles that F_4 and F_5 make with the equilibrant E as α and β, respectively (or as $-\alpha$ or $-\beta$ if the second solution is considered). Applying the law of cosines, we can determine the magnitudes of α and β:

$$F_4{}^2 = F_5{}^2 + E^2 - 2F_5E \cos \alpha$$

Solving for $\cos \alpha$, we get

$$\cos \alpha = \frac{F_5{}^2 + E^2 - F_4{}^2}{2F_5E}$$

Substituting for F_4, F_5, and E,

$$\cos \alpha = \frac{75^2 + 139^2 - 110^2}{2(75)(139)}$$

$$= \frac{5620 + 19,320 - 12,100}{20,850} = \frac{12,840}{20,850}$$

$$= 0.615$$

$$\therefore \ \alpha = 51.7°$$

Proceeding in the same way, we can determine the angle β:

$$F_5{}^2 = F_4{}^2 + E^2 - 2F_4E \cos \beta$$

Solving for $\cos \beta$, we get

$$\cos \beta = \frac{F_4{}^2 + E^2 - F_5{}^2}{2F_4E}$$

Substituting for F_4, F_5, and E,

$$\cos \beta = \frac{110^2 + 139^2 - 75^2}{2(110)(139)}$$

$$= \frac{12,100 + 19,320 - 5620}{30,580} = \frac{25,800}{30,580}$$

$$= 0.844$$

$$\therefore \ \beta = 32.5°$$

5. Determine the angles θ_{4_x} and θ_{5_x} that forces F_4 and F_5 make, respectively, with the x axis (see Figs. 3.61a and 3.61b).

$$\theta_{4_x} = \theta_{E_x} + \beta$$
$$= 35.6° + 32.5°$$
$$= 68.1°$$

Then, since $\alpha = \theta_{E_x} + \theta_{5_x}$,

$$\theta_{5_x} = \alpha - \theta_{E_x}$$
$$= 51.7° - 35.6°$$
$$= 16.1°$$

This completes the mathematical analysis of the given problem for a single value each for θ_{4_x} and θ_{5_x}.

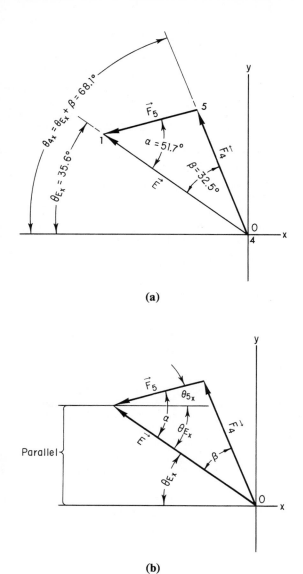

(a)

(b)

FIGURE 3.61

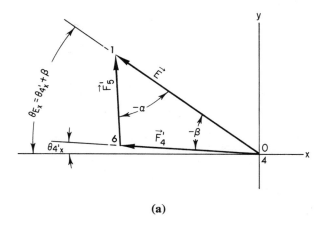

(a)

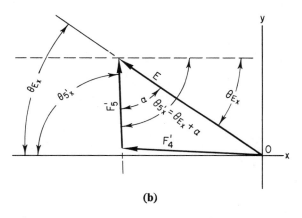

(b)

FIGURE 3.62

Also, from Fig. 3.62b,

$$\theta_{5'_x} = \theta_{E_x} + \alpha$$
$$= 35.6° + 51.7°$$
$$= 87.3°$$

EXAMPLE 3.15 _____

The equilibrium of a coplanar, concurrent force system of two unknowns.

Given: A weight $P = 100$ lb hanging from a weightless and completely flexible cable (BOC) fixed at points B and C, as shown in Fig. 3.63a.

Find: The forces F_1 and F_2 acting, respectively, in segments OB and OC of the cable, which maintain the given system in equilibrium.

There is another set of values for these angles that will satisfy the equilibrium conditions. These values can be determined as follows: α and β remain constant in value for the other possible directions of F_4 and F_5 (see Fig. 3.62). Thus, from Fig. 3.62a,

$$\theta_{E_x} = \theta_{4'_x} + \beta$$
$$\therefore\ \theta_{4'_x} = \theta_{E_x} - \beta$$
$$= 35.6° - 32.5°$$
$$= 3.1°$$

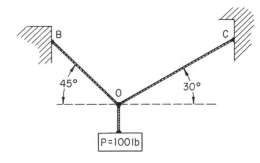

(a) Space Diagram

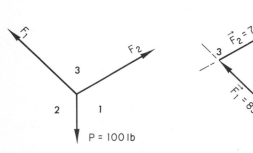

(b) Free-body Diagram

(c) Vector Diagram
Vector Scale: 1 in. = 50 lb

FIGURE 3.63

Graphical Analysis

1. For equilibrium, the vector diagram representing the given force system must be a closed polygon; thus, $\vec{F_1} + \vec{F_3} + \vec{P} = 0$.

2. Draw a free-body diagram of the point O, indicating the sense of the given action force P and the assumed senses of the reaction forces F_1 and F_2. From inspection of the free-body diagram (Fig. 3.63b), we can see that OB and OC will be in *tension*; therefore, the senses of F_1 and F_2 will head away from point O.

3. Draw the vector diagram, starting with the known force P (represented by vector $[\overrightarrow{1\text{--}2}]$, as shown in Fig. 3.63c.

4. Draw a line parallel to OB from point 2 and a line parallel to OC from point 1. These two lines intersect at point 3 (see Fig. 3.63c).

5. Indicate the senses of vectors $[\overrightarrow{2\text{--}3}]$ and $[\overrightarrow{3\text{--}1}]$, which must follow in consecutive order with the sense of the given load P.

6. Measure vectors $[\overrightarrow{2\text{--}3}]$ and $[\overrightarrow{3\text{--}1}]$ to the chosen vector scale:

$$[\overrightarrow{2\text{--}3}] = 73 \text{ lb} = F_1$$
$$[\overrightarrow{3\text{--}1}] = 89 \text{ lb} = F_2$$

7. Transfer the senses of vectors $[\overrightarrow{2\text{--}3}]$ and $[\overrightarrow{3\text{--}1}]$ to the free-body diagram to determine whether or not the senses we assumed for F_1 and F_2 are correct. We see that they check.

Mathematical Analysis

1. Draw a free-body diagram of the given force system, relating the action and reaction forces to a coordinate axis system (Fig. 3.64).

2. Assume that F_1 and F_2 act away from origin O.

3. For equilibrium, $\sum F_x = 0$ and $\sum F_y = 0$. Applying the principle of projections, we write

$$\sum F_x = -F_1 \cos 45° + F_2 \cos 30° = 0$$

(a) $$\therefore \quad -F_1\left(\frac{1}{\sqrt{2}}\right) + F_2\left(\frac{\sqrt{3}}{2}\right) = 0$$

and

$$\sum F_y = -P + F_1 \sin 45° + F_2 \sin 30° = 0$$

(b) $$\therefore \quad F_1\left(\frac{1}{\sqrt{2}}\right) + F_2\left(\frac{1}{2}\right) = 100$$

Solving equations (a) and (b) simultaneously (since they are two independent equations involving two unknowns), we find

(a) $$-\cancel{F_1}\left(\cancel{\frac{1}{\sqrt{2}}}\right) + F_2\left(\frac{\sqrt{3}}{2}\right) = 0$$

(b) $$\cancel{F_1}\left(\cancel{\frac{1}{\sqrt{2}}}\right) + F_2\left(\frac{1}{2}\right) = 100$$
$$\overline{\qquad\qquad\qquad\qquad}$$
$$F_2\left(\frac{\sqrt{3}}{2} + \frac{1}{2}\right) = 100$$

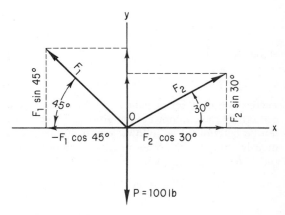

FIGURE 3.64

Free-body Diagram with Coordinate Axes

$$\therefore \ F_2 = \frac{100}{(\sqrt{3}+1)/2} = \frac{200}{\sqrt{3}+1}$$

$$= \frac{200}{2.73}$$

$$= 73.3 \ \text{lb}$$

4. Substituting $F_2 = 73$ lb in equation (a), we solve for F_1:

$$F_1 = F_2\left(\frac{\sqrt{3}}{2}\right)\left(\frac{\sqrt{2}}{1}\right) = F_2\left(\frac{\sqrt{3}}{\sqrt{2}}\right)$$

$$= (73.3 \ \text{lb})\left(\frac{\sqrt{3}}{\sqrt{2}}\right)$$

$$= 89.7 \ \text{lb}$$

NOTE: Values for both F_1 and F_2 are positive, indicating that the senses we assumed for these forces are correct.

EXAMPLE 3.16 _____

The equilibrium of a coplanar, concurrent force system of three unknowns.

Given: Bar AC hinged at point C and supported by a wire BD, as shown in Fig. 3.65a. Load $P = 100$ lb is applied at point A.

Find: A. The magnitude and type of force in the wire BD necessary to maintain the system in static equilibrium.
B. The horizontal and vertical components of the reaction R_C at point C.

Graphical Analysis

1. Lay out the structure diagram to scale (Fig. 3.65b).

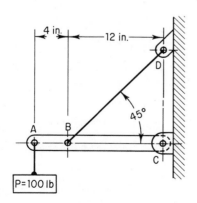

(a) Structure Diagram

FIGURE 3.65(a)

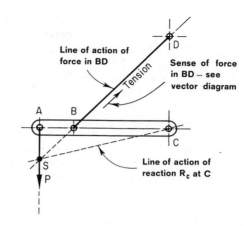

(b) Structure Diagram
Space Scale: $\frac{1}{8}$ in. $= 1$ in.

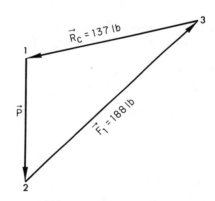

(c) Vector Diagram
Vector Scale: 1 in. $= 50$ lb

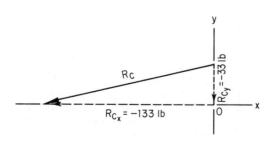

(d) Vector Diagram to Determine R_{C_x} and R_{C_y}
Vector Scale: 1 in. $= 50$ lb

FIGURE 3.65(b)–(d)

2. Extend the *known lines of action* of the applied load P and the reaction force F_1 in the wire BD (direction of F_1 must be that of BD) until they intersect at a point S (see Fig. 3.65b).

3. From point S, draw a line through point C. The line SC establishes the line of action of the reaction R_C at the hinge point C (see Fig. 3.65b). The line of action of R_C must pass through points C and S, since three forces in a plane must intersect at one point to be in equilibrium. Therefore, the *resultant* of the load P and the reaction load F_1 must be equal in magnitude, opposite in sense, and collinear in action to the reaction force R_C.

4. Using the lines of action of P, F_1, and R_C, draw the vector diagram, starting with the known force P (see Fig. 3.65c). For equilibrium, the vector diagram must close.

5. Measure the lengths (to the vector scale) of the vectors representing R_C and F_1:

$$[\overrightarrow{2\text{–}3}] = F_1 = 188 \text{ lb}$$
$$[\overrightarrow{3\text{–}1}] = R_C = 137 \text{ lb}$$

6. Transfer the arrows to the structure diagram to determine the type of load in the wire BD: the wire is in tension.

7. Graphically resolve R_C into its vertical and horizontal components R_{C_x} and R_{C_y}, respectively (see Fig. 3.65d). Measure the vectors representing R_{C_x} and R_{C_y} to the vector scale:

$$R_{C_x} = -133 \text{ lb}$$
$$R_{C_y} = -33 \text{ lb}$$

Mathematical Analysis

1. Draw a free-body diagram of the loaded bar. Since the direction of the reaction R_C at point C is not known, assume that the horizontal and vertical components of R_C act as shown in Fig. 3.66a.

2. If we attempt to solve this problem using the principle of projections, we obtain

(a) $\sum F_x = F_1 \cos 45° + R_{C_x} = 0$

(b) $\sum F_y = -P + F_1 \sin 45° + R_{C_y} = 0$

Equations (a) and (b) contain three unknowns (F_1, R_{C_x}, and R_{C_y}). Statically we cannot get more than two independent equations in a coplanar, concurrent force system; therefore, this approach will not lead us to a solution to the problem.

3. Applying Varignon's theorem in proper combination with the principle of projections, we can obtain a mathematical solution. Placing the coordinate axes with the origin at C (see Fig. 3.66a) and taking moments about the point C, we write

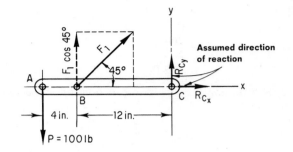

(a) Free-body Diagram

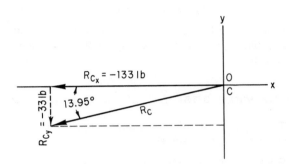

(b) Vector Diagram

FIGURE 3.66

$$\sum M_C = 0 \quad \text{(for equilibrium)}$$
$$\therefore \; \sum M_C = 16P - 12F_1 \cos 45° = 0$$

Transposing and solving for F_1, we get

$$F_1 = \frac{16P}{12 \cos 45°}$$
$$= \frac{16(100)}{12(1/\sqrt{2})} = \frac{1600(\sqrt{2})}{12}$$
$$= 188.6 \text{ lb}$$

4. Substituting this value of F_1 in equations (a) and (b), we can solve for R_{C_x} and R_{C_y}:

$$\sum F_x = (188.6 \text{ lb})(\cos 45°) + R_{C_x} = 0$$
$$\therefore \; R_{C_x} = -(188.6 \text{ lb})(\cos 45°)$$
$$= -(188.6 \text{ lb})\left(\frac{1}{\sqrt{2}}\right)$$
$$= -133.2 \text{ lb}$$

where the minus sign indicates that the sense of R_{C_x} is opposite to the assumed sense.

$$\sum F_y = -100 \text{ lb} + (188.6 \text{ lb})(\cos 45°) + R_{C_y} = 0$$
$$\therefore \; R_{C_y} = 100 \text{ lb} - (188.6 \text{ lb})(\cos 45°)$$

$$R_{C_y} = 100 \text{ lb} - (188.6 \text{ lb})\left(\frac{1}{\sqrt{2}}\right)$$

$$= 100 \text{ lb} - 133.2 \text{ lb}$$

$$= -33.2 \text{ lb}$$

where the minus sign indicates that the sense of R_{C_y} is opposite to the assumed sense.

5. From Fig. 3.66b, the magnitude of R_C is determined as follows:

$$R_C = \sqrt{R_{C_x}^2 + R_{C_y}^2}$$

$$= \sqrt{133.2^2 + 33.2^2}$$

$$= \sqrt{17,750 + 1100} = \sqrt{18,850}$$

$$= 137.5 \text{ lb}$$

6. The direction of R_C is defined by θ_{R_C} (see Fig. 3.66b):

$$\tan \theta_{R_C} = \frac{R_{C_y}}{R_{C_x}} = \frac{-33.2}{-133.2}$$

$$= 0.249$$

$$\therefore \theta_{R_O} = -13.95°$$

EXAMPLE 3.17 _____

The equilibrium of a coplanar, concurrent force system of three unknowns.

Given: Rigid bar AC supported at point A with a frictionless pin and loaded as shown in Fig. 3.67a. Load $P = 100$ lb. Pulleys at D and E are frictionless, and cables supporting loads P and Q are completely flexible and inextensible.

Find: A. The magnitude of the load Q necessary to maintain the equilibrium of bar AC in the given position.
   B. The magnitude, direction, and sense of the reaction R_A at the pin A.

Mathematical Analysis

1. Isolate the bar AC from its supports, and draw a free-body diagram, as shown in Fig. 3.67b, assuming coordinate axes x and y with origin at A.
2. Write the expression for $\sum M_A = 0$ by taking moments about point A. (By using this moment center, we are able to eliminate the immediate consideration of the two unknowns R_{A_x} and R_{A_y}, the rectangular components of R_A.)

$$\sum M_A = 0 \quad \text{(for equilibrium)}$$

$$= -3Q \cos 30° + 8P \cos 45° = 0$$

Transposing and solving for Q, we get

$$Q = \frac{8P \cos 45°}{3 \cos 30°}$$

$$= \frac{8(100)(1/\sqrt{2})}{3(\sqrt{3}/2)} = \frac{8(100)(2)}{3(\sqrt{3})(\sqrt{2})}$$

$$= \frac{8(100)(\sqrt{2})}{3\sqrt{3}}$$

$$= 217.5 \text{ lb}$$

3. Solve for R_{A_x} and R_{A_y} by writing expressions for $\sum F_x = 0$ and $\sum F_y = 0$ (see Fig. 3.68a).

$$\sum F_x = -Q + P \cos 75° - R_{A_x} = 0$$

$$\therefore R_{A_x} = P \cos 75° - Q$$

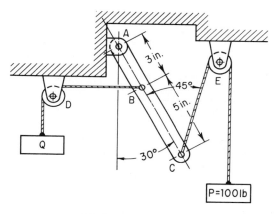

(a) Structure Diagram

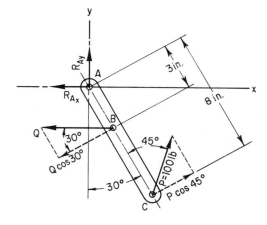

(b) Free-body Diagram

FIGURE 3.67

Substituting $Q = 217.5$ lb and $P = 100$ lb in the above equation for R_{A_x}, we get

$$R_{A_x} = (100 \text{ lb})(\cos 75°) - 217.5 \text{ lb}$$
$$= (100 \text{ lb})(0.259) - 217.5 \text{ lb}$$
$$= 25.9 \text{ lb} - 217.5 \text{ lb}$$
$$= -191.6 \text{ lb}$$

where the minus sign indicates that the sense is opposite to that assumed.

$$\sum F_y = R_{A_y} + P \sin 75° = 0$$
$$\therefore \ R_{A_y} = -P \sin 75°$$
$$= -(100 \text{ lb})(0.966)$$
$$= -96.6 \text{ lb}$$

where the minus sign indicates that the sense is opposite to that assumed.

4. Referring to Fig. 3.68b, determine the magnitude of R_A by

$$R_A = \sqrt{R_{A_x}^2 + R_{A_y}^2}$$
$$= \sqrt{(-191.6)^2 + (-96.6)^2}$$
$$= \sqrt{36{,}700 + 9300}$$
$$= \sqrt{46{,}000}$$
$$= 214.4 \text{ lb}$$

5. The direction of R_A is defined by θ_{R_A} (see Fig. 3.68b).

$$\tan \theta_{R_A} = \frac{R_{A_y}}{R_{A_x}}$$
$$= \frac{96.6}{191.6} = 0.498$$
$$\therefore \ \theta_{R_A} = 26.5°$$

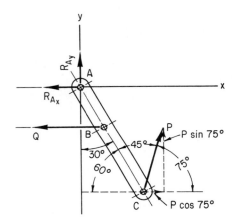

(a) Free-body Diagram

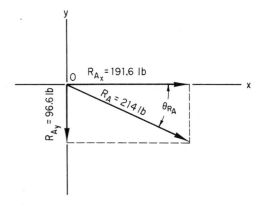

(b) Vector Diagram

FIGURE 3.68

Graphical Analysis

1. Lay out the free-body diagram to scale, and extend the known lines of action of forces P and Q until they intersect at point S (see Fig. 3.69a).
2. The line of action of reaction R_A must pass through point A (a known point on the line of action of R_A) and through point S, since the forces in a three-force system in equilibrium must be concurrent. This gives the directions of the lines of action of all the external forces in the given system.
3. Starting with known force P, draw the vector diagram with the directions of the vectors representing forces P, Q, and R_A parallel to the lines of action of these forces in the free-body diagram (see Fig. 3.69b).
4. Measure the length of vectors Q and R_A to the vector scale:

$$Q = 217 \text{ lb}$$

and

$$R_A = 214 \text{ lb}$$

5. Measure the angle θ_{R_A} that R_A makes with the x axis.

$$\therefore \ \theta_{R_A} = 26.5°$$

6. Transfer the arrow senses from the vector diagram to the space, or free-body, diagram.

NOTE: In the graphical analysis, we were able to solve this problem using only the vector diagram defining $\sum F_x = 0$ and $\sum F_y = 0$ for equilibrium. No moment analysis was necessary here, as it was in the mathematical analysis.

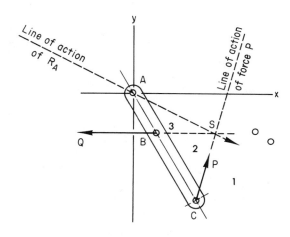

(a) Free-body Diagram with Structure to Scale
Space Scale: $\frac{1}{4}$ in. = 1 in.

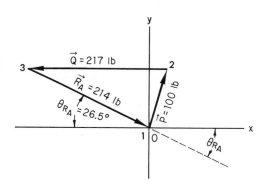

(b) Vector Diagram
Vector Scale: 1 in. = 100 lb

FIGURE 3.69

3.9 Equilibrium of Coplanar, Nonconcurrent Force Systems

A coplanar, nonconcurrent force system is in static equilibrium when it has *no resultant force* and when it has *no resultant moment*. Since these conditions must be satisfied, *three independent* equations are available to define a state of static equilibrium for such a system:

$$\sum F_x = 0 \qquad \sum F_y = 0 \qquad \sum M = 0$$

EXAMPLE 3.18 _____

Equilibrium; the general case of three coplanar, nonconcurrent forces.

Given: Coplanar, nonconcurrent forces $F_1 = 100$ lb, $F_2 = 150$ lb, and $F_3 = 75$ lb, as shown in Fig. 3.70a.

Find: The magnitude and the location of the equilibrant force F_E required to balance the given system in static equilibrium.

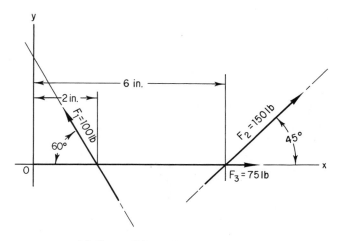

(a) Space Diagram
Space Scale: $\frac{1}{2}$ in. = 1 in.

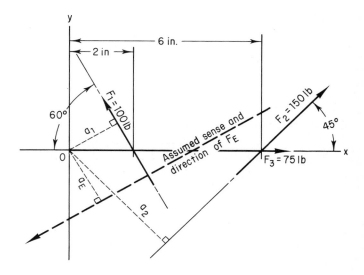

(b) Space Diagram

FIGURE 3.70

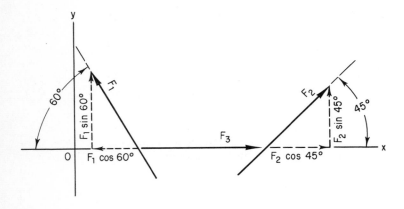

(a)

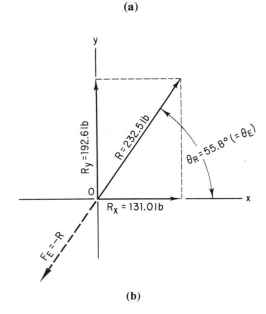

(b)

FIGURE 3.71

Mathematical Analysis

If we attempt to solve this problem directly by the equations of equilibrium ($\sum F_x = 0$, $\sum F_y = 0$, and $\sum M = 0$), we will not find a solution. This can be illustrated as follows:

a. From inspection of the given force system, we see that two forces (F_1 and F_2) have general directions and senses directed upward and force F_3 has a sense and direction to the right; therefore, assume that the line of action and the sense of the equilibrant F_E act downward and to the left, as shown in Fig. 3.70b.

b. Write the expressions defining static equilibrium conditions:

$$\sum F_x = 0$$

$$-F_1 \cos 60° + F_2 \cos 45° + F_3 - F_E \cos \theta_E = 0$$

$$\sum F_y = 0$$

$$F_1 \sin 60° + F_2 \sin 45° - F_E \sin \theta_E = 0$$

$$\sum M_O = 0$$

$$a_1 F_1 + a_2 F_2 - a_E F_E = 0$$

From these three independent equations, we see that four unknown quantities are involved: F_E, $\cos \theta_E$, $\sin \theta_E$, and a_E. Therefore, these equations cannot be solved simultaneously.

Using the resultant approach, as in Example 3.5, we can solve the problem mathematically (see Fig. 3.71a).

1. Determine the magnitude of the resultant force of the given system by the principle of projections:

$$\sum F_x = R_x = -F_1 \cos 60° + F_2 \cos 45° + F_3$$

$$= -(100 \text{ lb})\left(\frac{1}{2}\right) + (150 \text{ lb})\left(\frac{1}{\sqrt{2}}\right) + 75 \text{ lb}$$

$$= -50 \text{ lb} + 106 \text{ lb} + 75 \text{ lb}$$

$$= 131 \text{ lb}$$

$$\sum F_y = R_y = F_1 \sin 60° + F_2 \sin 45°$$

$$= (100 \text{ lb})\left(\frac{\sqrt{3}}{2}\right) + (150 \text{ lb})\left(\frac{1}{\sqrt{2}}\right)$$

$$= 86.6 \text{ lb} + 106 \text{ lb}$$

$$= 192.6 \text{ lb}$$

Then, referring to Fig. 3.71b,

$$R = \sqrt{R_x{}^2 + R_y{}^2}$$

$$= \sqrt{131^2 + 192.6^2}$$

$$= \sqrt{17{,}150 + 37{,}000}$$

$$= \sqrt{54{,}150}$$

$$= 232.5 \text{ lb}$$

$$\tan \theta_R = \frac{\sum F_y}{\sum F_x} = \frac{R_y}{R_x}$$

$$= \frac{192.6}{131.0}$$

$$= 1.471$$

$$\therefore \quad \theta_R = 55.8°$$

2. Since the equilibrant F_E is equal in magnitude, collinear in action, and opposite in sense to the resultant, we *reverse* the sense of the resultant to transform it into F_E (see Figs. 3.70b and 3.71b).

3. Determine the location of F_E relative to the given force system (and assumed coordinate system) by applying Varignon's theorem. Take moments of each

force in the system about origin O including the moment of F_E. From Fig. 3.70b,

$$\sum M_O = 0 \qquad \text{(for equilibrium)}$$

$$a_1 F_1 + a_2 F_2 - a_E F_E = 0$$

Solving for a_E, we write

$$a_E = \frac{a_1 F_1 + a_2 F_2}{F_E}$$

Magnitudes of moment arms a_1 and a_2 for forces F_1 and F_2 are determined, as indicated in Figs. 3.72a and 3.72b:

$$\sin 60° = \frac{a_1}{2} \qquad \sin 45° = \frac{a_2}{6}$$

$$a_1 = 2 \sin 60° \qquad a_2 = 6 \sin 45°$$

$$= 2\left(\frac{\sqrt{3}}{2}\right) \qquad = 6\left(\frac{1}{\sqrt{2}}\right)$$

$$= \sqrt{3} \text{ in.} \qquad = \frac{6}{\sqrt{2}} \text{ in.}$$

Substituting these values for a_1 and a_2 in the equation defining a_E, we get

$$a_E = \frac{(\sqrt{3} \text{ in.})(100 \text{ lb}) + (6/\sqrt{2} \text{ in.})(150 \text{ lb})}{232.5 \text{ lb}}$$

$$= \frac{173.2 \text{ lb-in.} + 636 \text{ lb-in.}}{232.5 \text{ lb}} = \frac{809.2}{232.5} \text{ in.}$$

$$= 3.48 \text{ in.}$$

4. To determine the point at which the equilibrant F_E intersects the x axis, we write the following expression (see Fig. 3.72c):

$$\sin \theta_E = \frac{a_E}{x_E}$$

$$\therefore x_E = \frac{a_E}{\sin \theta_E} = \frac{3.48 \text{ in.}}{0.827}$$

$$= 4.20 \text{ in.}$$

Graphical Analysis

1. Draw the vector diagram with the closing vector representing the equilibrant F_E of the given force system (see Fig. 3.73b). Measure the vector representing F_E to the vector scale: $F_E = 233$ lb.
2. Assume a pole 0 in the plane of the vector diagram, and draw the ray polygon (see Fig. 3.73b).
3. In the funicular polygon, draw the line of action of F_E parallel to vector $\overrightarrow{4-1}$ in the vector diagram through the point of intersection (P) of strings [0-1] and [0-4]. This locates the equilibrant F_E relative to the given forces and coordinate system. Measure the angle $\theta_E = 55.5°$ (see Fig. 3.73a).

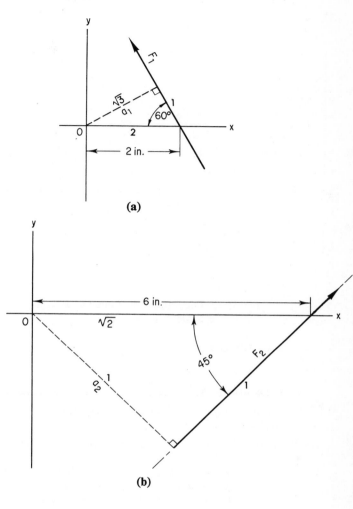

(a)

(b)

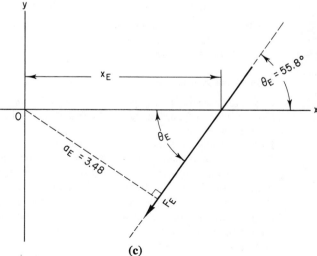

(c)

FIGURE 3.72

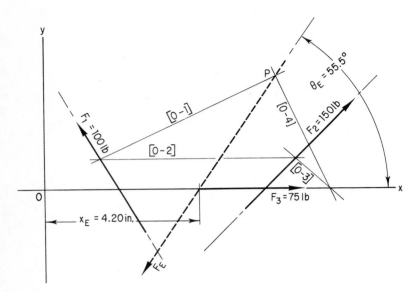

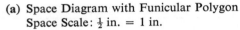

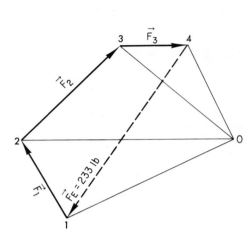

(a) Space Diagram with Funicular Polygon
Space Scale: $\frac{1}{2}$ in. = 1 in.

(b) Vector Diagram with Ray Polygon
Vector Scale: 1 in. = 50 lb

FIGURE 3.73

EXAMPLE 3.19 ─────────────

The coplanar, nonconcurrent force system as related to a structure in equilibrium.

Given: A structure loaded and supported as shown in Fig. 3.74. Assume frictionless hinges at points A, B, and C, and a frictionless pulley at point E. Cable supporting $F_2 = 700$ lb is perfectly flexible and inextensible. The weight of the supported beam is 800 lb.

Find: The magnitudes, senses, and directions (relative to a horizontal axis) of the reactions at A and B.

Graphical Analysis

1. In the space diagram (Fig. 3.75a), extend the *known lines of action* of applied forces F_1 and F_2 until they intersect at point U.
2. Graphically add the vectors representing F_1 and F_2 to determine their resultant R_{1+2} (see vector diagram in Fig. 3.75b). This resultant must act through point U (in the space diagram); therefore, transfer the line of action of the vector $\vec{R}_{1+2}$ from the vector diagram to the space diagram (Fig. 3.75a), and extend it through point U until it intersects the line of action of F_3 at point S.
3. Graphically determine $\vec{R}_{1+2+3}$, the resultant of $\vec{R}_{1+2}$ and $\vec{F}_3$ (Fig. 3.75b). Transfer the line of action

of $\vec{R}_{1+2+3}$ through point S from the vector diagram to the space diagram.
4. In the space diagram extend the line of action of R_{1+2+3} until it intersects the line of action of the force in member BC at point T (which is also the line of action of the reactive force F_B at B). (Since member BC is a two-force member, the line of action of the force in this member is assumed to act through the centerline of member BC.)
5. Now reduce the given system to a three-force coplanar system (R_{1+2+3}, F_A, and F_B). For static equilibrium, these three forces *must be concurrent*. Therefore, the line of action of the reaction at A *must* pass through point T (and point A).
6. Having established the line of action of reaction force F_A in the space diagram (Fig. 3.75a), and knowing the line of action of the reaction force F_B, complete the vector diagram, as shown in Fig. 3.75b.
7. Measure the vectors $[\overrightarrow{4\text{--}5}]$ and $[\overrightarrow{5\text{--}1}]$ representing the forces F_B and F_A:

$$F_B = 2010 \text{ lb} \qquad F_A = 1470 \text{ lb}$$

8. Measure the angle β that the reaction force F_A makes with the horizontal axis: $\beta = 3.25°$.

Mathematical Analysis

1. Draw the free-body diagram of the entire structure (see Fig. 3.76a).

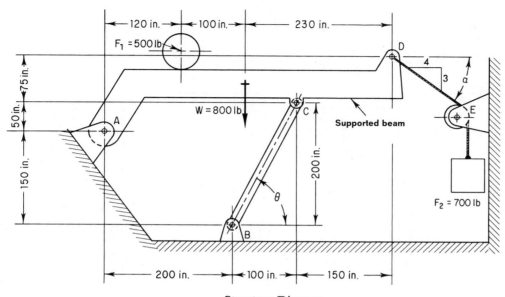

Structure Diagram
Space Scale: 1 in. = 100 in.

FIGURE 3.74

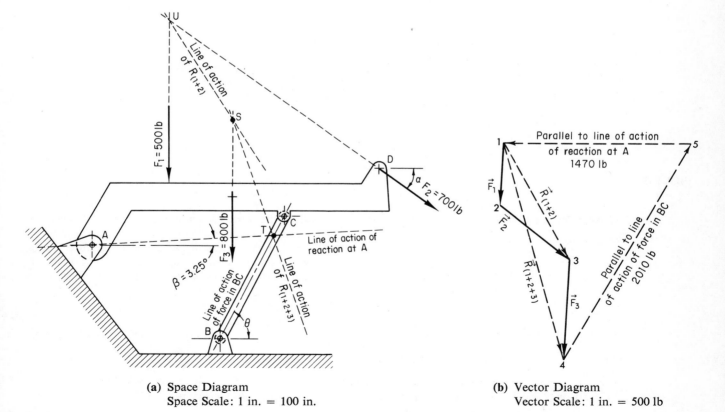

(a) Space Diagram
Space Scale: 1 in. = 100 in.

(b) Vector Diagram
Vector Scale: 1 in. = 500 lb

FIGURE 3.75

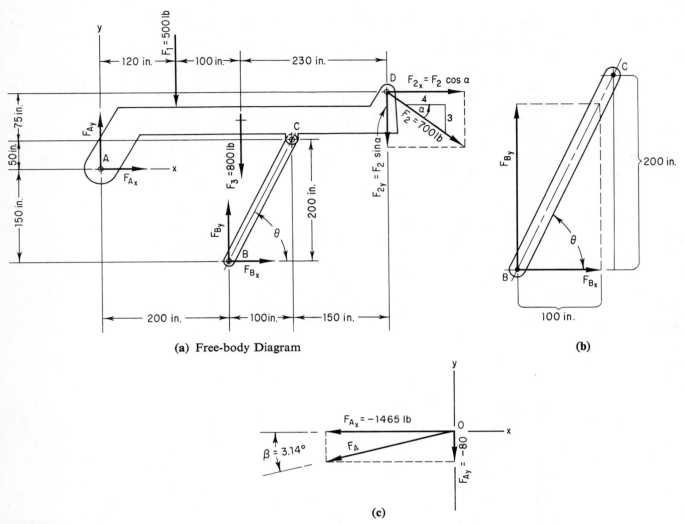

(a) Free-body Diagram

(b)

(c)

FIGURE 3.76

2. Applying the principle of projections, we write

$\sum F_x = 0$:

$$F_{A_x} + F_{B_x} + F_2 \cos \alpha = 0$$
$$F_{A_x} + F_{B_x} + (700\ \text{lb})(\tfrac{4}{5}) = 0$$

(a) $\quad F_{A_x} + F_{B_x} + 560\ \text{lb} = 0$

$\sum F_y = 0$:

$$F_{A_y} - F_1 - F_3 + F_{B_y} - F_2 \sin \alpha = 0$$
$$F_{A_y} - 500\ \text{lb} - 800\ \text{lb} + F_{B_y} - (700\ \text{lb})(\tfrac{3}{5}) = 0$$

(b) $\quad \therefore\ F_{A_y} + F_{B_y} - 1720\ \text{lb} = 0$

3. Since we have four unknowns (F_{A_x}, F_{A_y}, F_{B_x}, and F_{B_y}) and only two independent equations, we must obtain two additional independent equations from Varignon's theorem and from the geometry of the

given structure. For equilibrium, $\sum M = 0$. Since we know the line of action of force F_B and *do not know* the direction of the line of action of the force F_A, it will be convenient to use point A as a moment center. Taking moments about point A, we write

$\sum M_A = 0$

$$-120F_1 - 220F_3 + 150F_{B_x} + 200F_{B_y} - 450F_{2_y} - 125F_{2_x} = 0$$

Substituting

$$F_1 = 500\ \text{lb}, \quad F_3 = 800\ \text{lb},$$
$$F_{2_y} = F_2 \sin \alpha = (700\ \text{lb})(\tfrac{3}{5}),$$

and

$$F_{2_x} = F_2 \cos \alpha = (700\ \text{lb})(\tfrac{4}{5}),$$

we get

$$-(120 \text{ in.})(500 \text{ lb}) - (220 \text{ in.})(800 \text{ lb}) + (150 \text{ in.})(F_{B_x})$$
$$+ (200 \text{ in.})(F_{B_y}) - (450 \text{ in.})(700 \text{ lb})(\tfrac{3}{5})$$
$$- (125 \text{ in.})(700 \text{ lb})(\tfrac{4}{5}) = 0$$

$$-60{,}000 \text{ lb-in.} - 176{,}000 \text{ lb-in.}$$
$$+ (150 \text{ in.})(F_{B_x}) + (200 \text{ in.})(F_{B_y})$$
$$- 189{,}000 \text{ lb-in.} - 70{,}000 \text{ lb-in.} = 0$$

$$\therefore (150 \text{ in.})(F_{B_x}) + (200 \text{ in.})(F_{B_y})$$
$$- 495{,}000 \text{ lb-in.} = 0$$

Dividing through by 100 to reduce the coefficients, we get

(c) $(1.5 \text{ in.})(F_{B_x}) + (2.0 \text{ in.})(F_{B_y}) - 4950 \text{ lb-in.} = 0$

4. From the geometry of the given structure, we see that the structure and the forces F_{B_x} and F_{B_y} at the point B form similar triangles (see Fig. 3.76b). Using this relationship, we write

$$\tan \theta = \frac{200}{100} = \frac{F_{B_y}}{F_{B_x}}$$

(d) $\therefore F_{B_y} = 2F_{B_x}$

5. Substituting equation (d) in equation (c),

$$(1.5 \text{ in.})(F_{B_x}) + (2.0 \text{ in.})(2F_{B_x})$$
$$- 4950 \text{ lb-in.} = 0$$
$$(5.5 \text{ in.})(F_{B_x}) = 4950 \text{ lb-in.}$$

$$\therefore F_{B_x} = \frac{4950 \text{ lb-in.}}{5.5 \text{ in.}} = 900 \text{ lb}$$

Solving for F_{B_y},

$$F_{B_y} = 2F_{B_x}$$
$$F_{B_y} = 2(900 \text{ lb}) = 1800 \text{ lb}$$

6. Determine the magnitude of the reaction F_B:

$$F_B = \sqrt{F_{B_x}^2 + F_{B_y}^2}$$
$$= \sqrt{900^2 + 1800^2}$$
$$= \sqrt{810{,}000 + 3{,}240{,}000} = \sqrt{4{,}050{,}000}$$
$$= 2015 \text{ lb}$$

7. To solve for the reaction F_A, we substitute the above values for F_{B_x} and F_{B_y} in equations (a) and (b), respectively:

(a) $F_{A_x} + F_{B_x} + 560 \text{ lb} = 0$
$$F_{A_x} + 900 \text{ lb} + 560 \text{ lb} = 0$$
$$\therefore F_{A_x} = -1460 \text{ lb}$$

where the minus sign indicates that the direction of component force F_{A_x} is opposite to the direction we assumed.

(b) $F_{A_y} + F_{B_y} - 1720 \text{ lb} = 0$
$$F_{A_y} + 1800 \text{ lb} - 1720 \text{ lb} = 0$$
$$\therefore F_{A_y} = -80 \text{ lb}$$

where the minus sign indicates that the direction of component F_{A_y} is opposite to the direction we assumed.

8. Determine the magnitude of the reaction F_A:

$$F_A = \sqrt{F_{A_x}^2 + F_{A_y}^2}$$
$$= \sqrt{(-1460)^2 + (-80)^2}$$
$$= \sqrt{2{,}130{,}000 + 6400} = \sqrt{2{,}136{,}400}$$
$$= 1465 \text{ lb}$$

9. Determine the angle β that F_A makes with the x axis (see Fig. 3.76c):

$$\tan \beta = \frac{F_{A_y}}{F_{A_x}} = \frac{80}{1465}$$
$$= 0.057$$
$$\therefore \beta = 3.14°$$

3.10 Equilibrium of Coplanar, Parallel Force Systems

A coplanar, parallel force system is in static equilibrium when it has *no resultant force* ($\sum F_x = 0$ or $\sum F_y = 0$) and *no resultant moment* ($\sum M = 0$). Thus, there are *two independent* equations that may be used to solve for two unknown quantities.

EXAMPLE 3.20 _____

The coplanar, parallel force system applied to a structure in equilibrium.

Given: A beam simply supported and loaded as shown in Fig. 3.77. $F_1 = 500 \text{ lb}$, $F_2 = 300 \text{ lb}$. The weight of the beam is 1000 lb.

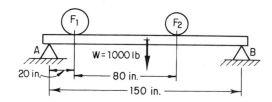

FIGURE 3.77

Structure Diagram
Scale: 1 in. = 50 in.

Find: The magnitudes of the reactions at the supporting points A and B.

Graphical Analysis

1. Draw a free-body diagram of the given loaded beam *to scale* (see Fig. 3.78a).
2. Draw a vector diagram showing the graphical addition of the known forces $(\vec{F_1} + \vec{F_2} + \overrightarrow{1000}$ lb) and the ray polygon, as shown in Fig. 3.78b.

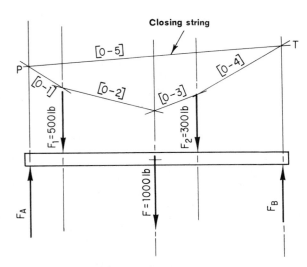

(a) Free-body Diagram with Equilibrium Diagram

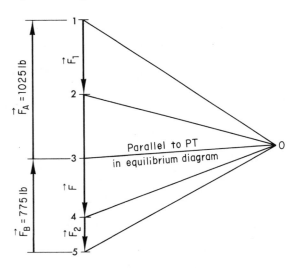

(b) Vector Diagram with Ray Polygon
Vector Scale: 1 in. = 500 lb

FIGURE 3.78

3. Draw the string polygon (equilibrium diagram) starting at point P on the line of action of one of the *unknown reactions*, F_A (see Fig. 3.78a). Since the given beam is in equilibrium, the string polygon must be a *closed polygon*. The closing string [0–5] is drawn from point T (where [0–4] intersects the line of action of F_B) to point P on the line of action of F_A. The *component directions* of F_A are defined by strings [0–1] and [0–5], and the component directions of F_B are defined by strings [0–4] and [0–5].
4. Draw a line from point 0 (in the ray polygon, Fig. 3.78b) *parallel* to PT in the string polygon (equilibrium diagram). The point 5 where this line intersects the vector diagram establishes the vector lengths of $\vec{F_A}$ and $\vec{F_B}$, since $\overrightarrow{[0-1]}$ and $\overrightarrow{[0-5]}$ are now the *components* of $\vec{F_A}$, and $\overrightarrow{[0-4]}$ and $\overrightarrow{[0-5]}$ the components of $\vec{F_B}$ (see Fig. 3.78b). The vector diagram now indicates equilibrium $(\sum F_y = 0)$, since $\vec{F_1} + \vec{F} + \vec{F_2} - \vec{F_B} - \vec{F_A} = 0$.
5. Measure the vector lengths for F_A and F_B:

$$F_A = 1025 \text{ lb} \qquad F_B = 775 \text{ lb}$$

Mathematical Analysis

1. Draw the free-body diagram of the given structure, showing the dimensions and including the x-y axes, as indicated in Fig. 3.79.
2. For equilibrium, $\sum F_y = 0$:

$$\therefore \ F_A - F_1 - F - F_2 + F_B = 0$$
$$F_A - 500 \text{ lb} - 1000 \text{ lb} - 300 \text{ lb} + F_B = 0$$

(a)
$$F_A + F_B - 1800 \text{ lb} = 0$$

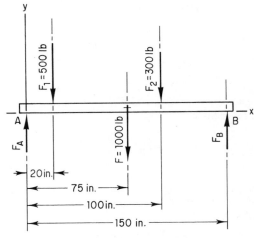

Free-body Diagram

FIGURE 3.79

3. Since there are two unknowns in equation (a), we must develop another independent equation based on the principle of statics. Since we know that $\sum M = 0$ for a structure in static equilibrium, we can take moments about point A and write

$$\sum M_A = 0$$

$$\therefore \ -(20 \text{ in.})F_1 - (75 \text{ in.})F$$
$$-(100 \text{ in.})F_2 + (150 \text{ in.})F_B = 0$$
$$-(20 \text{ in.})(500 \text{ lb}) - (75 \text{ in.})(1000 \text{ lb})$$
$$-(100 \text{ in.})(300 \text{ lb}) + (150 \text{ in.})F_B = 0$$
$$(-10,000 - 75,000 - 30,000) \text{ lb-in.}$$
$$+ (150 \text{ in.})(F_B) = 0$$

(b) $\qquad (150 \text{ in.})(F_B) - 115,000 \text{ lb-in.} = 0$

4. Solving for F_B,

$$F_B = \frac{115,000 \text{ lb-in.}}{150 \text{ in.}} = 767 \text{ lb}$$

5. Solve for F_A by substituting in equation (a) the value determined for F_B:

$$F_A + F_B - 1800 \text{ lb} = 0$$
$$\therefore \ F_A = 1800 \text{ lb} - F_B$$
$$= 1800 \text{ lb} - 767 \text{ lb}$$
$$= 1033 \text{ lb}$$

PROBLEMS

3.1 Given: A force system composed of forces $F_1 = 75$ lb, $F_2 = 90$ lb, $F_3 = 160$ lb, and $F_4 = 80$ lb acting in the x-y plane, as shown in Fig. 3.80.

Find: A. Graphically determine the magnitude and direction of the resultant of the given force system.
B. Check your results, using mathematical analysis.

3.2 Given: A force system composed of forces $F_1 = 150$ lb, $F_2 = 110$ lb, $F_3 = 95$ lb, and $F_4 = 105$ lb acting in the x-y plane, as shown in Fig. 3.81.

Find: A. Graphically determine the magnitude and direction of the resultant of the given force system.
B. Check your results, using mathematical analysis.

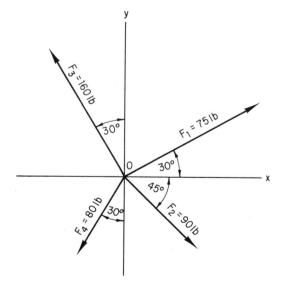

FIGURE 3.80

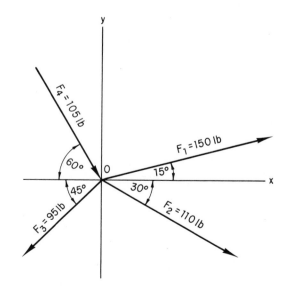

FIGURE 3.81

3.3 Given: Through experiment, it has been determined that to move weight W in Fig. 3.82, a horizontal force of 35 lb must be applied.

Find: A. Graphically determine the force F that is required to move weight W; also find the magnitude of the force in cable AC.

B. Check your results, using mathematical analysis.

3.4 Given: A pickup truck P weighing 2000 lb carrying a load $W = 1000$ lb, as shown in Fig. 3.83.

Find: The total load carried by each wheel of the truck:
A. Using mathematical analysis.
B. Using graphical analysis.

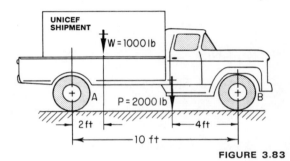

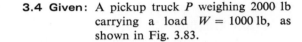

FIGURE 3.82

FIGURE 3.83

3.5 Given: A beam hinged at point A with a frictionless pin and supported at point C by a knife edge, as shown in Fig. 3.84. The beam is loaded with a vertical load of 100 lb and an inclined load of 150 lb.

Find: A. Using mathematical analysis, determine the magnitude and direction of the reaction forces at points A and C.
B. Check your answers, using graphical analysis.

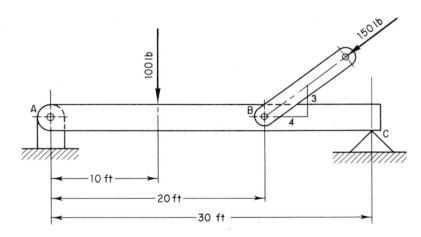

FIGURE 3.84

3.6 Given: A weightless beam supported and loaded as shown in Fig. 3.85. Assume that all hinges, pins, and pulleys are frictionless and that all cables are perfectly flexible and inextensible.

Find: A. Whether or not the given system is in static equilibrium, using mathematical analysis and graphical analysis.

B. If the system is not in equilibrium, what magnitude must W_1 have in order that it be in equilibrium?

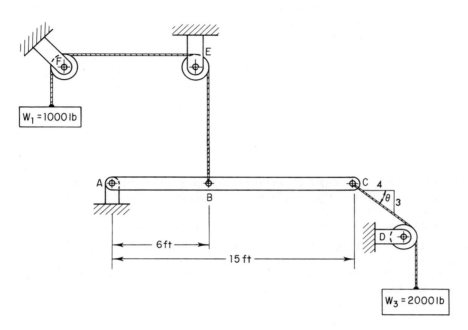

FIGURE 3.85

3.7 Given: The weightless plate of Fig. 3.86 supported with a frictionless hinge at point A, with weights $W_1 = 100$ lb, $W_2 = 400$ lb, and W_3 (magnitude unknown) applied at points B, C, and D, respectively.

Find: A. Using graphical analysis, determine the magnitudes of the reaction force at hinge A and the weight W_3 at D needed to maintain the plate in equilibrium in the given position.

B. Check your answers, using mathematical analysis.

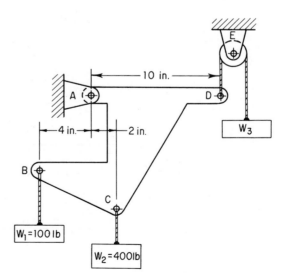

FIGURE 3.86

3.8 Given: A weightless bar loaded at its ends with equal and opposite loads ($W_1 = 1000$ lb and $W_2 = 1000$ lb) and supported with knife edges (points C and D), as shown in Fig. 3.87.

Find: A. Using graphical analysis, determine the magnitudes of the reaction forces at points C and D.
B. Check your answers by using mathematical analysis.

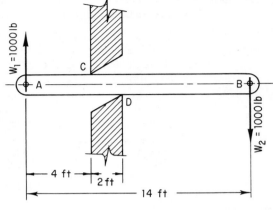

FIGURE 3.87

3.9 Given: A 1-ft section through a retaining wall (Fig. 3.88) resists a total pressure $P = 18h^2$ lb. The weight of the retaining wall is $Q = 0.5P$ lb. The line of action of force Q is located a distance $d = 0.271h$ from the vertical face of the wall. The base of the retaining wall is $b = 0.75h$.

Find: A. Using mathematical analysis, determine the reaction on the base and the point where its line of action intersects the base.
B. Assume a convenient value for h, and check your results using graphical analysis.

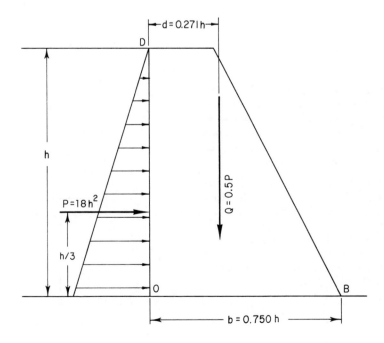

FIGURE 3.88

3.10 Given: The coplanar force system as shown in Fig. 3.89, where

$F_1 = 50$ lb,
$F_2 = 60$ lb,
$F_3 = 100$ lb,
$F_4 = 40$ lb.

Find: A. Using mathematical analysis, determine the magnitude of the resultant of the given force system.
B. Using mathematical analysis, locate the point at which the resultant crosses the x axis.
C. Check your results, using graphical analysis.

3.11 Given: The system of couples as shown in Fig. 3.90, where the couple vectors are

$C_1 = 50$ lb-ft,
$C_2 = 60$ lb-ft,
$C_3 = 100$ lb-ft,
$C_4 = 30$ lb-ft.

Find: The single additional couple C_E that must act in the given system to produce equilibrium.

Ans. 122.9 lb-ft

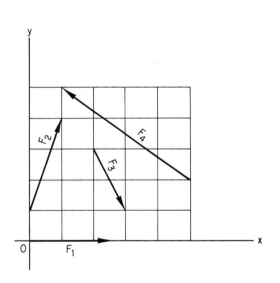

FIGURE 3.89

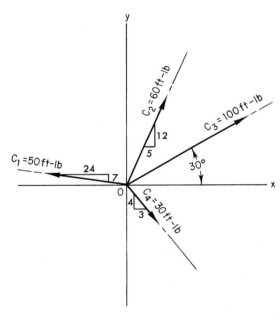

FIGURE 3.90

3.12 Given: A block weighing $P = 1000$ lb suspended in equilibrium by a system of weights and pulleys arranged as shown in Fig. 3.91. The weights W_1, W_2, and W_3 are connected to the block by weightless, perfectly flexible, and inextensible cables that pass over frictionless and weightless pulleys.

Find: Using graphical analysis, determine the magnitudes of weights W_1, W_2, and W_3 that maintain the system in equilibrium.

Ans. $W_1 = 471$ lb,
$W_2 = 667$ lb,
$W_3 = 1000$ lb.

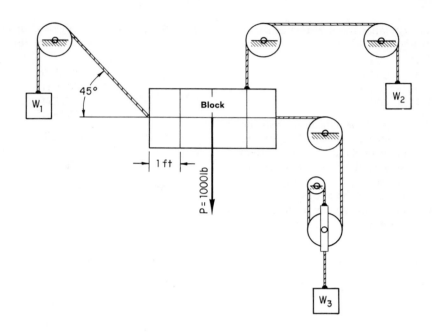

FIGURE 3.91

3.13 Given: The system of cables, pulleys, and beams shown in Fig. 3.92. The location of the vertical 1000-lb load on the weightless beam *CD* is *unknown*. The cables are perfectly flexible, inextensible, and weightless. The beams are weightless, and the pulleys are weightless and frictionless. All pulleys are 1 ft in diameter.

Find: A. The magnitude of the force *P* required to hold the given system in equilibrium.

B. The line of action of the 1000-lb load with respect to point *C*.

Ans.   *P* = 83.3 lb, and the 1000-lb load is located 2 ft from point *C*.

3.14 Using the answers to Prob. 3.13, determine the forces acting at points *A* and *B*.

Ans. $F_B = 700$ lb,
$F_A = 383.3$ lb.

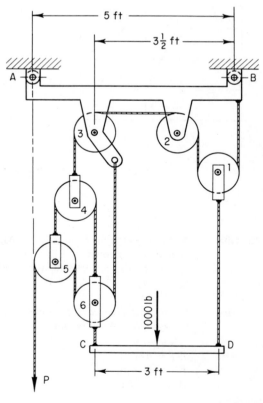

FIGURE 3.92

3.15 Given: The pinned structure in Fig. 3.93, with the applied load $F = 200$ lb.

Find: The magnitude of the forces acting at each lettered joint on the structure.

Ans. $F_A = 250$ lb,
$F_B = 160$ lb,
$F_C = 150$ lb,
$F_D = 134.5$ lb,
$F_E = 134.5$ lb.

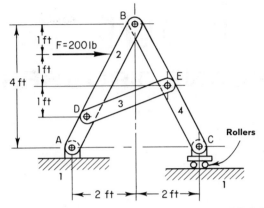

FIGURE 3.93

Four
PLANE TRUSSES

4.1 Introduction

A plane truss is a *rigid frame structure* made up of a number of *rigid bars* connected to each other at their ends. This type of structure is widely used in bridge construction, roof trusses, crane booms, etc. In Fig. 4.1 is shown a simple roof truss made of wood planks nailed together at their ends. This type of truss is used in small home construction.

The simplest plane truss is a *triangular frame* made of three rigid bars pinned at their ends (see Fig. 4.2). The triangular frame is obviously rigid, since the shape, or geometry, of a triangle cannot be altered without changing the lengths of the legs (in this case bars) of the triangle. Consequently, if they are to be rigid frame structures, all plane trusses must consist of combinations of triangles.

In this chapter, we discuss the *ideal plane truss* (rigid frame structure), which has the following characteristics (see Fig. 4.3):

1. The members (bars) of the plane truss are coplanar. In analyzing the plane truss, we usually represent its members by their centerlines.

2. The members (bars) of the plane truss are assumed to be *weightless*.

3. The joints of the plane truss, where the individual members of the truss are connected, are fastened to each other with *frictionless pins*.

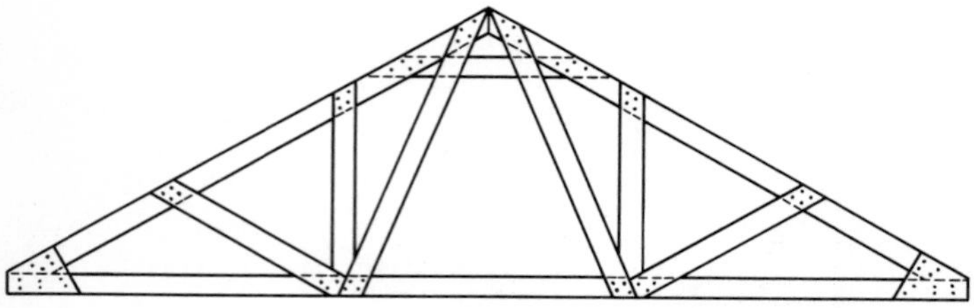

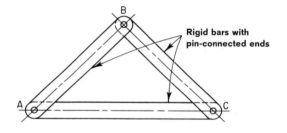

FIGURE 4.2

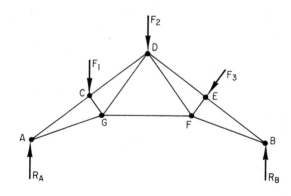

FIGURE 4.3

Pin-connected joints (apexes) are A, B, C, D, E, F, and G. External loading includes reactions R_A, R_B, and applied loads F_1, F_2, and F_3.

FIGURE 4.1

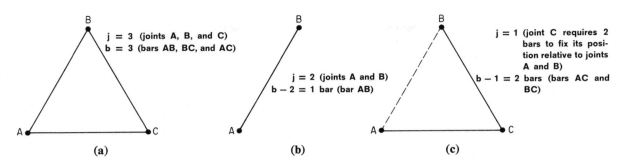

FIGURE 4.4

4. All external loads are applied at the joints of the truss through the connecting frictionless pins and are in the *same plane* as the truss itself.

5. All members (bars) in the plane truss are *two*-force members, since the external loads are applied at the ends of the members.

4.2 Redundant or Superfluous Members

In an externally loaded plane truss in equilibrium, every joint of the truss is also in equilibrium. Therefore, at each joint, there exists a coplanar, concurrent force system for which equilibrium can be defined by the *two* general equations $\sum F_x = 0$ and $\sum F_y = 0$. If there are more than two unknown forces at a joint, they cannot be determined by the principles of statics, and the plane truss is said to have a redundant member (or members) at that joint. Such members do not contribute to the rigidity of the truss.

To determine whether or not a particular plane truss contains redundant or superfluous members, we develop a simple relationship by considering the rigidity characteristics of a plane triangular frame (truss).

Figure 4.4a shows a plane triangular truss that consists of three joints A, B, and C and three bars AB, BC, and AC. Referring to Fig. 4.4b, we see that bar AB fixes two joints (A and B) relative to each other. From Fig. 4.4c, we see that joint C requires two bars AC and BC to fix its position relative to joints A and B.

Let j represent the number of joints and b the number of bars in the triangular truss. From Fig. 4.4b, we see that the two joints A and B require only one bar to fix their positions relative to each other, leaving $j - 2$ joints to be located with $b - 1$ bars. From the triangular truss, we see that $b - 1 = 2$ and $j - 2 = 1$. This means that there are two available bars to locate the single joint C.

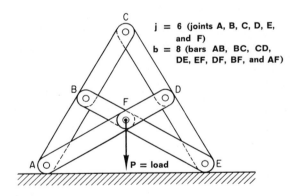

FIGURE 4.5

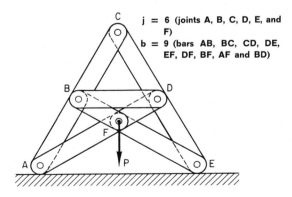

FIGURE 4.6

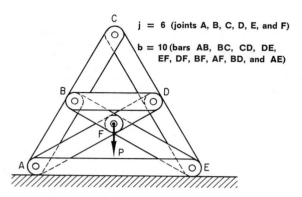

$j = 6$ (joints A, B, C, D, E, and F)

$b = 10$ (bars AB, BC, CD, DE, EF, DF, BF, AF, BD, and AE)

FIGURE 4.7

Since there are no other bars, we can write the following proportion:

$$\frac{b-1}{j-2} = \frac{2}{1}$$

or

$$b - 1 = 2(j - 2)$$
$$\therefore \ b = 2(j - 2) + 1$$
$$= 2j - 3$$

If b is *less than* $2j - 3$ for a particular plane truss, the plane truss contains *too few* bars for rigidity. If b is *greater than* $2j - 3$ for a particular plane truss, the plane truss has *more* bars than are necessary to establish a condition of rigidity, and we conclude that the truss contains a redundant member.

Consider the plane trusses shown in Figs. 4.5, 4.6, and 4.7. In Fig. 4.5 is shown a plane truss that consists of six joints and eight bars. To determine whether or not this truss is a rigid frame, we apply the equation $b = 2j - 3$:

$$b = 2(6) - 3 = 12 - 3 = 9$$

Therefore, we conclude that the given plane truss *is not* a rigid frame, since it has only eight bars.

We see in Fig. 4.6 a plane truss that is made of nine bars having six joints. Since $b = 2j - 3 = 2(6) - 3 = 9$, this plane truss *is* a rigid frame.

We see in Fig. 4.7 a plane truss with ten bars and six joints. Again using $b = 2j - 3$, we find $2(6) - 3 = 9$. Therefore, this plane truss has one *superfluous* bar. (If either *AE* or *BD* is removed, the structure will still be rigid.)

4.3 External Reactions to a Loaded Plane Truss

Before the loads carried by each member of an externally loaded truss can be analyzed, it is necessary to determine the directions, magnitudes, and senses of the reactions of the supports that maintain the plane truss in static equilibrium. The following example illustrates how this can be done graphically and mathematically.

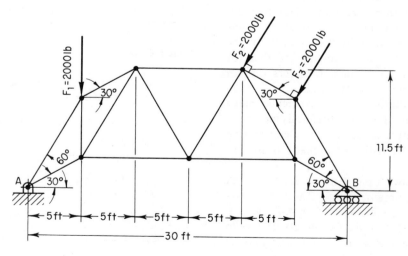

FIGURE 4.8

Scale: 1 in. = 6 ft

EXAMPLE 4.1

Determination of external reactions to a loaded plane truss.

Given: The loaded plane truss shown in Fig. 4.8.

Find: The reactions R_A and R_B at support points A and B, respectively, by using mathematical and graphical analysis.

Mathematical Analysis

1. Draw the free-body diagram of the entire plane truss, as shown in Fig. 4.9a.

2. Determine whether or not the given plane truss is a rigid frame. The truss has nine joints and fifteen bars. Applying the equation $b = 2j - 3$, we see that $b = 2(9) - 3 = 18 - 3 = 15$. Therefore, the given truss is a rigid frame with no superfluous members.

3. Determine the moments of each external and reaction load about support point A. From the geometry of the given truss and its external loading, we can determine the perpendicular distance from support point A to the line of action of each external load and reaction force (see Fig. 4.9b). The perpendicular distance from point A to the line of action of each force is as follows:

$$\text{to } F_1 = 5 \text{ ft}$$
$$\text{to } F_2 = \left(20 - \frac{11.5}{\tan 60°}\right)(\sin 60°) \text{ ft}$$
$$\text{to } F_3 = 20 \sin 60° \text{ ft}$$
$$\text{to } R_B = 30 \text{ ft}$$

4. Taking moments about point A, we get

$$\sum M_A = -F_1 5 - F_2\left(20 - \frac{11.5}{\tan 60°}\right)(\sin 60°)$$
$$- F_3(20 \sin 60°) + 30R_B = 0$$
$$= -F_1 5 - F_2(13.35 \sin 60°)$$
$$- F_3(20 \sin 60°) + 30R_B = 0$$

$$\therefore R_B = \frac{2000(5) + 2000(11.56) + 2000(17.32)}{30}$$
$$= \frac{10{,}000 + 23{,}120 + 34{,}640}{30} = \frac{67{,}760}{30}$$
$$= 2260 \text{ lb}$$

5. Considering the equilibrium conditions in the x and y directions, we can write:

$$\sum F_x = 0$$
$$-F_2 \cos 60° - F_3 \cos 60° + R_{A_x} = 0$$
$$\therefore R_{A_x} = F_2 \cos 60° + F_3 \cos 60°$$
$$= (2000 \text{ lb})(\tfrac{1}{2}) + (2000 \text{ lb})(\tfrac{1}{2})$$
$$= 1000 \text{ lb} + 1000 \text{ lb}$$
$$= 2000 \text{ lb}$$

$$\sum F_y = 0$$
$$R_{A_y} - F_1 - F_2 \sin 60° - F_3 \sin 60° + R_B = 0$$
$$\therefore R_{A_y} = F_1 + F_2 \sin 60° + F_3 \sin 60° - R_B$$
$$= 2000 \text{ lb} + (2000 \text{ lb})\left(\frac{\sqrt{3}}{2}\right)$$
$$+ (2000 \text{ lb})\left(\frac{\sqrt{3}}{2}\right) - 2260 \text{ lb}$$
$$= 2000 \text{ lb} + 1732 \text{ lb} + 1732 \text{ lb} - 2260 \text{ lb}$$
$$= 3204 \text{ lb}$$

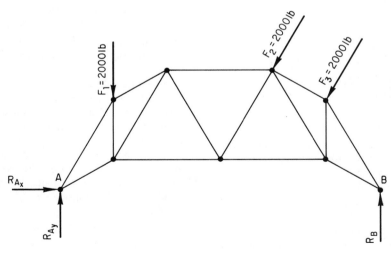

(a) Free-body Diagram

FIGURE 4.9(a)

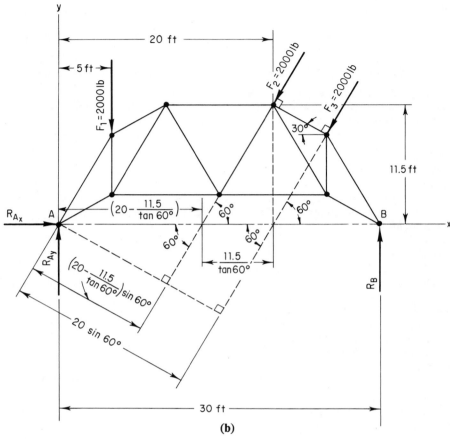

FIGURE 4.9(b)

6. Determine reaction R_A:

$$
\begin{aligned}
R_A &= \sqrt{R_{A_x}{}^2 + R_{A_y}{}^2} \\
&= \sqrt{2000^2 + 3204^2} \\
&= \sqrt{4,000,000 + 10,250,000} \\
&= \sqrt{14,250,000} \\
&= 3780 \text{ lb}
\end{aligned}
$$

Graphical Analysis I

1. Accurately draw the plane truss to a convenient space scale (in Fig. 4.10, we indicate a scale of 1 in. = 6 ft), showing the applied loads F_1, F_2, and F_3 and the *known* direction of reaction R_B (direction of R_A is unknown at this stage). (See Fig. 4.10.)

2. Using a convenient vector scale (in Fig. 4.10b, a scale of 1 in. = 2000 lb is shown), construct the vector diagram showing $\vec{F}_1 + \vec{F}_2 + \vec{F}_3$, and determine the *equilibrant* $\vec{E}$ necessary to maintain the given force system in equilibrium (see Fig. 4.10b).

3. Construct the ray polygon, using the known force vectors, $\vec{F}_1$, $\vec{F}_2$, and $\vec{F}_3$, and determine the location of the line of action of equilibrant $\vec{E}$ by the funicular polygon (examine carefully Figs. 4.10a and 4.10b).

4. Extend the line of action of equilibrant E until it intersects (at point P) the extended known line of action of R_B. Draw a line from point P to support point A, that defines the line of action of R_A (see Fig. 4.10a).

5. Using the *known* magnitude and direction of equilibrant E and the *known directions* of R_A and R_B, draw a vector diagram (superimposed on the initial vector diagram combining $\vec{F}_1$, $\vec{F}_2$, and $\vec{F}_3$) that closes to indicate an equilibrium condition between $\vec{E}$, $\vec{R}_A$, and $\vec{R}_B$. From this diagram, we can determine the magnitudes of $\vec{R}_A$ and $\vec{R}_B$ by measuring the vectors that represent these reactions: $R_A = 3780$ lb and $R_B = 2260$ lb (see Fig. 4.10b).

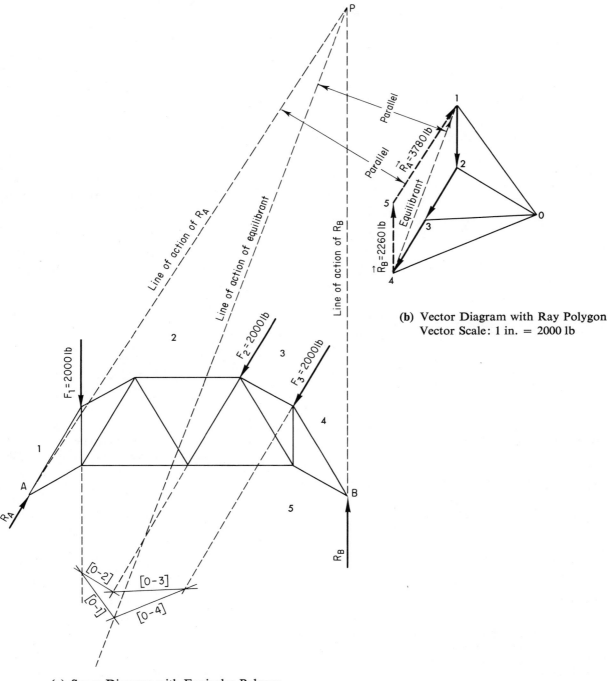

(b) Vector Diagram with Ray Polygon
Vector Scale: 1 in. = 2000 lb

(a) Space Diagram with Funicular Polygon
Space Scale: 1 in. = 6 ft

FIGURE 4.10

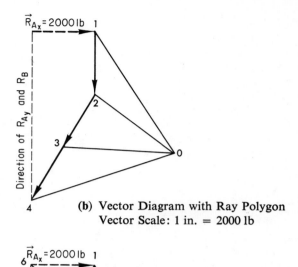

(b) Vector Diagram with Ray Polygon
Vector Scale: 1 in. = 2000 lb

(c) Vector Diagram with Ray Polygon—
Complete Vector Scale: 1 in. = 2000 lb

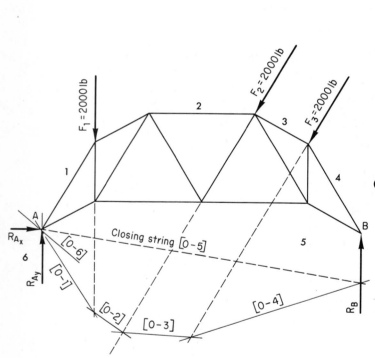

(a) Space Diagram with Funicular Polygon
Space Scale: 1 in. = 6 ft.

FIGURE 4.11

Graphical Analysis II

1. Accurately draw the plane truss to a convenient space scale (in Fig. 4.11a, we indicate a scale of 1 in. = 6 ft), showing the applied loads F_1, F_2, and F_3, the *direction* of R_B, and the x and y components of R_A (R_{A_x} and R_{A_y}, the magnitudes of which are unknown). (See Fig. 4.11a.)

2. Construct a vector diagram to a convenient vector scale (a scale of 1 in. = 2000 lb is shown in Fig. 4.11b), showing the addition of forces F_1, F_2, and F_3, and the

directions of $\vec{R}_B$, $\vec{R}_{A_y}$, and $\vec{R}_{A_x}$. From this diagram (Fig. 4.11b), we see that the magnitude of $\vec{R}_{A_x}$ can be determined directly by measurement ($R_{A_x} = 2000$ lb)
3. Construct the ray polygon $[0\vec{-}1]$, $[0\vec{-}2]$, $[0\vec{-}3]$, $[0\vec{-}4]$, and $[0\vec{-}6]$, as shown in Fig. 4.11c.
4. Starting at support point A in the space diagram, through which we know the reaction R_A passes (as do its components R_{A_x} and R_{A_y}), construct the funicular polygon for the *entire system* of external forces. The closing string $[0–5]$ is a component direction of R_B *and* a component of R_A. (This closing string indicates equilibrium for the given external force system. Fig. 4.11 shows all rays balanced.)
   5. Transfer the *direction* of the closing string $[0–5]$ in the funicular polygon to the vector diagram. This determines point 5 in the vector diagram and therefore the magnitudes of $\vec{R}_B$ and $\vec{R}_{A_y}$. (See Fig. 4.11c.)
6. Starting from point 5, draw $\vec{R}_A$ to point 1 in the vector diagram (see Fig. 4.11c). Measuring to the vector scale, we find $R_A = 3780$ lb and $R_B = 2260$ lb.
7. Transfer the direction of $\vec{R}_A$ to the space diagram to complete the solution.

4.4 Loads in Plane Truss Members

In designing a plane truss, it is necessary to determine the magnitude and the type of load carried by each bar in the truss under a specified external loading of the truss. There are three basic methods by which this can be done:

1. The method of joints, where the equilibrium conditions of each joint in the truss are analyzed systematically.

2. The method of sections, where "sections" of the truss are analyzed for equilibrium conditions.

3. The Maxwell diagram, where the entire truss is analyzed for equilibrium conditions through the use of a single all-inclusive vector diagram.

Each of these methods will be illustrated, using the externally loaded plane truss shown in Fig. 4.12a.

EXAMPLE 4.2 _____

The method of joints.

Given: An externally loaded plane truss supported at points A and B, as shown in Fig. 4.12a.

Find: The magnitude and the type of load carried by each member of the truss.

Mathematical Analysis

1. Determine whether or not the given plane truss is a rigid frame. From Fig. 4.12a, we see that $b = 7$ and $j = 5$. Substituting these values in $b = 2j - 3$, we get $b = 2(5) - 3 = 7$, which indicates that the given plane truss is a rigid frame and that it has no superfluous bars.
2. Draw the free-body diagram of the given loaded truss, as shown in Fig. 4.12b.
3. Determine the reactions at support points A and B (R_A and R_B, respectively) by taking moments about point A and algebraically summing the forces in the y direction.

$$\sum M_A = 0$$

$$-F_1 6 - F_2 12 - F_3 18 + R_B 24 = 0$$

$$\therefore \ R_B = \frac{F_1 6 + F_2 12 + F_3 18}{24}$$

$$= \frac{2000(6) + 4000(12) + 4000(18)}{24}$$

$$= \frac{132,000}{24}$$

$$= 5500 \text{ lb}$$

$$\sum F_y = 0$$

$$-F_1 - F_2 - F_3 + R_A + R_B = 0$$

$$\therefore \ R_A = F_1 + F_2 + F_3 - R_B$$

$$= 2000 \text{ lb} + 4000 \text{ lb} + 4000 \text{ lb} - 5500 \text{ lb}$$

$$= 4500 \text{ lb}$$

4. To expedite further calculations, we analyze the geometry of the given plane truss. From Fig. 4.13, we can determine the following useful relationships:

$$\tan \theta = \tfrac{8}{18} = 0.444$$

therefore, $\theta = 23.9°$. Using the slide rule, we see that

$$\sin \theta = 0.406 \quad \text{and} \quad \cos \theta = 0.913$$

From Fig. 4.13, we also see that

$$\sin \alpha = \tfrac{8}{10} \quad \text{and} \quad \cos \alpha = \tfrac{6}{10}$$

5. Consider the equilibrium of joint A by first sketching a free-body diagram of the joint to show what forces are acting there (see Fig. 4.14). Since the force

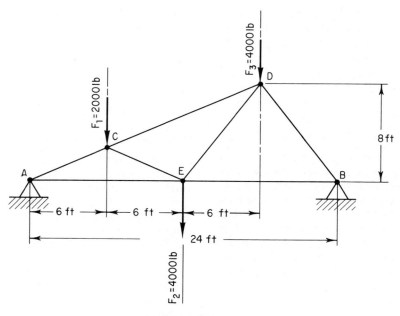

(a) Space Diagram
Scale: 1 in. = 5 ft

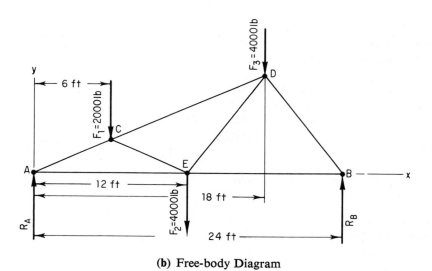

(b) Free-body Diagram

FIGURE 4.12

system at joint A is a coplanar, *concurrent* force system (as are *all* the joints of the truss), *two equations* of static equilibrium are available: $\sum F_x = 0$ and $\sum F_y = 0$. Therefore, referring to Fig. 4.14, we write

$$\sum F_x = -F_{AC} \cos \theta + F_{AE} = 0$$

and

$$\sum F_y = +R_A - F_{AC} \sin \theta = 0$$

From $\sum F_y = 0$, we get

$$R_A = F_{AC} \sin \theta$$

$$\therefore F_{AC} = \frac{R_A}{\sin \theta} = \frac{4500}{0.406} \text{ lb}$$
$$= +11,100 \text{ lb}$$

where the plus sign indicates that the assumed sense of F_{AC} is correct. The bar AC is in compression, since the sense is toward joint A.

From $\sum F_x = 0$, we get

$$F_{AE} = F_{AC} \cos \theta = (11,100 \text{ lb})(0.913)$$
$$= +10,130 \text{ lb}$$

where the plus sign indicates that the assumed sense of F_{AE} is the correct sense. The bar AE is in tension, since the sense of the force is away from joint A.

6. Consider the equilibrium of joint C by first sketching the free-body diagram of joint C, Fig. 4.15. (NOTE: The sense of the force in AC must be *toward* joint C, since we found bar AC to be in compression in step 4 above.) For equilibrium of joint C, $\sum F_x = 0$; thus,

$$F_{CD} \cos \theta + F_{CE} \cos \theta + F_{AC} \cos \theta = 0$$

Dividing both sides of this equation by $\cos \theta$, we get

$$F_{CD} + F_{CE} + F_{AC} = 0$$
$$\therefore F_{CD} + F_{CE} = -F_{AC} = -11,100 \text{ lb}$$

Also, $\sum F_y = 0$; hence,

$$-F_1 + F_{CD} \sin \theta - F_{CE} \sin \theta + F_{AC} \sin \theta = 0$$

Dividing both sides of this equation by $\sin \theta$ and substituting the known values for F_1 and F_{AC}, we get

$$\frac{2000 \text{ lb}}{0.406} + F_{CD} - F_{CE} + 11,100 \text{ lb} = 0$$

or

$$F_{CD} - F_{CE} = -6170 \text{ lb}$$

Solving the two above equations for F_{CD} and F_{CE} simultaneously for F_{CD},

$$F_{CD} + F_{CE} = -11,100 \text{ lb}$$
$$\underline{F_{CD} - F_{CE} = -6,170 \text{ lb}}$$
$$2F_{CD} = -17,270 \text{ lb}$$
$$\therefore F_{CD} = -8635 \text{ lb}$$

where the minus sign indicates that the sense of the force in the bar CD is *opposite* to that which was assumed (see Fig. 4.16). Substituting $F_{CD} = -8635$ lb in $F_{CD} - F_{CE} = -6170$ lb, we get

$$F_{CE} = 6170 \text{ lb} - 8635 \text{ lb}$$
$$= -2465 \text{ lb}$$

where the minus sign indicates that the sense of the force in bar CE is *opposite* to that which was assumed (see Fig. 4.16).

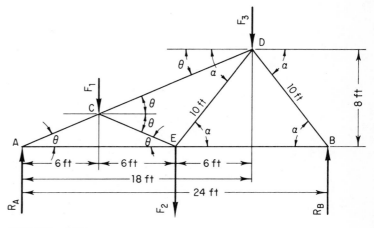

FIGURE 4.13

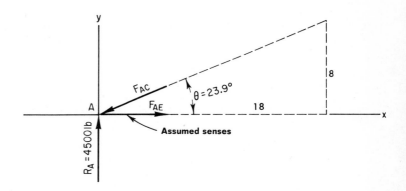

FIGURE 4.14

Free-body Diagram of Joint A

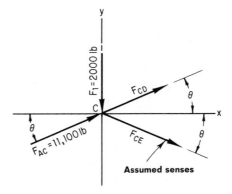

FIGURE 4.15

Free-body Diagram of Joint C

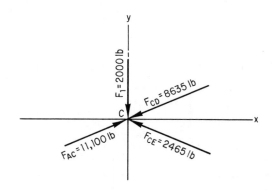

FIGURE 4.16

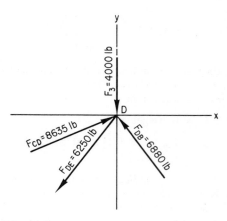

FIGURE 4.18

7. Consider the equilibrium of joint D by sketching the free-body diagram of this joint, Fig. 4.17. (NOTE: Since bar CD is pushing at joint C, for equilibrium it must push at joint D. Thus, the sense of the force in CD is *toward* joint D, and bar CD is in compression.)

For equilibrium at joint D, $\sum F_x = 0$:

$$F_{CD} \cos \theta + F_{DE} \cos \alpha - F_{DB} \cos \alpha = 0$$

Substituting the known values for F_{CD}, $\cos \theta$, and $\cos \alpha$, we get

$$(8635 \text{ lb})(0.913) + F_{DE}\tfrac{6}{10} - F_{DB}\tfrac{6}{10} = 0$$
$$\therefore \ 0.6F_{DE} - 0.6F_{DB} = -7880 \text{ lb}$$

Also, $\sum F_y = 0$:

$$- F_3 + F_{CD} \sin \theta + F_{DE} \sin \alpha + F_{DB} \sin \alpha = 0$$

Substituting the known values for F_3, F_{CD}, $\sin \theta$, and $\sin \alpha$, we get

$$-4000 \text{ lb} + (8635 \text{ lb})(0.406) + F_{DE}\tfrac{8}{10} + F_{DB}\tfrac{8}{10} = 0$$
$$\therefore \ 0.8F_{DE} + 0.8F_{DB} = 500 \text{ lb}$$

Solving simultaneously for F_{DE} and F_{DB}, we find that $F_{DE} = -6250$ lb, where the minus sign indicates that the sense of the force in bar DE is opposite to that which was assumed (see Fig. 4.18).

We also find that $F_{DB} = +6880$ lb, where the plus sign indicates that the sense of F_{DB} was correctly assumed (see Fig. 4.18).

8. Consider the equilibrium of joint B by sketching the free-body diagram of the joint, Fig. 4.19. (NOTE: Since bar DB is pushing at joint D, it must be pushing at joint B. Thus, the sense of the force in bar DB is *toward* joint B, and bar DB is in compression.)

For equilibrium at joint B, $\sum F_x = 0$ and $\sum F_y = 0$:

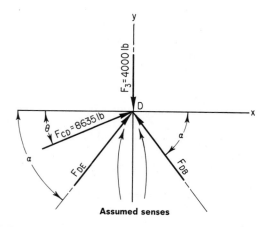

FIGURE 4.17
Free-body Diagram of Joint D

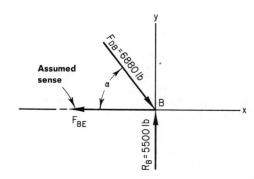

FIGURE 4.19
Free-body Diagram of Joint B

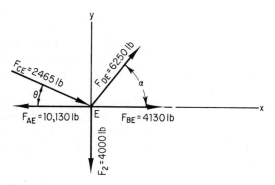

FIGURE 4.20

the accuracy of the preceding calculations in steps 1–7. Sketch a free-body diagram of joint E, Fig. 4.20. From this diagram, we see that

$$\sum F_y = -F_2 + F_{DE} \sin \alpha - F_{CE} \sin \theta = 0$$

Substituting the known values for F_2, F_{DE}, F_{CE}, $\sin \alpha$, and $\sin \theta$, we get

$$
\begin{aligned}
\sum F_y &= -4000 \text{ lb} + (6250 \text{ lb})(0.8) \\
&\quad - (2465 \text{ lb})(0.406) \\
&= -4000 \text{ lb} + 5000 \text{ lb} - 1000 \text{ lb} \\
&= -5000 \text{ lb} + 5000 \text{ lb} \\
&= 0
\end{aligned}
$$

which indicates that there is no significant error in the preceding calculations.

10. Considering the senses of the forces in the bars at each joint, determine whether each bar is in tension or compression. If the sense of a force acts *toward* a joint, the bar is *pushing* at the joint and therefore is in compression. If the sense is *away* from the joint, the bar is *pulling* at the joint and therefore must be in *tension*. Summarize the magnitudes and types of forces in each bar of the truss, as shown in Fig. 4.22.

$$\sum F_x = -F_{BE} + F_{DB} \cos \alpha = 0$$
$$\sum F_y = R_B - F_{DB} \sin \alpha = 0$$

Using the $\sum F_x$ equation, we can solve directly for F_{BE}:

$$
\begin{aligned}
F_{BE} &= F_{DB} \cos \alpha \\
&= (6880 \text{ lb})(\tfrac{6}{10}) \\
&= +4130 \text{ lb}
\end{aligned}
$$

That the sense has been correctly assumed is indicated by the plus sign.

9. No analysis is necessary for joint E, since the loads in the bars that are joined at E have been determined. However, an analysis of joint E serves as a *check* on

Graphical Analysis

1. Accurately lay out the truss to a convenient space scale (in Fig. 4.21a, we indicate 1 in. = 5 ft). Use Bow's notation. (See Fig. 4.21.)

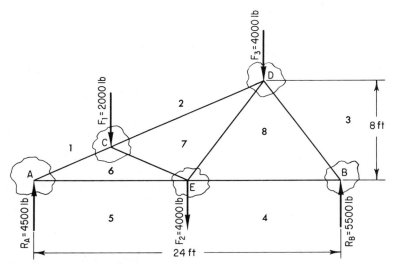

(a) Space Diagram
(see Fig. 4.12a for complete dimensions.)
Scale: 1 in. = 5 ft

FIGURE 4.21(a)

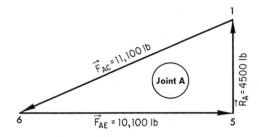

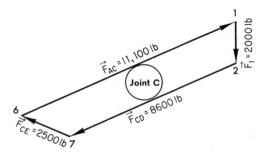

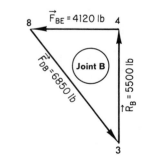

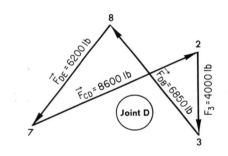

(b) Vector Diagrams of
Joints *A*, *B*, *C*, and *D*
Vector Scale: 1 in. = 3000 lb

FIGURE 4.21(b)

2. Starting with joint *A*, draw the vector diagram to a convenient scale that represents the equilibrium condition for joint *A*. (Vectors are parallel to R_A and bars *AC* and *AE*.) Measuring the vector lengths, we get $\vec{F}_{AC} = 11,100$ lb and $\vec{F}_{AE} = 10,100$ lb. (See Fig. 4.21b, joint *A*.)

3. Draw a vector diagram that represents the equilibrium condition at joint *C*, using a vector having the magnitude of $\vec{F}_{AC}$ but a sense *opposite* to that found in the vector diagram for joint *A*. (Since bar *AC* is pushing toward joint *A*, it must push toward joint *C* with equal magnitude. Vectors are parallel to bars *AC*, *CD*, and *CE* and to applied force F_1.) Analyzing joint *D* in the same manner and measuring the vector lengths, we get $\vec{F}_{DE} = 6200$ lb and $\vec{F}_{DB} = 6850$ lb. (See Fig. 4.21b, joint *D*.)

4. Draw a vector diagram that represents the equilibrium condition at joint *B*, using a vector having the magnitude of $\vec{F}_{DB}$ but a sense opposite to that found in the vector diagram for joint *D*. (Vectors are parallel to bars *DB* and *BE* and to reaction R_B.) Measuring the vector lengths, we get $\vec{F}_{BE} = 4120$ lb.

5. Transfer the senses of the vectors from each vector diagram to the respective joints of the plane truss, and record the magnitudes and types of load carried by each member of the truss, as shown in Fig. 4.22. Values determined by mathematical analysis are indicated in this figure with boldface numbers. Indicated also (in regular typeface), for purposes of comparison, are the values determined by graphical analysis.

The Maxwell diagram is a compact and comprehensive graphical method of determining the magnitude and type of load in an externally loaded plane truss. This method actually unifies the graphical analysis illustrated in Example 4.2, where the individual vector diagrams, defining the equilibrium condition of each joint in a truss, are combined into one diagram.

EXAMPLE 4.3

The Maxwell diagram: loads carried by the bars of an externally loaded plane truss.

Given: The externally loaded plane truss shown in Fig. 4.23a.

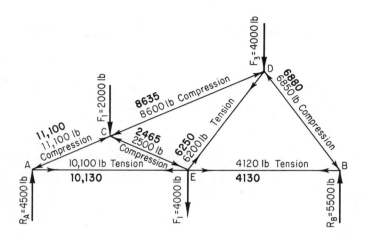

FIGURE 4.22

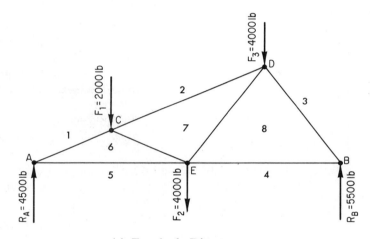

(a) Free-body Diagram
Space Scale: 1 in. = 5 ft

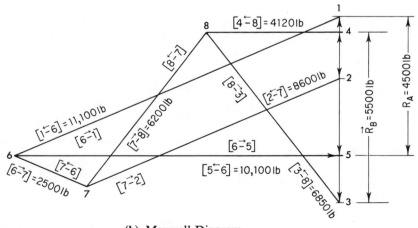

(b) Maxwell Diagram
Vector Scale: 1 in. = 2000 lb

FIGURE 4.23

Find: Using the Maxwell diagram, determine the magnitude and type of load carried by each bar of the given truss.

Maxwell Diagram Analysis

1. Accurately lay out the plane truss to a convenient space scale.

2. Apply Bow's notation to the external loads and reactions and to the bars of the plane truss (see Fig. 4.23a).

3. Since $R_A = 4500$ lb and $R_B = 5500$ lb (from previous calculations), we can draw the vector diagram of the known loads and reactions to a convenient scale (1 in. = 2000 lb), as shown in Fig. 4.23b. The vector diagram [1–2], [2–3], [4–5], and [5–1] closes for equilibrium.

4. Starting with joint A in the space diagram and continuing around each joint in a *clockwise* direction, list (according to Bow's notation) the forces acting at each joint:

> Joint A: [5–1], [1–6], [6–5]
>
> Joint C: [6–1], [1–2], [2–7], [7–6]
>
> Joint D: [7–2], [2–3], [3–8], [8–7]
>
> Joint B: [8–3], [3–4], [4–8]
>
> Joint E: [8–4], [4–5], [5–6], [6–7], [7–8]

5. Starting in the vector diagram at point 5 (with the known load $[\overrightarrow{5-1}] = R_A = 4500$ lb), lay off vectors that are parallel to the bars that join at joint A (see Fig. 4.23b). That is, lay off the vectors going from 5 to 1, 1 to 6, and 6 to 5. The intersection of $[\overrightarrow{5-6}]$ and $[\overrightarrow{1-6}]$ determines point 6 in the diagram. (Note that this "loop" closes, indicating that joint A is in static equilibrium.) Note the senses of the vectors $[\overrightarrow{5-1}]$, $[\overrightarrow{1-6}]$, and $[\overrightarrow{6-5}]$.

6. Starting at point 6, lay off vectors that are parallel to the bars that join at joint C. That is, lay off the vectors going from 6 to 1, 1 to 2, 2 to 7, and 7 to 6. The intersection of $[\overrightarrow{2-7}]$ and $[\overrightarrow{6-7}]$ determines point 7.

7. Starting at point 7, lay off vectors that are parallel to the bars at joint D, going from 7 to 2, 2 to 3, 3 to 8, and 8 to 7. The intersection of $[\overrightarrow{3-8}]$ and $[\overrightarrow{8-7}]$ determines point 8.

8. Starting at point 8, lay off vectors that are parallel to the bars at joint B, going from 8 to 3, 3 to 4, and 4 to 8. This last vector $[\overrightarrow{4-8}]$ is the closing vector for the entire diagram and indicates an equilibrium condition for all the joints in the plane truss.

9. To the vector scale, measure all the vectors in the Maxwell diagram; these vectors represent forces in the bars of the given plane truss:

Bar	Vector	Magnitude
AC	[$\overrightarrow{1-6}$]	11,100 lb
CD	[$\overrightarrow{2-7}$]	8,600 lb
DB	[$\overrightarrow{3-8}$]	6,850 lb
BE	[$\overrightarrow{4-8}$]	4,120 lb
DE	[$\overrightarrow{7-8}$]	6,200 lb
CE	[$\overrightarrow{6-7}$]	2,500 lb
AE	[$\overrightarrow{6-5}$]	10,100 lb

10. To determine whether a bar is in tension or compression, read the numbers in the Maxwell diagram in a clockwise direction (which is the direction assumed for Bow's notation). For example, at joint C in Fig. 4.23a, the forces are [$\overrightarrow{6-1}$], [$\overrightarrow{1-2}$], [$\overrightarrow{2-7}$], and [$\overrightarrow{7-6}$]. Referring to the Maxwell diagram and reading (in a clockwise direction) from 6 to 1, 1 to 2, 2 to 7, and 7 to 6, we see that the sense of vector [$\overrightarrow{6-1}$], when transferred to joint C, acts *toward* joint C. Therefore, bar AC is in *compression*. We may continue this analysis as follows:

   a. Read from 2 to 7: vector [$\overrightarrow{2-7}$] has a sense *toward* joint C, indicating that bar CD is in *compression*.

   b. Read from 7 to 6: vector [$\overrightarrow{7-6}$] has a sense *toward* joint C, indicating that bar CE is in *compression*.

At joint D, we have forces [$\overrightarrow{7-2}$], [$\overrightarrow{2-3}$], [$\overrightarrow{3-8}$], and [$\overrightarrow{8-7}$]. Referring to the Maxwell diagram, we proceed as follows:

   c. Read from 7 to 2: the bar CD is in *compression*, since the sense of [$\overrightarrow{7-2}$] is *toward* joint D.

   d. Read from 3 to 8: the bar DB is in *compression*, since the sense of [$\overrightarrow{3-8}$] is *toward* joint D.

   e. Read from 8 to 7: the bar DE is in *tension*, since the sense of [$\overrightarrow{8-7}$] is *away* from joint D.

Continuing around the truss and the Maxwell diagram in this manner, we can determine the type of load each bar in the truss carries. (In summary form, these results would appear as shown previously in Fig. 4.22.)

The *method of sections*, as the name implies, deals with sections of a plane truss rather than with the individual bars at each joint of the truss. This method utilizes an *imaginary cutting plane*

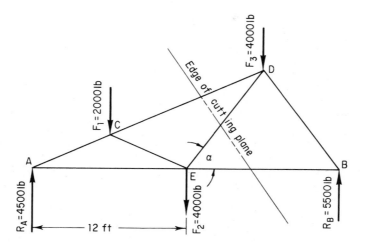

FIGURE 4.24

that usually "cuts" a *maximum* of *three* bars at one time. This forms a coplanar, nonconcurrent force system that can be analyzed by means of three equilibrium equations:

$$\sum F_x = 0, \quad \sum F_y = 0, \quad \text{and} \quad \sum M = 0$$

The advantage of the method of sections is that the loads carried by a *specific* bar, or bars, can be determined without the analysis of all the bars in the truss. Thus, the results of this method can be found quickly and used as a quick check against the results obtained by other methods of analysis.

EXAMPLE 4.4 ─────────────

The method of sections: loads carried by the bars of an externally loaded plane truss.

Given: The externally loaded truss shown in Fig. 4.24, which is the same truss as that used in Examples 4.2 and 4.3.

Find: Using the method of sections, determine the magnitude and type of load, carried by the bar *DE* of the given truss.

Method of Sections Analysis

1. Cut bars *CD*, *DE*, and *BE* of the given plane truss with a *cutting plane* as shown in Fig. 4.24.
2. Consider the equilibrium of the *left section* of the plane truss. For convenience, *assume* that the forces in *CD*, *DE*, and *BE* are tensile forces. (See Fig. 4.25.)

Taking moments about joint *A*,

$$
\begin{aligned}
\sum M_A &= -(6 \text{ ft})(F_1) - (12 \text{ ft})(F_2) \\
&\quad + (12 \text{ ft})(\sin \alpha)F_{DE} = 0 \\
&= -(6 \text{ ft})(2000 \text{ lb}) - (12 \text{ ft})(4000 \text{ lb}) \\
&\quad + (12 \text{ ft})(\tfrac{8}{10})(F_{DE}) \\
&= -12{,}000 \text{ lb-ft} - 48{,}000 \text{ lb-ft} \\
&\quad + (9.6 \text{ ft})F_{DE} \\
\therefore \ F_{DE} &= \frac{60{,}000 \text{ lb-ft}}{9.6 \text{ ft}} \\
&= +6250 \text{ lb}
\end{aligned}
$$

The plus sign indicates that we assumed the correct sense; bar *DE* is in tension.

3. If loads in other bars are to be determined, additional cutting planes can be used. Careful choice of sections can expedite calculations.

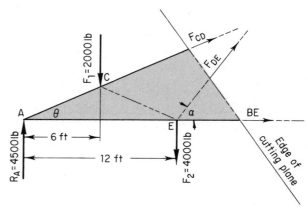

FIGURE 4.25

PROBLEMS _____

4.1 Given: A simple triangular truss of three bars joined with frictionless pins. A vertical load $W = 2000$ lb is applied to the truss, as shown in Fig. 4.26.

Find: Using graphical analysis and the method of joints, determine the magnitude and type (tension or compression) of load in each member.

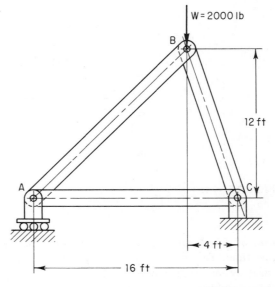

FIGURE 4.26

4.2 Given: The pin-connected truss shown in Fig. 4.26.

Find: The magnitude and type (tension or compression) of load in each bar of the given truss.
A. Use mathematical analysis and the method of joints.
B. Use mathematical analysis and the method of sections.
C. Compare answers in parts A and B with your answer in Prob. 4.1.

4.3 Given: The truss shown in Fig. 4.26.

Find: Using the Maxwell diagram, determine the magnitude and type of load in each member of the given truss.

4.4 Given: A pin-connected truss carrying a load of 12,000 lb, as shown in Fig. 4.27.

Find: Using graphical analysis and the method of joints, determine the magnitude and type of load (tension or compression) in each member of the truss.

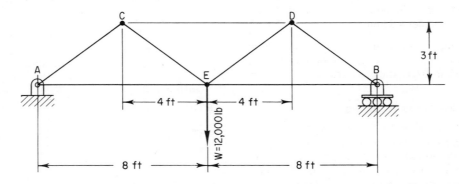

FIGURE 4.27

118

4.5 Given: The truss shown in Fig. 4.28.

Find: Using mathematical analysis and the method of joints, determine the magnitude and type of load in each member of the given truss.

4.6 Given: The truss shown in Fig. 4.27.

Find: Using mathematical analysis and the method of sections, determine the magnitude and type of load in members *CD*, *DE*, and *EB*.

4.7 Given: The truss shown in Fig. 4.27.

Find: Using the Maxwell diagram, determine the magnitude and type of load in each member of the given truss.

4.8 Given: A pin-connected truss carrying loads $W_1 = 1000$ lb and $W_2 = 3000$ lb, as shown in Fig. 4.28.

Find: The magnitude and type of load in members *DC* and *AD* of the given truss, using mathematical analysis and the method of sections.

4.9 Given: The pin-connected truss shown in Fig. 4.28.

Find: Using the Maxwell diagram, determine the magnitude and type of load in each member of the given truss.

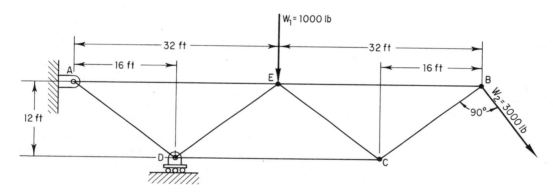

FIGURE 4.28

4.10 Given: A pin-connected truss with a 5000-lb load and a 20-ton load applied, as shown in Fig. 4.29.

Find: The forces exerted by supports *A* and *B*. (Before starting your solution, check the truss for superfluous members.)

Ans. Force at point *A* = 9.71 tons, force at point *B* = 10.63 tons.

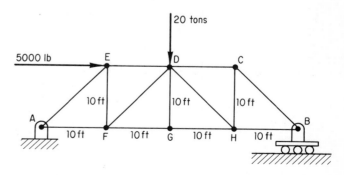

FIGURE 4.29

4.11 Given: The pin-connected truss shown in Fig. 4.30.

Find: Using the method of joints, determine which members of the given truss can be removed without affecting the rigidity of the structure. (Before starting your solution, check the truss for superfluous members.)

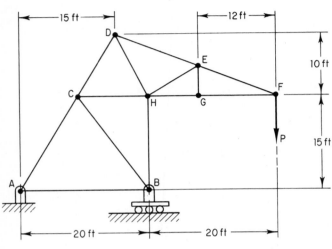

FIGURE 4.30

4.12 Given: A pin-connected truss with applied loads 3000 lb, 7000 lb, and 5000 lb as shown in Fig. 4.31.

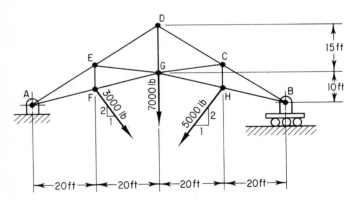

FIGURE 4.31

Find: Using Graphical Analysis II (see page 108), determine the forces exerted by the supports on the given truss at points A and B. (Use a vector scale of 1 in. = 3000 lb and a space scale of 1 in. = 16 ft.)

Ans. F_A = 6720 lb, F_B = 7380 lb

4.13 Find: The type and magnitude of the load in each member of the truss in Prob. 4.10. Use the method of joints.

Ans. DC = 10.62 tons compression,
CH = 10.62 tons tension,
GH = 21.25 tons tension,
CB = 15.05 tons compression,
HB = 10.63 tons tension,
GF = 21.25 tons tension,
ED = 11.88 tons compression,
AE = 13.25 tons compression,
EF = 9.38 tons tension,
AF = 11.88 tons tension,
FD = 13.25 tons compression,
GD = 0,
DH = 15.05 tons compression.

4.14 Determine the type and magnitude of the load in member DH of the truss given in Prob. 4.11. Let the load P = 10,000 lb, and use the method of sections.

Ans. 31,400 lb compression.

4.15 Make a Maxwell diagram for the truss given in Prob. 4.12, using a vector scale of 1 in. = 3000 lb. Record the magnitude and type (tension or compression) of force in each member. Check your results by using another method of analysis.

Five

THREE-DIMENSIONAL FORCE SYSTEMS

5.1 Introduction

A force system in three-dimensional space is called a *noncoplanar* force system. It is one in which the lines of action of the forces in the system do *not* lie in one plane. Force systems in space are commonly found in such mechanical structures as machines and aircraft. Some examples of simple three-dimensional force systems are loaded tripods, poles, towers braced by guy wires, three-member wall brackets, and certain cranes and derricks.

There are three general types of force systems in three-dimensional space:

1. Concurrent, noncoplanar.
2. Parallel.
3. Nonconcurrent and nonparallel.

5.2 Concurrent, Noncoplanar Force Systems

The analysis of a tripod structure can be used to illustrate the general approach used to solve statics problems of concurrent, noncoplanar force systems.

Consider the tripod in Fig. 5.1. It carries a load *P* placed at *O* (the apex of the tripod) and, by assumption, has weightless legs *OL*, *OM*, and *ON*. Such a physical structure represents a system of concurrent noncoplanar forces.

For static equilibrium of this loaded tripod, *internal* forces in legs *OL*, *OM*, and *ON* must balance the *external* load *P* so that the apex *O*

does not move. Thus, the algebraic sum of all the forces (external and internal) in the given system must equal zero: $\sum F = 0$. In terms of rectangular components (projections on the *x-y-z* axes) the equilibrium condition is expressed as $\sum F_x = 0$, $\sum F_y = 0$, and $\sum F_z = 0$. If we take moments of the individual forces in the given system about any point, we can express the equilibrium condition as $\sum M = 0$. In terms of the rectangular components or projections of the moments as vectors on the *x-y-z* axes (assuming the moment center does not lie on any of the axes) we can express the condition of equilibrium as $\sum M_x = 0$, $\sum M_y = 0$, and $\sum M_z = 0$.

From the above, we see that *three independent equations* are necessary to define an equilibrium condition for a *concurrent*, noncoplanar force system:

$$\sum F_x = 0$$
$$\sum F_y = 0$$
$$\sum F_z = 0$$

or

$$\sum M_x = 0$$
$$\sum M_y = 0$$
$$\sum M_z = 0$$

Since only *three independent* equations are available, we can solve for only *three unknowns* (using statics principles) in a given spatial force system of *concurrent*, noncoplanar forces. The moment equations do not add any new information, since they *repeat* the fact that apex *O* of the tripod does not move if it is in a state of static equilibrium. Therefore, $\sum M = 0$ and $\sum F = 0$ say the same things about apex *O* and are *not* independent of each other. In solving spatial

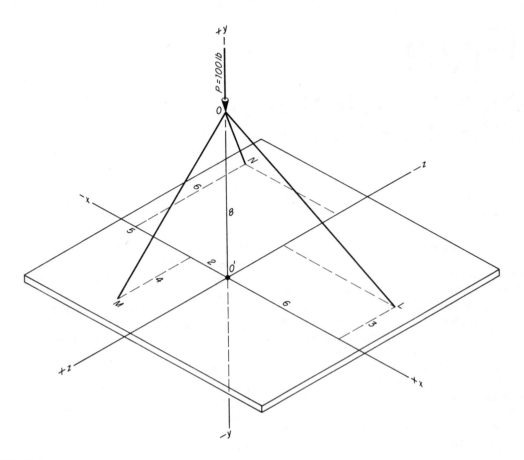

FIGURE 5.1

Loaded Tripod

statics problems, we may use a combination of force and moment equations, provided that no more than three independent equations are used.

Graphically, the vector diagram indicating the vector sum of the forces in a concurrent, non-coplanar force system must *close* for equilibrium conditions. Therefore, the resultant force of the system is equal to zero ($\sum F = 0$) and the system is *balanced*.

EXAMPLE 5.1 _____

The static equilibrium analysis of a loaded tripod.

Given: A tripod with weightless legs OL, OM, and ON acted on by an externally applied vertical downward load $P = 100$ lb, as shown in Fig. 5.2.

Find: The magnitude and type of reaction force exerted by each leg of the tripod to support the load P.

Mathematical Analysis

1. Consider point O (apex of the given tripod) the free body, and let the compressive forces in legs OL, OM, and ON be represented by A, B, and C (see Fig. 5.2). When all the forces in the system are in equilibrium, their resultant is zero, and therefore, $\sum F_x = 0$, $\sum F_y = 0$, and $\sum F_z = 0$.

2. If we project the concurrent, noncoplanar forces A, B, and C on the x-z plane, then $\sum F_x = 0$ and $\sum F_z = 0$ must be satisfied for equilibrium. If we project these three forces on the y axis, then $\sum F_y = 0$ must also be satisfied. The *three unknown* forces A, B, and C can then be found by forming the *three equations* $\sum F_x = 0$, $\sum F_y = 0$, and $\sum F_z = 0$ and by solving them *simultaneously*.

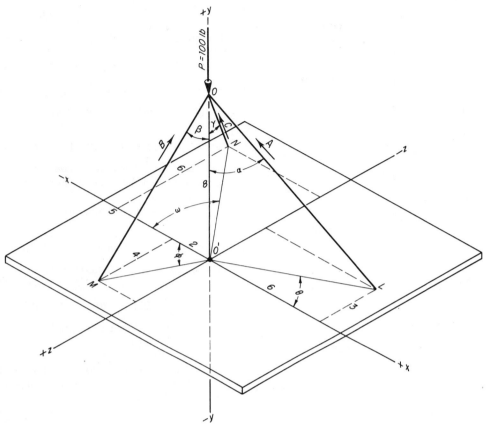

FIGURE 5.2

3. To write $\sum F_y = 0$, we must determine the angle that each force makes with the y axis, as well as with the x and z axes.

4. Referring to Fig. 5.2, we see that

$$\tan \alpha = \frac{O'L}{O'O} = \frac{O'L}{8}$$

$$O'L = \sqrt{6^2 + 3^2}$$
$$= \sqrt{36 + 9} = \sqrt{45}$$
$$= 6.71$$

$$\therefore \ \tan \alpha = \frac{6.71}{8} = 0.838$$

Therefore, $\alpha = 39.9°$, $\cos \alpha = 0.767$, and $\sin \alpha = 0.642$. Next,

$$\tan \beta = \frac{O'M}{O'O} = \frac{O'M}{8}$$

$$O'M = \sqrt{4^2 + 2^2} = \sqrt{16 + 4}$$
$$= \sqrt{20}$$
$$= 4.47$$

$$\therefore \ \tan \beta = \frac{4.47}{8} = 0.560$$

Therefore, $\beta = 29.25°$, $\cos \beta = 0.872$, and $\sin \beta = 0.489$. Finally,

$$\tan \gamma = \frac{O'N}{O'O} = \frac{O'N}{8}$$

$$O'N = \sqrt{6^2 + 5^2} = \sqrt{36 + 25}$$
$$= \sqrt{61}$$
$$= 7.81$$

$$\tan \gamma = \frac{7.81}{8} = 0.976$$

Therefore, $\gamma = 44.3°$, $\cos \gamma = 0.716$, and $\sin \gamma = 0.698$.

5. Writing the equation for $\sum F_y = 0$, we obtain, as shown in Fig. 5.3a,

$$A \cos \alpha + B \cos \beta + C \cos \gamma - 100 = 0$$

$A \cos 39.9° + B \cos 29.25°$
$$+ C \cos 44.3° - 100 = 0$$

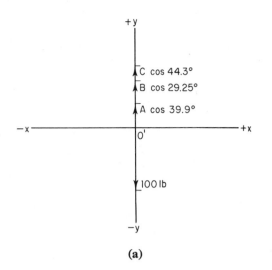

(a)

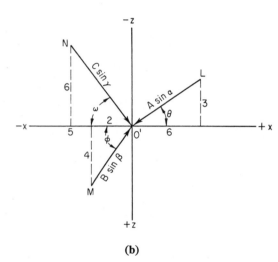

(b)

FIGURE 5.3

(a) $A(0.767) + B(0.872) + C(0.716) - 100 = 0$

which is the *first* of *three* equations required to find the three unknowns.

6. Determine the angles θ, φ, and ω that the projections of the forces A, B, and C make respectively with the x axis in the x-z plane (see Fig. 5.3b).

$$\tan \theta = \tfrac{3}{6} = 0.500$$

Therefore, $\theta = 26.55°$, $\cos \theta = 0.894$, and $\sin \theta = 0.447$.

$$\tan \varphi = \tfrac{4}{2} = 2.00$$

Therefore, $\varphi = 63.4°$, $\cos \varphi = 0.447$, and $\sin \varphi = 0.894$.

$$\tan \omega = \tfrac{6}{5} = 1.20$$

Therefore, $\omega = 50.2°$, $\cos \omega = 0.640$, and $\sin \omega = 0.768$.

7. Writing the equation for $\sum F_x = 0$, we get

$$-A \sin \alpha \cos \theta + B \sin \beta \cos \varphi + C \sin \gamma \cos \omega = 0$$

$$-A(0.642)(0.894) + B(0.489)(0.447) \qquad\qquad + C(0.698)(0.640) = 0$$

(b) $-A(0.574) + B(0.218) + C(0.447) = 0$

(see Fig. 5.3b). This is the *second* of *three* equations required to find the three unknown forces A, B, and C.

8. For the third equation, we write $\sum F_z = 0$ (see Fig. 5.3b):

$$A \sin \alpha \sin \theta - B \sin \beta \sin \varphi + C \sin \gamma \sin \omega = 0$$

$$A(0.642)(0.447) - B(0.489)(0.894) \qquad\qquad + C(0.698)(0.768) = 0$$

(c) $A(0.287) - B(0.437) + C(0.536) = 0$

This is the *third* and last equation needed to find forces A, B, and C.

9. To find forces A, B, and C, we solve equations (a), (b), and (c) simultaneously. First, we eliminate A in equations (a) and (b) by multiplying equation (b) by $0.767/0.574 = 1.332$:

(a) $0.767A + 0.872B + 0.716C - 100 = 0$

(b) $(-0.574A + 0.218B + 0.447C)(1.332) = 0$

or

$$-0.767A + 0.291B + 0.597C \qquad = 0$$
$$\underline{0.767A + 0.872B + 0.716C - 100 = 0}$$
$$1.163B + 1.313C - 100 = 0$$

We have reduced an equation with three unknowns to an equation with only two unknowns (B and C). Therefore, we need another equation containing the same unknowns. With this pair of equations, we will be able to find both unknowns. Then, by substituting these results into one of the *original* equations containing the three unknowns, we will be able to find the third unknown.

10. Next, we eliminate A from equations (b) and (c) by multiplying equation (c) by $0.574/0.287 = 2.000$:

(b) $-0.574A + 0.218B + 0.447C = 0$

(c) $(0.287A - 0.437B + 0.536C)(2.000) = 0$

or

$$0.574A - 0.874B + 1.072C = 0$$
$$\underline{-0.574A + 0.218B + 0.447C = 0}$$
$$-0.656B + 1.519C = 0$$

11. Solve the two equations with two unknowns B and C simultaneously:

$$1.163B + 1.313C = 100$$
$$-0.656B + 1.519C = 0$$

Eliminate B by multiplying the second equation by the factor $1.163/0.656 = 1.772$:

$$1.163B + 1.313C = 100$$
$$(-0.656B + 1.519C)(1.772) = 0$$

or

$$1.163B + 1.313C = 100$$
$$\underline{-1.163B + 2.690C = 0}$$
$$4.003C = 100$$
$$\therefore C = \frac{100}{4.003}$$
$$= 24.9 \text{ lb}$$

By substituting $C = 24.9$ lb in the equation $-0.656B + 1.519C = 0$, we get

$$0.656B = 1.519C$$
$$B = \frac{1.519C}{0.656}$$
$$= \frac{1.519(24.9 \text{ lb})}{0.656}$$
$$= 57.7 \text{ lb}$$

Find A by substituting $B = 57.7$ lb and $C = 24.9$ lb in equation (b):

$$-0.574A + 0.218B + 0.447C = 0$$
$$0.574A = 0.218B + 0.447C$$
$$A = \frac{0.218B + 0.447C}{0.574}$$
$$= \frac{0.218(57.7 \text{ lb}) + 0.447(24.9 \text{ lb})}{0.574}$$
$$= \frac{12.58 \text{ lb} + 11.13 \text{ lb}}{0.574}$$
$$= \frac{23.71 \text{ lb}}{0.574}$$
$$= 41.3 \text{ lb}$$

12. To check the solutions for A, B, and C, substitute their values into any of the three equations. If they are correct, the two sides of the equation will be equal. To demonstrate this, the values of A, B, and C will be substituted into equation (c).

(c) $0.287A - 0.437B + 0.536C = 0$

$0.287(41.3 \text{ lb}) - 0.437(57.7 \text{ lb}) + 0.536(24.9 \text{ lb}) = 0$

$11.85 \text{ lb} - 25.20 \text{ lb} + 13.35 \text{ lb} = 0$

$25.20 \text{ lb} - 25.20 \text{ lb} = 0$

Graphical Analysis

1. Draw the top and front orthographic views of the given loaded tripod to a convenient *space scale* (1 in. = 5 ft is indicated in Fig. 5.4a). (These views—the space diagrams—fix the geometry of the tripod in space.)

2. Since there are three unknown forces (A, B, and C), a new orthographic view of the loaded tripod must be established so that a vector diagram, whose vectors are *parallel* to the *legs* of the tripod and to the line of action of the load P can be constructed to close for equilibrium conditions.[1] In Fig. 5.4a, the auxiliary view is such an orthographic view, with the plane formed by legs OL and ON shown as an edge.

3. Apply Bow's notation in the auxiliary view, placing a number in the spaces on either side of the known load P and then in consecutive order placing numbers on either side of each leg of the tripod. (In Fig. 5.4a, leg ON has been *symbolically* "moved" and noted as a zig-zag line ON_s in order that a *space* could be seen between itself and OL, since in this view both these legs appear as one line.)

4. Construct a vector diagram whose vectors are *parallel* to the legs of the tripod in the top and auxiliary views of the space diagram. (The vector scale indicated in Fig. 5.4b is 1 in. = 30 lb.) This results in two new views (top and auxiliary) of the vector diagram that are necessary to define the vectors in a three-dimensional space. For equilibrium, the vector diagram *must close*.

5. Measure the true lengths of the vectors representing the forces A, B, and C in legs OL, OM, and ON (the vectors are numbered $[\overrightarrow{4\text{–}1}]$, $[\overrightarrow{2\text{–}3}]$, and $[\overrightarrow{3\text{–}4}]$, respectively, in the vector diagram). (See Fig. 5.4b.)

$$\text{true length of } [\overrightarrow{4\text{–}1}] = A = 42 \text{ lb}$$
$$\text{true length of } [\overrightarrow{2\text{–}3}] = B = 58 \text{ lb}$$
$$\text{true length of } [\overrightarrow{3\text{–}4}] = C = 24 \text{ lb}$$

5.3 Noncoplanar, Nonconcurrent, Nonparallel Force Systems

With the law of superposition, the parallelogram law, and the representation of moments of couples as vectors, it is possible to show how any general

---

[1] Steve M. Slaby, *Fundamentals of Three-Dimensional Descriptive Geometry* (New York: Harcourt, Brace & World, 1966), Chapter IX.

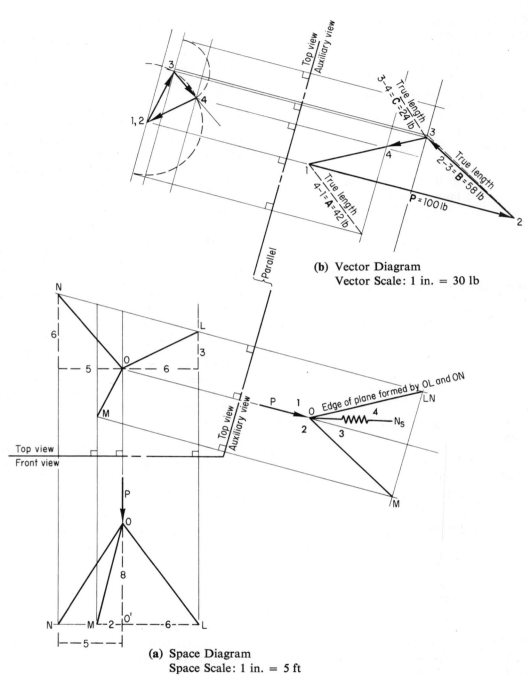

(b) Vector Diagram
Vector Scale: 1 in. = 30 lb

(a) Space Diagram
Space Scale: 1 in. = 5 ft

FIGURE 5.4

noncoplanar, nonconcurrent, nonparallel force system can be reduced to a resultant force *and* a resultant couple.

Since a general noncoplanar system is a three-dimensional space system, the resultant force and the resultant couple, as represented by force and moment vectors, respectively, have projections on the *x*, *y*, and *z* axes. Further, there is a total of *six projections* in the general case $\sum F_x$, $\sum F_y$, and $\sum F_z$ for the vector representing the resultant force and $\sum M_x$, $\sum M_y$, and $\sum M_z$ for the vector representing the resultant couple; therefore, for static equilibrium, *six conditions* must be satisfied. These conditions are

$$\sum F_x = 0 \qquad \sum M_x = 0$$
$$\sum F_y = 0 \qquad \sum M_y = 0$$
$$\sum F_z = 0 \qquad \sum M_z = 0$$

Thus, we have *six independent* equations available for solving static equilibrium problems of noncoplanar, nonconcurrent, nonparallel force systems.

The equations for finding the resultant force and couple of a noncoplanar, nonconcurrent, nonparallel force system are

$$R = \sqrt{(\sum F_x)^2 + (\sum F_y)^2 + (\sum F_z)^2}$$
$$\cos \theta_x = \frac{\sum F_x}{R}$$
$$\cos \theta_y = \frac{\sum F_y}{R}$$
$$\cos \theta_z = \frac{\sum F_z}{R}$$
$$M_C = \sqrt{(\sum M_x)^2 + (\sum M_y)^2 + (\sum M_z)^2}$$

where θ is the angle that resultant R makes with the x, y, and z axes. The *senses* of the resultant force and the resultant couple are indicated by the sign convention in the summations under the radical sign in the equations.

In order to obtain equilibrium in any force system, the resultant must equal *zero*. In a noncoplanar, nonconcurrent, nonparallel system, both the force resultant R and the moment or couple resultant M_C must equal zero.

For the resultant force to be zero,

$$R = \sqrt{(\sum F_x)^2 + (\sum F_y)^2 + (\sum F_z)^2} = 0$$

Since each term under the radical sign is squared, it must be positive. In order for the sum of the terms under the radical to be zero, then, each one must itself be equal to zero. Therefore,

$$\sum F_x = 0, \qquad \sum F_y = 0, \quad \text{and} \quad \sum F_z = 0$$

If the same reasoning is applied to the equation of the resultant couple,

$$M_C = \sqrt{(\sum M_x)^2 + (\sum M_y)^2 + (\sum M_z)^2} = 0$$

there result three more equations required for equilibrium:

$$\sum M_x = 0, \quad \sum M_y = 0, \quad \text{and} \quad \sum M_z = 0$$

If, in a spatial force system, the six equations of equilibrium are satisfied, the body that is acted upon by a number of forces and moments is not being moved or *translated* in any direction parallel to the assumed three coordinate axes (x, y, and z) and is also not being *rotated* about any of these axes.

EXAMPLE 5.2 _____

The static equilibrium of a noncoplanar, nonconcurrent, nonparallel force system.

Given: Three noncoplanar, nonconcurrent, nonparallel forces: $A = 100$ lb acting in the $-x$ direction; $B = 75$ lb acting in the $-z$ direction; and $C = 50$ lb acting in the $-y$ direction (see Fig. 5.5).

Find: Using mathematical analysis, determine the equilibrant force E and the equilibrant couple M_E necessary to place the given force system in static equilibrium.

NOTE: In this problem, the resultant will be found by resolving each force into an equal parallel force

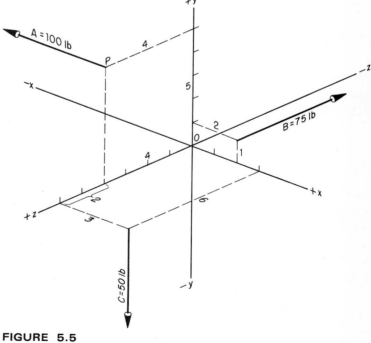

FIGURE 5.5

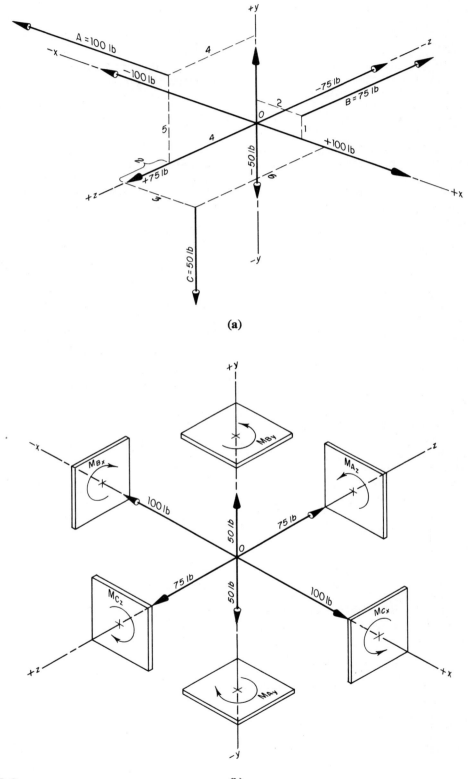

(a)

FIGURE 5.6

(b)

and a couple. For convenience, the equal parallel force will be passed through the origin of the co-ordinate axes. Each force A, B, and C, will be moved to an axis parallel to itself and will be replaced by its moments about the appropriate axes. As before, the usual sign convention for moments will be used: a moment is positive if it tends to produce counter-clockwise rotation as viewed when looking from the positive end of the axis to the origin.

1. Replace force A by the same force on the x axis and its moments about two axes (see Fig. 5.6a): $M_{A_z} = 5A$; $M_{A_y} = -4A$.

2. Replace force B by the same force on the z axis and its moments about two axes (see Fig. 5.6a): $M_{B_y} = 2B$; $M_{B_x} = -B$.

3. Replace force C by the same force on the y axis and its moments about two axes (see Fig. 5.6a): $M_{C_z} = -3C$; $M_{C_x} = 6C$.

The noncoplanar, nonconcurrent, nonparallel force system has now been replaced by a noncoplanar, concurrent system with center at origin O of the x-y-z coordinate system and a series of moments (see Fig. 5.6b).

4. Since $\sum F_x = -100$, $\sum F_y = -50$, and $\sum F_z = -75$, the magnitude of the resultant force R of the noncoplanar, concurrent system is

$$R = \sqrt{(\sum F_x)^2 + (\sum F_y)^2 + (\sum F_z)^2}$$
$$= \sqrt{(-100)^2 + (-50)^2 + (-75)^2}$$

$$R = \sqrt{10{,}000 + 2500 + 5625}$$
$$= \sqrt{18{,}125}$$
$$= 134.5 \text{ lb}$$

The equilibrant E is equal in magnitude to the resultant R but *opposite* in sense: $E = 134.5$ lb.

5. If the angles that the equilibrant E makes with the x, y, and z axes are α, β, and γ, respectively, then

$$\cos \alpha = \frac{\sum F_x}{E} = \frac{100}{134.5} = 0.744$$

$$\cos \beta = \frac{\sum F_y}{E} = \frac{50}{134.5} = 0.372$$

$$\cos \gamma = \frac{\sum F_z}{E} = \frac{75}{134.5} = 0.558$$

and therefore

$$\alpha = 42°$$
$$\beta = 68.2°$$
$$\gamma = 56.1°$$

Angles α, β, and γ are called the *direction angles* of a force in space (see Fig. 5.7). Since they are the angles that a force F makes with the x, y, and z axes, respectively, the x, y, and z components of a force may be written as follows:

$$F_x = F \cos \alpha$$
$$F_y = F \cos \beta$$
$$F_z = F \cos \gamma$$

Then, since F_x, F_y, and F_z are the three edges of a rectangular parallelepiped of which the force F is the diagonal, and since, from geometry, the square of

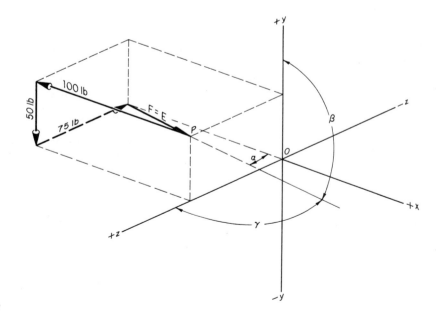

FIGURE 5.7

the diagonal is equal to the sum of the squares of the three edges,

$$F^2 = F_x{}^2 + F_y{}^2 + F_z{}^2$$
$$= (F \cos \alpha)^2 + (F \cos \beta)^2 + (F \cos \gamma)^2$$
$$= F^2 \cos^2 \alpha + F^2 \cos^2 \beta + F^2 \cos^2 \gamma$$
$$= F^2(\cos^2 \alpha + \cos^2 \beta + \cos^2 \gamma)$$

Finally, since the sum of the squares of the cosines of the direction angles are equal to one,

$$1 = \cos^2 \alpha + \cos^2 \beta + \cos^2 \gamma$$

This equation can be applied to the cosines of the angles of the equilibrant E in order to check that our computed values $\cos \alpha = 0.744$, $\cos \beta = 0.372$, and $\cos \gamma = 0.558$ are correct:

$$\cos^2 \alpha = 0.744^2 = 0.555$$
$$\cos^2 \beta = 0.372^2 = 0.138$$
$$\cos^2 \gamma = 0.558^2 = \underline{0.312}$$
$$1.005$$

(NOTE: Discrepancy due to "rounding off" of decimals.)

6. The magnitude of the resultant couple is (see Fig. 5.6)

$$M_C = \sqrt{(\textstyle\sum M_x)^2 + (\textstyle\sum M_y)^2 + (\textstyle\sum M_z)^2}$$
$$\textstyle\sum M_x = 6C - 1B$$
$$\textstyle\sum M_y = 2B - 4A$$
$$\textstyle\sum M_z = 5A - 3C$$

Since $A = 100$ lb, $B = 75$ lb, and $C = 50$ lb, we get

$$\textstyle\sum M_x = 6(50) \text{ lb-ft} - 75 \text{ lb-ft}$$
$$= 300 \text{ lb-ft} - 75 \text{ lb-ft} = 225 \text{ lb-ft}$$
$$\textstyle\sum M_y = 2(75) \text{ lb-ft} - 4(100) \text{ lb-ft}$$
$$= 150 \text{ lb-ft} - 400 \text{ lb-ft} = -250 \text{ lb-ft}$$
$$\textstyle\sum M_z = 5(100) \text{ lb-ft} - 3(50) \text{ lb-ft}$$
$$= 500 \text{ lb-ft} - 150 \text{ lb-ft} = 350 \text{ lb-ft}$$
$$\therefore M_C = \sqrt{225^2 + (-250)^2 + 350^2}$$
$$= \sqrt{50,625 + 62,500 + 122,500}$$
$$= \sqrt{235,625}$$
$$= 485 \text{ lb-ft}$$

Equilibrant couple $M_E = 485$ lb-ft (see Fig. 5.8).

5.4 Spatial Noncoplanar, Parallel Force Systems

The principles discussed in Sec. 3.4 and Sec. 3.9 for determining the resultant and equilibrant of *coplanar* force systems can be extended to *noncoplanar*, parallel force systems by examining the *projections* of the vectors of forces in such a system on two or more orthographic projection planes. The projections of these vectors can be handled as if they were *representations of coplanar*, parallel force systems in each projection plane. By projectively relating each projection of the resultant (or equilibrant) of the given force system, it is possible to determine the *actual* space location of the resultant (or equilibrant), if one exists, in the given system.

As in a coplanar, parallel force system, there are three possible conditions:

1. A single resultant force ($\textstyle\sum F = R$).

2. No resultant force (where the system is in equilibrium; $\textstyle\sum F = 0$ and $\textstyle\sum M = 0$).

3. A resultant couple ($\textstyle\sum F = 0$ but $\textstyle\sum M \neq 0$).

Example 5.3 illustrates case 1; the same approach can also be applied to cases 2 and 3.

EXAMPLE 5.3 ———————————

The equilibrant of a noncoplanar, parallel force system.

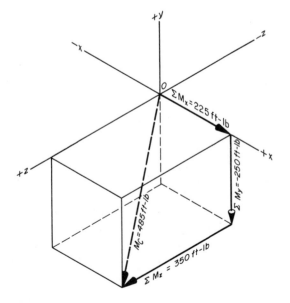

FIGURE 5.8

Given: Noncoplanar, parallel forces $A = 100$ lb, $B = 75$ lb, and $C = 90$ lb, as shown in Fig. 5.9.

Find: Using graphical and mathematical analysis, determine and locate (relative to the given forces) the equilibrant E of the given force system.

Graphical Analysis

1. Draw the top view and front view—the horizontal and frontal projections—of the given force system to an assumed space scale (1 in. = 3 ft is indicated in Fig. 5.10). This is the space diagram of the given force system (see Fig. 5.10).

2. Draw a vector diagram (I in Fig. 5.11) showing the graphical addition of the forces as represented by vectors **A**, **B**, and **C** to determine the resultant **R** of the given system; also draw the ray polygon, as shown in Fig. 5.11 ($R = 65$ lb).

3. Draw the string polygon (I in Fig. 5.11) starting on the line of action of force A in the front view of the space diagram. (Point M on A is used as a starting point.) The closing strings $[P-1]$ and $[P-4]$ intersect at point N, through which the equilibrant passes. (The sense of the equilibrant is opposite to that of the resultant in the vector diagram.) (See Fig. 5.11.)

4. Since we are dealing with a three-dimensional force system, we must determine the location of the equilibrant in at least two projectively related views before its position in space can be specifically defined. Draw a *second* space view in projection with one of the original views, showing the parallel lines of action of forces A, B, and C (auxiliary view in Fig. 5.11).

5. Draw another vector diagram (II in Fig. 5.11), again showing the graphical addition of the vectors representing forces A, B, and C, where the vectors are *parallel* to the new space view of the given forces. Draw a ray polygon based on the new orientation of the vector diagram (II in Fig. 5.11).

6. Draw the string polygon (II in Fig. 5.11), starting on the line of action of force A at an assumed point S. The closing strings $[P'-1]$ and $[P'-4]$ in the auxiliary view intersect at point N', which is the point through which the equilibrant passes in this view.

7. Project the equilibrant line of action from the front view to the top view and from the auxiliary view to the top view. The intersection of the projectors from these views in the top view determines the actual location of the equilibrant E in space relative to the given forces.

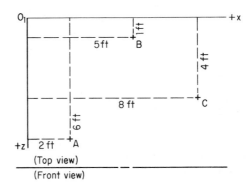

FIGURE 5.9

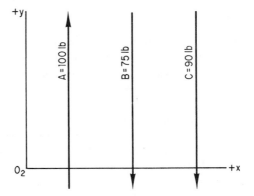

FIGURE 5.10

Space Diagram
Space Scale: 1 in. = 3.0 ft

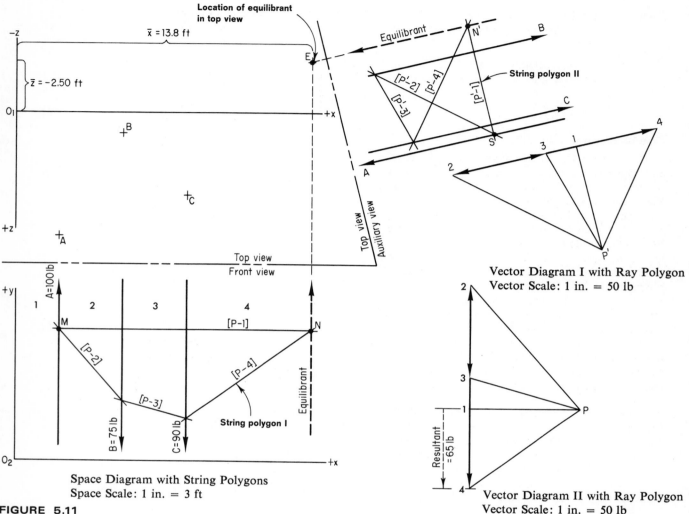

Space Diagram with String Polygons
Space Scale: 1 in. = 3 ft

FIGURE 5.11

Vector Diagram I with Ray Polygon
Vector Scale: 1 in. = 50 lb

Vector Diagram II with Ray Polygon
Vector Scale: 1 in. = 50 lb

In the above solution, the given force system has been projected onto two projection planes (the front and auxiliary views) where the lines of action of the forces are seen as *parallel lines*. Each of these views represents a *coplanar picture* of the given force system, and by combining these two coplanar pictures by means of orthographic projection, we are able to determine the *third dimension* that locates the equilibrant relative to the given forces.

-------------------- **EXAMPLE 5.3 (cont'd.)**

Mathematical Analysis

1. The *resultant* of a noncoplanar, parallel force system is the algebraic sum of all the forces in the system. The *equilibrant* is equal in magnitude and opposite in sense to the resultant.

2. The *position* of the line of action of the resultant force (and also the equilibrant) is found by applying Varignon's theorem. Moments can be taken with respect to each axis that is perpendicular to the forces. If the resultant is a single force, the equations for finding the resultant are

$$R = \sum F$$
$$R\bar{x} = \sum M_z$$

where $\bar{x}$ is the perpendicular distance between the forces and the z axis, and

$$R\bar{z} = \sum M_x$$

where $\bar{z}$ is the perpendicular distance between the forces and the x axis.

3. Referring to Fig. 5.11, we get, from $R = \sum F$,

$$R = A - B - C$$

where upward forces are positive and downward forces are negative. Substituting the given values for A, B, and C,

$$R = 100 \text{ lb} - 75 \text{ lb} - 90 \text{ lb}$$
$$= -65 \text{ lb}$$

4. The summation of moments about the z axis is represented by $R\bar{x} = \sum M_z$. Substituting the given values for A, B, and C and their perpendicular distances (moment arms) from the z axis, we get

$$(65 \text{ lb})\bar{x} = (75 \text{ lb})(5 \text{ ft}) + (90 \text{ lb})(8 \text{ ft}) - (100 \text{ lb})(2 \text{ ft})$$

using the sign convention where counterclockwise rotation is positive. Therefore,

$$\bar{x} = \frac{375 \text{ lb-ft} + 720 \text{ lb-ft} - 200 \text{ lb-ft}}{65 \text{ lb}} = \frac{895}{65} \text{ ft}$$
$$= 13.8 \text{ ft}$$

5. The summation of moments about the x axis is represented by $R\bar{z} = \sum M_x$. Substituting the given values for A, B, and C and their perpendicular distances from the x axis, we get (using the same sign convention as above)

$$(65 \text{ lb})\bar{z} = (75 \text{ lb})(1 \text{ ft}) + (90 \text{ lb})(4 \text{ ft}) - (100 \text{ lb})(6 \text{ ft})$$

Therefore,

$$\bar{z} = \frac{75 \text{ lb-ft} + 360 \text{ lb-ft} - 600 \text{ lb-ft}}{65 \text{ lb}} = \frac{-165}{65} \text{ ft}$$
$$= -2.54 \text{ ft}$$

6. Since the equilibrant E has the same line of action as the resultant R, it has the same position (location) in space as the resultant R; its sense is *opposite* that of R (see Figs. 5.12 and 5.13).

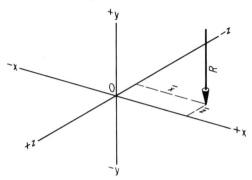

FIGURE 5.12

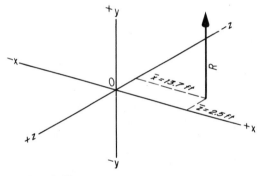

FIGURE 5.13

PROBLEMS

5.1 **Given:** Three concurrent, noncoplanar forces $F_1 = 100$ lb, $F_2 = 2000$ lb, and $F_3 = 1000$ lb, as shown in Fig. 5.14.

  Find: Using mathematical analysis, determine the magnitude and position (relative to the x, y, and z axes) of the resultant force of the given forces.

5.2 **Given:** Forces $F_1 = 1000$ lb, $F_2 = 2000$ lb, and $F_3 = 1000$ lb, as shown in Fig. 5.14.

  Find: Using graphical analysis, determine the magnitude of the resultant force of the given force system.

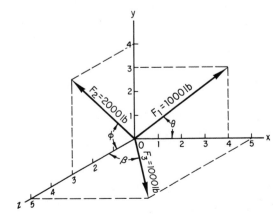

FIGURE 5.14

133

5.3   **Given:** A force F that passes through the origin of an x-y-z coordinate system making angles of θ_x, θ_y, and θ_z with the three coordinate axes, as shown in Fig. 5.15.

      Find: Show that the components of the force F are

$$F_x = F \cos \theta_x$$
$$F_y = F \cos \theta_y$$
$$F_z = F \cos \theta_z$$

and that

$$F = \sqrt{F_x{}^2 + F_y{}^2 + F_z{}^2}$$

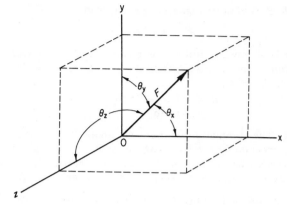

FIGURE 5.15

5.4   **Given:** Three concurrent forces $F_1 = 1000$ lb, $F_2 = 4000$ lb, and $F_3 = 5000$ lb, as shown in Fig. 5.16.

      Find: Using mathematical analysis, determine the magnitude and position of the resultant force of the given force system.

5.5   **Given:** Forces $F_1 = 1000$ lb, $F_2 = 4000$ lb, and $F_3 = 5000$ lb, as shown in Fig. 5.16.

      Find: Using graphical analysis, determine the magnitude and position of the resultant force of the given force system.

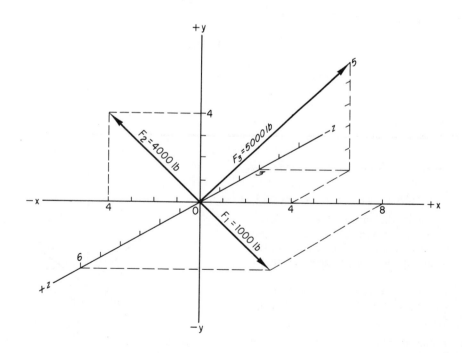

FIGURE 5.16

5.6 **Given:** Three concurrent, noncoplanar forces $F_1 = 3000$ lb, $F_2 = 1500$ lb, and $F_3 = 1000$ lb, as shown in Fig. 5.17.

Find: Using mathematical analysis, determine the magnitude and position of the force required to keep the given force system in equilibrium. (Define the position by the angles θ_x, θ_y, and θ_z that the required force makes with the coordinate axes.)

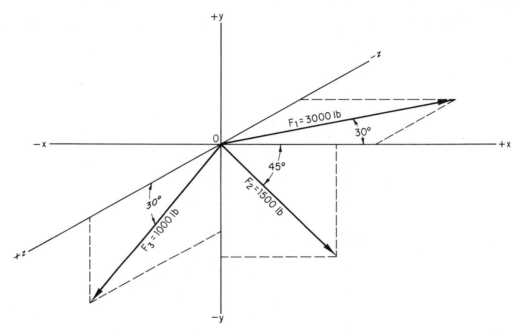

FIGURE 5.17

5.7 **Given:** A force of 4000 lb supported by three cables OA, OB, and OC attached to a ceiling, as shown in Fig. 5.18.

Find: Using mathematical analysis and the translational equilibrium criteria ($\sum F_x = 0$, $\sum F_y = 0$, and $\sum F_z = 0$), determine the magnitude and type of load that each cable must support.

Ans. Load $F_{OA} = 1650$ lb tension, load $F_{OB} = 1150$ lb tension, load $F_{OC} = 2450$ lb tension

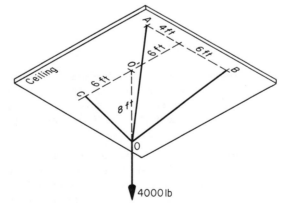

FIGURE 5.18

5.8 **Given:** A tripod with weightless legs attached to a vertical plane by ball and socket joints. This tripod is acted upon at its apex V by forces F_1 and F_2, as shown in Fig. 5.19. These forces are perpendicular and parallel, respectively, to the vertical plane.

Find: Using mathematical analysis, determine the magnitude and type of load each leg in the tripod must support for static equilibrium.

Ans. Load $F_{VA} = 105$ lb compression, load $F_{VB} = 105$ lb compression, load $F_{VC} = 322$ lb tension

5.9   **Given:** The loaded tripod shown in Fig. 5.19.

      Find: Using graphical analysis, determine the magnitude and type of load in each leg of the given tripod.

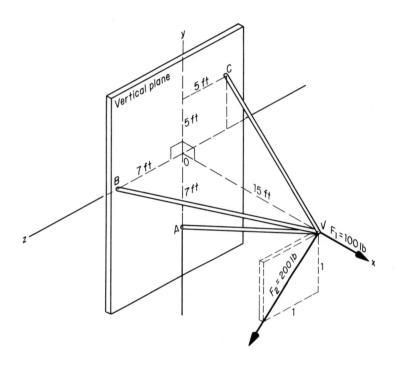

FIGURE 5.19

5.10 Given: A general noncoplanar, nonconcurrent, nonparallel force system composed of forces $F_1 = 200$ lb, $F_2 = 200$ lb, and $F_3 = 300$ lb, as shown in Fig. 5.20.

      Find: Using mathematical analysis, determine the complete resultant of the given force system with respect to point D. (Would the answer be the same if the complete resultant was evaluated with respect to any other point?)

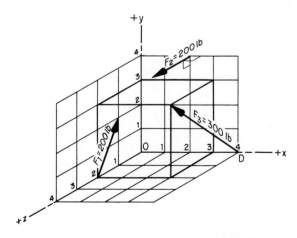

FIGURE 5.20

5.11 Given: Three noncoplanar, nonconcurrent, nonparallel forces $F_1 = 100$ lb, $F_2 = 300$ lb, and $F_3 = 200$ lb, as shown in Fig. 5.21.

Find: Using mathematical analysis, determine the complete resultant of the given force system with respect to the origin O of the coordinate axes. Show in a sketch how this complete resultant may be represented.

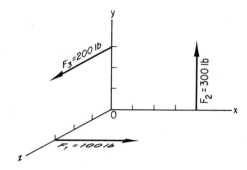

FIGURE 5.21

5.12 Given: Three noncoplanar, parallel forces $F_1 = 100$ lb, $F_2 = 800$ lb, and $F_3 = 300$ lb, as shown in Fig. 5.22.

Find: Using mathematical analysis, determine the magnitude of the resultant force of the given force system and its location relative to the x and z axes.

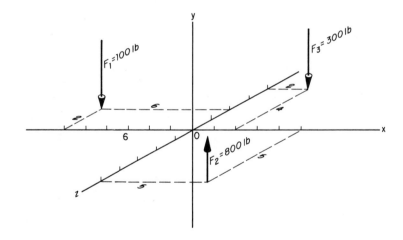

FIGURE 5.22

5.13 Given: Three noncoplanar, parallel forces, as shown in Fig. 5.22.

Find: Using graphical analysis, determine the magnitude of the resultant force of the given force system and its location relative to the x and z axes.

5.14 Given: A Texas-tower structure is subjected to the dead weight, loads $F_1 = 7$ tons, $F_2 = 50$ tons, $F_3 = 30$ tons, and $F_4 = 25$ tons, as shown in Fig. 5.23.

Find: Using mathematical analysis, determine the force that each of the three legs of the tower must exert to support the platform in static equilibrium.

Ans. Leg A 42.5 tons, leg B 37.8 tons, leg C 31.7 tons

5.15 **Given**: A loaded Texas-tower structure, as shown in Fig. 5.23.

Find: Using graphical analysis, determine the force that each of the three legs of the tower must exert to support the platform in static equilibrium.

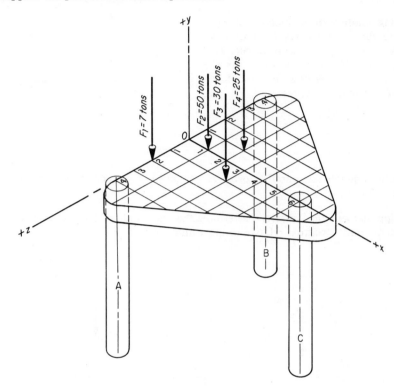

FIGURE 5.23

Six
STATIC AND KINETIC FRICTION

6.1 Introduction

When the surfaces of two bodies are in contact, any motion of one surface over the other is resisted or retarded by *tangential* forces called *frictional* forces. These frictional forces act parallel to the contacting surfaces and opposite to the direction of impending motion. The *resultant* of all the frictional forces is referred to as *friction*. (See Fig. 6.1.)

There are several different types of friction:

1. *Static friction*: one surface in contact with another surface where *no motion* occurs between the surfaces, such as a block at *rest* on an inclined surface.

2. *Kinetic friction*: one surface in contact with another surface where *motion does occur*, such as a block *sliding* down an inclined surface.

3. *Rolling friction*: one surface, such as a wheel, rolls on another surface.

Static friction exists between two contacting surfaces that are at *rest* relative to each other. It is the friction that is present *up to* the point of actual motion (impending motion) between the two surfaces. (Sometimes static friction is referred to as the friction of *repose* or rest.)

Kinetic friction is the friction that exists *after* motion between two contacting surfaces has commenced. This friction is present as long as motion between the two surfaces continues. (In general, the magnitude of the kinetic-friction force is *less* than that of the static-friction force.)

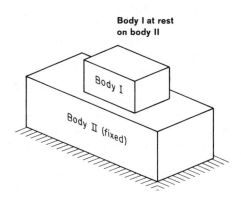

FIGURE 6.1

6.2 Static Friction

In order to illustrate some of the basic concepts of friction, let us consider the static-equilibrium condition of a force P' applied to a particle K *at rest* on a rough surface.[1] (See Fig. 6.2.)

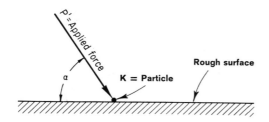

FIGURE 6.2

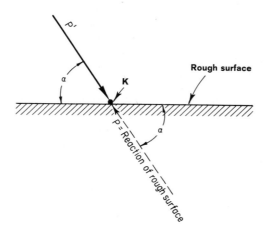

FIGURE 6.3

Since particle K is in equilibrium, the *reaction force P* of the rough surface must be equal and opposite to P'. Therefore, the line of action of the reaction force P is at the same angle α with the rough surface as is that of force P' (see Fig. 6.3).

If, as in Fig. 6.4, we resolve the applied force P' and the reaction force P into components that are *tangential* to the rough surface (F' and F, respectively) and perpendicular to the rough surface

---

[1] "Rough surface" means a surface that imparts frictional resistance to motion; a "smooth surface" can only resist motion in a direction *perpendicular* to itself.

(N' and N, respectively), we can write the following expressions for equilibrium:

$$\mathbf{F'} - \mathbf{F} = 0 \quad \text{and} \quad \mathbf{N'} - \mathbf{N} = 0$$

Using the angle θ that the applied and reaction forces make with the perpendicular forces N' and N, we can write the following equations for the components of the applied force P':

$$F' = P' \sin \theta$$
$$N' = P' \cos \theta$$

Similarly, the components of the reaction force P may be written as follows:

$$F = P \sin \theta$$
$$N = P \cos \theta$$

The F' component of P' tends to cause particle K to slide along the rough surface. This motion is prevented by the F component of the reaction force P, which is the *friction* force.

From the above expressions, we see that

$$\frac{P \sin \theta}{P \cos \theta} = \tan \theta = \frac{F}{N}$$

Thus, when a particle is in equilibrium on a rough surface, the tangent of the angle θ between the reaction force P and the perpendicular force N is equal to the ratio of the friction force F to the perpendicular force N.

Two finite, rough-surfaced bodies in contact actually touch each other at many points (see Fig. 6.5). If a force P' is applied to body I as shown in Fig. 6.6, the force P' is distributed over all the points of contact between the rough surfaces of bodies I and II. The reaction force is also distributed over all the points of contact and for equilibrium must be equal and opposite to the distributed applied force (see Fig. 6.7).

If we consider the perpendicular (N) and tangential (F) components of the distributed *reaction* forces at each contacting point (1, 2, 3, 4, . . ., etc.), we see that for equilibrium each reaction force makes an angle θ with its associated perpendicular (N) component (see Fig. 6.8). The tangent of each of the angles (θ_1, θ_2, θ_3, θ_4, . . ., etc.) is equal to the ratios F_1/N_1, F_2/N_2, F_3/N_3, F_4/N_4, . . ., etc. Between any two given surfaces, this ratio is a *constant up to impending motion*, since each point of contact on each body is in

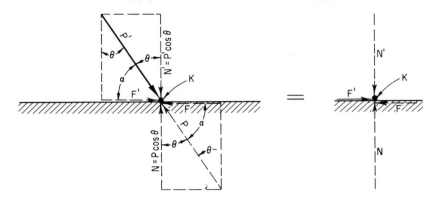

FIGURE 6.4

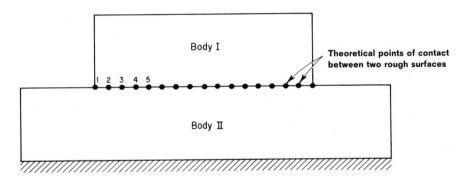

FIGURE 6.5

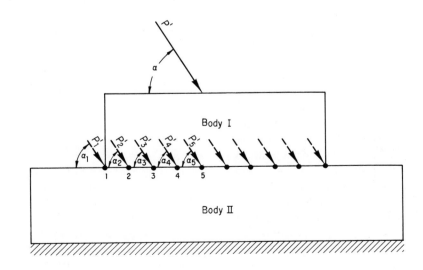

FIGURE 6.6

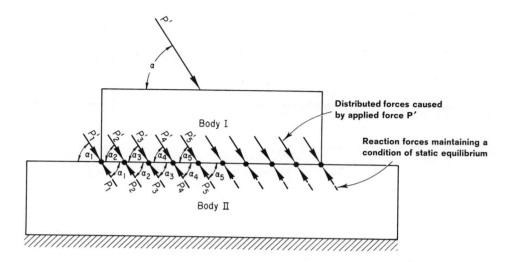

FIGURE 6.7

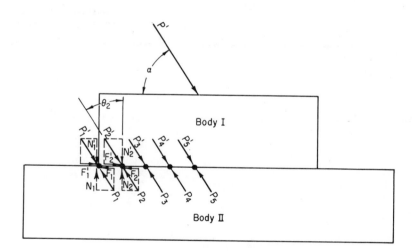

FIGURE 6.8

static equilibrium. As the number of contact points increases (for example, assume that the total *area* of contact is increased), the perpendicular force N (for a *given* applied load) at each point *proportionally* decreases (proportionally less force per unit area) as does the individual tangential forces. But the *sum* of the individual perpendicular and tangential forces remains the same.

As a corollary, if the perpendicular forces increase, the frictional forces increase proportionately. Thus, taking the total (resultant)

of the individual N_i and F_i forces, we obtain

$$\sum N_i = N \quad \text{and} \quad \sum F_i = F$$

and the proportion $\tan \theta = F/N$ holds.

From this discussion, it should be apparent that friction is *independent* of the area of contact of two surfaces. Therefore, we can treat two contacting rough surfaces as a *point* resting on a rough surface with an applied force acting on the point and the rough surface resisting motion to maintain static equilibrium.

6.3 Coefficient of Static Friction

The angle θ that the reaction force P makes with the perpendicular component N can be determined experimentally. At the *instant* of *impending motion*, this angle reaches a limiting *maximum* value, which is usually designated as ϕ. This limiting angle of resistance is called the *angle of friction* or *angle of repose*.

Experimental procedure

1. Place a block of solid, homogeneous material (like a block of wood) of a known weight W on a flat surface, as shown in Fig. 6.9.

2. Attach a spring balance to the block so that the applied force F' can be measured at the instant motion begins.

3. Slowly increase force F'. At the *instant* the block moves, record the magnitude of F' on the spring balance. (F' is equal to the resisting frictional force F.)

4. Knowing W and F', determine the resultant P' of W and F': $\mathbf{P'} = \mathbf{W} + \mathbf{F'}$.

5. The tangent of the angle ϕ that the resultant P' makes with the perpendicular component N is

$$\tan \phi = \frac{F'}{N}$$

Since frictional force is *independent* of the area of contact between two surfaces, the resisting force is dependent only upon the *material* of the block and the material of supporting plane surface Therefore, the *angle of friction* varies according to the type of material. Within the limits of experimental error, the angle of friction—and thus the ratio F/N—is constant for any given material. The ratio F/N is defined as the coefficient of static friction and is designated by μ (Greek *mu*). Thus, $\mu = F/N = \tan \phi$. Values of μ for several common materials are given in Table 6.1.

The coefficient of static friction μ may be determined by another method using a solid block of given material with a known weight W and an inclined plane, as shown in the following procedure.

Experimental procedure

1. Place a block of known weight W at the right end of a plane AB of length L (see Fig. 6.10).

Table 6.1
COEFFICIENT OF STATIC FRICTION μ

Wood on Wood	0.25–0.65
Metals on Metals	0.15–0.30
Metals on Wood	0.20–0.60
Wood on Leather	0.25–0.50
Metals on Leather	0.30–0.60

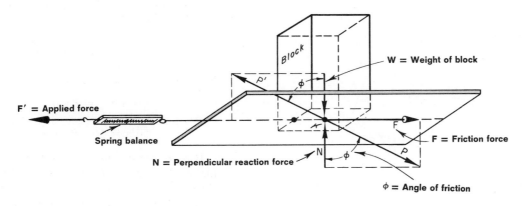

FIGURE 6.9

2. Raise the right end (*B*) of the plane until the block just starts to slide.

3. At the instant of *impending motion*, the plane makes an angle ϕ with the horizontal. The tangent of angle ϕ is y/x. (See Fig. 6.10.)

4. Consider the static equilibrium conditions of the block at the instant of impending motion. For equilibrium to exist at this instant, there must be a force *P* equal in magnitude and opposite in sense to weight *W*.

5. Resolve *P* into components *N* and *F* that are perpendicular and tangential, respectively, to the inclined plane (see Fig. 6.11.) The resulting component *F* is the frictional force resisting downward motion of the block along the plane.

6. From the geometry, as shown in Fig. 6.12, it is evident that the angle the line of action of *W* makes with the perpendicular component *N* is equal to ϕ, the angle of friction.

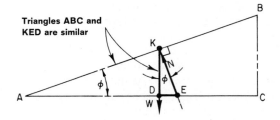

FIGURE 6.12

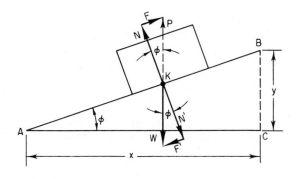

FIGURE 6.13

Using similar-triangle relationships, we can write (see Fig. 6.13)

$$\frac{F'}{N'} = \frac{F}{N} = \frac{y}{x}$$

Therefore, the coefficient of static friction is

$$\mu = \frac{F}{N} = \tan \phi = \frac{y}{x}$$

7. Writing *F*, *N*, *F'*, and *N'* in terms of ϕ, we get (see Fig. 6.14)

$$F' = W \sin \phi \quad \text{and} \quad N' = W \cos \phi$$
$$F = P \sin \phi \quad \text{and} \quad N = P \cos \phi$$

Since $F' = F$ and $N' = N$ for equilibrium,

$$W \sin \phi = P \sin \phi$$

and

$$W \cos \phi = P \cos \phi$$

If we *rotate* the line of action of *W*, which makes the angle ϕ with the normal *N*, through a full 360°, we generate a cone that is called the *cone of friction* (see Fig. 6.15). As long as the line of action of the force *W*

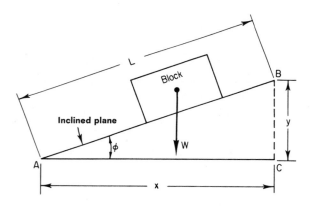

FIGURE 6.10

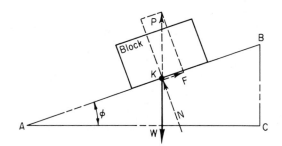

FIGURE 6.11

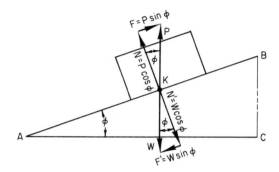

FIGURE 6.14

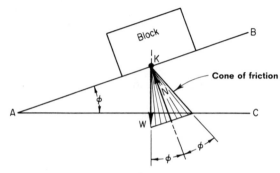

FIGURE 6.15

(or the resultant of a number of forces applied to the block) lies *within* the angle ϕ, the block will remain at rest.

6.4 Basic Laws of Friction

The discussion above can be summarized by listing some of the basic laws of friction:

1. Within the limits of experimentation, the *total frictional force F* (at impending motion) between two contacting surfaces is *proportional* to the *total perpendicular force N* exerted by one surface on the other. Mathematically,

$$F = \mu N$$

2. The *total* frictional force between two contacting surfaces is *independent* of the area of contact.

3. Static frictional forces are *greater* than kinetic frictional forces (which can be proven by experiment).

EXAMPLE 6.1

The force required to start moving a block up a rough, inclined plane.

Given: A block having weight $W = 100$ lb on a plane inclined at 30° to the horizontal. A force Q that makes an angle of 30° with the inclined plane is applied to the block, as in Fig. 6.16. ($\mu = 0.50$.)

Find: The force Q necessary to start the given block up the inclined plane.

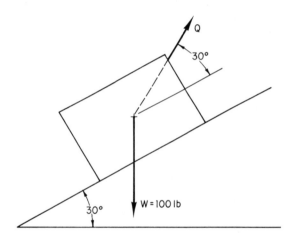

FIGURE 6.16

Mathematical Analysis
Using P Directly

1. Draw the free-body diagram of the given block (Fig. 6.17). In Fig. 6.17b, the resultant of forces W and Q is balanced by force P at point K. Force P has been resolved into F and N.

2. Considering the equilibrium condition of the entire system at impending motion, we write the equation for $\sum F_x = 0$:

$$Q \cos 30° - W \sin 30° - P \sin \phi = 0$$

$$Q\left(\frac{\sqrt{3}}{2}\right) = 100\left(\frac{1}{2}\right) \ P\left(\frac{1}{\sqrt{5}}\right) = 0$$

$$\frac{Q\sqrt{3}}{2} - 50 - \frac{P}{\sqrt{5}} = 0$$

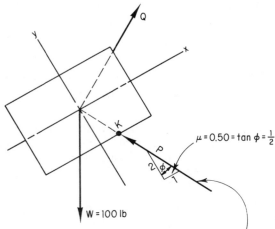

$\mu = 0.50 = \tan \phi = \frac{1}{2}$

W = 100 lb

P = Reaction force maintaining equilibrium at impending motion

(a) Free-body Diagram

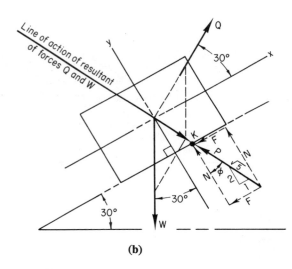

Line of action of resultant
of forces Q and W

30°

30°

30°

W

(b)

FIGURE 6.17

Next, for $\sum F_y = 0$,

$$Q \sin 30° - W \cos 30° + P \cos \phi = 0$$

$$Q\left(\frac{1}{2}\right) - 100\left(\frac{\sqrt{3}}{2}\right) + P\left(\frac{2}{\sqrt{5}}\right) = 0$$

$$\frac{Q}{2} - 50\sqrt{3} + \frac{2P}{\sqrt{5}} = 0$$

3. Having two unknowns (P and Q) and two equations, we can find Q:

$$2\left(\frac{Q\sqrt{3}}{2}\right) - 2(50) - 2\left(\frac{P}{\sqrt{5}}\right) = 0$$

$$\frac{Q}{2} - 50\sqrt{3} + \frac{2P}{\sqrt{5}} = 0$$

$$\overline{Q\sqrt{3} + \frac{Q}{2} - 100 - 50\sqrt{3} = 0}$$

$$\therefore Q = \frac{100 + 50\sqrt{3}}{\sqrt{3} + \frac{1}{2}}$$

$$= 83.6 \text{ lb}$$

**Mathematical Analysis
Using F and N Directly**

From the free-body diagram in Fig. 6.17b, we write

1. $\sum F_x = 0$:

$$Q \cos 30° - W \sin 30° - F = 0$$
$$\therefore F = Q \cos 30° - W \sin 30°$$

For $\sum F_y = 0$,

$$Q \sin 30° - W \cos 30° + N = 0$$
$$\therefore N = W \cos 30° - Q \sin 30°$$

2. Since $F = \mu N$,

$$F = 0.50N$$

and

$$Q \cos 30° - W \sin 30°$$
$$= 0.50(W \cos 30° - Q \sin 30°)$$

Substituting known values for W, $\sin 30°$, and $\cos 30°$,

$$Q\left(\frac{\sqrt{3}}{2}\right) - 100\left(\frac{1}{2}\right) = 0.50 \left[100\left(\frac{\sqrt{3}}{2}\right) - Q\left(\frac{1}{2}\right)\right]$$

$$\frac{Q\sqrt{3}}{2} - 50 = 25\sqrt{3} - 0.25Q$$

$$\frac{Q\sqrt{3}}{2} + 0.25Q = 25\sqrt{3} + 50$$

$$1.12Q = 93.3$$

$$\therefore Q = \frac{93.3}{1.12} = 83.4 \text{ lb}$$

Graphical Analysis

1. Draw $W = 100$ lb to a convenient vector scale (1 in. = 50 lb is indicated in Fig. 6.18).

2. Since the directions of **Q** and **P** are known (with $\tan \phi = 0.50$, the direction of **P** can be determined), we can draw a vector diagram that closes for equilibrium (see Fig. 6.18). Measuring the vectors **Q** and **P**, we find that $Q = 84$ lb and $P = 50$ lb.

3. Resisting force P can be resolved into F and N components, since the direction of these components are known. By measurement, we get $F = 23$ lb and $N = 46$ lb. (See Fig. 6.18.)

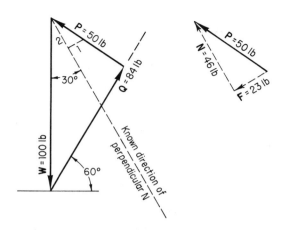

FIGURE 6.18

Vector Diagrams
Vector Scale: 1 in. = 50 lb

EXAMPLE 6.2 _____

The friction torque of a solid, flat pivot.

Given: A flat pivot having radius r and weight W with two applied opposite, equal, and parallel forces Q tending to cause the pivot to rotate, as shown in Fig. 6.19.

Find: An expression that defines the resisting frictional torque of the pivot at the instant of *impending* rotation.

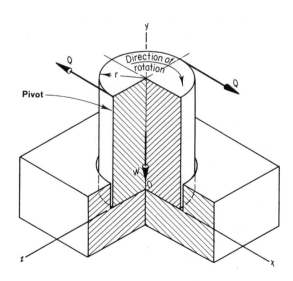

FIGURE 6.19

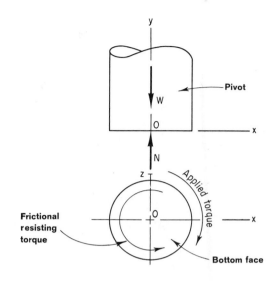

FIGURE 6.20

Mathematical Analysis

1. Draw the free-body diagram of the pivot at impending rotation, as shown in Fig. 6.20.
2. For equilibrium at *impending rotation*, the following static equilibrium expressions must be satisfied: $\sum F_y = 0$ and $\sum M_y = 0$, since we are concerned with only vertical loads (W and N) and torque. Therefore,

$$\sum F_y = W - N = 0$$

and

$\sum M_y$ = applied torque
$\qquad\qquad$ − frictional resisting torque = 0

3. To determine the resisting torque due to friction, we divide the circular *flat end face* of the pivot into small triangular elements. The frictional forces acting on each triangular element, at the instant of impending rotation, can be considered parallel forces distributed over the *area* of each triangular element. The *resultant* of each parallel force system therefore passes through the *centroid*[2] of each triangular element. (The centroid is located $\frac{2}{3}r$ from the vertex of each triangular element; which in this case is measured from the origin O.) (See Figs. 6.21 and 6.22.)

_____

[2] The centroid of a plane figure corresponds to the center of gravity of a three-dimensional body. See Chapter 7 for a complete discussion of centroids.

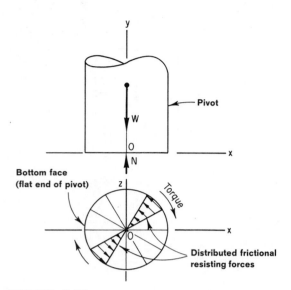

FIGURE 6.21

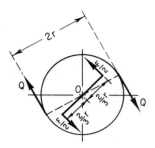

FIGURE 6.23

Since the magnitude of the total frictional force F is independent of the area of contact, we can assume that F is concentrated at a point K that is $\frac{2}{3}r$ from the *center* of the circular flat end face of the pivot (see Fig. 6.22).

With this information, we write

$$\sum M_y = \sum M_O = \tfrac{2}{3}rF - 2rQ = 0$$

Since $F = \mu N$, we can substitute in the above equation and write

$$\tfrac{2}{3}r\mu N - 2rQ = 0$$

$$\therefore \ \ \tfrac{2}{3}r\mu N = 2rQ$$

$$= \text{frictional resisting torque}$$

4. Since the torque due to the two applied parallel forces Q is actually caused by a *couple* whose moment is $2rQ$, the frictional resisting torque can be

regarded as a couple formed by two $F/2$ forces that have a perpendicular distance between them equal to $\frac{4}{3}r$ (see Fig. 6.23). Therefore, we can write

$$2rQ = \tfrac{4}{3}r\left(\frac{F}{2}\right)$$

$$= \tfrac{2}{3}rF$$

$$= \tfrac{2}{3}r\mu N$$

which is the same result obtained in step 3 above.

6.5 Static Rolling Friction and Rolling Resistance

A cylindrical roller with radius r and weight W rolling on a horizontal flat plane surface *ideally* makes a *line contact* with the plane surface. If both the roller and plane surfaces are rigid bodies, deformation of neither takes place: the cylinder maintains perfect roundness and the plane perfect flatness. (See Fig. 6.24.)

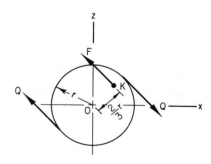

FIGURE 6.22

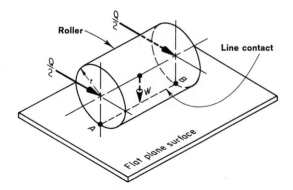

FIGURE 6.24

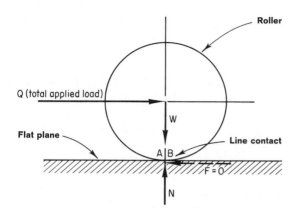

FIGURE 6.25

phenomenon, it is necessary to regard the roller and the flat plane as *nonrigid* bodies that *do* deform under a load. Under these circumstances, the roller and the flat plane make a surface (area) contact with each other, rather than a line contact. (See Fig. 6.26.)

Considering the equilibrium of the roller at the instant of impending rolling, we see from the free-body diagram of the roller (Fig. 6.27a) that forces Q and W are kept in equilibrium by the reaction force P. Resolving P into components that are tangential and perpendicular

If two forces $Q/2$ applied to the axis of the roller (as shown in Fig. 6.24) cause motion (rolling at a constant velocity *without* slipping), the roller will move, and the plane surface will *not* offer any resistance to this motion.

Referring to Fig. 6.25, we see that the only resistance the flat plane offers to the roller under these idealized conditions is the perpendicular force N. Thus, the static frictional force F is equal to zero (since we have assumed no slipping or sliding between the roller and the plane surface). Therefore, the roller will continue to roll on the flat plane at a constant velocity.

From experience, we know that a roller rolling on a horizontal flat surface does in fact slow down and eventually stop. To analyze the reason for this

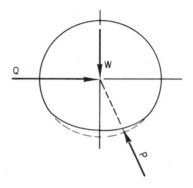

(a) Free-body Diagram

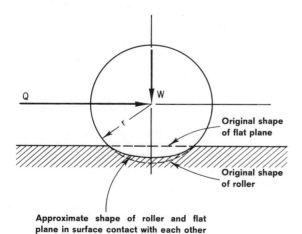

FIGURE 6.26

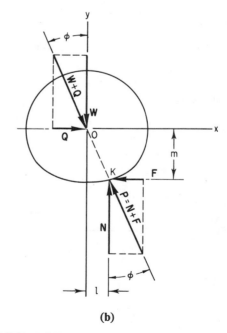

(b)

FIGURE 6.27

(F and N, respectively) to the flat plane surface (see Fig. 6.27b), we see that

$$\sum F_x = 0$$
$$\therefore \mathbf{Q} - \mathbf{F} = 0$$
$$\mathbf{F} = \mathbf{Q}$$

and

$$\sum F_y = 0$$
$$\therefore -\mathbf{W} + \mathbf{N} = 0$$
$$\mathbf{W} = \mathbf{N}$$

and

$$\sum M_O = 0$$
$$\therefore l\mathbf{N} - m\mathbf{F} = 0$$
$$m\mathbf{F} = l\mathbf{N}$$

from which

$$\mathbf{F} = \frac{l\mathbf{N}}{m}$$

For very small deformations, m is very close in magnitude to radius r, and since $\mathbf{W} = \mathbf{N}$ (from $\sum F_y = 0$), we may write the above equation as

$$F = \frac{lW}{r}$$

which defines the *rolling resistance* force F that slows down the roller. (NOTE: The distance l is determined experimentally for various types of materials. For softer materials it can be seen that l gets larger.)

EXAMPLE 6.3

The rolling resistance of a roller between two flat, bearing surfaces.

Given: A cylindrical roller (weightless and having a radius r) between two flat, bearing surfaces of similar material. The top bearing plate (I) has weight W and is acted upon by a horizontal load Q. The lower bearing plate (II) is stationary. (See Fig. 6.28).

Find: The magnitude of force Q necessary to move the top bearing plate (I).

Mathematical Analysis

1. The loads applied to the roller are Q and W. The resultant R of these two loads is transmitted by the top bearing plate to the roller, as shown in Fig. 6.29.
2. Draw the free-body diagram of the roller, as shown in Fig. 6.30.
3. For equilibrium, at the instant of impending rolling, $\sum F_x = 0$, $\sum F_y = 0$, and $\sum M_O = 0$. Therefore,

$$\sum F_x = Q - F = 0$$
$$\therefore \mathbf{F} = \mathbf{Q}$$

and

$$\sum F_y = W - N = 0$$
$$\therefore \mathbf{W} = \mathbf{N}$$

and, since the moment arm of F is very close to r,

$$\sum M_O = 2l\mathbf{N} - 2r\mathbf{F} = 0$$
$$\therefore \mathbf{F} = \frac{2l\mathbf{N}}{2r} = \frac{l\mathbf{N}}{r}$$

Since $\mathbf{W} = \mathbf{N}$, we can write

$$F = \frac{lW}{r}$$

Also, since $\mathbf{F} = \mathbf{Q}$, we can write

$$Q = \frac{lW}{r}$$

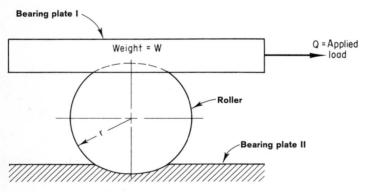

FIGURE 6.28

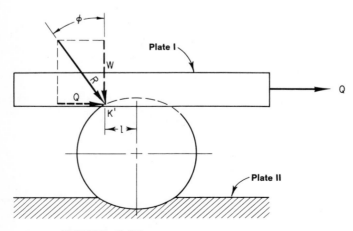

FIGURE 6.29

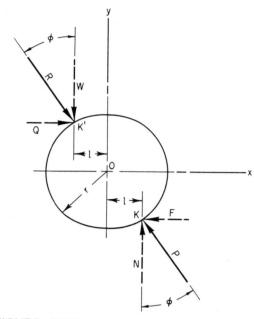

FIGURE 6.30

Free-body Diagram of the Roller

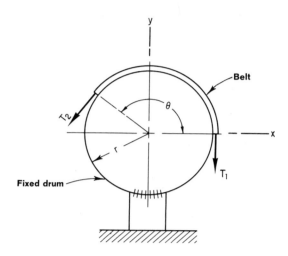

FIGURE 6.31

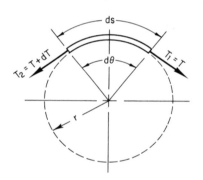

FIGURE 6.32

6.6 Belt Friction

Belt friction (or band friction) occurs in many engineering systems that involve power transmission from motors to machinery, and engines to generators, through belts and pulleys. In this section, we will develop an expression for the relationship between two tensions T_1 and T_2 on a belt in contact with a fixed drum. Slipping between the drum and the belt is *impending* because one tension (T_2) is greater in magnitude than the other tension (T_1). (See Fig. 6.31.) The expression will be derived from the equilibrium conditions of the given force system and the relationship between the perpendicular and frictional forces acting on the fixed drum and the belt.

Consider an elemental length of the belt, ds, that subtends an angle $d\theta$. Assume that at one end of ds (toward the T_1 end of the belt) the tension is T and that at the other end of ds the tension is $T + dT$. Thus, we have assumed that there is a greater tension at the T_2 end of the belt. (See Fig. 6.32.) (NOTE: These assumed tensions exist under the condition of *impending* slipping between the drum and the belt.)

The free-body diagram of the elemental length ds (Fig. 6.33) shows that both $T + dT$ and T are kept in equilibrium (at impending slipping) by the elemental frictional force dF and the elemental perpendicular force dN. Therefore, for equilibrium, we write

$$\sum F_x = -(T + dT)\cos\frac{d\theta}{2} + T\cos\frac{d\theta}{2} + dF = 0$$

$$\sum F_y = dN - (T + dT)\sin\frac{d\theta}{2} - T\sin\frac{d\theta}{2} = 0$$

$$\sum M_O = r(T + dT) - r\,dF - rT = 0$$

From the $\sum M_O$,

$$\sum M_O = rT + r\,dT - r\,dF - rT = 0$$
$$\therefore\ dF = dT$$

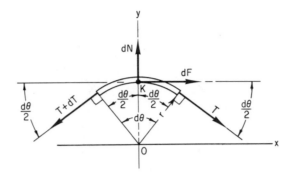

(a) Free-body Diagram

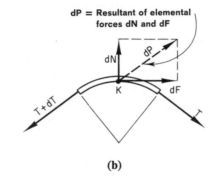

(b)

FIGURE 6.33

Thus, the elemental tension in ds is equal to the elemental friction force acting on ds.

From $\sum F_y = 0$,

$$dN = (T + dT) \sin \frac{d\theta}{2} + T \sin \frac{d\theta}{2}$$

$$= T \sin \frac{d\theta}{2} + dT \sin \frac{d\theta}{2} + T \sin \frac{d\theta}{2}$$

$$= 2T \sin \frac{d\theta}{2} + dT \sin \frac{d\theta}{2}$$

For extremely small angles, $\sin d\theta/2$ is approximately equal to $d\theta/2$ in *radians*. Therefore,

$$dN = 2T \frac{d\theta}{2} + dT \frac{d\theta}{2}$$

Since $(dT)(d\theta/2)$ is a product of two infinitesimals (resulting in a second-order infinitesimal), it can be neglected. Therefore, we can finally write

$$dN = T \, d\theta$$

Since $dF = dT = \mu \, dN$ at impending slipping, we can multiply both sides of $dN = T \, d\theta$ by μ to get

$$\mu \, dN = \mu T \, d\theta$$

Substituting dT for $\mu \, dN$,

$$dT = \mu T \, d\theta$$

$$\therefore \frac{dT}{T} = \mu \, d\theta$$

which defines the ratio of the tension in an elemental length ds of the belt to the total tension T in the belt. To determine the relation between T_1 and T_2, we integrate $dT/T = \mu \, d\theta$ between the limits of T_1 and T_2 and between the limits of $0°$ and $\theta°$ for the angle of contact between the drum and the belt, as follows:

$$\int_{T_1}^{T_2} \frac{dT}{T} = \mu \int_0^\theta d\theta$$

$$\therefore [\log_e T]_{T_1}^{T_2} = \mu [\theta]_0^\theta$$

$$\therefore \log_e T_2 - \log_e T_1 = \mu \theta$$

or

$$\frac{T_2}{T_1} = e^{\mu\theta}$$

If logarithms to the base 10 are used, the relation between T_1 and T_2 can be written as follows:

$$\log_{10} \frac{T_2}{T_1} = \mu\theta(\log_{10} e) = \mu\theta(0.434)$$

Another useful form is

$$\log_{10} T_2 - \log_{10} T_1 = 0.434 \, \mu\theta$$

If θ is measured in degrees, the relationship between T_1 and T_2 can be expressed as

$$\log_{10} T_2 - \log_{10} T_1 = 0.00758 \, \mu\theta.$$

EXAMPLE 6.4 ⎯⎯⎯⎯⎯⎯⎯⎯⎯⎯

Belt friction.

Given: A rope wrapped around a drum with radius $r = 10$ in., as shown in Fig. 6.34. A load of 200 lb is applied to one end of the rope, and a load of 5000 lb is applied to the other end. $\mu = 0.30$.

Find: The number of times the rope must be wrapped around the drum in order for the 200 lb load to be able to support the 5000 lb load in static equilibrium.

Mathematical Analysis

1. Let $T_2 = 5000$ lb, $T_1 = 200$ lb, and $\mu = 0.30$. Substituting these values into $\log_{10} T_2 - \log_{10} T_1 = 0.00758\mu\theta$, we get

$$\log_{10} 5000 - \log_{10} 200 = 0.00758\mu\theta$$

$$\therefore \quad \theta = \frac{\log_{10} 5000 - \log_{10} 200}{0.00758(0.30)}$$

$$= \frac{3.69897 - 2.30103}{0.002274}$$

$$= \frac{1.39794}{0.002274}$$

$$= 603°$$

Thus, the rope must be wrapped around the drum

$$\frac{603°}{360°/\text{revolution}} = 1.68 \text{ revolutions}$$

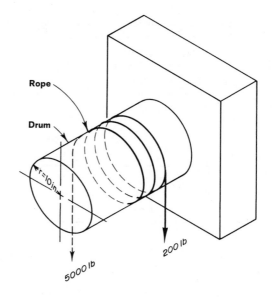

FIGURE 6.34

PROBLEMS

6.1 **Given:** A block weighing 30 lb resting on a horizontal surface. A horizontal force of 10 lb acting on the block causes motion. (See Fig. 6.35.)

Find: The coefficient of friction μ between the block and the horizontal supporting surface.
A. Use mathematical analysis.
B. Use graphical analysis.

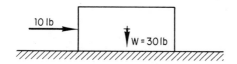

FIGURE 6.35

6.2 **Given:** A block weighing 20 lb resting on a horizontal surface. A force of 6 lb acting on the block makes an angle of 30° with the horizontal surface. (See Fig. 6.36.)

Find: The coefficient of static friction μ between the block and the horizontal supporting surface.
A. Use mathematical analysis.
B. Use graphical analysis.

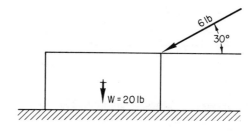

FIGURE 6.36

6.3 **Given:** A block weighing 20 lb resting on a horizontal surface. A force of 6 lb pulling on the block makes an angle of 30° with the horizontal surface. (See Fig. 6.37.)

153

Find: The coefficient of static friction μ between the block and the horizontal supporting surface.
A. Use mathematical analysis.
B. Use graphical analysis.
C. Compare your answers to those in Prob. 6.2.

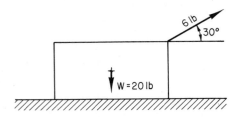

FIGURE 6.37

6.4 Given: A block weighing 100 lb resting on an inclined surface that makes an angle of 30° with the horizontal, as shown in Fig. 6.38.

Find: The coefficient of static friction μ between the block and the inclined surface necessary to keep the block from moving.
A. Use mathematical analysis.
B. Use graphical analysis.

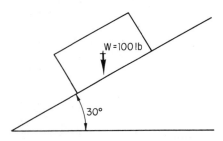

FIGURE 6.38

6.5 Given: A block weighing 200 lb on an inclined plane with a force P acting on the block, as shown in Fig. 6.39. $\mu = 0.40$.

Find: Using mathematical analysis, determine the full range of values that the force P may assume while the block remains in equilibrium.

Ans. $P = 6.3$ lb acting to the left to $P = 179$ lb acting to the right

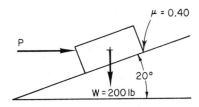

FIGURE 6.39

6.6 Given: A block weighing 200 lb on an inclined plane with a force P acting on the block, as shown in Fig. 6.39. $\mu = 0.40$.

Find: Using graphical analysis, determine the full range of values that force P may assume while the block remains in equilibrium. (Check your answers with Prob. 6.5.)

6.7 Given: A block of weight W resting on a horizontal surface where $\mu = 0.3$. A force of 50 lb acts on the block, as shown in Fig. 6.40.

Find: Graphically determine the magnitude and location of the perpendicular force acting on the block and the weight of the block when motion is impending.

Ans. Weight of block $= 171$ lb; the location of the perpendicular force is 0.6 ft from the line of action of the weight of the block.

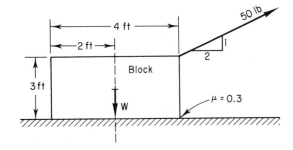

FIGURE 6.40

6.8 Given: A block of weight W resting on a horizontal surface where $\mu = 0.3$. A force of 50 lb acts on the block, as shown in Fig. 6.40.

Find : Using mathematical analysis determine the magnitude and location of the perpendicular force acting on the block and the weight of the block when motion is impending. (Check your answers with Prob. 6.8.)

6.9   Given : Two blocks weighing 100 lb and 75 lb, respectively, resting on two surfaces and on each other, as shown in Fig. 6.41. A horizontal force P acts on the 100-lb block, as shown. All surfaces have the same coefficient of static friction, $\mu = 0.25$.

Find : Using mathematical analysis, determine the magnitude of the force P that causes impending motion to the right.

Ans.   88.5 lb

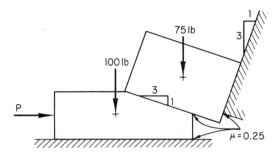

FIGURE 6.41

6.10   Given : The two blocks shown in Fig. 6.41, with all conditions remaining the same.

Find : Using graphical analysis, determine the magnitude of the force P that causes impending motion to the right.

6.11   Given : Two blocks having weights 1000 lb and W_1, respectively, connected to each other with a weightless, perfectly flexible cable passing over a fixed cylinder and resting on inclined planes, as shown in Fig. 6.42. The coefficient of static friction between the blocks and the planes on which they rest and between the cable and the fixed cylinder is $\mu = 0.3$.

Find : The magnitude of the weight W_1 that causes motion of the 1000 lb block to impend.

Ans.   2540 lb

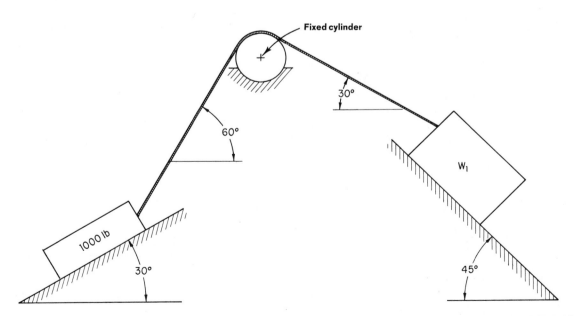

FIGURE 6.42

6.12 Given: A block of weight W_b resting on an inclined surface making 45° with the horizontal and acted upon by a 1000-lb force, as shown in Fig. 6.43. The coefficient of static friction between the block and the inclined surface is $\mu = 0.50$.

Find: The weight W_b of the block necessary to prevent impending motion upward.
A. Use mathematical analysis.
B. Use graphical analysis.

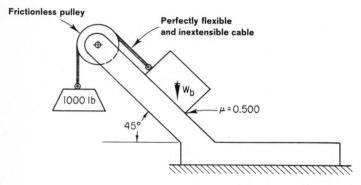

FIGURE 6.43

6.13 Given: A force of 200 lb applied to a crate weighing 1000 lb, as shown in Fig. 6.44.

Find: Whether the crate will slide, remain stationary, or tip over.

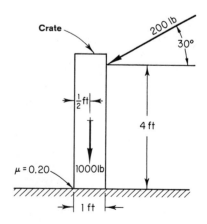

FIGURE 6.44

6.14 Given: A 25-lb cylinder that rests on an inclined plane having a resilient surface. The plane is inclined until the cylinder begins to roll down the plane, as shown in Fig. 6.45.

Find: The approximate magnitude of the rolling resistance.

Ans. 0.218 lb

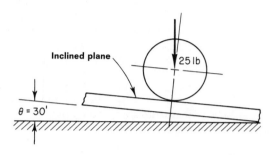

FIGURE 6.45

6.15 Given: A 10-in. diameter pivot supported and externally loaded with a load $W = 1000$ lb, as shown in Fig. 6.46. The coefficient of static friction between the pivot and the supporting surfaces is $\mu = 0.30$.

Find: The torque Q in pound-inches that must be applied to the pivot, at its circumference to cause impending rotation.

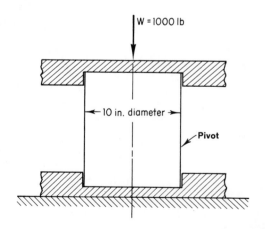

FIGURE 6.46

Seven

DISTRIBUTED FORCE SYSTEMS: FLUID STATICS AND CENTROIDS

7.1 Introduction

Distributed force systems are systems in which a number of forces act on an *area* or a volume. These force systems include parallel and nonparallel forces, coplanar and noncoplanar forces, forces of equal and unequal magnitudes, and forces spread uniformly and nonuniformly over an area. Some examples of distributed force systems are gravity forces acting on bodies, snow loads on roofs, water or fluid pressure on submerged bodies, internal air or gas pressure in tanks, atmospheric pressure, forces acting on bearings of rotating shafts, loaded floor joists, and loaded reinforced concrete beams.

This chapter is concerned with distributed force systems of parallel forces and shows how the concepts of parallel force systems (both coplanar and noncoplanar) presented in earlier chapters can be applied to the analysis of *distributed* force systems.

7.2 Center of Parallel Force Systems

In Chapter 3, it was shown that the line of action of the resultant force of a coplanar, parallel force system with a single resultant force could be located by Varignon's theorem—through either graphical or mathematical analysis. For example, the resultant of the parallel force system in Fig. 7.1 can be located relative to the y axis by summing up the moments of force about the origin O of the given coordinate system, as follows:

$$x_c R = x_1 F_1 + x_2 F_2 + x_3 F_3$$

$$\therefore \; x_c = \frac{x_1 F_1 + x_2 F_2 + x_3 F_3}{R}$$

where x_c is the distance from the y axis to the line of action of the resultant force. If the *same* downward parallel forces F_1, F_2, and F_3 in Fig. 7.1 are applied to the plane figure at the same respective points of application, and if the plane figure and the coordinate axes are rotated through and angle of $90°$, as shown in Fig. 7.2, the re-

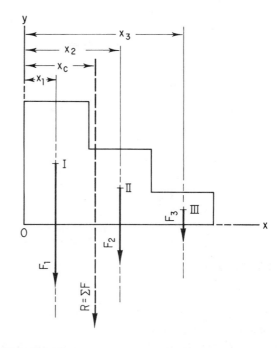

FIGURE 7.1

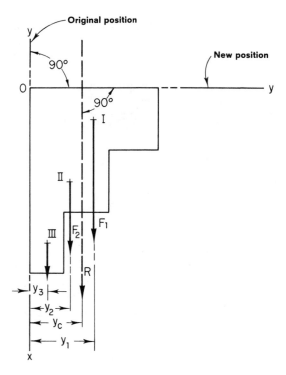

FIGURE 7.2

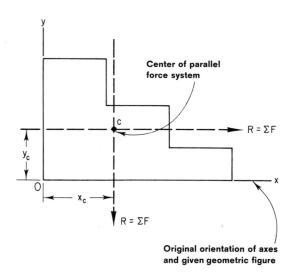

FIGURE 7.3

sultant force R could be located again. This time, instead of being parallel to the y axis, the resultant R makes an angle of $90°$ with the new y axis. Summing the moments of the forces about

the origin of the new coordinate position, we may locate the resultant relative to the x axis as follows:

$$y_c R = y_1 F_1 + y_2 F_2 + y_3 F_3$$

$$\therefore \ y_c = \frac{y_1 F_1 + y_2 F_2 + y_3 F_3}{R}$$

In determining x_c and y_c, we have fixed a point c through which the line of action of the resultant R will pass, regardless of the angle through which the plane geometric figure is rotated (in the x-y plane), provided that the applied forces act continually downward, toward the bottom of this page. This fixed point is defined as the *center* of the given parallel force system (see Fig. 7.3).

7.3 Center of Gravity and Centroids

Early in this book a "particle" was visualized as being a small, solid sphere whose diameter approaches zero—this is an *idealized* physical concept of the smallest possible body having mass. In a similar way, we may regard a rigid body as consisting of a great number of individual particles. When a rigid body is acted upon by gravity forces (which are assumed to be parallel forces), these forces are distributed over each particle in the body. The *force of gravity* on each particle is *proportional to the mass of each particle*. Since a particle is considered infinitesimal in size, the forces of gravity act through the center of each particle of mass in the body. The *center of gravity*, then, is a point in the rigid body through which the *resultant* of the *distributed parallel gravity forces* passes. No matter how the body is oriented relative to the earth, *the resultant of the distributed parallel gravity forces will always pass through this same point.*

The concept of the center of a parallel force system can be conveniently used to determine the *center of gravity* of both geometric figures (having no mass) and three-dimensional solid bodies (having mass). In Fig. 7.4 we see a rectangular plane figure $ABCD$ whose area has been subdivided into n smaller areas ΔA. These subareas can be imagined to represent *particles of area*, whose

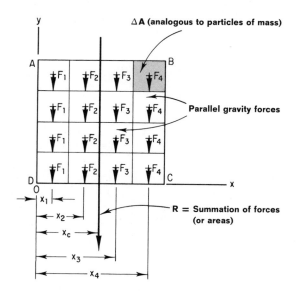

FIGURE 7.4

sum comprises the total area of the rectangular figure ($\sum \Delta A_n$ = total area) shown in Fig. 7.5. Since the gravity forces act through the center of each particle of area, we can sum all the moments of these gravity forces relative to the y axis and divide this sum by the number of particles of area into which the rectangular figure has been subdivided, thus determining the *average distance* (x_c) from each particle of area to the y axis:

$$x_c = \frac{\sum x_n F_n}{\sum F_n}$$

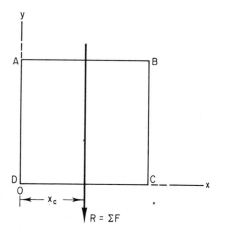

FIGURE 7.5

Rotating the rectangular figure in the x-y plane through an angle of 90° (see Fig. 7.6), we can sum the moments (relative to the x axis) of the gravity forces (assuming n number of forces) acting on n individual particles of area and thus determine y_c:

$$y_c = \frac{\sum y_n F_n}{\sum F_n}$$

Since gravity forces are *proportional* to the *mass* of each particle in a body, and since the total mass of a body is proportional to the *size* of the body, it is possible to say, by analogy, that the "mass" of a plane figure is proportional to its total area. Therefore, we can rewrite the above expressions for x_c and y_c by substituting the elemental sub-areas ("particles" of areas into which the plane figure has been divided) into these expressions in place of the gravity forces (see Fig. 7.7):

$$x_c = \frac{\sum x_n \Delta A_n}{\sum \Delta A_n}$$

$$y_c = \frac{\sum y_n \Delta A_n}{\sum \Delta A_n}$$

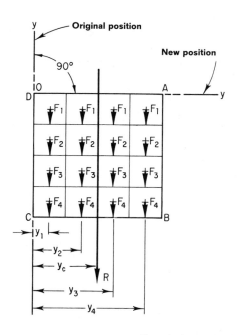

Since each particle of area is equal, $F_1 = F_2 = F_3 = F_4$

FIGURE 7.6

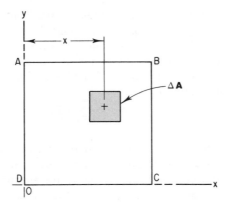

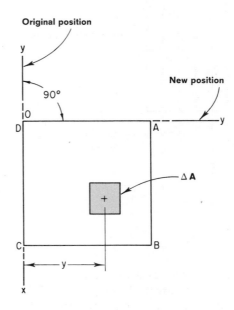

FIGURE 7.7

In these expressions, x_n and y_n are the moment arms from the y and x axes, respectively, and ΔA represents the subareas into which the plane figure has been divided. If the size of the elemental subareas (dA) approaches zero and the *number* of these elements approaches infinity, we can write the above equations in terms of the calculus (see Fig. 7.8)

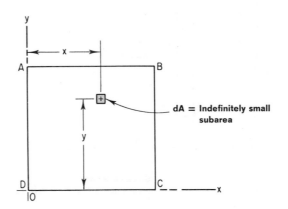

FIGURE 7.8

$$x_c = \frac{\int x\, dA}{\int dA} \quad \text{and} \quad y_c = \frac{\int y\, dA}{\int dA}$$

These expressions define the *centroid* of an area and are known as *first moment of area* equations, since the integral $\int x\, dA$ defines all the moments of the elemental areas about the y axis and $\int y\, dA$ represents all the moments of these areas about the x axis. The integral $\int dA$ represents the *total area* of the plane figure.

7.4 Axes of Symmetry

A plane figure is said to have an *axis of symmetry* if it can be divided by a longitudinal plane into two similar, congruent halves. In Fig. 7.9a, we see that the sides AB and CD are *bisected* by the axis of symmetry. Actually, any line in the plane figure *parallel* to lines AB and CD will be bisected by the axis of symmetry.

In evaluating $x_c = \int x\,dA / \int dA$ for the plane figure in Fig. 7.9b, we see that the first moment of area taken to the right of the axis of symmetry cancels the first moment of area taken to the left of this axis. Thus, the centroid of the figure (which has the y axis as an axis of symmetry) must be located on the axis of symmetry of the figure. Further, if a plane figure has *two* axes of symmetry (see Fig. 7.10) the centroid is located at the point where the two axes intersect.

If a plane figure has a congruent axis of symmetry, the figure can usually be "folded" on this axis such that the right half corresponds

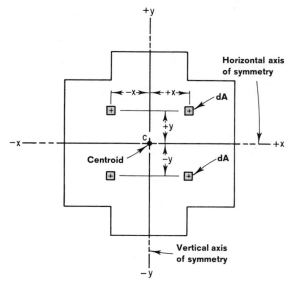

FIGURE 7.10

with its left half. On the other hand, the concept of symmetry applies to plane figures that are symmetrical about axes about which the figures *cannot* be folded so that the right half corresponds with the left half. For example, the diagonals of a rectangle (or any parallelogram) can be considered to be axes of symmetry since the two diagonals of a rectangle *bisect* each other and any line that is parallel to the bisected diagonal in the plane of the rectangle. This also holds for triangular plane figures.

Certain properties of symmetry are illustrated in Fig. 7.11. In all the illustrations, the centroid of each plane figure is located on the axis of symmetry.

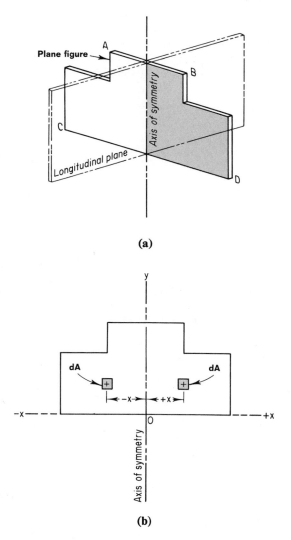

(a)

(b)

FIGURE 7.9

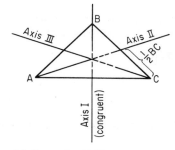

(a) Isosceles Triangle
(Three Axes of Symmetry)

FIGURE 7.11(a)

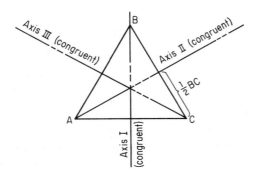

(b) Equilateral Triangle
(Three Axes of Symmetry)

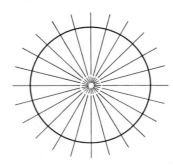

(c) Circle
(Infinite Number of Axes of Symmetry)

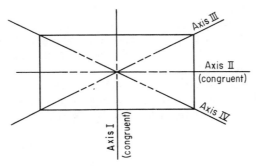

(d) Rectangle—or Any Parallelogram
(Four Axes of Symmetry)

FIGURE 7.11(b)–(d)

7.5 Center of Symmetry

The *center of symmetry* of a plane figure is the point in the figure where *all lines* drawn (in its plane) through this point and terminated by the sides of the figure are *bisected* by the point (see Fig. 7.12). From the definition of a centroid, it can

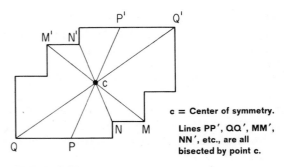

c = Center of symmetry.

Lines PP′, QQ′, MM′, NN′, etc., are all bisected by point c.

FIGURE 7.12

be seen that *if* a plane figure has a center of symmetry it corresponds to the centroid.

It is also important to note that a plane figure may have a center of symmetry but not necessarily an axis of congruent symmetry, and vice versa (a plane figure can have an axis of congruent symmetry but no center of symmetry). Illustrated in Figs. 7.13a–c are a few typical cases of plane figures involving centers and axes of symmetry.

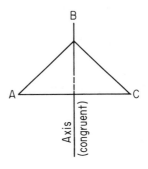

(a) Isosceles Triangle
(One Axis of Congruent Symmetry—*No* Center of Symmetry)

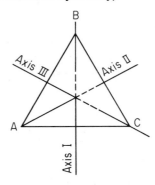

(b) Equilateral Triangle
(Three Axes of Congruent Symmetry—*No* Center of Symmetry)

FIGURE 7.13(a), (b)

c = Center of symmetry.

Lines LL', NN', QQ',
MM', PP', etc., are
bisected by point c.

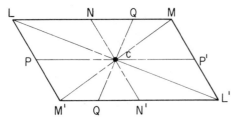

(c) Parallelogram
(Center of Symmetry—*No* Congruent
Axes of Symmetry)

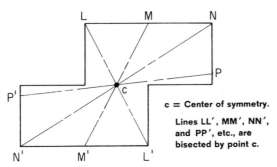

c = Center of symmetry.

Lines LL', MM', NN',
and PP', etc., are
bisected by point c.

(d) Composite Figure
(Center of Symmetry—*No* Congruent
Axes of Symmetry)

FIGURE 7.13(c), (d)

7.6 Locating Centroids

Examples 7.1, 7.2, and 7.3 illustrate how the centroids of basic geometric shapes are determined graphically and mathematically. After the centroid for each shape is located, the centroids of composite areas that are composed of a combination of various geometric shapes can be determined.[1]

EXAMPLE 7.1 ――――――――――

The centroid of an oblique triangle.

Given: Oblique triangle *RST* (see Fig. 7.14).

――――――――――

[1] The centroids of basic geometric shapes are tabulated in engineering handbooks and in a number of the textbooks listed in the bibliography at the end of this book.

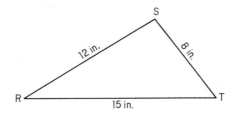

FIGURE 7.14

Find: The location of the centroid of triangle *RST*, using graphical and mathematical analysis.

Graphical Analysis

1. Construct triangle *RST* to a convenient scale.
2. Any line *parallel* to *RT* in triangle *RST* (such as 1–2 in Fig. 7.15a) is bisected by the line drawn from

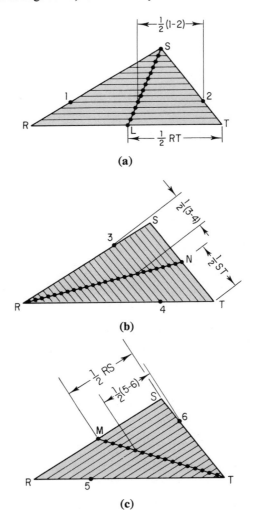

FIGURE 7.15

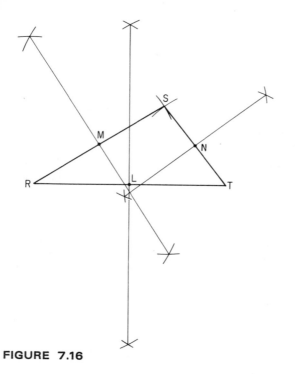

FIGURE 7.16

5. Measuring the distance from the vertex R to the centroid c, we find that the centroid is at a point two thirds of the distance from vertex R to midpoint N. This is also true of the distances from vertex S to midpoint L and from vertex T to midpoint M.

Mathematical Analysis

Using geometric relationships:

1. As in Fig. 7.18, draw triangle RST and the lines from each vertex to the midpoints of the respective opposite sides (RN, SL, TM). These lines intersect at point c.

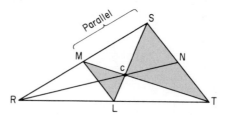

FIGURE 7.18

vertex S to midpoint L (of RT). Similarly, any line parallel to ST (such as 3–4 in Fig. 7.15b) is bisected by the line from vertex R to midpoint N (of ST), and any line parallel to RS (such as 5–6 in Fig. 7.15c) is bisected by the line from vertex T to midpoint M (of RS). Since the center (or centroid) of each parallel line (1–2, 3–4, 4–5, etc.) is determined by the bisecting line drawn from the vertex of the triangle to the midpoint of the opposite side, the centroid of the triangle must be located at the intersection of the three lines.

3. Therefore, to find the centroid, *bisect* side RT (point L), bisect side RS (point M), and bisect side ST (point N) (see Fig. 7.16).

4. Then connect the vertexes of triangle RST with the midpoints L, M, and N of sides RT, RS, and ST. Intersection c is the centroid of the given triangle. (See Fig. 7.17.)

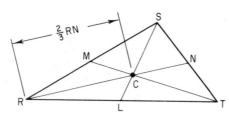

FIGURE 7.17

2. Connect midpoints L and M with a straight line. Since L and M are midpoints of RT and RS, respectively, the line LM is parallel to side ST of triangle RST.

3. From plane geometry, note that triangles RML and RST are similar and that the triangles LcM and TcS are also similar, since the alternate interior angles, determined here by lines SL and TM, between two parallel lines (LM and ST) are equal.

4. From similar triangle relationships, $LM = \frac{1}{2}ST$, since LM is parallel to ST through the midpoints M and L of lines RS and RT, respectively.

5. Again from similar triangle relationships,

$$\frac{LM}{ST} = \frac{cL}{cS}$$

Substituting $LM = \frac{1}{2}ST$ in the above relationship,

$$\frac{ST}{2ST} = \frac{cL}{cS}$$

$$\therefore \frac{1}{2} = \frac{cL}{cS} \quad \text{or} \quad cS = 2cL$$

Thus, the distance from c to S is *twice* that from c to L, and the centroid c of the given triangle is located *two thirds* of the distance from S to L, measured from vertex S. (See Fig. 7.19.) The centroid can be located relative to any vertex of the given triangle in the same way.

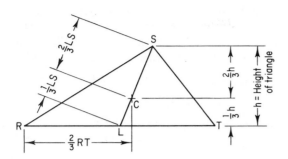

FIGURE 7.19

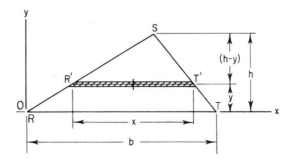

FIGURE 7.21

Mathematical Analysis

Using the calculus:

1. Relate the given oblique triangle *RST* to the *x* and *y* axes, as shown in Fig. 7.20.

2. Mark off a horizontal *elemental strip* of area $dA = x\,dy$ (see Fig. 7.20).

3. The centroid of the *elemental strip* of area is located a distance *y* above the *x* axis.

4. The expression that defines the location (relative to the *x* axis) of the *entire area* of the triangle is

$$y_c = \frac{\int y\,dA}{\int dA}$$

5. Substitute $dA = x\,dy$ and $\int dA =$ total area of triangle $= \frac{1}{2}bh$ (where $b =$ base and $h =$ height of triangle), to get

$$y_c = \frac{\int y\,dA}{\int dA}$$
$$= \frac{\int y(x)\,dy}{\frac{1}{2}bh}$$
$$= \frac{2}{bh}\int y(x)\,dy$$

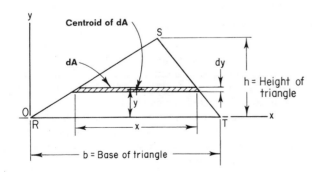

FIGURE 7.20

To sum all the individual horizontal elemental strips of area in the triangle, integrate this last expression between the limits $y = 0$ and $y = h$. But first get *x* in terms of *y* by considering the geometric relationships of the given triangle and the elemental strips of area.

6. From Fig. 7.21 and similar triangle relationships between triangles *RST* and *R′ST′*, we can write

$$\frac{h}{b} = \frac{h - y}{x}$$

$$\therefore \ x = \frac{b}{h}(h - y)$$

7. Substitute $x = \frac{b}{h}(h - y)$ into $y_c = \frac{2}{bh}\int yx\,dy$ to get

$$y_c = \frac{2}{bh}\int y\left[\frac{b}{h}(h - y)\right]dy$$
$$= \frac{2}{bh}\left(\frac{b}{h}\right)\int (yh - y^2)\,dy$$
$$= \frac{2}{h^2}\int (yh - y^2)\,dy$$

8. Integrating from $y = 0$ to $y = h$,

$$y_c = \frac{2}{h^2}\left[\frac{hy^2}{2} - \frac{y^3}{3}\right]_0^h = \frac{2}{h^2}\left[\frac{h^3}{2} - \frac{h^3}{3}\right]$$
$$= h - \frac{2}{3}h$$
$$= \frac{h}{3}$$

9. Since the centroid of the given triangle is located on the line from vertex *S* to the midpoint of the opposite side *RT*, and since we have calculated that $y_c = h/3$, we can locate the centroid *c* relative to the *y* axis (see Fig. 7.22). To quickly determine an expression for x_c, analyze the geometry of the given triangle on the basis of the geometric relationships

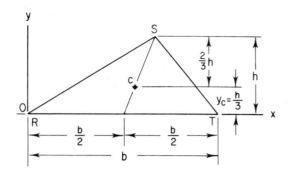

FIGURE 7.22

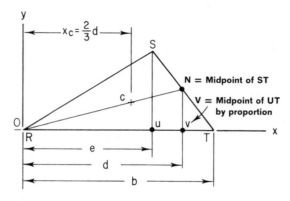

FIGURE 7.23

developed up to this point. (See Fig. 7.19.) From Fig. 7.23, the following relationship, based on geometry, can be written:

$$d = \frac{b + e}{2}$$

$$\therefore \frac{2}{3}d = \frac{2}{3}\left(\frac{b + e}{2}\right) = \frac{b + e}{3}$$

Since $x_c = \frac{2}{3}d$, we can substitute and write

$$x_c = \frac{b + e}{3}$$

The centroid of a *straight line segment* is, by symmetry, located at the midpoint of the line. If the line is a *curved line*, the centroid is *not* on the line itself; the centroid can be located by dividing the line into *elemental lengths* Δl, where the centroids of the *individual* elemental lengths are very closely located at the midpoints of each Δl.

By regarding each Δl as being *proportional* to its "mass," we can take moments, relative to the y axis, of each Δl at its centroid (see Fig. 7.24). Expressing this in mathematical terms, we get

$$\sum M_y = x_c L = x_1 \, \Delta l_1 + x_2 \, \Delta l_2 + x_3 \, \Delta l_3 + \cdots + x_n \, \Delta l_n$$

where x_c is the location of the centroid of the entire line relative to the y axis and $L = \Delta l_1 + \Delta l_2 + \Delta l_3 + \cdots + \Delta l_n$ is the total length of the given curved line. Rewriting the expression for $\sum M_y$ and solving for x_c, we get

$$x_c = \frac{x_1 \, \Delta l_1 + x_2 \, \Delta l_2 + x_3 \, \Delta l_3 + \cdots + x_n \, \Delta l_n}{\Delta l_1 + \Delta l_2 + \Delta l_3 + \cdots + \Delta l_n}$$

$$= \frac{\sum x \, \Delta l}{\sum \Delta l} = \frac{\sum x \, \Delta l}{L}$$

Similarly, taking moments relative to the x axis, we find

$$y_c = \frac{\sum y \, \Delta l}{L}$$

If the curved line segment is part of a circular arc, the above expressions for x_c and y_c can be applied to derive a general expression for the location of its centroid.

EXAMPLE 7.2 _____

The centroid of a line segment.

Given: A circular arc with radius r subtending an angle θ, as shown in Fig. 7.25, and a semi-circular arc as shown in Fig. 7.29.

Find: The location of the centroid in terms of radius r and angle θ.

Mathematical Analysis

Using geometric relationships:

1. As oriented in Fig. 7.25, the x axis is the axis of symmetry of the circular arc segment.

2. Divide the given circular arc into elemental lengths Δl, as shown in Fig. 7.26. (Only a few Δl lengths are illustrated for clarity.)

3. By symmetry, the centroid of each Δl is at the center of each elemental length (c_1, c_2, c_3, c_4, etc.). Taking moments relative to the x and y axes, we get the familiar expressions

$$x_c = \frac{\sum x \, \Delta l}{L} \quad \text{and} \quad y_c = \frac{\sum y \, \Delta l}{L}$$

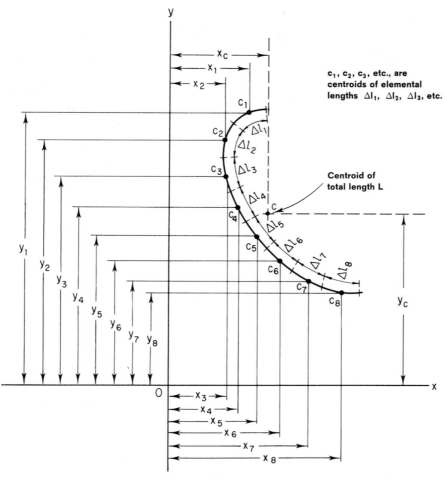

FIGURE 7.24

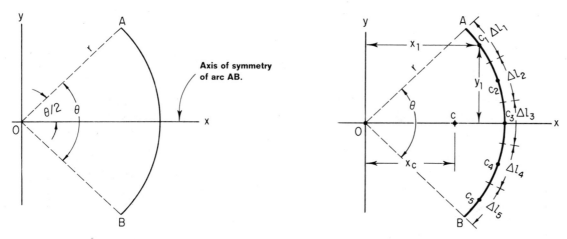

FIGURE 7.25   **FIGURE 7.26**

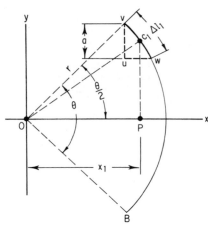

FIGURE 7.27

4. Consider one elemental length Δl, as shown in Fig. 7.27. The vertical projection of Δl_1 is UV. Since triangles OPC and VUW are similar (from geometry), we can write

$$\frac{UV}{VW} = \frac{OP}{Oc_1}$$

Since $Oc_1 = r$, $OP = x_1$, $VW = \Delta l_1$, and $UV = a$, we can write the above equation as

$$\frac{a}{\Delta l_1} = \frac{x_1}{r}$$

Rearranging terms, we obtain the expression

$$x_1 \, \Delta l_1 = ra$$

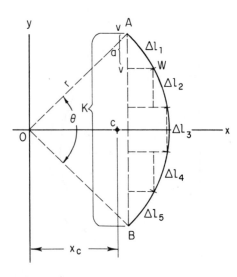

FIGURE 7.28

which shows that the moment of Δl_1 about the y axis is equal to the product of the radius r of the given circular arc and the vertical projection a of Δl_1.

5. Substituting ra for $x \, \Delta l$ in $x_c = \sum x \, \Delta l / L$, we get

$$x_c = \frac{\sum ra}{L}$$

6. Since, as noted in Fig. 7.28, $\sum a = K$, the *chord length AB*, and since r is a constant, we can write

$$x_c = \frac{\sum ra}{L}$$

$$= \frac{r \sum a}{L}$$

$$= \frac{rK}{L}$$

7. For a *semicircular* arc with the x axis as the axis of symmetry, $\theta = \pi$ (in radians), $L = \pi r$, and $K = 2r$ (see Fig. 7.29):

$$x_c = \frac{rK}{L}$$

$$= \frac{r(2r)}{\pi r}$$

$$= \frac{2r}{\pi}$$

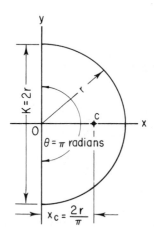

FIGURE 7.29

Mathematical Analysis

Using calculus to determine the centroid of a semicircular arc:

1. The following is known about the arc in Fig. 7.30.

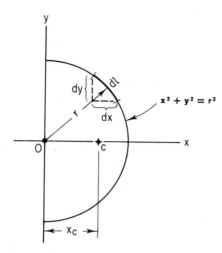

FIGURE 7.30

Equation of a circle: $x^2 + y^2 = r^2$

Circumference of a semicircular arc: πr

2. Divide the semicircular arc into infinitesimal segments dl (see Fig. 7.30).

3. The location of the centroid x_c relative to the y axis is defined as

$$x_c = \frac{\int x \, dl}{\int dl}$$

(where dl has been substituted for Δl and $\int dl$ for L in $x_c = \sum x \, \Delta l / L$).

4. Since πr is the length of the semicircular arc, πr may be substituted for $\int dl$:

$$x_c = \frac{\int x \, dl}{\pi r}$$

5. Integrate $\int x \, dl$ over the entire length of the semicircular arc (and thus sum the moments of all the infinitesimal segments relative to the y axis). Before this integration can be done, dl must be expressed in terms of y, since the summation will take place between the limits of $y = +r$ and $y = -r$. To give dl in terms of y, consider the differentials dx and dy. From Fig. 7.31,

$$(dl)^2 = (dx)^2 + (dy)^2$$

Using this relationship, derive an expression to permit the integration operation above. Divide both sides of the above relationship by $(dy)^2$:

$$\frac{(dl)^2}{(dy)^2} = \frac{(dx)^2}{(dy)^2} + \frac{(dy)^2}{(dy)^2}$$

Thus,

$$\frac{dl}{dy} = \sqrt{1 + \left(\frac{dx}{dy}\right)^2}$$

6. Since $x^2 + y^2 = r^2$ (the equation of a circle), $\frac{dx}{dy}$ can be determined by differentiation with respect to y:

$$2x\frac{dx}{dy} + 2y = 0$$

$$\therefore \frac{dx}{dy} = -\frac{y}{x}$$

Substitute

$$\frac{dx}{dy} = -\frac{y}{x} \quad \text{in} \quad \frac{dl}{dy} = \sqrt{1 + \left(\frac{dx}{dy}\right)^2}$$

$$\frac{dl}{dy} = \sqrt{1 + \frac{y^2}{x^2}}$$

$$= \sqrt{\frac{x^2 + y^2}{x^2}} = \sqrt{\frac{r^2}{x^2}}$$

$$= \frac{r}{x}$$

From this, $dl = (r/x) \, dy$.

7. Substitute

$$dl = \left(\frac{r}{x}\right) dy \quad \text{in} \quad x_c = \frac{\int x \, dl}{\pi r}$$

$$x_c = \frac{\int x(r/x) \, dy}{\pi r}$$

$$= \frac{\int dy}{\pi}$$

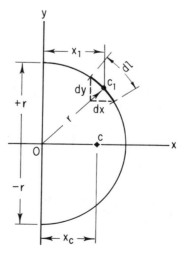

FIGURE 7.31

8. Now integrate this expression between the limits of $y = +r$ and $y = -r$:

$$x_c = \frac{\int_{-r}^{+r} dy}{\pi}$$

$$= \frac{[y]_{-r}^{+r}}{\pi} = \frac{[r - (-r)]}{\pi}$$

$$= \frac{2r}{\pi}$$

EXAMPLE 7.3 _____

The centroid of a *sector* (area) of a circle.

Given: A semicircular sector having radius r, as shown in Fig. 7.32.

Find: The location of the centroid of the given semicircular sector relative to the y axis.

Mathematical Analysis

Using geometric relationships:

1. As shown in Fig. 7.32, divide the given semicircular sector into a number of elemental radial sections. (If these sections are small enough, they approximate triangular shapes.)
2. The centroid of each elemental triangular shape (radial section) is located two thirds the distance from the vertex (origin O) of each triangular section to the midpoint of the base of each triangle (see Fig. 7.32). Therefore the centroids of all the elemental triangular sections form a semicircular arc with radius $r_1 = \frac{2}{3}r$.

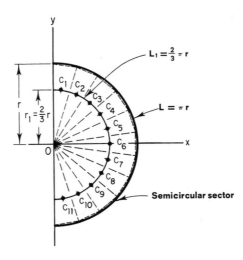

FIGURE 7.32

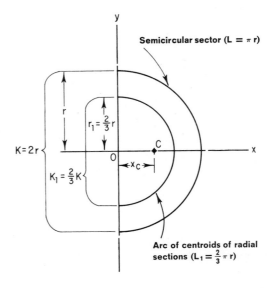

FIGURE 7.33

3. Since $r_1 = \frac{2}{3}r$, the chord length K_1 of the semicircular arc is $\frac{2}{3}K$, where $K = 2r$ is the chord length of the given semicircular area (see Fig. 7.33). Similarly, the length of the semicircular arc L_1 is $\frac{2}{3}L$, where L is the length of the circumference of the semicircular sector. Since $L = \pi r$, then $L_1 = \frac{2}{3}L = \frac{2}{3}\pi r$.
4. Determine the centroid of the semicircular arc (radius r_1), using the expression $x_c = rK/L$, which can be written as

$$x_c = \frac{r_1 K_1}{L}$$

Making the proper substitutions for r_1, K_1, and L_1,

$$x_c = \frac{\frac{2}{3}r(\frac{2}{3}K)}{\frac{2}{3}L}$$

$$= \frac{\frac{2}{3}r(\frac{2}{3})(2r)}{\frac{2}{3}\pi r} = \frac{\frac{4}{3}r^2}{\pi r}$$

$$= \frac{4r}{3\pi}$$

This final expression for x_c represents the *average* of the centroids of the elemental triangular sections, which actually defines the location of the centroid for the given semicircular sector.

Mathematical Analysis

Using calculus:

1. Regard the given semicircular sector as being divided into an infinite number of indefinitely small

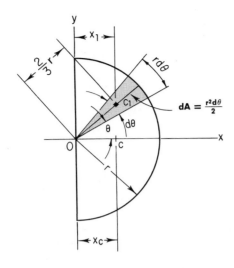

FIGURE 7.34

triangular sections (one of these sections is shown in Fig. 7.34).

2. The centroid c_1 of one of these infinitesimal triangular sections is located a distance $\frac{2}{3}r$ from the origin O or x_1 from the y axis, as shown in Fig. 7.34.

3. Applying the basic equation for x_c of an area,

$$x_c = \frac{\int x \, dA}{\int dA}$$

where x represents the moment arm to the centroid of each infinitesimal triangular section, dA represents the area of each triangular section, and $\int dA$ repre-

sents the entire area of the semicircular sector. From Fig. 7.34,

$$dA = \frac{r(r \, d\theta)}{2} = \frac{r^2 \, d\theta}{2}$$

and

$$x = \tfrac{2}{3}r \cos \theta$$

which is a general expression for all the moment arms for all the triangular sections, and

$$\int dA = \frac{\pi r^2}{2}$$

(the area of a semicircle). Substitute these expressions in the x_c equation, introducing the limits of integration from $\theta = +\pi/2$ to $\theta = -\pi/2$:

$$x_c = \int_{-\pi/2}^{+\pi/2} \frac{\frac{2}{3}r(\cos \theta)(r^2/2) \, d\theta}{\pi r^2/2}$$

Combining terms and rewriting,

$$x_c = \frac{2r}{3\pi} \int_{-\pi/2}^{+\pi/2} \cos \theta \, d\theta$$

Integrating,

$$x_c = \frac{2r}{3\pi} \left[\sin \theta \right]_{-\pi/2}^{+\pi/2}$$

$$= \frac{2r}{3\pi} \left[1 - (-1) \right] = \frac{2r}{3\pi} \ (2)$$

$$= \frac{4r}{3\pi}$$

EXAMPLE 7.4 _____

The centroid of a composite area.

Given: The plane figure shown in Fig. 7.35.

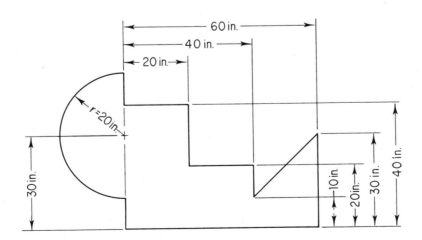

FIGURE 7.35

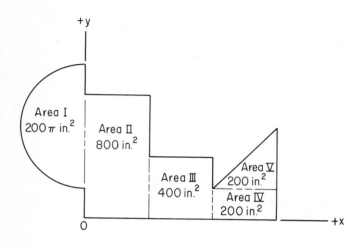

FIGURE 7.36

Find: The location of the centroid of the given figure, using mathematical and graphical analysis.

Mathematical Analysis

1. Relate the given plane figure to the x-y axes, and divide it into basic geometric component shapes (I, II, III, IV, and V), as shown in Fig. 7.36.

2. Determine the area of each component geometric shape.

$$I = \frac{\pi r^2}{2} = 200\pi \text{ in.}^2$$

$$II = 20 \times 40 = 800 \text{ in.}^2$$

$$III = 20 \times 20 = 400 \text{ in.}^2$$

$$IV = 10 \times 20 = 200 \text{ in.}^2$$

$$V = \frac{20 \times 20}{2} = 200 \text{ in.}^2$$

3. Using the property of symmetry, locate the centroids of the rectangular area components (see Fig. 7.37).
4. Locate the centroids relative to the x-y axes for the semicircular and triangular component areas, using known information about the centroids of these geometric shapes (see Fig. 7.37).
5. Since $x_c = \sum x\, \Delta A / \sum \Delta A,$

$$x_c = \frac{x_I A_I + x_{II} A_{II} + x_{III} A_{III} + x_{IV} A_{IV} + x_V A_V}{A_{\text{total}}}$$

Substitute the proper values for the individual moment arms and areas (keeping in mind that the *signs* of the individual $x\,\Delta A$ products must be considered, since part of the composite figure is to the left of the y axis):

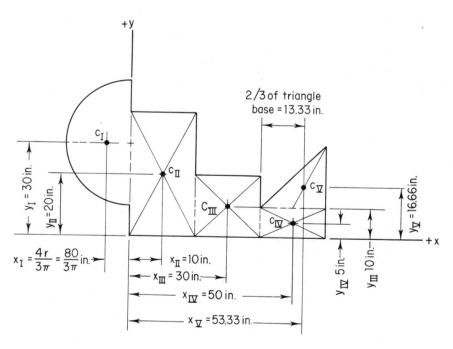

FIGURE 7.37

$$x_c = \frac{-\dfrac{80}{3\pi}(200\pi) + 10(800) + 30(400)}{200\pi + 800 + 400 + 200 + 200}$$

$$+ \frac{50(200) + 53.33(200)}{200\pi + 800 + 400 + 200 + 200}$$

$$= \frac{-5333 + 8000 + 12,000 + 10,000 + 10,666}{2228}$$

$$= \frac{35,333}{2228}$$

$$= 15.8 \text{ in.}$$

6. Using $y_c = \sum y\,\Delta A / \sum \Delta A$, make the proper substitutions and solve for y_c:

$$y_c = \frac{y_I A_I + y_{II} A_{II} + y_{III} A_{III} + y_{IV} A_{IV} + y_V A_V}{A_{\text{total}}}$$

$$= \frac{30(200\pi) + 20(800) + 10(400)}{2228}$$

$$+ \frac{5(200) + 16.66(200)}{2228}$$

$$= \frac{18,850 + 16,000 + 4000 + 1000 + 3332}{2228}$$

$$= \frac{43,182}{2228}$$

$$= 19.3 \text{ in.}$$

For convenience, record the individual calculations in Table 7.1.

The substitutions of $\sum \Delta A$, $\sum x\,\Delta A$, and $\sum y\,\Delta A$ can then be made conveniently in the equations for x_c and y_c.

7. In Fig. 7.38 is shown the location of the centroid c of the given composite area.

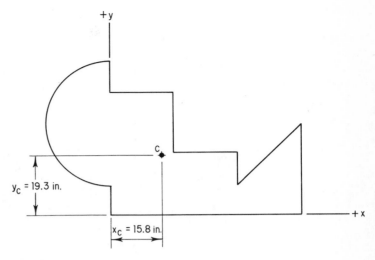

FIGURE 7.38

Graphical Analysis

NOTE: Graphically, we can use the vector concept to determine the centroids of composite plane figures by making an analogy between a vector quantity and an area and by applying the vector diagram (with a ray polygon) and the funicular polygon.

1. Draw the composite plane figure to a convenient space scale (see Fig. 7.39).
2. Divide the given plane figure into its basic geometric component areas, calculate the area of each component in square inches, and locate the centroids of each component area. (This step is similar to the approach taken in the mathematical analysis above. See Fig. 7.37.)

Table 7.1

SUMMARY OF MATHEMATICAL ANALYSIS FOR EXAMPLE 7.4

Component Area	Actual Area, in.^{2} ΔA	x Coordinates of Centroids of Component Areas, in.	x ΔA, in.^{3}	y Coordinates of Centroids of Component Areas, in.	y ΔA, in.^{3}
I	200π	$-80/3\pi$	$-5,333$	30	18,850
II	800	10	8,000	20	16,000
III	400	30	12,000	10	4,000
IV	200	50	10,000	5	1,000
V	200	53.33	10,666	16.66	3,332
	$\sum \Delta A = 2228$		$\sum x\,\Delta A = 35,333$		$\sum y\,\Delta A = 43,182$

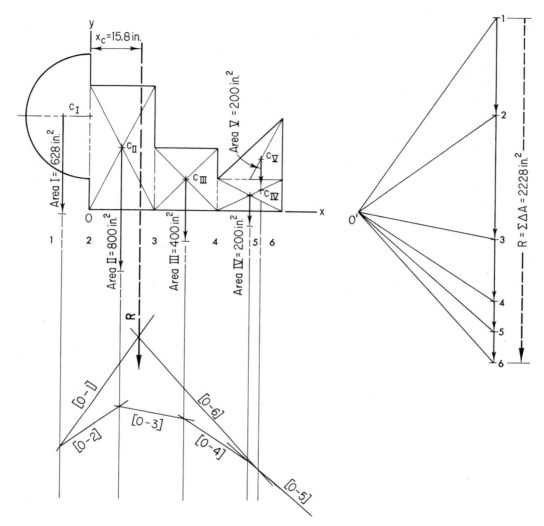

FIGURE 7.39

Space Diagram
Space Scale: 1 in. = 20 in.
Funicular Polygon
Vector Diagram with Ray Polygon
Vector Scale: 1 in. = 400 in.²

3. Assume a convenient vector scale, where the magnitude of the vectors represents area. Draw vectors that represent the component areas (I, II, III, IV, and V) and whose lines of action go through the centroids of the respective areas. (See Fig. 7.39.)

4. Draw the vector diagram (with a ray polygon, pole $0'$) to the assumed vector scale, showing the summation $\sum \Delta A = R$ of the component areas and using Bow's notation.

5. Construct the funicular polygon to locate resultant R. ($x_c = 15.8$ in. from the y axis).

6. Rotate the vectors in the space diagram through an angle of 90° (see Fig. 7.40).

7. Construct the vector diagram (with a ray polygon, pole $0''$) and the funicular polygon to locate resultant R in this orientation. (Based on the scale indicated in Fig. 7.40, $y_c = 19.5$ in. from the x axis.)

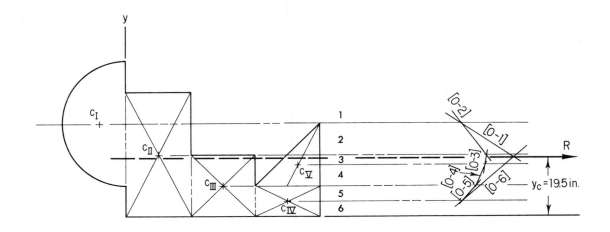

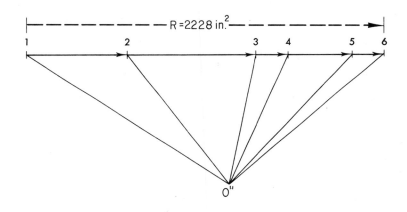

FIGURE 7.40

Space Diagram
Space Scale: 1 in. = 20 in.
Funicular Polygon
Vector Diagram with Ray Polygon
Vector scale: 1 in. = 400 in.^{2}

7.7 Uniformly Distributed Parallel Forces

In most engineering (and architectural) structures, parallel forces are distributed over an *area*. Such force systems occur in machinery, buildings, airplanes, and ships. Load diagrams, which are graphical representations of distributed parallel force systems, have the following characteristics:

1. They show the *intensity* (load per *unit* length of application) of an applied load at any point.

2. The centroid of a load diagram is at the center of the parallel distributed forces and is the point through which the resultant of the total distributed force system passes.

3. The area of a load diagram is equal to the

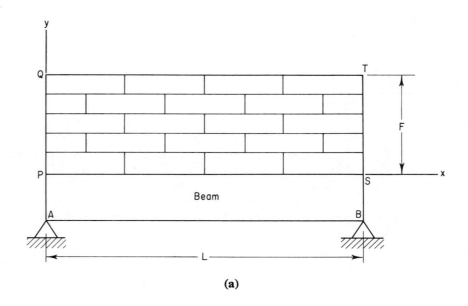

(a)

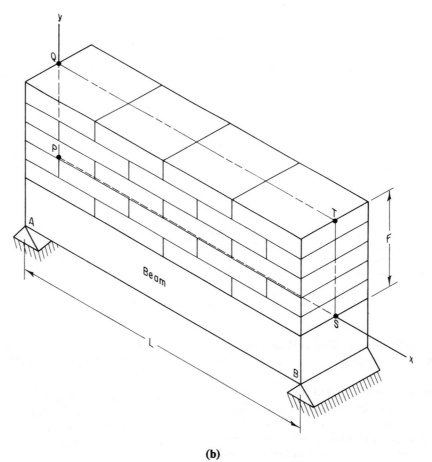

(b)

FIGURE 7.41

magnitude of the resultant of the distributed force system it represents.

Let us consider a simply supported beam AB carrying a uniformly distributed load—a load of tightly stacked bricks, as shown in Fig. 7.41.

It is reasonable for us to assume that the distributed forces caused by the bricks are concentrated in the central plane $PQTS$ of the load of bricks, since the weight of each brick (all of which have the same size and shape) can be considered to be concentrated at the centroid (or center of gravity) of each brick; therefore the centroids all lie in a vertical plane (see Fig. 7.42). We can further assume (for purposes of analysis) that the distributed load is applied along the line PS (see Fig. 7.42a) with an intensity of F pounds per unit length of PS. Thus, the resultant R of the whole load of bricks is

$$R = \left(\frac{F}{\text{unit length of } PS}\right)(\text{total length of } PS)$$

Assuming that the unit length is 1 ft, we can write

$$R = \left(\frac{F\,\text{lb}}{\text{ft}}\right)(L\,\text{ft})$$

where L is the total length of PS, and therefore

$$R = FL\ \text{lb}$$

which equals the *area* of the central plane (F lb being treated as a vector length).

If the algebraic sum of the moments of each unit force F is taken relative to the y axis (see Fig. 7.43), we obtain the center of the applied parallel force system, which locates the resultant R of the given system. This also locates the line on which the centroid of the load diagram lies, since

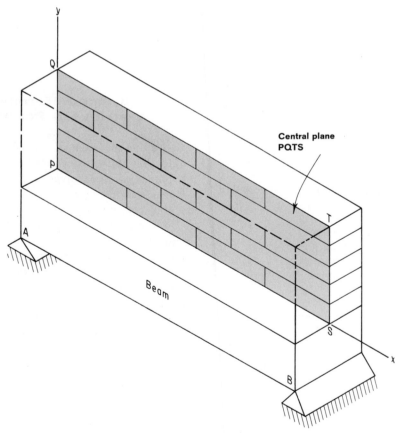

(a)

FIGURE 7.42(a)

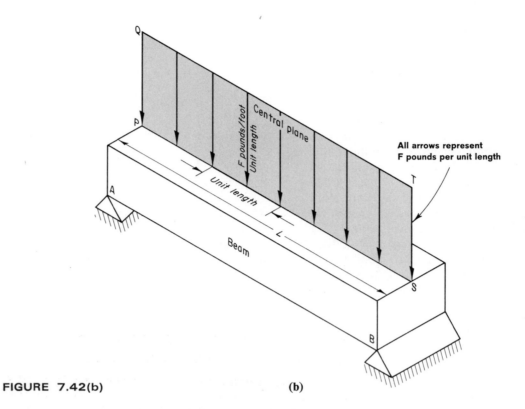

FIGURE 7.42(b)   **(b)**

$$\sum M_y = x_c R = \sum xF$$

$$\therefore\ x_c = \frac{\sum xF}{R} = \frac{\sum xF}{\sum F}$$

which is the familiar expression for the location of the centroid of a plane figure. (In Fig. 7.43, the load diagram is a rectangle whose centroid has been located by symmetry.)

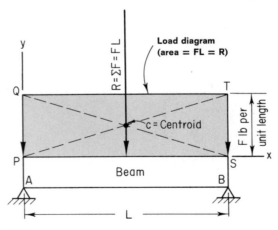

FIGURE 7.43

7.8 Nonuniformly Distributed Parallel Forces

Using the approach of Sec. 7.7, we can develop load diagrams that represent *nonuniformly* distributed parallel forces acting on a structure. Consider a beam CD having a length L and loaded with a varying load, as shown in Fig. 7.44.

Assume that the intensity of the load at the left end of the beam (at C) is zero pounds per foot and that this load varies uniformly to a maximum of F pounds per foot at the right end of the beam (at D). Thus, the applied load varies uniformly along the x axis.

Next, consider the central plane of the distributed load, as shown in Fig. 7.45, where

F = load per unit length (pounds per lineal foot, for example) at the right end of the beam

F_1 = load per unit length (pounds per lineal foot) at any intermediate position on the beam

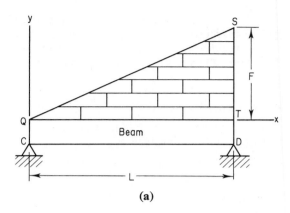

(a)

$$\frac{F}{L} = \frac{F_1}{x}$$

$$\therefore \ F_1 = \frac{Fx}{L}$$

Substituting $\dfrac{Fx}{L}$ for F_1 in $R = \displaystyle\int_0^L F_1 \ dx$, we get

$$R = \int_0^L \frac{F}{L} x \ dx = \frac{F}{L} \int_0^L x \ dx = \frac{F}{L}\left[\frac{x^2}{2}\right]_0^L$$

$$= \frac{FL}{2}$$

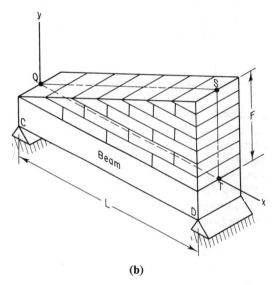

(b)

FIGURE 7.44

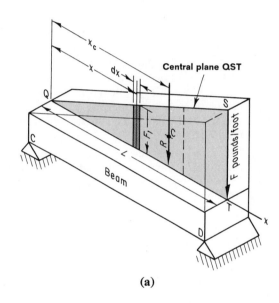

(a)

R = resultant of the entire distributed load

L = length of the beam

dx = infinitesimal segment of L (in feet)

Since F_1 = pounds per foot and dx = feet, $F_1 \ dx$ = pounds of load at x_1. ($F_1 \ dx$ also equals the area dR of the infinitesimal strip that is dx wide.) Therefore, the total load acting on the beam is

$$R = \int_0^L dR = \int_0^L F_1 \ dx$$

To integrate this expression for R, it is necessary to express F_1 in terms of F, L, and x. From similar triangle relationships (see Fig. 7.45b),

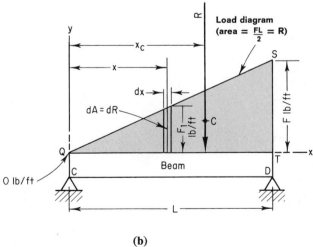

(b)

FIGURE 7.45

From Fig. 7.45, we see that $FL/2$ is the area of the *load diagram QST*. Since the centroid of a triangle is located two thirds the distance from the vertex to the opposite base, the resultant R is at $x_c = \frac{2}{3}L$.

The use of the load diagram concept facilitates the analysis of equilibrium conditions of rigid bodies that are subjected to distributed parallel forces, since the entire applied force system can be reduced to a single force (or couple) whose magnitude and location are easily determined.

EXAMPLE 7.5

Static equilibrium analysis of a body subjected to a distributed load.

Given: A flat, rectangular plate 1 ft wide and 24 ft long submerged in water and supported as shown in Fig. 7.46. (Assume that the flat plate and the supporting bars AB and AC are weightless and that all joints are frictionless pin joints.)

Find: Using a load diagram, determine the magnitudes and types of load in bars AB and AC necessary to maintain static equilibrium.

NOTE: Water pressure acting on a submerged rigid body represents a distributed parallel force system that *always* acts perpendicular to the surface of the body. (The density of water is approximately 62.5 lb/ft³.)

Mathematical Analysis

1. Determine the intensity F of the water pressure at the bottom of the submerged plate:

$$F = \text{(depth of water)(density of water)}$$
$$= (20 \text{ ft})(62.5 \text{ lb/ft}^3)$$
$$= 1250 \text{ lb/ft}^2$$

2. The water pressure at the top of the flat plate is zero.

3. Sketch the load diagram that represents the distributed water pressure over the surface of the flat plate (see Fig. 7.47).

4. Determine the magnitude of the resultant R of the distributed water pressure by calculating the area of the load diagram:

$$R = (\tfrac{1}{2} \text{ ft})(24 \text{ ft})(1250 \text{ lb/ft}^2)$$
$$= 15{,}000 \text{ lb}$$

5. Locate the line of action of R by determining the centroid of the load diagram (see Fig. 7.48).

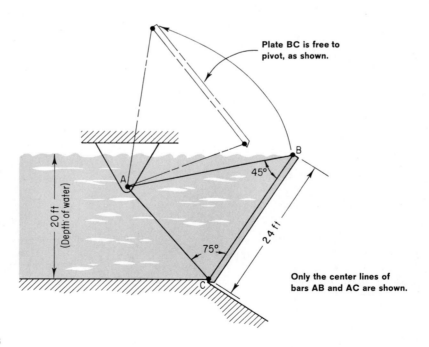

Plate BC is free to pivot, as shown.

Only the center lines of bars AB and AC are shown.

FIGURE 7.46
Space Scale: 1 in. = 10 ft.

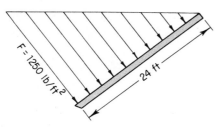

FIGURE 7.47

Load Diagram

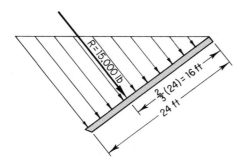

FIGURE 7.48

Load Diagram

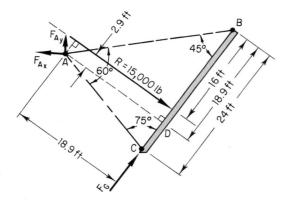

FIGURE 7.49

Free-Body Diagram of Flat Plate and Supporting Bars

6. Draw the free-body diagram of the given flat plate, as shown in Fig. 7.49.

7. Take moments about point A to determine F_G at the bottom of the flat plate. To determine the moment arm for R and F_G relative to point A, apply the law of sines:

$$\frac{BC}{\sin 60°} = \frac{AB}{\sin 75°}$$

$$\therefore \quad AB = \frac{BC \sin 75°}{\sin 60°} = \frac{(24 \text{ ft})(0.966)}{0.866}$$

$$= 26.8 \text{ ft}$$

Now find the *projection* of AB on BC (which gives the distance BD from A to B, measured along BC). (See Fig. 7.49.)

$$BD = AB \cos 45° = (26.8 \text{ ft})(0.707)$$

$$= 18.9 \text{ ft}$$

Therefore, the moment arm for R relative to point A is 18.9 ft − 16 ft = 2.9 ft. Similarly, the perpendicular moment arm from A to force F_G is

$$AD = AB \cos 45° = (26.8 \text{ ft})(0.707)$$

$$= 18.9 \text{ ft}$$

With this information, sum the moments about point A:

$$\sum M_A = (-2.9 \text{ ft})R + (18.9 \text{ ft})F_G = 0$$

$$\therefore \quad F_G = \frac{(2.9 \text{ ft})R}{18.9 \text{ ft}} = \frac{2.9(15,000 \text{ lb})}{18.9}$$

$$= 2310 \text{ lb}$$

8. Draw the free-body diagram (Fig. 7.50) of the flat plate isolated from its supports.

9. To determine the load F_C in bar AC, sum the moments about point B:

$$\sum M_B = (16 \text{ ft})R - (24 \text{ ft})F_C \sin 75° = 0$$

$$\therefore \quad F_C = \frac{(16 \text{ ft})R}{24 \sin 75° \text{ ft}} = \frac{16(15,000 \text{ lb})}{24(0.966)}$$

$$= 10,380 \text{ lb [tension]}$$

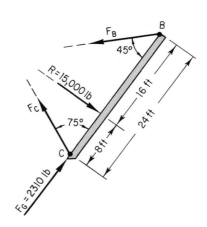

FIGURE 7.50

Free-Body Diagram of Flat Plate

10. To determine the load F_B in bar AB, sum the moments about point C:

$$\sum M_C = (-8 \text{ ft})R + (24 \text{ ft})F_B \sin 45° = 0$$

$$\therefore \; F_B = \frac{(8 \text{ ft})R}{24 \sin 45° \text{ ft}} = \frac{8(15{,}000 \text{ lb})}{24(0.707)}$$

$$= 7080 \text{ lb [tension]}$$

7.9 Center of Gravity of Solid Bodies

The center of gravity (c.g.) of a solid three-dimensional homogeneous body is at the center of the distributed parallel, *noncoplanar* gravity force system acting on the body. The method for determining the centroids of two-dimensional bodies (the concept of distributed parallel,

coplanar forces) can be applied to determine the center of gravity of solid three-dimensional bodies.

Experimentally, the center of gravity of a solid body can be located, as shown in Fig. 7.51, by suspending a solid block by a string, first from one point on the body (A) and then from another (B). The lines AC and BD shown in the figure are the lines through which the resultant R of the gravity forces acting on the body passes in each position of suspension. Thus, the intersection of AC and BD is the c.g. of the block (AC and BC lying in the *central plane ABCD* of the block). (In Fig. 7.51, a symmetrical block was used to illustrate the concept of center of gravity because of its geometric simplicity and also because it emphasized the idea of the central plane $ABCD$.)

As in our discussion of the load diagram, we can assume that the gravity forces acting on a

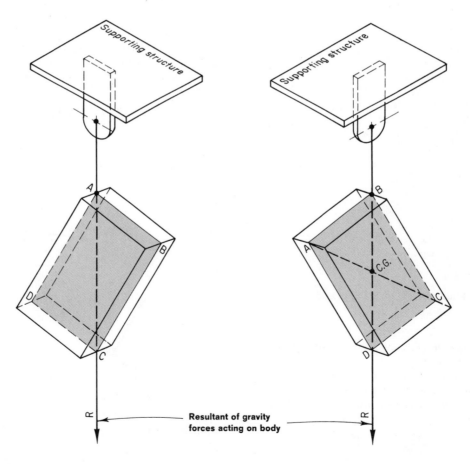

Resultant of gravity forces acting on body

FIGURE 7.51

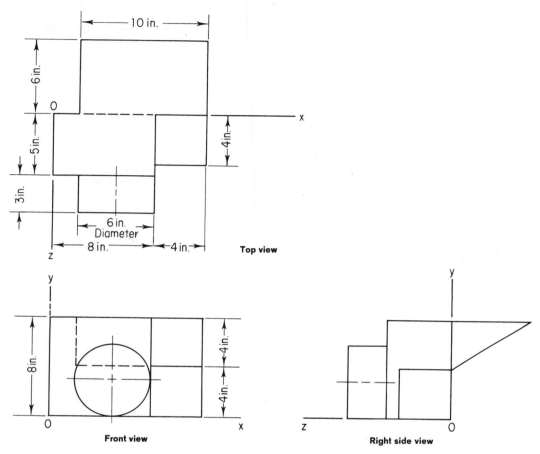

FIGURE 7.52
Space Scale: 1 in. = 5 in.

regular body are concentrated in the central plane of the body. By locating the centroid of the central plane, we can determine the point through which the resultant of the gravity forces passes. In the case of three-dimensional bodies, we make an analogy between the *volume* of the body and the gravity forces acting on it. Thus, in the expressions for centroids,

$$x_c = \frac{\int x\, dA}{\int dA} \quad \text{and} \quad y_c = \frac{\int y\, dA}{\int dA}$$

we substitute infinitesimal units of volume dV for dA and get

$$x_{C.G.} = \frac{\int x\, dV}{\int dV} \quad \text{and} \quad y_{C.G.} = \frac{\int y\, dV}{\int dV}$$

and because we are now dealing with a three-dimensional object, we must also express the third coordinate of the center of gravity by

$$z_{C.G.} = \frac{\int z\, dV}{\int dV}$$

EXAMPLE 7.6 _____

The center of gravity of a composite three-dimensional body.

Given: Three orthographic views (front, top, and right side) and a pictorial representation of a three-dimensional body, as shown in Figs. 7.52 and 7.53. (Dimensioning does not follow standard practice in order to facilitate the solution of this problem.)

Find: The center of gravity (c.g.) of the given body, using graphical and mathematical analysis.

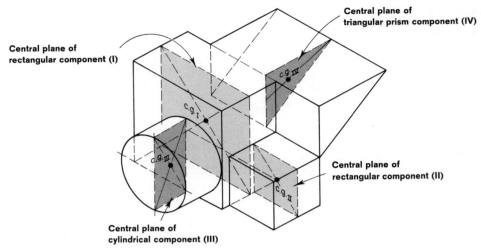

FIGURE 7.53

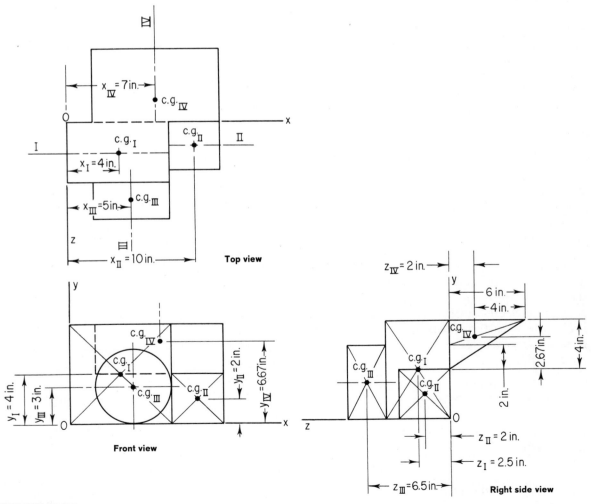

FIGURE 7.54

Mathematical Analysis

1. Relate the given composite body to the x-y axes, as shown in Fig. 7.52.

2. Divide the composite body into its basic geometric components (I, II, III, and IV) consisting of one cylindrical component (III), one triangular prism component (IV), and two right parallelopiped components (I and II). (See Figs. 7.52 and 7.53.)

3. Calculate the volume of each component:

$$V_\text{I} = 8 \text{ in.} \times 8 \text{ in.} \times 5 \text{ in.} = 320 \text{ in.}^3$$

$$V_\text{II} = 4 \text{ in.} \times 4 \text{ in.} \times 4 \text{ in.} = 64 \text{ in.}^3$$

$$V_\text{III} = \pi r^2 h = \pi(3 \text{ in.})^2(3 \text{ in.}) = 85 \text{ in.}^3$$

$$V_\text{IV} = \tfrac{1}{2}bhR = \tfrac{1}{2}(6 \text{ in.})(4 \text{ in.})(10 \text{ in.}) = 120 \text{ in.}^3$$

$$V_\text{total} = 589 \text{ in.}^3$$

4. From the geometry of the individual component volumes and from the symmetry of the figures, locate the central planes (and their centroids relative to the x-y-z axes) of the components (see Figs. 7.53 and 7.54).

$x_\text{I} = 4 \text{ in.}, \quad x_\text{II} = 10 \text{ in.}, \quad x_\text{III} = 5 \text{ in.}, \quad x_\text{IV} = 7 \text{ in.}$

$y_\text{I} = 4 \text{ in.}, \quad y_\text{II} = 2 \text{ in.}, \quad y_\text{III} = 3 \text{ in.}, \quad y_\text{IV} = 6.67 \text{ in.}$

$z_\text{I} = 2.5 \text{ in.}, \quad z_\text{II} = 2 \text{ in.}, \quad z_\text{III} = 6.5 \text{ in.}, \quad z_\text{IV} = 2 \text{ in.}$

5. Determine $x_\text{C.G.}$, $y_\text{C.G.}$, and $z_\text{C.G.}$ of the given body by taking moments of the respective component volumes relative to the x-y-z axes.

$$x_\text{C.G.} = \frac{\sum x\,\Delta V}{\sum \Delta V}$$

$$= \frac{x_\text{I}V_\text{I} + x_\text{II}V_\text{II} + x_\text{III}V_\text{III} + x_\text{IV}V_\text{IV}}{V_\text{total}}$$

$$= \frac{4(320) + 10(64) + 5(85) + 7(120)}{589}$$

$$= \frac{3185 \text{ in.}^4}{589 \text{ in.}^3} = 5.4 \text{ in.}$$

$$y_\text{C.G.} = \frac{\sum y\,\Delta V}{\sum \Delta V}$$

$$= \frac{y_\text{I}V_\text{I} + y_\text{II}V_\text{II} + y_\text{III}V_\text{III} + y_\text{IV}V_\text{IV}}{V_\text{total}}$$

$$= \frac{4(320) + 2(64) + 3(85) + 6.67(120)}{589}$$

$$= \frac{2463 \text{ in.}^4}{589 \text{ in.}^3} = 4.17 \text{ in.}$$

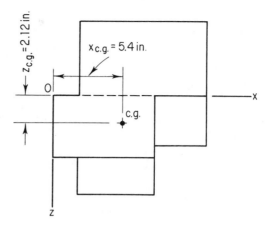

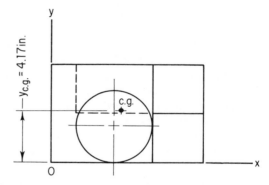

FIGURE 7.55

$$z_\text{C.G.} = \frac{\sum z\,\Delta V}{\sum \Delta V}$$

$$= \frac{z_\text{I}V_\text{I} + z_\text{II}V_\text{II} + z_\text{III}V_\text{III} + z_\text{IV}V_\text{IV}}{V_\text{total}}$$

$$= \frac{2.5(320) + 2(64) + 6.5(85) - 2(120)}{589}$$

$$= \frac{1241 \text{ in.}^4}{589 \text{ in.}^3}$$

$$= 2.12 \text{ in.}$$

[NOTE: For the product $z_\text{IV}V_\text{IV}$, the sign is negative.] In Fig. 7.55 is shown the location of the center of gravity of the given body.

7.10 Suspended Cables

Suspended cables—such as the cables used in suspension bridges—usually carry distributed loads. The loading of such cables includes the

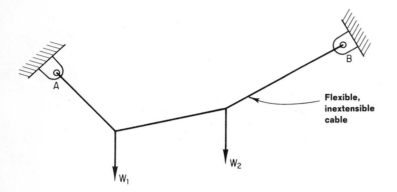

FIGURE 7.56

weight of the cable itself (uniformly distributed along its entire length) and the vertical load (uniformly distributed along the *horizontal*) transmitted to the cables by the hangers that support the roadway structure. This section deals with some general principles of static equilibrium of suspended cables assumed to be weightless, perfectly flexible, and inextensible. (Such idealized cables have the property of being able to carry tension loads *only*.) Also developed in this section are some general equations for these cable conditions, and illustrated is a cable subjected to vertical loading uniformly distributed along the horizontal direction.[2]

Let us consider the idealized weightless, perfectly flexible, and inextensible cable suspended from two points and loaded as shown in Fig. 7.56. By considering the static equilibrium conditions of a segment of this cable, we can determine an expression which will define the tension at any point in the cable.

In Fig. 7.57 is shown a free-body diagram of a segment of the given cable from some point O to any other point K to the right on the cable. The shape of the cable is fixed in its *equilibrium shape* and may now be treated as a rigid body. The *x-y* axes in Fig. 7.57 have been placed so that the origin coincides with point O. The tension in the cable at point O is represented by its horizontal and vertical components T_H and T_V, respectively.

The following conditions must be satisfied if the segment is to be in static equilibrium:

----

[2] Detailed developments of other types of cable loading may be found in a number of the textbooks listed in the bibliography at the end of this book.

$$\sum F_x = 0$$

$$\therefore \ T_K \cos \theta - T_H = 0$$

$$\therefore \ T_H = T_K \cos \theta$$

and

$$\sum F_y = 0$$

$$\therefore \ T_K \sin \theta + T_V - W_1 - W_2 = 0$$

$$\therefore \ T_K \sin \theta = W_1 + W_2 - T_V$$

The two preceding equations cannot be solved, since there are *four* unknowns (T_H, T_V, T_K, and θ) and only two equations. Consideration of moment equilibrium conditions will not improve the situation, since *three* equations ($\sum F_x = 0$, $\sum F_y = 0$, and $\sum M_O = 0$) cannot be solved for *four* unknowns. Therefore, we must obtain further information by considering the equilibrium of a *part* of the given system and the geometry of that part.

Imagine a cable that carries external vertical loads in a way that places a portion of the cable in a horizontal position, as shown in Fig. 7.58. If point O is located on the horizontal segment of the cable, then there will be *no* vertical component of the cable tension acting at that point. (In other words, at point O the tension in the cable acts in a horizontal direction only.)

In Fig. 7.59 is shown a free-body diagram of a segment of this cable from point O to any other point K to the right on the cable. Considering the horizontal static equilibrium conditions of this segment, we can write

$$\sum F_x = 0$$

$$\therefore \ T_H = T_K \cos \theta$$

From this (and the horizontal summation performed for the cable segment in Fig. 7.57) we see that the *horizontal* component of the tension at any point on the cable has a *constant* magnitude.

Considering the vertical static equilibrium conditions of the cable segment in Fig. 7.59, we can write

$$\sum F_y = 0$$

$$\therefore \ T_K \sin \theta = W_1 + W_2$$

From this equation, we derive the following significant fact: the *vertical* component of the tension at any point in a cable is equal to the sum of the external loads that act upon the cable

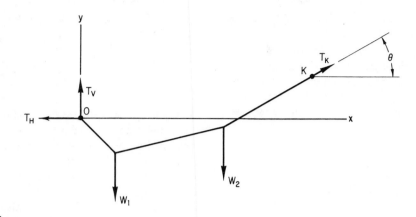

FIGURE 7.57

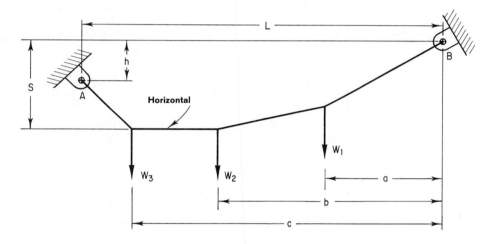

FIGURE 7.58

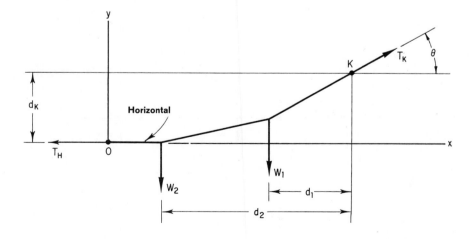

FIGURE 7.59

between that point and the point that is on the *horizontal* portion of the cable.

Considering the moment equation for equilibrium of the cable segment, we can assume that point K is located at point B, which is at the right end of the cable (see Fig. 7.58). Using $d_1 = a$, $d_2 = b$, and $d_K = s$ (see Figs. 7.58 and 7.59), we can write

$$\sum M_B = 0$$

$$\therefore \ T_H s = W_1 a + W_2 b$$

For this cable segment, there are only *three* unknowns (T_H, T_K, and θ) and *three* independent equations involving these unknowns. We can therefore find these unknowns.

The angle θ that results from any external vertical loading may be determined by reducing the total given force system (which is set up as a coplanar, nonconcurrent system) to a coplanar, concurrent force system (see Fig. 7.60).

We can reduce a system of parallel, external forces, such as W_1 and W_2, to a single resultant R, which will be parallel to the given external forces. The line of action of R can be determined by considering the moments of W_1 and W_2 about an assumed point. Referring to Fig. 7.60, let d_T be the required moment arm for R, and using the origin B as a moment center, we can write

$$W_1 a + W_2 b = R d_T$$

$$\therefore \ d_T = \frac{W_1 a + W_2 b}{R}$$

$$= \frac{W_1 a + W_2 b}{W_1 + W_2}$$

After replacing the external loads W_1 and W_2 by their resultant R, we see that the entire force system involves *three forces* (T_H, T_B, and R). Three forces, as we know, can be in equilibrium only if they are *concurrent*. Since T_H and T_B become concurrent at point P (see Fig. 7.60), the line of action of R must also pass through point P. The distance d_T in Fig. 7.60, which locates point P, is the same distance as the moment arm d_T of the force R.

The angle θ can now be determined from the right-triangle relationship (which is evident from Fig. 7.60), as follows:

$$\tan \theta = \frac{S}{d_T} = \frac{S}{\dfrac{W_1 a + W_2 b}{W_1 + W_2}}$$

$$= \frac{S(W_1 + W_2)}{W_1 a + W_2 b}$$

or

$$\theta = \tan^{-1} \left[\frac{S(W_1 + W_2)}{W_1 a + W_2 b} \right]$$

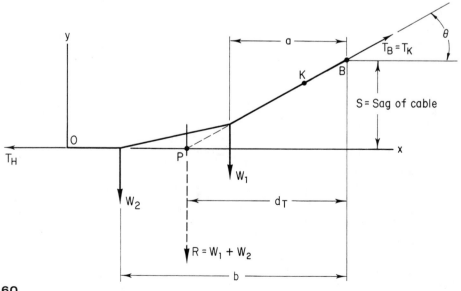

FIGURE 7.60

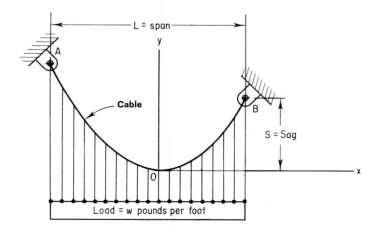

FIGURE 7.61

If the vertical loading is distributed uniformly along the horizontal (W pounds per horizontal foot), the equilibrium shape of the cable will be a definite *curve*. In Fig. 7.61 is shown a suspended cable subjected to such a uniformly distributed load. (Assume that the load is applied continuously to the cable by an infinite number of weightless hangers.)

Consider a segment of the cable starting from its lowest point O to an assumed point K to the right of O (see Fig. 7.62). For static equilibrium analysis, we consider the cable to be "frozen" into the shape it has assumed under the applied load. Draw a free-body diagram of the segment OK (see Fig. 7.63). Construct the vector diagram, indicating equilibrium conditions for the given segment (see Fig. 7.64).

From the vector diagram, we see that

$$T_K{}^2 = R^2 + T_H{}^2$$

$$\therefore T_K = \sqrt{R^2 + T_H{}^2}$$

Also from this diagram, we see that

$$\tan \theta = \frac{R}{T_H}$$

Similarly, $T_H = T_K \cos \theta$, which is constant for a given uniformly distributed loading (and which

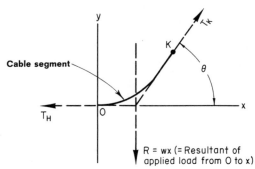

FIGURE 7.63

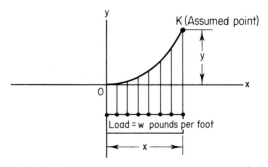

FIGURE 7.62

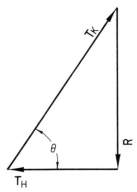

FIGURE 7.64
Vector Diagram

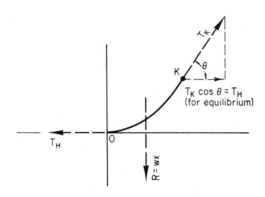

FIGURE 7.65

also agrees with one of the general equations). (See Fig. 7.65.)

To determine the shape of the curve the cable takes under the given loading, it is necessary to derive an expression that will define the *slope* of the curve at any point. (The slope of the curve is defined as the *tangent* to the curve at any point.) (See Fig. 7.66.)

We see from Fig. 7.66 that the tangent (relative to the *x* axis) at point *K* is

$$\frac{dy}{dx} = \tan \theta$$

From the vector diagram shown in Fig. 7.64, we see that

$$\tan \theta = \frac{R}{T_H}$$

$$\therefore \frac{dy}{dx} = \frac{R}{T_H}$$

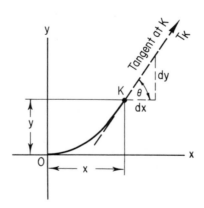

FIGURE 7.66

EXAMPLE 7.7

The suspended cable loaded with a uniform load.

Given: A weightless, perfectly flexible, and inextensible cable supported between two supports *A* and *B*. The span between the supports is $L = 150$ ft, the sag of the cable = 30 ft, and the support *B* is 90 ft below support *A*. (See Fig. 7.67.) The applied load is 800 lb per horizontal foot.

Find: The tension in the cable at its lowest point and at the supports *A* and *B*.

Mathematical Analysis

1. Since the loading applied to the cable is a uniform load, the cable curve takes the shape of a parabola whose equation is $y = wx^2/2T_H$. Place the origin of the *x-y* axes at the lowest point on the cable curve. The *y* axis is therefore located a distance *l* from support *B* and a distance 150 ft − *l* from support *A*. (See Fig. 7.68.)

Since $R = wx$ (see Figs. 7.62 and 7.63), we can substitute and write

$$\frac{dy}{dx} = \frac{wx}{T_H}$$

which defines the slope of the given cable curve at any point. To determine the equation of this curve, we must rewrite the expression, as follows

$$dy = \frac{wx \, dx}{T_H}$$

and integrate both sides:

$$\int_0^y dy = \int_0^x \frac{wx \, dx}{T_H}$$

$$\therefore y = \frac{wx^2}{2T_H} + C_1$$

To determine the value of the constant of integration C_1, we note that the origin of the *x-y* axes is located at the lowest point on the cable curve. Therefore, at origin *O*, when $x = 0$ then $y = 0$. This is a known "boundary condition" that can be substituted in the equation for *y*, and from which we determine that $C_1 = 0$. Therefore, the equation for the cable curve is

$$y = \frac{wx^2}{2T_H}$$

This is the equation of a *parabola* whose axis is vertical and whose parameter is $w/2T_H$.

2. Since points *A* and *B* are on the parabolic curve of

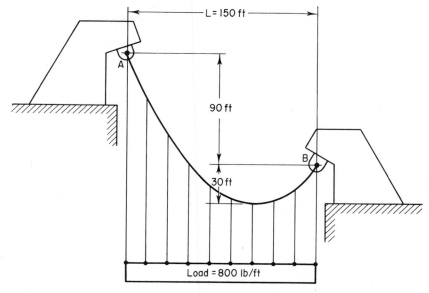

FIGURE 7.67

the cable, their coordinates relative to the x-y axes are defined as (x_1, y_1) and (x_2, y_2), respectively (see Fig. 7.68), where $x_1 = l$, $y_1 = 30$ ft, $x_2 = (150$ ft $- l)$, and $y_2 = 120$ ft. Substitute these values in the equation for the parabola:

$$y_1 = \frac{wx_1{}^2}{2T_H}$$

$$\therefore \ 30 = \frac{800l^2}{2T_H}$$

from which

$$3T_H = 40l^2$$

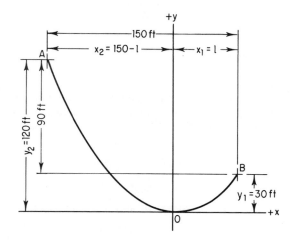

FIGURE 7.68

Similarly,

$$y_2 = \frac{wx_2{}^2}{2T_H}$$

$$\therefore \ 120 = \frac{800(150 - l)^2}{2T_H}$$

from which

$$3T_H = 10(150 - l)^2$$

3. This gives two equations that can be solved simultaneously for T_H and l:

$$3T_H = 40l^2$$

$$-3T_H = -10(150 - l)^2$$

$$\overline{ 0 = 40l^2 - 10(22{,}500 - 300l + l^2)}$$

Transpose and rearrange terms:

$$30l^2 + 3000l - 225{,}000 = 0$$

Divide both sides of this equation by 30:

$$l^2 + 100l - 7500 = 0$$

This is a quadratic equation that can be solved for l by the quadratic formula:

$$l = \frac{-b \pm \sqrt{b^2 - 4ac}}{2a}$$

$$= \frac{-100 \pm \sqrt{100^2 - 4(1)(-7500)}}{2(1)}$$

$$l = 50 \text{ ft}$$

4. Substitute $l = 50$ ft in $3T_H = 40l^2$:

$$3T_H = 40(50)^2$$

$$\therefore \ T_H = \frac{40(50)^2}{3}$$

$$= 33,333 \ \text{lb}$$

5. Draw the free-body diagram of the cable curve from origin O to support B (see Fig. 7.69). From this diagram, draw the vector diagram that indicates the static equilibrium conditions for segment OB (see Fig. 7.70).

6. Using the vector diagram, solve for T_B. From Fig. 7.70,

$$T_B^2 = R_{OB}^2 + T_H^2$$

$$\therefore \ T_B = \sqrt{R_{OB}^2 + T_H^2}$$

Substitute:

$$T_B = \sqrt{40,000^2 + 33,333^2}$$

$$= 52,100 \ \text{lb}$$

7. Draw the free-body diagram of the segment of the cable curve from origin O to support A (see Fig.

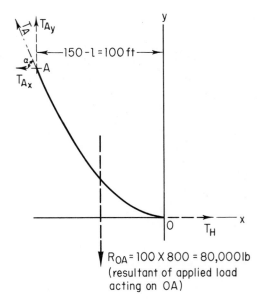

FIGURE 7.71

$R_{OA} = 100 \times 800 = 80,000$ lb
(resultant of applied load acting on OA)

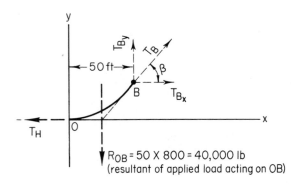

FIGURE 7.69

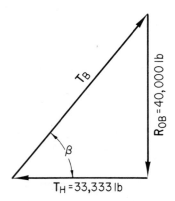

FIGURE 7.70
Vector Diagram

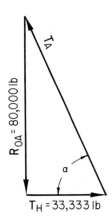

FIGURE 7.72
Vector Diagram

7.71). From this diagram, draw the vector diagram that indicates the static equilibrium conditions for segment OA (see Fig. 7.72).

8. From Fig. 7.72,

$$T_A^2 = R_{OA}^2 + T_H^2$$

$$\therefore \ T_A = \sqrt{R_{OA}^2 + T_H^2}$$

Substitute $R_{OA} = 80,000$ lb and $T_H = 33,333$ lb:

$$T_A = \sqrt{80,000^2 + 33,333^2}$$

$$= 86,800 \ \text{lb}$$

7.1 **Given:** A triangular cross section with a square cutout, as shown in Fig. 7.73.

Find: The location of the centroid of the given cross section relative to the x axis.
A. Use graphical analysis.
B. Use mathematical analysis.

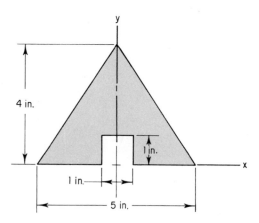

FIGURE 7.73

7.2 **Giver.:** An irregular cross section, as shown in Fig. 7.74.

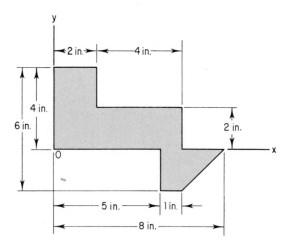

FIGURE 7.74

Find: The location of the centroid of the given cross section relative to the x and y axes.
A. Use mathematical analysis.
B. Use graphical analysis.

7.3 **Given:** A circular cross section with an irregular cutout, as shown in Fig. 7.75.

Find: The location of the centroid of the given circular cross section relative to the x and y axes.
A. Use mathematical analysis.
B. Use graphical analysis.

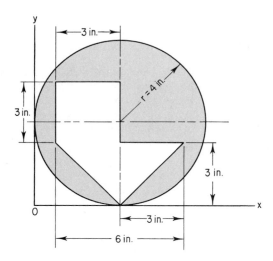

FIGURE 7.75

7.4 **Given:** A hinged sluice gate acted upon by 10 ft of water, as shown in Fig. 7.76. Assume the gate to be weightless and the hinge to be frictionless. Density of water $= 62.5$ lb/ft³.

Find: The minimum force P required to keep the sluice gate closed.
A. Use mathematical analysis.
B. Use graphical analysis.

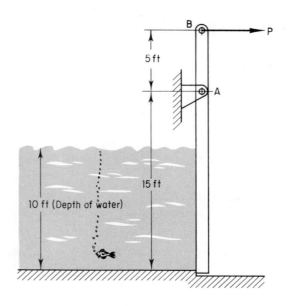

FIGURE 7.76

7.5 **Given:** A half-cycle of the sine wave $y = A \sin x$, as shown in Fig. 7.77.

Find: The centroid of the area enclosed by the sine wave and the x axis relative to the given x-y axes.

Ans. $x_c = \pi/2$, $y_c = \pi A/8$.

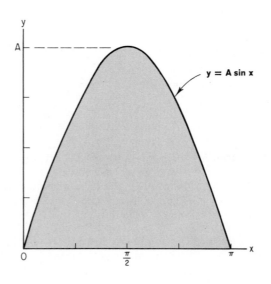

FIGURE 7.77

7.6 **Given:** A quarter-cycle of a cosine wave $y = \cos x$, as shown in Fig. 7.78.

Find: The centroid of the shaded area with respect to the x-y axes.

Ans. $x_c = [2\pi/4(\pi - 2)] - 1$,
$y_c = \pi A/8(\pi/2 - 1)$.

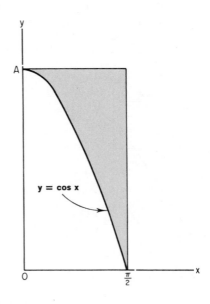

FIGURE 7.78

7.7 **Given:** A triangle of metal rods of the same cross section and density, as shown in Fig. 7.79.

Find: The centroid of the triangle with respect to point A, first using graphical analysis and then by mathematical analysis.

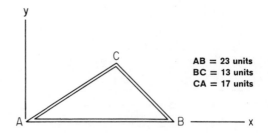

AB = 23 units
BC = 13 units
CA = 17 units

FIGURE 7.79

7.8 **Given:** The area of a *surface of revolution* can be determined if the length of the generating element is known and if the distance traveled by the centroid of the generating element is also known. Shown in Fig. 7.80 is a generating element *ABCDE*.

Find: The surface area that results when element *ABCDE* is rotated through an angle of 360° about an axis passing through points *A* and *E*.

Ans. 53.6 ft².

7.9 **Given:** Earth fill has been placed over a tunnel of semicircular cross section, as shown in Fig. 7.81. At the y axis, the distributed load of the fill has its maximum value $W_{max} = 1000$ lb/ft.

Find: The magnitude and location (relative to the y axis) of the resultant force exerted by the fill. (Do not use calculus to solve this problem.)

Ans. Resultant = 5945 lb, x_c = 4.36 ft.

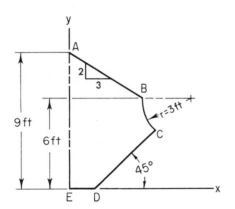

FIGURE 7.80

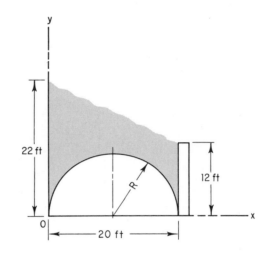

FIGURE 7.81

7.10 **Given:** A steel wire having a diameter of 0.10 in. and a density of 0.283 lb/in.³ supported over two frictionless pulleys of equal diameter and loaded as shown in Fig. 7.82. Assume the supports for the sagging portion of the wire to be 100 ft apart. If a wire (or cable) is subjected to sufficient tension, its sag will be so small that its weight could be assumed to be uniformly distributed along its length.

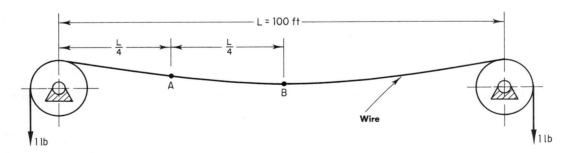

FIGURE 7.82

Find: The maximum slope angle attained by the wire and the amount of sag at the points A and B indicated in Fig. 7.82.

Ans. Maximum slope angle $= 0°\ 46'$, sag at $A = 3.0$ in., sag at $B = 4.0$ in.

7.11 Given: A one-piece homogeneous metal aircraft bracket, as shown in Fig. 7.83.

Find: Using mathematical analysis, determine the location of the center of gravity of the given bracket relative to the x, y, and z axes. (HINT: Calculate the volume of each basic geometric shape that comprises the bracket, and handle these volumes as vectors.)

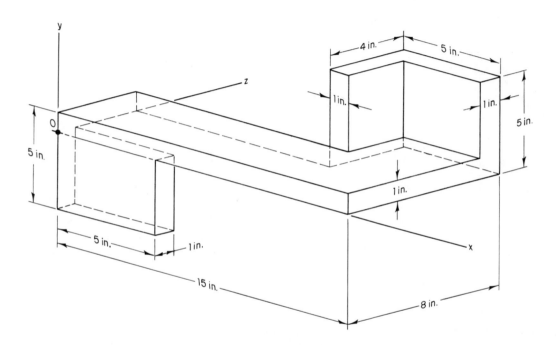

FIGURE 7.83

7.12 Given: The bracket shown in Fig. 7.83 and described in Prob. 7.11.

Find: Using graphical analysis, determine the location of the center of gravity of the bracket relative to the x, y, and z axes.

7.13 Given: A rectangular box, supported by three legs, containing a volume of dry sand piled in one corner, as shown in Fig. 7.84.

Find: If the sand weighs 100 lb/ft³, determine the magnitude of the force that each supporting leg must exert to hold the box in equilibrium.

Ans. $F_A = 25$ lb, $F_B = 62.5$ lb, $F_C = 12.5$ lb.

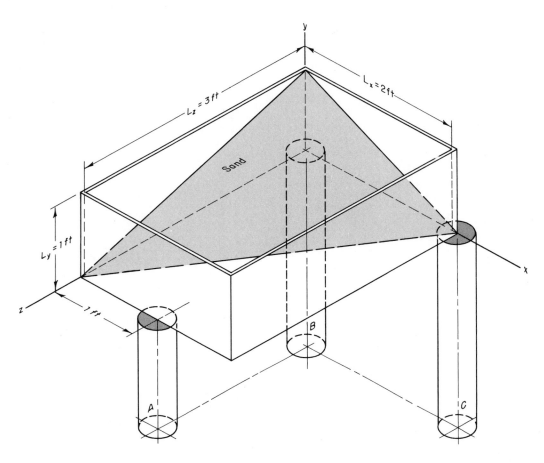

FIGURE 7.84

7.14 Given: The box shown in Fig. 7.84 and described in Prob. 7.13.

  Find: If the lengths L_x and L_z of the rectangular box can have any values, would it be possible for the sand, when piled in the corner as shown, to overturn the box?

7.15 Given: A weightless, perfectly flexible cable supporting a uniformly distributed horizontal load, as shown in Fig. 7.85.

  Find: Using only geometric relationships (no calculus), obtain the equation for the curve assumed by the given cable.

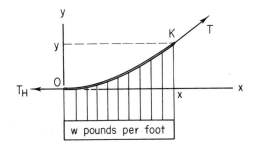

FIGURE 7.85

Part Two

INTRODUCTION TO STRENGTH OF MATERIALS

Eight

ENGINEERING MATERIALS AND THEIR PROPERTIES

8.1 Introduction

Man has always been interested in the materials from which he makes his tools and structures. The development from the earliest primitive man to his modern counterpart has been marked by the use of new materials and has been identified by the materials used. Thus, we refer to the Stone Age, the Bronze Age, and the Iron Age. Civilizations were distinguished both by their architecture and engineering and by the kinds of materials used for tools and artifacts.

In 12 A.D., Vitruvius, a Roman architect, described the use of building materials in a way that resembles a modern materials specification. Much like modern waterfront construction, early Roman harbor structures were built on timber piles driven into the ocean bottom. The life of extensive harbor installations depended upon the strength and durability of their foundations. Vitruvius, in an effort to improve the strength and life of these structures, organized the data—gained from successes and failures—on suitable pile timber. Today, almost two thousand years later, engineers designing harbor and river structures write timber-pile specifications in much the same manner.

Not until the Italian Renaissance in the fifteenth and sixteenth centuries, however, did men of science give serious attention to the mechanical properties of engineering materials. Galileo prepared one of the earliest known discussions on the strength of beams and aroused interest in what was then the new field of strength of materials. Robert Hooke, by his discovery of the relationship between force and the change of shape of a material, in 1678, made a great stride forward in the understanding of material behavior and enabled others to make rapid progress. Bernoulli's work on beams and Euler's study of beams and columns were important milestones. Coulomb, better known for his work in electricity, did significant work in studying beam stresses and developing torsion theory. In 1807, the English physicist Thomas Young put Hooke's law into quantitative form and set the cornerstone of modern engineering design. Navier (who studied the bending of beams) and Coulomb are credited with organizing the science of strength of materials as we know it today.

8.2 Strength of Materials Defined

A machine or a structure is made up of parts or bodies consisting of small particles, or molecules, and is designed to resist or support external forces. When an external load or force is applied to a body, two things happen: (1) changes in the shape of the body, called *deformations*, are caused, and (2) internal forces called *stresses* are set up between the molecules of the body and resist the changes in shape.

Strength of materials is the branch of mechanics that deals with the *stresses within a body* caused by external forces, the *changes of shape and size* caused by external forces, and the *physical properties* of the material of a body that enable it to resist the action of external forces. In the first part of this book, we have been concerned only with *external* forces and the equilibrium between them. In this part, we will examine the relationships between *externally applied forces and internally induced stresses* in simple machine parts and structural members.

Design and analysis

A knowledge of strength of materials is essential to the engineer, the architect, and the technician in the solution of two kinds of problems: design and analysis. Problems in physical *design* deal with the determination of the material, the size, and the shape of a body required to effectively and economically resist the action of external forces. In *analysis*, on the other hand, we begin with assumed, estimated, or known loading, size, shape, and material and find the internal resisting forces or stresses in the component parts. From this information, we can decide whether the size of the member is adequate to carry the required load. If material, size, and shape are fixed, analysis will reveal the maximum load that the part can safely carry.

But the engineer, the architect, and the technician, in discharging their responsibilities, need to know more than basic design requirements. To make proper and efficient use of materials, they must know the mechanical and physical properties of the engineering materials with which they work: wood, ferrous and nonferrous metals, and such inert materials as stone and concrete.

8.3 Applications

Modern engineering is challenged by the requirements for new materials with special properties. Solid fuels for nuclear reactors and thick shielding were problems of the past decade. The A-11 supersonic aircraft was made possible by the use of titanium as a skin material that is able to withstand enormous stress and heat in flight. Jet engines and high-speed turbines have spurred the search for rotor materials that can be subjected to tremendous gas temperatures and rotational speeds without losing their shape or strength. Space flight created the practical problem of developing a material for heat shielding that would resist the heat generated by friction on the re-entry of a space vehicle into the earth's atmosphere.

Less spectacular but no less demanding are the material-strength problems yet to be solved to prevent boiler explosions, water-main breaks, machine destruction, or collapse of a building or a bridge. Material failures, while not the sole cause of structural catastrophes, are of great concern to physicists, metallurgists, and engineers. Together, these specialists are working to obtain the *theoretical* strengths of many engineering materials—strengths that are vastly larger than the *actual* strengths.

Why do the actual strengths of various materials fall far short of the theoretical strengths? Why is a single strand of spider web stronger than steel of the same size? Metallurgist John J. Gilman, in an article in *Scientific American* (February 1960), claims that all materials contain minute cracks that open up under stress. He states that a drinking glass made of *ideal* glass only $\frac{1}{64}$ in. thick, lying on its side, could support the weight of a 200-lb man. For *ordinary* glass to carry the same load, it must be $\frac{1}{4}$ in. thick.

The principles of strength of materials are widely applied in the fields of *structural engineering* and *machine design*. The first is concerned with such matters as the strength of structures and structural members: buildings and bridges and their parts—beams, columns, bars, joints, plates, shells, bolts, and rivets. In machine design, some of the problems investigated are stresses in flywheels, chains, connecting rods, pistons, piping, pressure vessels, rotating machine elements, fittings, and bars of intricate shapes, as well as the effect of nonuniform heating and fatigue of metals.

8.4 Properties of Materials

The term *properties* (of a material), as used in this book, refers to the factors that indicate desirable or undesirable characteristics of the material. Many types of characteristics are exhibited by materials. Electrical, magnetic, thermal, acoustical, and optical properties are indicated by a material under the action of an electrical potential, a magnetic field, heat, sound, and light, respectively. Mechanical properties are characteristics exhibited by a material subjected to loads or forces, and they are thus the main concern to structural engineers and machine designers.

In a specific problem, the designer determines the ideal properties required and compares them with the properties of available materials. He then determines the properties and calculates the sizes of the structural or machine members to produce the appropriate strength requirements. In this way, he also finds an economical solution by proportioning members for a minimum amount of material.

Mechanical properties of materials are generally determined by testing and experimentation. Methods for testing have been developed and standardized over many years. Specifications for testing and specifications for materials have been prepared by a number of technical societies, including the American Society for Testing Materials (ASTM). Published *ASTM Standards* are available for a vast number of engineering materials. This literature is available to technicians, engineers, architects, and students. Regardless of your field of specialization, you should be familiar with the wide range of information and service available from ASTM. One useful reference is *Selected*

FIGURE 8.2

Olsen electro-mechanical universal testing machine. This model can apply tensile, compressive, or bending loads up to 10,000 lb.

ASTM Engineering Materials Standards for Use in College Curricula.

Several different laboratory tests are used to determine the numerical values of mechanical properties. Standard test methods and procedures minimize the variation in test results for a given material by such factors as the way the testing equipment is set up, the size and shape of the sample, and the speed of loading.

The *tensile test* is of special importance in determining the mechanical properties of materials. It tests the ability of a material to resist being pulled apart. In the tensile test of a metal, a standard size round bar (Fig. 8.1) is placed in the grips of a universal testing machine, such as that shown in Figs. 8.2 and 8.3. The universal testing

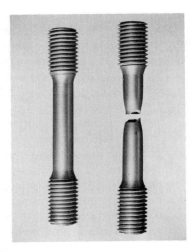

FIGURE 8.1

Left: Standard tension sample before test. *Right:* After rupture.

FIGURE 8.3

Southwark universal testing machine. 3,000,000 lb capacity.

machine differs from a single-purpose machine in its ability to perform a number of different tests: tensile, compressive, and bending. Some universal machines are capable of applying loads in excess of one million pounds. Much college laboratory work is done with 60,000-lb and 120,000-lb testers.

After the sample has been securely gripped by the testing machine, a device for measuring the change in the length of the sample is fastened to it. One device, which measures the change of length by mechanical or electrical means, is called an *extensometer* (see Fig. 8.4). Changes

in the sample's length caused by the application of load are read on a dial gage. In recent years, *electric resistance strain gages* have become popular. This gage operates on the principle that the electrical resistance of wire changes when its diameter and length change. Electric strain gages are firmly cemented to the sample and act as if they were part of the sample. These gages are connected electrically to a remote electronic indicator that uses small changes in electrical resistance to show the corresponding strain.

When the strain gage is in place, the testing machine slowly applies to the specimen a load or pulling force of known value shown on the dial. This tensile load is gradually increased until the specimen breaks in two, as shown in Fig. 8.1. During the test, measurements of the load and the corresponding change in length or *elongation* of the sample are made. From these data a *stress-strain diagram* is plotted. On the y axis of the graph is plotted the *stress*, which is obtained by dividing the applied load by the cross-sectional area of the sample. On the x axis of the graph is plotted the *strain*, or change in each linear inch of length of the sample. A typical stress-strain curve for a mild steel in tension is shown in Fig. 8.5.

Analysis of this graph reveals several important properties of materials. Comparison of the stress-strain curves for several different materials indicates the differences in some of their mechanical properties.

Let us examine the stress-strain diagram in Fig. 8.5. The curve begins slightly above the origin, indicating that the sample is subjected to a small initial load; this assures us that the sample is gripped firmly in the universal tester and that the extensometer is in position to indicate error-free elongations. From this point, the graph rises in a straight line until it reaches the point at which it curves to the right and flattens out. The straight-line section shows a proportional relationship between stress and strain. That is, stress is proportional to strain, and an increase or decrease in stress produces a corresponding increase or decrease in strain. When the load and the stress are reduced to zero, the strain also becomes zero, indicating that the sample has returned to its original length. Stresses within the straight-line region of the curve for this material are said to be within the *elastic range*.

Just beyond the straight-line part is the curved, horizontal part of the stress-strain diagram. In this region, the strain increases at a faster rate than in the elastic range. The sample stretches with little or no increase in load. When the load (and stress) is reduced, the strain does not return to zero; the material does not return to its original length. The material does not behave as it did in the elastic range and is therefore considered to be in the *inelastic* or *plastic region*.

With continued increase in load and stress, the curve rises to a maximum point, called the *ultimate stress* or *ultimate strength*, and then drops off under additional loading to a point at which the sample is broken. Standard practice requires the values of stress obtained during the test to be computed from the original cross-sectional area of the specimen. The diameter of the sample does, of course, decrease slightly as the load is increased. This is called *necking-down* (see Fig. 8.1).

From the stress-strain curve, it is evident that certain materials may have both an elastic range and a plastic range, while others may behave inelastically. From Fig. 8.6, we see that brass has both an elastic and a plastic range, whereas cast iron exhibits only plastic behavior. From the slope, the curvature, the area under the stress-strain curve, and certain key points, it is possible to determine

FIGURE 8.4

Left: Olsen mechanical adjustable extensometer for 2-in. gage length. *Right:* Olsen electrical adjustable extensometer. An electric signal activates a stress-strain recorder and can produce a complete stress-strain diagram.

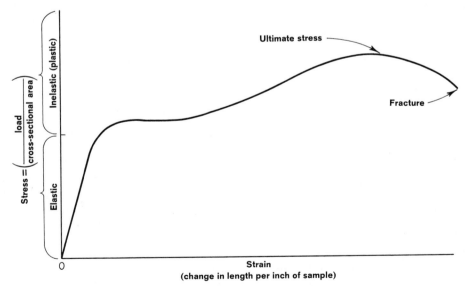

FIGURE 8.5

Stress-strain diagram for a mild steel in tension.

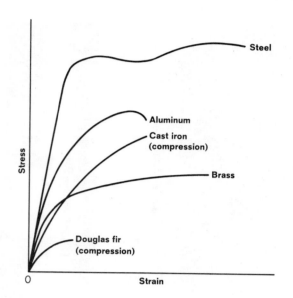

FIGURE 8.6

Stress-strain diagram for typical specimens of steel, aluminum, cast-iron, brass, and wood.

such mechanical properties as strength, stiffness, elasticity, ductility, and toughness.

8.5 Mechanical Properties

Since the study of strength of materials is fundamentally concerned with the properties of materials that are significant under the application of external loading, it is necessary that mechanical properties be examined in more detail.

Mechanical properties include the following:

Strength	Toughness
Stiffness	Ductility
Elasticity	Malleability
Creep	Hardness
Endurance limit	Plasticity
Resilience	Machinability

The properties listed on the left represent measures of *resistance* to the breaking of a material under various types of loading. Those listed on the right are related to the ease with which we can cut or remove materials during various manufacturing processes used to change the size or shape of engineering materials, particularly metals.

Strength

The strength of a material is its load-carrying capacity, or its ability to resist force. Since external forces create internal resisting forces, or stresses, strength can also be defined as the ability to resist stress. Its measure is generally considered the maximum stress that occurs on the stress-strain diagram for the material. This measure is called *ultimate stress*, the largest force *per unit* of cross-sectional *area* that the material can withstand before the sample breaks. It is found by dividing the maximum load that a sample can withstand by its original cross-sectional area. Ultimate stress is sometimes called *ultimate strength* or even simply *strength*.

Stiffness

Stiffness is the property of a material that enables it to resist deformation, or change of shape. The measure of stiffness is called the *modulus of elasticity*. It is obtained by dividing the change in stress by the corresponding change in strain, and is actually the slope of the straight-line part of the stress-strain diagram. If equal-sized specimens of steel and aluminum are subjected to the same pull, the aluminum specimen becomes longer than the steel. The elongation and therefore the strain of the aluminum will be larger than that of the steel. From this we conclude that steel is stiffer than aluminum.

Stiffness is desirable when deformation must be kept to a minimum, as in precision machine tools, heavy machinery containing rollers for production of sheet metal or paper, and such structural members as beams and columns.

Elasticity

When subjected to loads, all materials change in size and shape. The property of a body that enables it to return to its original size and shape after the load is removed is called *elasticity*. If the body recovers its original shape completely, it is said to be *perfectly elastic*. A material subjected to stress above a certain value will not return to its original dimensions when the load is removed. This stress is called the *elastic limit* and occurs just before the stress-strain diagram becomes curved.

A measure of the elasticity of a material is the strain at the elastic limit. In all structures and machine parts subjected to continuously changing loads, this property of elasticity is extremely important.

The opposite quality to elasticity is called *plasticity*. A perfectly plastic material, unlike a perfectly elastic one, will not return to its original dimensions when the external load is removed. Such materials are not suitable for structural purposes. Elastic materials, when stressed beyond their elastic limit, enter a plastic range and exhibit the property of plasticity. The permanent deformation that a plastic material under load and an elastic material stressed into its plastic range undergo is called *permanent set*.

Creep

Creep is the progressive, *inelastic* deformation of a material that continues as long as stress exists in the material and results in permanent set and possible damage. It is a dangerous property because it may occur under relatively low stresses at such an extremely slow rate that it may not be detected until substantial damage or even fracture has occurred. Creep usually occurs at relatively high temperatures (above 750°F for steel), especially at temperatures near the melting point of the material. The rate of creep increases as either the temperature or the stress increases. The *creep strength* (or the *creep limit*) of a material at any given elevated temperature is the highest stress that can be developed in it during a fixed length of time without causing more than a given deformation. The time required for a creep test can range up to 100,000 hr. The given test deformation is usually 1% of the original length. The results are then translated to the effect that would occur in 20 years. For machine parts, commonly used values are a strain of 0.01 in./in. in 100,000 hr and 0.01 in./in. in 10 years at the operating temperature of the member.[1] The creep limit generally used is the maximum stress at which the deformation will not exceed 1% in 100,000 hr under constant stress.

---

[1] Charles E. O'Rourke, *General Engineering Handbook* (New York: McGraw Hill, 1940), p. 145.

Creep strength is of great importance in components of machines operating at high temperatures: certain pressure vessels, gas engines, internal combustion engines, boilers, steam turbines, oil-refining equipment, and chemical tanks. However, for specific softer metals, such as tin, lead, and zinc, it may occur at ordinary temperatures. Lead, for example, will creep under a stress of 150 lb/in.[2] at room temperature. Creep in lead is sufficiently large to cause structural damage in some lead-sheathed cables. To a minor extent, creep also occurs at ordinary temperatures in concrete and timber under constant stress over an extended period of time.

Endurance Limit

If a load is applied to a material and then released and then reapplied millions of times, the material may fail by fracture or complete rupture without advance warning. A tiny crack starts at one or more points in the member and gradually, under repetition of the load, spreads from the edge of the crack, reducing the cross-sectional area of the member and causing it to break suddenly into two parts. This is actually breaking by progressive fracture. Unlike breaking by creep, it does not involve plastic flow of the member.

The measure of a material to resist this type of load is the *endurance limit*. The endurance limit is defined as the highest stress that can be repeated millions of times without causing the material to rupture. It is assumed that the stress is continually reversed—that is, that the load alternates from a push to a pull, causing the stress to change from compression to tension.

This type of loading occurs in railroad bridge members; railroad rails; crankshafts of aircraft and automobile engines; automobile springs and axles; industrial line shafting; steam engine piston rods, connecting rods, and crankshafts; and steam turbine shafts and blades. Research on repeated loading indicates that

1. The endurance limits of nonferrous metals are not as well defined as those of wrought ferrous metals (iron and steel).

2. The number of cycles of stress required for failure of nonferrous metals is greater than that for ferrous metals.

3. A notch, a hole, or another break in a continuous member severely reduces its endurance limit.

4. Corrosion or pitting in a material greatly reduces its endurance limit and leads to early fracture and rupture.

8.6 Energy Loads

Strength of materials, as mentioned earlier, is concerned with the resistance of a part of a machine or a structure to an external force. In many situations, the load is applied gradually, is fixed in value, and remains at rest. But some parts of engineering structures and machines also have to resist loads that are applied suddenly by moving bodies. When the loads are moving and are applied suddenly, however, static conditions of strength as discussed above are no longer valid, because the moving body has energy of motion, called *kinetic energy*. When a load is applied suddenly, the machine part or structure must be able to absorb the kinetic energy. In absorbing energy, the member will develop stresses and deformations.

In certain situations, the ability of a body to absorb energy may be more important than its ability to resist stress, and an appropriate material must be selected. A bar of cast iron, for instance, will support a larger static load than a bar of wood the same size; but the wood will resist a greater energy load than the cast iron. If the energy load delivered to a resisting member is relatively large, the dimensions and properties of the resisting member must be considerably different from those that are required to resist a static load of the same magnitude.

Only part of the energy of a moving body is absorbed by the resisting member. Some of the energy is spent in other ways. For example, most of the kinetic energy of an airplane that is landing goes to its landing gear and axle, the remainder being absorbed in the distortion of the aircraft frame, the flattening of its tires, the deformation of its wheel spokes, and the impact on the runway surface material.

Resilience

Resilience is the ability of a material to absorb energy without permanent set. For example, the roadway surface that regains its original shape is resilient. Resilience is sometimes referred to as *elastic toughness*. If a bar is stressed and elongated in simple tension, work is done on the bar, and therefore energy is stored in the bar. If the bar is not stressed beyond its elastic limit, it will return to its original length when the load is removed. The measure of resilience, the *modulus of resilience*, is the amount of energy a unit volume (one cubic inch) of the material has absorbed after being stressed to its elastic limit. It is represented by the area under the straight-line portion of the stress-strain diagram.

A high modulus of resilience is desirable in materials used for all types of springs—automobile, railroad car, aircraft landing gear—and for all parts where energy must be absorbed quickly without causing a change in dimensions when the load is removed. The ideal material adapted to resist energy loads without permanent distortion would have a high modulus of resiliency (a high elastic limit) and a low modulus of elasticity.

Toughness

Toughness is the ability of a material to resist fracture under a suddenly applied load, or *impact load*. Toughness, therefore, is the measure of the maximum amount of energy that a unit volume (1 in.^{3}) of a material will absorb without fracture, usually above its elastic limit. Most of this work or energy is converted into heat and causes some permanent deformation of the material. Only a small part of this energy can be recovered when the stress is removed. Toughness is indicated by the entire area under the stress-strain diagram.

A material must be tough to resist energy loads when it is likely to be stressed beyond its elastic limit. Because it can be bent into any shape without breaking, wrought iron is considered a tough material.

Normally, the stresses in such structural members as beams or parts of trusses remain within their elastic ranges, where size is restored when the load is removed. But when such a part is stressed beyond the elastic range, some reserve strength is needed to avoid the danger of total failure. A building in a windstorm or earthquake, a car or a train colliding with a bridge, and a minor airplane crash are situations where toughness is needed in materials.

A comparison of the toughness, or resistance to fracture, of similar materials under impact loads can be determined by the Charpy and Izod tests. In these standardized tests, the energy required to fracture a standard specimen by means of a weighted swinging pendulum is measured. An Olsen universal impact tester, which can be used for these tests, is shown in Fig. 8.7.

8.7 Other Properties

The seven properties discussed above—strength, stiffness, elasticity, creep, endurance, resilience, and toughness—are measures of a material's resistance to failure under various types of loading—static, repeated, and impact. In this section, we will discuss properties that are not directly related to the strength of a material but that are still important in engineering.

Basically, these properties are related to the *workability* of materials. Workability is the ease or difficulty with which a material can be shaped. Since there are a variety of methods for shaping materials, several different properties are used to indicate the workability of engineering materials. Among the most important of these are ductility, malleability, plasticity, hardness, and machinability.

Ductility

A ductile material is one that can be stretched from its elastic range into the plastic range, undergoing appreciable change of shape without rupture. This property is properly applied only to metals. Wood and concrete, for example, cannot be considered ductile. Aluminum, pure iron, and copper, which can be drawn into wires, are the most ductile of the common engineering materials; structural steel is one of the most ductile of the commonly used construction materials.

FIGURE 8.7

Olsen universal impact tester. This model can make Charpy, Izod, and Tension impact tests.

Ductility is an important measure of workability. It is essential for such operations as shaping, bending, pressing, stamping, punching, and other types of fabrication. The safety of structures depends in part on this property. Ductility is desirable in components subjected to sudden large loads. It permits a bridge, a building, or a machine to deform slightly and redistribute high stress that might occur in a small area and cause fracture.

Ductility is measured in one of three ways:

1. From the percentage of elongation of a 2-in. or 8-in. length of a specimen in a tension test after the specimen has been ruptured.

2. From the percentage of reduction in cross-sectional area at rupture in a tension test

(the greater the percentage of reduction, the greater the ductility).

3. From a standard ASTM cold-bend test.

In the cold-bend test, a test piece of material at room temperature is bent around a dowel; the greater the angle of bend without cracking, the greater the ductility. Method 1, however, is probably the one most commonly used today.

The opposite of ductility is *brittleness*. A material that fails suddenly with little deformation when stressed beyond its ultimate strength is said to be brittle. Such materials fail without warning. Plate glass is an example of an extremely brittle material. Cast iron, a tough material, is also quite brittle.

Malleability

Malleability is the capacity of a material to be rolled or hammered into a thin sheet. A malleable material can be plastically deformed under the action of a compressive force without failing. Ductile materials are generally malleable, and materials that are neither malleable nor ductile are brittle. Among the common engineering materials, copper, aluminum, tin, and wrought iron are the most malleable. The rolling of steel into structural shapes is possible because of its malleability. Gold, the most malleable of all materials, can be worked into extremely thin sheets called gold leaf.

Hardness

Hardness is the ability of a material to resist indentation, abrasion, cutting, plastic deformation, or scratching. It is, therefore, not a single property but a group of related properties. For this reason, several different methods of measurement have been developed; the method used depends upon the phase of hardness being tested.

The hardness of such materials as stone and brick is determined by standardized ASTM abrasion tests. Hardness of materials for structural work is not very significant, but it is important in machine components subject to wear, such as bearings and shafts. Here, hardness of metals is a key factor, and a number of standardized tests are available for comparison of different metals. The

tests are the Brinell, the Rockwell, and the Shore scleroscope.

Hardness of metals is commonly measured by the Brinell test. In this test, conducted on a machine like that shown in Fig. 8.8, a hardened steel ball 10 mm in diameter is forced into the sample being tested by a load of 3000 kg for ferrous metals and a load of 500 kg for nonferrous metals for a period of 15 sec. The Brinell hardness number is then computed as the load or force (in kilograms) divided by the surface area of the spherical indentation (in square millimeters) in the sample caused by the load.

A second method for determining the hardness of metals is the Rockwell test, in which the depth of penetration of a standard diamond cone or steel ball point is measured (see Fig. 8.9). A load of 10 kg increased to 150 kg (100 kg for the steel ball) is applied, and the depth of penetration is measured by a dial micrometer calibrated to read the hardness number directly. The higher the Rockwell

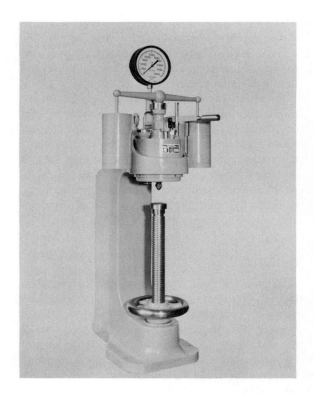

FIGURE 8.8
Brinell Hardness Tester.

hardness number, the greater the hardness. Additional information can be found in the ASTM specifications *Methods of Brinell Hardness Testing* and *Rockwell Hardness Testing of Metallic Materials.*

The Shore scleroscope test measures the rebound, or bounce, of a small weight dropped upon the sample from a standard height. The height of the rebound on an arbitrary scale is the scleroscope number. Since this test is also affected by the resilience of the material, it is not as widely used as the other methods.

For each test, there is a formula or relationship that converts the hardness number into the strength of the material. Formulas are also available for the conversion of the Brinell hardness number into the corresponding Rockwell and scleroscope numbers. While hardness is a prime factor in machinability and wear, it is also related to such properties as tensile strength, impact strength, and fatigue.

Plasticity

Plasticity is the opposite of elasticity. It is a material's capacity to undergo large inelastic deformation under a relatively small stress. This property is important for materials that are shaped in power press operations such as punching, stamping, coining, or drawing.

There are few perfectly plastic engineering materials. Lead is one. An example of plasticity in a metalworking operation is the forming of a tumbler (drinking glass) made of aluminum. The operation begins with a thick disk of the metal. In successive operations on a punch press, the disk is made thinner as the material is forced first into a dish shape, then into a cup, and finally into the deep shape with thin walls, resembling a drinking glass. The plasticity of the aluminum permits it, without fracture, to be greatly changed in shape.

Machinability

Machinability is the ease with which a material can be shaped with cutting tools. Since most machining operations involve the removal of metal, machinability is an indication of the ease with which the metal can be removed with such

FIGURE 8.9
Rockwell Hardness Tester.

normal industrial cutting tools as those used in a lathe, a shaper, a milling machine, or a drill press.

Copper, while soft and ductile, has poor machinability, since it does not respond well to cutting tools. The material is likely to rip instead of forming metal chips. A number of plastics have poor machinability because they are extremely abrasive to cutting tools and tend to dull them and impair their operation.

8.8 Common Engineering Materials

To make proper use of engineering materials, the engineer, the architect, and the engineering technician must know the basic properties of the common materials of engineering and construction—ferrous and nonferrous metals, inert materials, and woods. For a more detailed treatment of materials than that given below and for extensive tabulations of data, examine the bibliography and become familiar with the books available in the library.

8.9 Ferrous Metals

Cast iron, wrought iron, and steel are generally derived from iron ore, which is found in large quantities near the surface of the earth's crust. The bulk of the ore mined in the United States comes from the Lake Superior region in Minnesota.

Cast iron

The class of metals known as cast iron includes a variety of materials with a range of mechanical and physical properties resulting from different compositions. Cast iron, which contains from 2% to 4.25% carbon, is produced by refining pig iron, the product that results from smelting iron ore in a blast furnace. Pig iron is the raw material for practically all iron and steel products. Molten pig iron, together with additional carbon and silicon, is poured into molds, usually of sand or metal, to produce castings of the required size. Cast iron is an alloy of iron containing so much carbon that it is not malleable. See Figure 8.10.

There are two kinds of cast iron: gray cast iron and white cast iron. Gray cast irons have most of the carbon in the form of graphite flakes. They shrink less in casting and are softer and weaker than white cast irons. The free graphite flakes give gray cast iron its unique properties: resistance to wear and corrosion; machinability; and dampening ability. The latter is the ability to absorb vibration energy, and for this reason, gray cast iron serves well for machinery frames.

White cast iron, also called chilled cast iron because it has been cooled rapidly, is extremely hard and brittle and is highly resistant to abrasion. Its commercial use is limited to castings of railway car wheels, which must resist abrasion. It is also used to produce malleable cast iron. Malleable cast iron has strength, in addition to softness and ductility. The combination of strength and ductility makes malleable castings shock-resistant. The toughness of malleable cast iron is about seventy times that of gray cast iron.

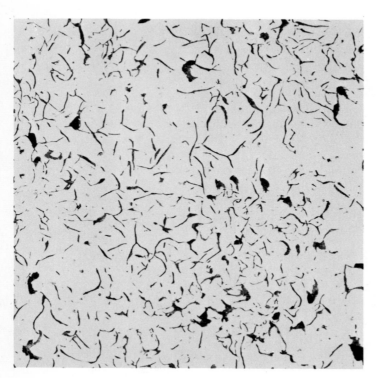

FIGURE 8.10

Photomicrograph of gray cast iron showing free graphite flakes (× 100).

Wrought iron

Wrought iron has a carbon content of less than 0.15% and contains small quantities of such impurities as limestone and silica. Its composition and manner of production give to it the desirable properties of ductility, malleability, and toughness. Wrought iron is thus ideal for machine parts that are fabricated by forging (hammering) or rolling. It can also be welded with ease.

Steel

There are two basic types of steel: plain *carbon steel* and *alloy steel*. Steel is produced from pig iron by the removal of impurities. Carbon steels are made by refining pig iron, the output of the blast furnace. In the refining process—conducted in open hearth or basic oxygen furnaces—carbon, silicon, phosphorus, and impurities are removed from the pig iron to yield a steel that contains from 0.008% to 1.7% carbon with traces of other elements. A carbon content of 1.7% makes the steel less tough and less ductile, but increases the ultimate strength and hardness. The *modulus of elasticity* (approximately 30,000,000 lb/in.^{2}), however, is not greatly altered. Structural steel with a carbon content from about 0.20% is used to produce various structural shapes by a rolling operation. These steels combine ductility with toughness and have an ultimate strength of about 60,000 lb/in.^{2}. Machine steel has a carbon content of 0.40% and an ultimate strength of about 80,000 lb/in.^{2}. A 0.75%-carbon steel is called *spring* steel, with an ultimate strength of 100,000 lb/in.^{2}; an increase to 1% carbon content yields a tool steel with an ultimate strength of about 250,000 lb/in.^{2}.

Alloy steels are created by the addition of small quantities of other metals to carbon steel to produce appreciable property changes in the steel. Nickel, chromium, manganese, silicon, tungsten, molybdenum, and vanadium are the commonly used alloying metals. Nickel increases the toughness of steel, and its beneficial effects are increased by the addition of chromium. High-nickel steels are strong and ductile at low temperatures and are used in equipment operating at low temperatures. High-chrome steels (over 10% chromium) are corrosion resistant and are called *stainless steels*. The addition of manganese in the manufacture of steel increases the tensile strength and hardness of the steel and reduces its ductility, toughness, and machinability. A manganese content of from 11% to 15% produces manganese steel, which, after heat treating, results in a tough steel with great shock and abrasion resistance but poor machinability.

Silicon increases the electrical resistance, the magnetic induction, and the permeability of steel. An acid-resistant steel is produced by the addition of silicon up to a content of about 12%. The addition of tungsten to steel, while increasing its brittleness, enables it to retain its hardness at high temperatures and therefore makes it suitable for high-speed tools and exhaust valves. Molybdenum increases the tensile strength of steel without impairing its machinability and is used for automotive parts. Vanadium and chromium added to steel produce a steel with the properties of chrome-nickel steels. In general, the addition of these alloying metals alone or in combinations increases the strength and hardness of the steel without decreasing the useful properties of plain carbon steel. The effects of several different alloys are summarized in Table 8.1 on page 214.

8.10 Control of Properties of Ferrous Metals

From Sec. 8.9, it is apparent that properties of ferrous metals can be modified by changing the carbon content. In this way, plain carbon steel can be given properties especially suited to particular uses.

The addition of alloying elements, another method of altering the properties of ferrous metals, was also mentioned in Sec. 8.9. By this method, the addition of combinations of alloys to carbon steel produces such materials as chrome-steel and chrome-vanadium steel, which are harder and tougher than the plain carbon steel.

The Society of Automotive Engineers (SAE) has set up a classification system for alloy steels in order to standardize the nomenclature of special alloy steels. As originally designed, the SAE alloy designation number consists of four digits. The first digit indicates the major alloying element or classification of the steel; the second digit indicates the approximate percentage of the principal alloying element other than carbon; and the last two digits indicate the "points" of carbon, each point representing 0.01% of carbon.

With the introduction of many new alloys, the original SAE system became inadequate, and the American Iron and Steel Institute (AISI) and SAE jointly produced a modified identification system known as the AISI-SAE system. This new system is basically the same as the old one, except that the first and second digits are related to an arbitrary table. The second digit indicates the approximate percentage of the main alloying element. Sometimes, a letter prefix is added to the four-digit number to indicate the process used to produce the steel. For example, B: acid Bessemer carbon; C: basic open-hearth carbon steel; and E: electric-furnace alloy steel.

Some examples of designations for plain carbon steels and alloy steels are

1045 A plain carbon steel with 0.45% carbon.

2320 An open-hearth alloy steel containing approximately 3.50% nickel and 0.20% carbon.

4140 A chrome-molybdenum steel with 0.40% carbon, 1.00% chromium and 0.20% molybdenum.

6150 A chrome-vanadium steel of 0.50% carbon, 0.80% manganese, 0.95% chromium, and 0.15% vanadium.

9255 A silico-manganese steel with approximately 2.00% silicon, 0.80% manganese, and 0.55% carbon.

There are two other methods of controlling and improving the properties of ferrous metals: heat treatment and shaping operations.

Table 8.1

THE EFFECTS OF ALLOYING METALS ON STEEL: INDEX OF PHYSICAL PROPERTIES[a]

Types of Steel (Approximately 0.40% carbon)	Breaking Strength	Elas- ticity	Duc- tility	Hard- ness	Distinguishing Characteristics	Typical Uses
Plain Carbon (C 0.40%)	100	100	100	100		Railroad track bolts, automobile axles, and brake levers
Medium Manganese (Mn 1.75%)	145	155	58	138	Good strength and workability	Logging and road and agricultural machinery
Straight Chromium (Cr 0.95%)	157	177	63	147		Springs, shear blades, and wood cutting tools
3.5% Nickel (C 0.30%, Ni 3.5%)	202	224	63	192	Toughness	Rock drill and air hammer parts, and crankshafts
Carbon-Vanadium (C 0.50%, V 0.18%)	158	179	68	153	Resists impact	Locomotive parts
Carbon-Molybdenum (C 0.20%, Mo 0.68%)	149	162	53	164	Resists heat	Boiler shells and high pressure steam equipment
High Silicon Sheets (Si 4.00%)	Electrical properties of prime importance				High electrical efficiency	Transformers, motors and generators
Silicon-Manganese (Si 2.00%, Mn 0.75%)	198	224	42	180	Springiness	Automobile and railroad car springs
Chromium-Nickel (Cr 0.60%, Ni 1.25%)	115	125	94	120	Surface easily hardened	Automobile ring gears, pinions, piston pins, and transmissions

Heat treatment

As a metal solidifies, its atoms arrange themselves in a regularly repeating pattern, which is known as a crystal structure. The arrangement of atoms within the solid crystal structure is called the microstructure. Most metals crystallize in one of two main geometric shapes: cubic or hexagonal. By controlling the microstructure of a metal, we can control its strength and toughness.

When the stress in steel exceeds the yield point (the point just beyond the top of the straight-line portion of the stress-strain diagram), a plastic flow occurs from the movement of disordered atomic arrangements within the steel crystal structure. In the soft phase of steel formation, this *dislocation* occurs at low stress levels. In steel, dislocations are prevented by very hard particles within the crystal structure, and consequently the yield strength of steel is relatively high. Yield strength is thus determined by the number, spacing, and size of these particles. And these three factors are controlled by the production and heat treatment of the steel.

Heat treatment consists in controlling the rate of change of the temperature of the metal and

Table 8.1 (continued)

Types of Steel (Approximately 0.40% carbon)	Breaking Strength	Elasticity	Ductility	Hardness	Distinguishing Characteristics	Typical Uses
Chromium-Vanadium (Cr 0.95%, V 0.18%)	202	229	52	225	High strength and hardness	Automobile gears, propeller shafts, and connecting rods
Chromium-Molybdenum (Cr 0.95%, Mo 0.20%)	130	135	94	125	Resists impact, fatigue, and heat	Aircraft forgings and fuselages
Nickel-Molybdenum (Ni 1.75%, Mo 0.35%)	155	177	68	153	Resists fatigue	Railroad roller bearings and automobile transmission gears
Manganese-Molybdenum (Mn 1.30%, Mo 0.30%)	158	177	68	151	Resists impact and fatigue	Dredge buckets, rock crushers, and turbine parts
Nickel-Chromium-Molybdenum (Ni 1.75%, Cr 0.65%, Mo 0.35%)	158	203	63	161	Resists twisting	Diesel engine crankshafts
High-Speed Steel (Tugsten 18%, Cr 4%, V 1.0%)	Cutting properties of prime importance				Stays hard at high temperatures	High-speed metal-cutting tools
Cobalt Magnet Steels (Co 35.0%)	Magnetic properties of prime importance				High magnetic strength	Permanent magnets in electrical apparatus
18–8 Stainless (Cr 18%, Ni 8%) (Cold worked)	207	219	53	165	Resists corrosion	Surgical instruments, food machinery, and kitchenware

[a] Adapted from E. Paul DeGarmo, *Materials and Processes in Manufacturing* (New York: Macmillan, 1960), pp. 132, 133.

FIGURE 8.11
Microstructure of a slowly cooled steel (× 1000).

changing its structure by reheating. The way in which a metal is cooled from an extremely high temperature to room temperature affects its final microstructure and its properties. The large variety of properties of irons and steels, then, depends upon the control of the cooling process and on changes in the microstructure that can be attained by reheating. Most steel heat-treating processes involve continuous cooling through various critical temperature ranges. Figure 8.11 shows the microstructure of a slowly cooled steel.

Shaping

Shaping is the process of changing the form of a metal. Cast iron, as its name implies, is shaped by casting. Wrought iron is shaped by forging and rolling. Steel, on the other hand, can be shaped by a variety of methods: casting, rolling, forging, or drawing. Each of these methods has a unique effect upon the properties of the steel.

Castings are made when molten metal is poured into molds of the required shape. Different parts of complex industrial shapes cool at different rates, resulting in internal nonuniformity and internal stress. For this reason, cast steel is weaker than rolled steel.

Rolled steel is shaped by being passed through a number of rolls that force it gradually into the required shape. Structural sections such as H- and I-beams and channels are rolled while red hot, and the pressure exerted increases the strength of the steel. Metal rolled at room temperature is said to be cold-rolled and has the advantage of increased strength at the expense of decreased ductility. *Forging* is a hammering or pressing operation done by a power press with enough force to make the metal (by plastic flow) take the desired shape of the mold formed by the press hammer and anvil. As with rolling, forging can be done while the metal is hot or cold. Forging has the same effect on ferrous metals as does rolling. A material that is drawn has been pulled through an opening in a die. Generally, this shaping operation is used for the production of wire and rods. *Drawing* can be done while the metal is hot or cold, but cold-drawn material must be heat-treated between operations to keep it from becoming too brittle.

Generally, methods that increase tensile strength tend to decrease ductility and toughness.

8.11 Nonferrous Metals

The main nonferrous metals used by engineers, architects, and technicians are aluminum, copper, lead, zinc, tin, nickel, and magnesium. Properties of these metals and their alloys can be changed by mechanical working. Nonferrous metals, however, are not altered as much by heat treatment as are the ferrous metals. An important characteristic of the nonferrous group is its resistance to corrosion.

Aluminum

Aluminum is widely used in the manufacture of items that must be light. Its other significant properties are malleability, electrical conductivity, and resistance to corrosion. Aluminum alloyed with magnesium has a higher tensile strength than pure aluminum but is still very ductile. Wrought aluminum alloys are drawn, rolled, and forged into wire, sheets, structural sections, and machine parts. They have ultimate strengths as high as 68,000 lb/in.² An alloy of copper and aluminum (in which copper is the major component) is extremely resistant to corrosion and is used extensively for cast parts. Also used for corrosion-resistant cast parts are aluminum-silicon alloys. For use in aircraft construction, sheets of aluminum alloyed with copper, for strength, are coated with pure aluminum, for corrosion resistance.[2] A cast aluminum alloy with 10% magnesium combines high strength and toughness.

Copper

Copper has the desirable properties of malleability, electrical conductivity, and corrosion resistance; but in its pure form it does not possess structural qualities. Copper alloyed with zinc (*brass*) is harder and stronger than copper and has copper's malleability, ductility, and corrosion resistance. Copper-tin alloys (*bronze*) are harder than brass, and because of their wear and corrosion resistance are widely used as materials for machine bearings.

Nickel

In its pure form, nickel is occasionally used as tubing where a high resistance to heat and corrosion is required. A major use of nickel is as an alloy with copper, aluminum, and iron, known as *Monel metal*. The alloy resists corrosive liquids at high temperatures.

Magnesium

When alloyed with other metals, magnesium has moderate strength and light weight (112 lb/ft³). Alloyed with manganese, it has good workability,

---

[2] For additional aluminum alloys and their specifications, see *Structural Aluminum Handbook*, published by the Aluminum Company of America.

good corrosion resistance, and medium tensile strength. Alloyed with 4% aluminum, the magnesium-manganese metal has increased tensile strength and ductility.

Zinc

The major use of zinc is for galvanizing. Its other use is for alloys, the main one being the brasses—the alloys with copper. Brass used in casting contains about 35% zinc.

Tin

Tin is used mainly as a plating material. It is also used as an alloying material, particularly with copper to produce bronze.

Lead

Lead is the heaviest of the metals (706 lb/ft³). It is quite malleable and will creep under a relatively low stress. Because of its corrosion resistance, it is used for pipes, conduits, and the lining of chemical tanks. Solder and pewter are lead-tin alloys. A lead-antimony alloy is used as a bearing material. Other lead alloys have extremely low melting points.

8.12 The Inert Materials

Stone, brick, and concrete are considered *inert* materials because they are not chemically active as are many metals. These materials are generally used in structural applications, particularly in large masses, such as building foundations, piers, and structural frames. Inert materials have high compressive strengths and low tensile strengths.

Stone

Stone is a natural material and is classified as *igneous*, *sedimentary*, or *metamorphic*, depending upon its origin: from volcanic or molten deposits, from layers deposited by wind or water, or from deposits that have been changed by heat and pressure. Strength and durability are the prime mechanical properties of stone. Lack of uniformity causes properties of stones of the same type to vary from one location to another. Limestone, granite, sandstone, marble, and slate are widely utilized today. Their main applications are decorative work, foundations, and roofing materials in building construction. The compressive strength of stone is about 8000 lb/in.².

Brick

Brick is a clay product in four groups: *paving brick, fire brick, sand-lime brick,* and *architectural terra cotta.* The strength and durability of clay products are adversely affected by their porosity. Desirable properties are also minimized by defects in the manufactured material that reduce strength, durability, and toughness. The compressive strength of brick masonry is affected by the type and hardness of the brick used, the type of mortar—a mixture of cement, sand, and water —used between bricks, and the skill with which the bricks are laid. The compressive strength of brick ranges from 1500 lb/in.² to 24,000 lb/in.² for special applications. For use outdoors, brick with a compressive strength of 4500 lb/in.² is recommended.

Concrete

Its strength, its ease of production and molding to any desired form, and its fire resistance make Portland cement concrete one of the most important structural materials. A mixture of cement, sand, gravel, and water, concrete can be considered artificial stone. It is quite strong in compression, is resistant to abrasion, is fireproof, relatively waterproof, and readily available in large quantities almost everywhere in the world. Its expansion due to an increase in temperature is about the same as that of steel.

While concrete is considered rigid and undeformable, tests have shown that concrete under a load maintained over a long period of time continues to deform by plastic flow. The effect of this action is to reduce the compressive stress in the concrete. When a sustained load is removed, the concrete paritally returns to its original shape after a long period of time.

Concrete is produced by mixing cement, sand, and gravel (aggregate) with water in proportions by volume to obtain the required strength. The strength of concrete is specified as the compressive strength that a standard cylinder (height twice its diameter) would have at the end of twenty-eight days. Concrete strengths vary from about 2000 lb/in.² to 8000 lb/in.². The lower-value-strength concrete is used in large foundations, piers, and dams. For structural frames in buildings and bridges, concrete of 4000-lb/in.² strength is used.

Concrete mixtures are given as proportions by volume. 1:2:4 concrete indicates that 1 ft³ of cement is used for every 2 ft³ of sand and 4 ft³ of gravel. A 1:2:4 mixture should produce a 2500-lb/in.² concrete. A mixture of 1:3:5 or 1:3:6 is used for structural components requiring high strength. Concrete for engineering and architectural construction used to be specified by the mixture ratio. A more recent method of specifying concrete is by the compressive strength that it is required to develop.

Like most stone products, which are weak in tension, concrete subjected to tensile stresses must be reinforced with strong tension members in the form of steel rods embedded in the concrete. Concrete in floor slabs, the bottom of simply supported beams, and the top of continuous beams at supports is subjected to tensile stresses.

Reinforced concrete building frames are monolithic—one continuous structure—and can distribute over the entire structure stresses due to the loads that are carried.

Two modern developments in reinforced concrete construction are precast concrete and prestressed concrete. In the former, structural members are cast in factory yards to design specifications and, after a curing period to attain high strength, are delivered to the job site where they are hoisted into position. This eliminates the need for elaborate wood and metal forms on the job site. Prestressed concrete beams, a European development, consist of concrete members with reinforcing steel rods, under a large tensile stress, cast within the concrete. The steel, in tension, applies a compressive stress to the bottom of the beam, which is normally in tension. When the beam is loaded, the compression at the bottom of the unloaded members is simply reduced, while the compression in the top of the member goes from a low value to a moderate value. This technique has made it possible to span distances of hundreds of feet with concrete members of only 2 to 3 ft in depth.

8.13 Structural Woods

The favorable mechanical properties of wood are its strength, stiffness, and hardness. There is, however, a great variation in its mechanical properties. There is also a marked difference between properties parallel to the grain of wood and those at right angles to the grain. For these reasons, the lumber industry, through the National Lumber Manufacturers' Association, has established rules for classifying structural woods, their mechanical properties, and their uses.

The woods most commonly used for structural purposes are southern cypress, Douglas fir, western hemlock, white hickory, oak, southern pine, and eastern spruce. Southern longleaf pine, one of the strongest woods, has a modulus of elasticity of approximately 1,600,000 lb/in.^{2}, a compressive strength of about 8440 lb/in.^{2}, parallel to the grain, and an allowable working stress of about 1700 lb/in.^{2}. Spruce, at the lower end of the scale, has a modulus of elasticity of about 1,000,000 lb/in.^{2}, a compressive strength slightly higher than 2000 lb/in.^{2}, and an allowable working stress of about 1000 lb/in.^{2}. White oak is the hardest of the structural woods; spruce is the softest. Hardness of wood is measured as the load in pounds required to embed a 0.444-in.-diameter steel ball to one half its diameter.

Southern cypress is light, strong, and decay resistant; it is commonly used for finish and siding purposes. Douglas fir, one of the most useful of the structural woods, is strong, hard, and durable, but has a tendency to split; a major use of it is timber piling. Hickory has a desirable combination of mechanical properties: strength, stiffness, resilience, and toughness; but it has poor decay resistance. Hickory is used mainly for spokes, rims, shafts, and poles. Oak is strong, stiff, and hard and is the heaviest of the common structural woods. In addition to its domestic use in furniture, flooring, and trim, oak is used as piling and structural timber. Southern pine is strong and hard and has wide structural use. Eastern spruce is strong, stiff, and tough and has good workability; its major use is for general millwork.

For major building construction, timber is used in the form of glued, laminated beams and arches. In this type of building component, small boards are glued together to form large cross sections that are fabricated in a shop and shipped to the job. Among the advantages of this are the following:

1. Large, high-strength cross sections and lengths can be fabricated.

2. Nonstructural grade lumber can be used to produce cross sections stronger than solid, one-piece lumber.

3. High fire resistance.

4. The quality of the gluing, heating, and application of pressure in the production of laminated members can be controlled.

PROBLEMS

8.1 What is the difference between statics and strength of materials?

8.2 What is the difference between a stress and a force?

8.3 How is the work of Hooke and Young related?

8.4 What is meant by the expression "properties of a material"?

8.5 What is the difference between properties and material characteristics?

8.6 How do mechanical properties differ from physical properties?

8.7 How are mechanical properties of materials generally determined?

8.8 What is meant by *ASTM Standards*?

8.9 List ten mechanical properties of materials.

8.10 What is the principle of the Rockwell and Brinell hardness tests?

8.11 Under what conditions is the Shore scleroscope hardness test useful?

8.12 How are the properties of strength and stiffness related to each other?

8.13 What is the difference between an energy load and a static load?

8.14 Define the terms *analysis* and *design*.

8.15 What is meant by the "workability of materials"?

8.16 List three properties of metallic materials.

8.17 A "rule-of-thumb" calculation states that the numerical value of the tensile strength of steel is 500 times its Brinell hardness number. How do you suppose this relationship was discovered? How can it be utilized?

8.18 What is steel?

8.19 What is the essential difference between cast iron, wrought iron, and steel?

8.20 What are some of the physical properties of white cast iron and wrought iron?

8.21 Define *alloy steel*, and give four examples.

8.22 Describe the AISI-SAE system of steel classification.

8.23 For each of the following AISI-SAE steel classifications, list the principal alloy, its approximate percentage, and the approximate carbon content: 1035, 2330, 6140, 9250.

8.24 How is the strength of steel affected by the addition of alloys?

8.25 How does the strength of a steel vary with its carbon content and hardness?

8.26 Compare the strength of cast steel with that of rolled steel.

8.27 Can a work-hardened piece of steel be as hard as one that was heat treated?

8.28 What are the similarities between magnesium and aluminum?

8.29 What is brass? What is bronze?

8.30 How is the machinability of metals related to their microstructures?

8.31 What is tempering? What is its purpose?

8.32 What is the general purpose of heat treating metals?

8.33 Explain why the following engineering components, devices, or elements are made of the indicated materials.

A   Hardened-steel ball bearings.
B   Alloy-steel automobile rear axle.
C   Structural-steel building girder.
D   Forged-steel tool holder for tool bit.
E   Brass water pipe.
F   Magnesium fittings for aircraft components.
G   Cast-iron air-compressor bases.
H   Brass machine screws.
I   Pressed-steel transmission pulleys.
J   AISI-SAE 9250 steel valve springs.

8.34 Give an application of Monel metal.

8.35 What is a major use of copper-tin alloys?

8.36 How many different materials can you name that are required in the production of

(1) electronic computers and
(2) super highways?

8.37 List three inert materials.

8.38 What is the essential difference between cement, concrete, and mortar?

8.39 Define *reinforced concrete*, and give two applications.

8.40 List the woods most commonly used for structural purposes.

8.41 How is the strength of timber related to grain direction?

8.42 Describe laminated timber components, and list their advantages.

Nine

SIMPLE STRESSES AND STRAINS

9.1 Introduction

In many assignments, the engineer, the architect, and the engineering technician apply the basic principles of statics and their knowledge of strength of materials. Three basic problems that they often encounter are the following:

1. How to find the *stresses* produced by the loads acting on a body and determine if they would damage the material and therefore the body.

2. How to find the *strains* in the body caused by given loads or the loads required to produce given strains.

3. How to select engineering materials with appropriate physical properties for use in machine members and structures.

In practical problems of design, any one of these factors—stress, strain, or physical properties—may be the controlling factor. In the design of bridges, buildings, ships, and aircraft, stress is often the major factor. In the design of such precision machine tools as lathes and grinders—where accuracy of dimension of the output of the machine depends upon the accuracy of the parts of the machine tool—strain becomes the governing factor. Further, with the increasing complexity, size, and cost of machines and structures, reliability becomes a prime consideration. Finally, economic competition has placed new emphasis on cost factors in design. For all these reasons, the designer's job has become more demanding.

This chapter will examine simple stress and strain, working stresses, stress distribution in machine parts and structures, and the use of the mechanical properties of materials.

9.2 Dimensional Analysis

Equations must be both mathematically and physically consistent. You are already familiar with the accuracy of *mathematical* numerical results: when numerical values are substituted for their symbols in an equation, both sides of the equation are reduced to the same quantity. To be *physically* correct, an equation must be *dimensionally homogeneous;* that is, both sides of the equation must be reducible to the same dimensional units. For example, the units in an equation used to find a length, when simplified by the same kind of manipulation as that on the numerical values, will result in length units (inches). As another example, consider the following equation for the centroid of a composite area:

$$x_c = \frac{x_1 A_1 + x_2 A_2}{A}$$

where x_1 is the center of gravity of area A_1, x_2 is the center of gravity of area A_2, and A is the total area. In one set of units, x_1 and x_2 are in inches and A_1, A_2, and A are in square inches. Substituting these units for the symbols in the equation above, we get

$$x_c = \frac{(\text{in.})(\text{in.}^2) + (\text{in.})(\text{in.}^2)}{\text{in.}^2}$$

$$= \frac{(\text{in.}^3) + (\text{in.}^3)}{\text{in.}^2}$$

$$= \frac{\text{in.}^3}{\text{in.}^2}$$

$$= \text{in.}$$

which indicates that the centroid is expressed in inches. This is consistent, since centroid is measured in length units, or inches.

For easy reference, we have listed in Table 9.1 the standard symbols and the corresponding units used in the study of strength of materials. The most common abbreviations for the units are given in parentheses.

9.3 Types of Loading

As noted in Chapter 8, there are three types of loads: *static*, *repeated*, and *impact*. A static load—

Table 9.1

SYMBOLS USED FOR MECHANICS OF SOLID BODIES INCLUDING STRENGTH OF MATERIALS

Symbol	Name	Units
δ	Total deformation (elongation or shortening)	inches (in.)
ϵ	Unit deformation (strain)	inches/inch (in./in.)
P	Applied force or load (concentrated)	pounds (lb)
E	Modulus of elasticity	pounds/square inch (lb/in.^{2})
s	Stress	pounds/square inch (lb/in.^{2})
L	Length	inches (in.)
A	Cross-sectional area	square inches (in.^{2})
W	Weight load	pounds (lb)
ρ	Density	pounds/cubic inch (lb/in.^{3})
M	Moment of force; bending moment	pound-inches (lb-in.)
W	Work	inch-pounds (in.-lb)
N	Factor of safety	dimensionless
G	Modulus of elasticity in shear; modulus of rigidity	pounds/square inch (lb/in.^{2})
t	Temperature	degrees Fahrenheit (°F)
δ_t	Thermal expansion	inches (in.)
α	Coefficient of linear thermal expansion	inches/inch-degree Fahrenheit (in./in.-°F)
h	Thickness; height	inches (in.)
c	Distance from neutral axis to extreme fiber	inches (in.)
U	Strain energy	inch-pounds (in.-lb)
k	Radius of gyration	inches (in.)
I	Moment of inertia	inches^4 (in.^{4})
Σ	Sigma (sum of)	none
$\int$	Integral (sum of)	none
V	Shearing force in a beam section	pounds (lb)
y_c	Centroid distance from y axis	inches (in.)
x_c	Centroid distance from x axis	inches (in.)
μ	Poisson's ratio	dimensionless

such as the weight of a building—is applied slowly and remains in one location on the member or structure. Static loads are occasionally called steady or dead loads. A repeated load—such as that applied to an automobile spring—is one that is applied and removed millions of times in the life of the part; it causes a stress that is continuously changing. Impact loads are applied suddenly: a body in motion comes into contact with a resisting body. Here energy is delivered to the resisting body by the moving body. A summary of the properties that measure the resistance to the three types of loading is given in Table 9.2.

Each type of loading develops a different kind of resistance in a member designed to resist the load. Moderate values of repeated and impact loads can produce results more severe than a large static load. A 1-lb weight falling on a beam from a height of 1 ft can cause as much stress as a static load of over a thousand pounds.

Loads are also classified as *concentrated* or *distributed*. A concentrated load is one in which the area of contact with the resisting body is extremely small compared to the area of the body. A weight hung on a chain attached to a beam is a concentrated load. A distributed load, which may be uniform or nonuniform, is spread over a large area. Water in a flat-bottomed tank acts as a *uniformly distributed* load; a cone-shaped pile of sand in a flat-bottomed bin is a *nonuniformly distributed* load.

Loads may be further classified by their points of application on the resisting members. If the line of action of a concentrated or distributed load is perpendicular to the cross-sectional area of the resisting member, goes through the centroid of the member, and acts along the axis of the member, the load is said to be an *axial load*. If the line of action does not coincide with the centroid of the cross-sectional area of the member, the load is called an *eccentric load*.

9.4 Stresses Due to Axial Loads

Stress is defined as force per unit of area. The stress is equivalent to an internal force that is in equilibrium with the external load P.

There are two basic stresses that may occur in a body: *normal stress* and *shearing stress*. If the stress is perpendicular to the cross-sectional area of the body, the stress is called a normal stress; if the stress is parallel to the stressed surface, it is called a shearing stress. All other stresses are a combination of these two basic stresses.

Normal stresses can be either *tensile* or *compressive*. When two equal and opposite axial forces tend to stretch or elongate a body, the body is said to be in tension (see Fig. 9.1). When

Table 9.2

ENGINEERING PROPERTIES THAT MEASURE THE RESISTANCE OF MATERIALS TO FAILURE

Type of Failure	LOADING		
	Steady	*Repeated*	*Impact*
Fracture	Ultimate strength, lb/in.²	Endurance limit, lb/in.²	Modulus of toughness, in.-lb/in.³
Slip	Elastic strength, lb/in.²		Modulus of resilience in.-lb/in.³
Creep	Creep limit, lb/in.²		

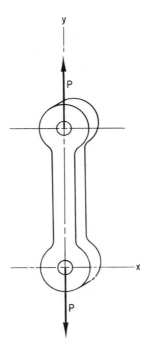

FIGURE 9.1

Tensile Stress

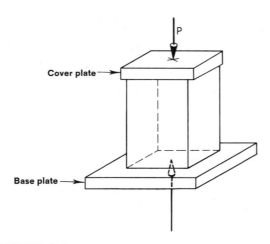

FIGURE 9.2

Compressive Stress

the axial forces push on the member and cause it to shorten, as in Fig. 9.2, the body is in compression. Tension forces create normal tensile stresses; compression forces create normal compressive stresses.

In Fig. 9.1 is shown a straight eye-bar of cross-sectional area A subjected to a tensile load P.

Since, by definition, the stress in the eye-bar is force per unit area, we may write

$$(1) \qquad s = \frac{P}{A}$$

where s is the stress in pounds per square inch, P is the load in pounds, and A is the cross-sectional area in square inches.

In solving design and analytical problems, this equation is useful in two equivalent forms that are obtained by simple algebra:

$$(2) \qquad P = sA$$

and

$$(3) \qquad A = \frac{P}{s}$$

Equation (1), as well as its other forms (2) and (3), is a general equation and can be applied to all basic stresses: tensile, compressive, and shearing. When the stress is tensile, the subscript t is added to s and A; when the stress is compressive or shearing, the subscript c or s is added, respectively. Thus,

$$s_t = \frac{P}{A_t} \qquad s_c = \frac{P}{A_c} \qquad s_s = \frac{P}{A_s}$$

Bearing

When two bodies are joined in compression, the compressive stress exerted by one body on the other over the area of contact is called the *bearing stress*. The surface over which the compressive load is applied is said to be "in bearing." The bearing stress is determined in the same manner as the compressive stress, and it can be represented by the equation

$$s_b = \frac{P}{A_b}$$

The bearing surface between two bodies in compression is not necessarily equal to the area in compression. Generally, bearing surfaces are designed to distribute compressive loads to a supporting body of lesser strength or hardness and to produce only minor surface deformations. For these reasons, the base support of many structures, like the base plate in Fig. 9.3, has a larger cross section than the post or column it supports.

The compression stress in the column in Fig. 9.3 is given by

$$s_c = \frac{P}{A_c}$$

and the bearing stress in the base plate is

$$s_b = \frac{P}{A_b}$$

Since $P = P$ and A_b is larger than A_c, s_b is smaller than s_c, which means that the base plate reduces the bearing stress that the underlying support must bear. For this reason, it is possible for sand with a bearing capacity of 2 tons/ft² to support a structural column with a load of 100 tons.

Shear stress

A body is said to be in shear when it is acted upon by two equal and opposite forces whose lines of action do not coincide but are parallel and are only a small distance apart. When a member is subjected to a shearing force, the area under stress is parallel to the direction of the force. The stressed plane lies parallel to the direction of stress, rather than perpendicular to it as in tension and compression. Shearing forces tend to cause one part of the body to slide with respect to the other on a shearing plane located between the two forces. In the household scissors, or "shears," for example, a cutting action is produced by actually shearing the material to which the parallel blades are applied. Figure 9.4 shows two flat plates held together by a rivet and subjected to shearing forces P. The plates are held in equilibrium against the forces P by an internal resisting force in the rivet, which prevents both horizontal motion and rotation. The shearing forces are balanced by the shearing stress. From Fig. 9.4d and the equilibrium conditions,

$$\sum F_x = 0$$

and therefore

$$P' = s_s A_s = P$$

or

$$s_s = \frac{P}{A_s}$$

Unlike normal stresses in tension and compression, the shearing stress s_s acts *in the plane A_s*, which cuts the rivet into two parts. Again it is assumed for simplicity that the shearing stress in

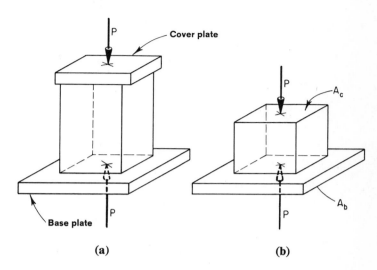

FIGURE 9.3

the shear plane A_s is uniformly distributed over the entire area. It is also assumed that friction, which would result from the force with which the plates are compressed by the rivet and which would normally aid in preventing the plates from being pulled apart, does not act. Actually, the rivet begins to work in shear only after the friction force is overcome. In this example, however, we neglect friction and consider only shear, thereby simplifying the stress analysis in a riveted joint.

If the rivet is not large enough or if its material is not strong enough to resist the load P as shown in the free-body diagram, failure will occur due to "sliding" of the material of the rivet, as shown in Fig. 9.4c, in which the material has failed on a single plane. In this case, the rivet was stressed on one shear area and it is said to be in *single shear*. When a rivet, a bolt, or a pin has two shear areas under stress, it is considered in *double shear*. This occurs in the riveted joint shown in Fig. 9.5.

For single shear, the resisting area A_s of a cylindrical member is a circular cross-sectional area,

$$A_s = \frac{\pi d^2}{4}$$

where d is the diameter of the rivet, expressed in inches. From the shear equation,

$$s_s = \frac{P}{n A_s}$$

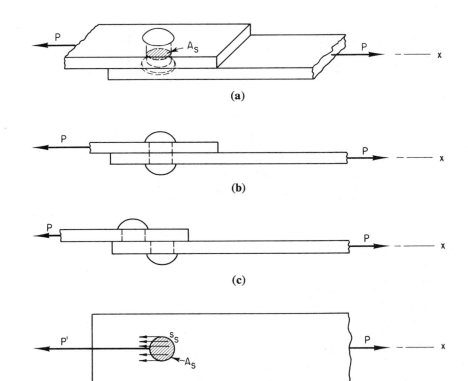

FIGURE 9.4

Simple Riveted Joint

where n is the number of rivets in the joint and nA_s equals the total shearing area. Therefore,

$$s_s = \frac{P}{n\pi d^2/4}$$

or

$$(4) \qquad s_s = \frac{4P}{n\pi d^2}$$

For double shear, where two similar shear areas are stressed,

$$A_s = 2\left(\frac{\pi d^2}{4}\right) = \frac{\pi d^2}{2}$$

for each rivet, and therefore,

$$s_s = \frac{P}{n\dfrac{\pi d^2}{2}}$$

$$(5) \qquad s_s = \frac{2P}{n\pi d^2}$$

From equation (4), the required rivet, pin, or bolt diameter can be found if the load and allowable shear stress are known:

For single shear,

$$s_s = \frac{4P}{n\pi d^2}$$

$$d^2 = \frac{4P}{n\pi s_s}$$

$$d = \sqrt{\frac{4P}{n\pi s_s}}$$

$$(6) \qquad d = 2\sqrt{\frac{P}{n\pi s_s}}$$

For double shear,

$$s_s = \frac{2P}{n\pi d^2}$$

$$d^2 = \frac{2P}{n\pi s_s}$$

$$d = \sqrt{\frac{2P}{n\pi s_s}}$$

$$(7) \qquad d = 1.414\sqrt{\frac{P}{n\pi s_s}}$$

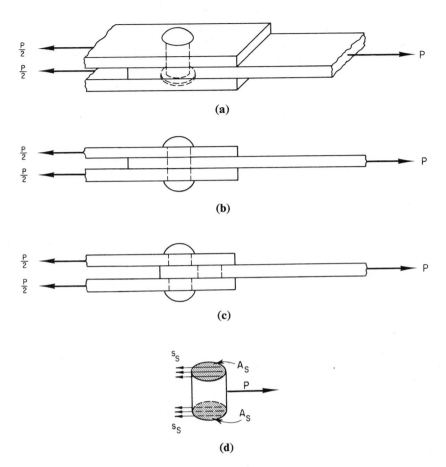

(a)

(b)

(c)

(d)

FIGURE 9.5

Riveted Joint in Double Shear

9.5 Solving Stress Problems

The stress formula was shown to be

$$s = \frac{P}{A}$$

where P is the external load in pounds, A is the stressed area in square inches, and s is the stress (average) in pounds per square inch. With this equation, it is possible to solve simple problems in analysis and design. Given P and A, we may find s; given s and A, we may find P. In these two solutions, a given part or member with known stress area A is *analyzed* to find the stress s produced by a load P, or to find the load-carrying capacity P. A simple *design* problem would be the determination of the cross-sectional area A re-

quired to resist a known load P without exceeding a given stress s. Here we are given P and s and are required to find A. From this cross-sectional area, various combinations of dimensions may be selected to produce the required area.

The first step in solving a direct-stress problem is the drawing of a simple free-body diagram. With such a diagram, it is possible to show the internal forces (see the rules for drawing free-body diagrams). Then, by applying the equations of equilibrium, we can determine the internal forces and the stresses produced by the external loads. Free-body diagrams will usually show the body cut in two parts by a section passing through the area on which the stress involved is acting.

While many of the free-body diagrams in this section are drawn in three dimensions for clarity, two-dimensional sketches are adequate. They should be fully labeled, including subscripts *t*, *c*, *b*, and *s* on stresses and areas to indicate tension, compression, bearing, and shear.

Finally, always include the *units* of each quantity in writing an equation. Ten thousand pounds should be written as 10,000 lb, not merely 10,000; a stress of five thousand pounds per square inch should be 5000 lb/in.², not 5000 psi or 5000. Energy or work should be indicated as 425 in.-lb, not merely 425. If this rule is followed, the units can be manipulated algebraically as are the symbols and the numerical values. Thus, the dimensions or units can be simplified, and the units of the final result can be checked against the correct units. If, for example, a problem requires a stress, the units reached after manipulation and simplification should be lb/in.². If the resulting units are not lb/in.², there is probably an error in the units of the given data of the problem, in the algebraic solution, or in the use of conversion factors, such as feet to inches or inches to feet. Incorrect units on a numerical result are a signal that you should check your work for method, units, and accuracy.

EXAMPLE 9.1 _____

Given: A short, concrete pier with cross-sectional dimensions of 12 × 18 in. supports a central load of 80,000 lb, as shown in Fig. 9.6.

Find: The stress in the pier.

Solution

The pier is in compression. Therefore,

$$s = s_c = \frac{P}{A_c}$$

$$P = 80,000 \text{ lb}$$

$$A_c = (18 \text{ in.})(12 \text{ in.}) = 216 \text{ in.}^2$$

$$s_c = \frac{80,000 \text{ lb}}{216 \text{ in.}^2}$$

$$s_c = 371 \text{ lb/in.}^2$$

EXAMPLE 9.2 _____

Given: An 8 × 8-in. (nominal) short post of a structural grade of longleaf southern pine with actual dimensions of $7\frac{1}{2} \times 7\frac{1}{2}$ in. is used to carry a compressive load, as shown in Fig. 9.7. The load is parallel to the grain of wood, and the allowable stress is 1200 lb/in.².

Find: The maximum load the post will support.

Solution

Since the post is in compression,

$$s = s_c = \frac{P}{A_c}$$

We are given that

$$s_c = 1200 \text{ lb/in.}^2$$

and, using the actual, not nominal, dimensions,

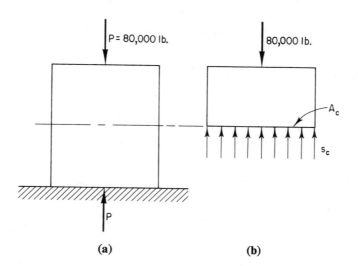

(a)   (b)

FIGURE 9.6

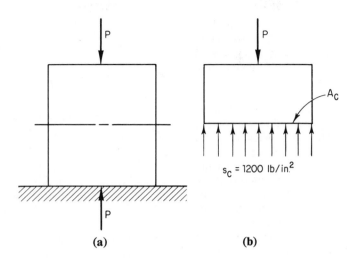

FIGURE 9.7

$$A_c = (7.5 \text{ in.})(7.5 \text{ in.}) = 56.25 \text{ in.}^2$$

Therefore, the maximum load is

$$P = s_c A_c$$
$$= (1200 \text{ lb/in.}^2)(56.25 \text{ in.}^2)$$
$$= 67,500 \text{ lb}$$

EXAMPLE 9.3 _____

Given: A short connecting rod $2\frac{1}{2}$ in. in diameter is attached to a 10-in.-diameter piston of a steam engine, as shown in Fig. 9.8a. The steam pressure on the piston head is 125 lb/in.².

Find: The stress in the connecting rod.

Solution

This problem is solved in much the same way as other direct-stress problems. However, a number of intermediate steps must be taken. The problem illustrates how a dynamic situation can be handled by means of the principles of statics and strength of materials.

First, following the procedure recommended previously, a number of sketches are drawn. Figure 9.8a shows the connecting rod and the piston acted upon by a pressure of 125 lb/in.². In order to find the stress in the connecting rod, it is necessary to find the *total force* or *load* that it must resist. This load is actually the total force P on the piston (see Fig. 9.8b). By the laws of static equilibrium, a reaction force P' also acts on the connecting rod.

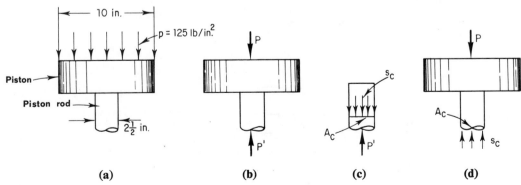

FIGURE 9.8

Next, we draw a free-body diagram of the bottom part of the connecting rod (Fig. 9.8c). This free-body diagram shows that the reaction force P' is resisted by the compressive stress s_c. From this diagram, the problem can be solved by the direct-stress formula.

We could have, of course, chosen to draw other free-body diagrams. In Fig. 9.8d, for example, the upper part of the connecting rod and the piston are considered the free body. Here the forces acting to maintain equilibrium are the total force P on the piston and the internal resisting force resulting from the compressive stress s_c in the connecting rod. As in Fig. 9.8c, the compressive force P is balanced by the effect of the compressive stress s_c. Therefore, the numerical results obtained by analyzing the free-body diagram in Fig. 9.8d would be the same as that obtained by analyzing the free-body diagram in Fig. 9.8c.

Now we proceed with the solution. Since the pressure p is expressed in pounds per square inch, the total force P created by the pressure is found from

$$P = pA$$

where p is the pressure of 125 lb/in.², A is the total area of the piston in square inches, and P is the equivalent central load in pounds. The area of the piston is the area of a circle 10 in. in diameter:

$$A = \frac{\pi d^2}{4} = 0.7854 d^2$$

$$= 0.7854(10 \text{ in.})^2$$

$$= 0.7854(100 \text{ in.}^2)$$

$$= 78.54 \text{ in.}^2$$

Therefore, the total force on the piston is

$$P = pA$$

$$= (125 \text{ lb/in.}^2)(78.54 \text{ in.}^2)$$

$$= 9800 \text{ lb}$$

Next, to find the stress s_c in the connecting rod, we refer to Fig. 9.8c, noting that

$$s_c = \frac{P}{A_c}$$

Since

$$P = 9800 \text{ lb}$$

and

A_c = cross-sectional area of connecting rod

$$= \frac{\pi d^2}{4} = 0.7854 d^2$$

$$= 0.7854(2.5 \text{ in.})^2$$

$$= 0.7854(6.25 \text{ in.}^2)$$

$$= 4.91 \text{ in.}^2$$

the compressive stress in the connecting rod is therefore

$$s_c = \frac{9800 \text{ lb}}{4.91 \text{ in.}^2}$$

$$= 2000 \text{ lb/in.}^2$$

EXAMPLE 9.4

Given: The rod and yoke joint shown in Fig. 9.9; the pin is $\frac{3}{4}$ in. in diameter, and the rod diameter at point A is 1 in. A tensile load of 10,000 lb is applied to the joint.

Find: A. The tensile stress in the rod.
B. The shearing stress in the pin.

Solution

First, find the tensile stress in the rod:

$$s_t = \frac{P}{A_t}$$

Since

$$P = 10,000 \text{ lb}$$

and

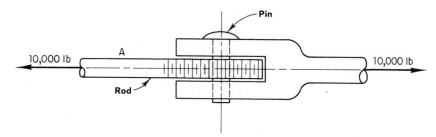

10,000 lb   A   Pin   10,000 lb

Rod

FIGURE 9.9

A_t = area of circular cross section of rod

$$= \frac{\pi d^2}{4}$$

$$= \frac{\pi}{4}(1 \text{ in.})^2$$

$$= 0.7854 \text{ in.}^2$$

the stress is

$$s_t = \frac{10,000 \text{ lb}}{0.7854 \text{ in.}^2}$$

$$= 12,720 \text{ lb/in.}^2$$

Next, find the shearing stress in the pin. The pin is in *double shear*, since it is stressed at two of its cross-sectional areas. If it were overstressed to failure, it would fail as shown in Fig. 9.10a. Draw a free-body diagram of the center portion C of the pin, as shown in Fig. 9.10b. From the laws of equilibrium,

$$\Sigma F_x = 0$$

$$P = 2s_s A_s$$

and

$$s_s = \frac{P}{2A_s}$$

$$= \frac{P}{2\pi d^2/4}$$

$$= \frac{2P}{\pi d^2}$$

which is the same as equation (5), which indicates shear stress in double shear. Substituting the given values ($P = 10,000$ lb and $d = 0.75$ in.) in this equation.

$$s_s = \frac{2(10,000 \text{ lb})}{\pi(0.75 \text{ in.})^2}$$

$$s_s = \frac{20,000 \text{ lb}}{\pi(0.5625 \text{ in.}^2)}$$

$$= 11,350 \text{ lb/in.}^2$$

[NOTE: This result could have been found directly from equation (6), although it is not necessary to depend slavishly on specialized formulas to solve many direct-stress problems. A knowledge of the basic direct-stress equation and the laws of equilibrium is sufficient.]

As an additional exercise, solve part B of this problem by using as the free body the bottom or top part of the pin in Fig. 9.10a. Note that the load on the top or bottom is $P/2$, since the full value of the load is transferred equally to both parts of the yoke.

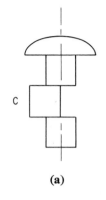

(a)

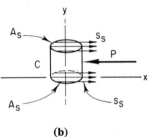

(b)

FIGURE 9.10

EXAMPLE 9.5 _____

Given: A square, wrought aluminum-alloy rod is required to carry a tensile load of 25,000 lb, as shown in Fig. 9.11.

Find: The required dimensions of the rod if its stress is not to exceed 15,000 lb/in.².

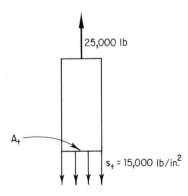

FIGURE 9.11

Free-body Diagram of Rod

Solution

From the direct-stress equations $s_t = P/A_t$,

$$A_t = \frac{P}{s_t}$$

$$= \frac{25{,}000 \text{ lb}}{15{,}000 \text{ lb/in.}^2}$$

$$= 1.67 \text{ in.}^2$$

If the side of the square rod is L,

$$A = L^2$$

and therefore

$$L^2 = 1.67 \text{ in.}^2$$

$$L = \sqrt{1.67 \text{ in.}^2}$$

$$= 1.295 \text{ in.}$$

The actual size required for the rod is 1.295 in., which is approximately $1\frac{5}{16}$ in. If the problem had asked for a bar of *nominal* size, the answer would have to be the next larger available stock size above $1\frac{5}{16}$ in. This information is generally found in materials handbooks published by manufacturers or distributors of the specific materials.

EXAMPLE 9.6 _____

Given: The 24-in.-diameter pulley in Fig. 9.12, which transmits a torque (turning moment) to a 2-in.-diameter shaft. The tension in the continuous pulley belt is 600 lb at top and 100 lb at bottom. Relative motion between the pulley and the shaft is prevented by a flat, metal key measuring $3 \times \frac{3}{4} \times \frac{1}{2}$ in., as shown in Fig. 9.12.

Find: A. The shearing stress in the key if the hub of the pulley is 3 in. wide and the key extends the full length of the hub.
   B. The bearing stress on the key.

Solution

In order to find the shearing stress in the key, we first must find the force exerted on the key. In effect, the key transmits the torque from the pulley to the shaft. Thus, if we know the torque on the pulley, we know the torque on the shaft, and from this we can find the force and the stress acting on the key.

1. Find the torque on the pulley. Torque (or moment) is the product of a force and its distance or lever arm (or moment arm). In this example, the force is provided by the tensions in the pulley belt. The *net force* operating here is the difference between

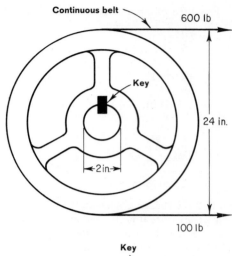

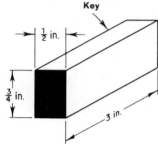

FIGURE 9.12

the tensions shown. The force then is 600 lb − 100 lb = 500 lb. The lever arm is the distance from the force to the center of rotation, in this case the radius of the pulley, or 12 in.

$$T = (500 \text{ lb})(12 \text{ in.}) = 6000 \text{ lb-in.}$$

2. Find the force on the key. The torque of 6000 lb-in. on the pulley is transmitted to the shaft, and therefore the torque on the shaft is also 6000 lb-in.

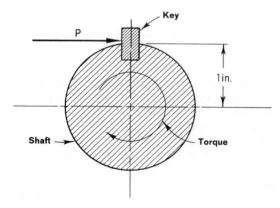

FIGURE 9.13

Since the torque on the shaft is the product of the force on the key (P) and its lever arm (1 in.) (see Fig. 9.13), the force acting on the key may be determined as follows:

$$T_{\text{shaft}} = P(1 \text{ in.}) = T_{\text{pulley}}$$

$$P(1 \text{ in.}) = 6000 \text{ lb-in.}$$

$$\therefore \ P = \frac{6000 \text{ lb-in.}}{1 \text{ in.}}$$

$$= 6000 \text{ lb}$$

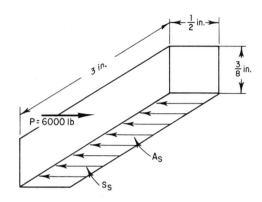

FIGURE 9.14

Shearing Stress in a Key
Free-body Diagram of Top Half of Key

3. Find the shearing stress in the key. The internal shearing force must balance the external shearing force of 6000 lb (see Fig. 9.14). Thus, the shearing stress on the key may be determined as follows:

$$s_s = \frac{P}{A_s} = \frac{6000 \text{ lb}}{(\frac{1}{2} \text{ in.})(3 \text{ in.})}$$

$$= \frac{6000 \text{ lb}}{1.5 \text{ in.}^2}$$

$$= 4000 \text{ lb/in.}^2$$

4. Find the bearing stress on the key. Draw the free-body diagram of the key, as in Fig. 9.15. Force P exerted by the pulley presses against the top of the key. The shaft reacts by pressing with force P' against the bottom half of the key. Force P, therefore, tends to crush the key across the stressed plane A_b. The same conditions occur on the upper part of the other side. Thus, the bearing stress is

$$s_b = \frac{P}{A_b}$$

$$= \frac{6000 \text{ lb}}{\frac{1}{2}(\frac{3}{4} \text{ in.})(3 \text{ in.})}$$

$$= \frac{6000 \text{ lb}}{1\frac{1}{8} \text{ in.}^2}$$

$$= 5330 \text{ lb/in.}^2$$

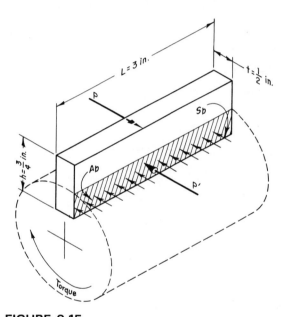

FIGURE 9.15

Bearing Stress on a Key

EXAMPLE 9.7 _____

Given: The 1-in.-diameter, square-headed steel bolt in Fig. 9.16 is subjected to an axial pull of 10,000 lb. The bolt head measures $1\frac{1}{2} \times 1\frac{1}{2} \times \frac{5}{8}$ in.

Find: A. The tensile stress in the shank of the bolt.

B. The *average* shear stress in the bolt head, assuming that the shear area is a cylindrical surface that would be created by the hole left if the shank were pulled out of the head.

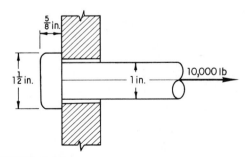

FIGURE 9.16

Stresses on a Bolt

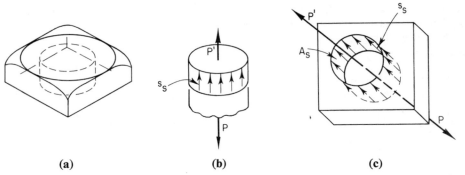

(a)   **(b)**   **(c)**

FIGURE 9.17

Shearing Stresses on Bolt Head and Shank

C. The bearing stress created by the contact between the bolt head and the plate.

Solution

1. Find the tensile stress.

$$s_t = \frac{P}{A_t}$$

A_t = cross-sectional area of shank

$$= \frac{\pi d^2}{4}$$

$$= 0.7854(1 \text{ in.})^2$$

$$= 0.7854 \text{ in.}^2$$

$$\therefore \ s_t = \frac{10{,}000 \text{ lb}}{0.7854 \text{ in.}^2}$$

$$= 12{,}729 \text{ lb/in.}^2$$

2. Find the shear stress.

$$s_s = \frac{P}{A_s}$$

A_s = cylindrical surface between shank and head (see Fig. 9.17)

$$= (\text{circumference})(\text{height})$$

$$= (\pi d)h$$

$$= (\pi 1.00 \text{ in.})(\tfrac{5}{8} \text{ in.})$$

$$= 1.96 \text{ in.}^2$$

$$\therefore \ s_s = \frac{10{,}000 \text{ lb}}{1.96 \text{ in.}^2}$$

$$= 5100 \text{ lb/in.}^2$$

3. Find the bearing stress

$$s_b = \frac{P}{A_b}$$

where A_b (shown cross-hatched in Fig. 9.18) is the bearing area between the bolt head and the steel plate. The area A_b is the difference between the square area of the head and the area of the hole in the plate; *normally, it is not the shank area*. In this problem, we assume that the hole is the same size as the bolt shank. The bearing area is then

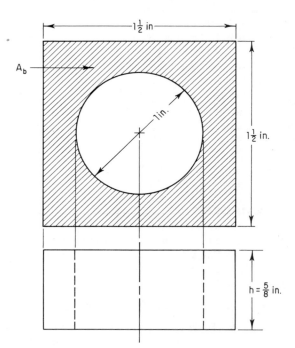

FIGURE 9.18

Bearing Stress on Bolt Head

A_b = (area of square) − (area of circle)

$$= (1.5 \text{ in.})^2 - \frac{\pi(1 \text{ in.})^2}{4}$$

$$= 2.25 \text{ in.}^2 - 0.7854 \text{ in.}^2 = 1.465 \text{ in.}^2$$

$$\therefore \; s_b = \frac{P}{A_b}$$

$$= \frac{10,000 \text{ lb}}{1.465 \text{ in.}^2} = 6800 \text{ lb/in.}^2$$

A bolt such as the one in Example 9.7 can fail in three ways: in tension across the shank area, causing rupture of the shank; in shear by the shank being pulled out of the head; and in bearing by the crushing of the head. Since the allowable shear stress is less than the tensile or bearing stress, shear should be the major factor in determining the allowable load on the bolt.

EXAMPLE 9.8

Given: A $\frac{3}{8}$-in.-thick, low-carbon structural steel plate with a shearing stress of 45,000 lb/in.².

Find: The force required to punch a hole 2 in. in diameter in the steel plate.

Solution

Draw the free-body diagram of the slug of material that is to be punched out of the plate, as shown in Fig. 9.19. The area over which the shearing stress occurs is the outside of the slug created by the punch, forming a cylindrical surface. Thus, the shearing area is

A_s = area of cylinder

$$= (\text{circumference})(\text{height})$$

$$= \pi dh = (\pi 2 \text{ in.})(\tfrac{3}{8} \text{ in.}) = 2.35 \text{ in.}^2$$

Therefore, the required force is

$$P = s_s A_s$$

$$= (45,000 \text{ lb/in.}^2)(2.35 \text{ in.}^2)$$

$$= 106,000 \text{ lb}$$

EXAMPLE 9.9

Given: The small, commercial building frame shown in Fig. 9.20, consisting of two stories and a basement. The dead load (D.L., weight of the structure) for each floor and roof is 75 lb/ft². The live load (L.L.) is set at 75 lb/ft². All the footings are the same size and are in the shape of truncated pyramids, 12 in. square on top and 36 in. square at the bottom.

Find: The bearing pressure on the foundation bed under the interior footings in pounds per square inch and tons per square foot.

Solution

As shown by the dashed lines in Fig. 9.20b, each interior column carries the load imposed by the floor above for a distance of half a bay in all directions. Thus, the footings supporting the interior columns support the load of the area enclosed by the dashed lines for all floors and roof above the footings. Therefore, the total load supported by the interior footings is computed as follows.

load per floor = (area)(total load per square foot)

total load/ft² = live load + dead load

$$= 75 \text{ lb/ft}^2 + 75 \text{ lb/ft}^2$$

$$= 150 \text{ lb/ft}^2$$

Since the floor area is 3 bays long and 2 bays wide,

floor area = $(3 \times 15 \text{ ft})(2 \times 15 \text{ ft})$

$$= 1350 \text{ ft}^2$$

Then

total load per floor = $(1350 \text{ ft}^2)(150 \text{ lb/ft}^2)$

$$= 202,500 \text{ lb}$$

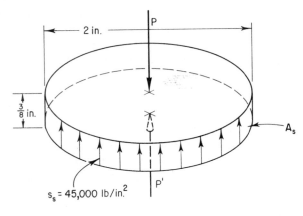

FIGURE 9.19
Forces on Punched Material

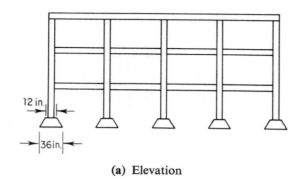

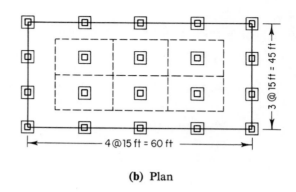

(a) Elevation   (b) Plan

FIGURE 9.20

Small Building Frame

total load for both floors and roof = 3(202,500 lb)

$$= 607,500 \text{ lb}$$

which is the total load P.

Next, find the bearing area A_b:

Bearing area per footing

$$= (36 \text{ in.})(36 \text{ in.})$$

$$= 1296 \text{ in.}^2$$

total bearing area A_b

$$= (\text{number of footings})(\text{area per footing})$$

$$= 6(1296 \text{ in.}^2)$$

$$= 7770 \text{ in.}^2$$

Finally, find the bearing stress s_b:

$$s_b = \frac{P}{A_b}$$

$$= \frac{607,500 \text{ lb}}{7770 \text{ in.}^2}$$

$$= 78.2 \text{ lb/in.}^2$$

In pounds per square foot,

$$s_b = (78.2 \text{ lb/in.}^2)(144 \text{ in.}^2/\text{ft}^2)$$

$$= 11,250 \text{ lb/ft}^2$$

In tons per square foot,

$$s_b = \frac{11,250 \text{ lb/ft}^2}{2000 \text{ lb/ton}}$$

$$= 5.62 \text{ tons/ft}^2$$

Tables of allowable bearing capacities of various foundation beds indicate that coarse gravel has a bearing capacity of 6 tons/ft², which means that a gravel foundation bed would be appropriate for this building.

9.6 Deformation Due to Central Loads

Engineeering materials are not rigid. When subjected to a force, they undergo a change in size or shape. A bar in tension is elongated, and a bar in compression is shortened.

Changes in dimensions are called *deformations*. When a body, such as the bar in Fig. 9.21a, is stretched by the tensile load P, its total deformation (or elongation) is represented by δ, the Greek letter *delta*. The total deformation δ is the change in length between any two given points on a member with uniform cross section. It is therefore equal to the difference between original length L (between points 1 and 2) and the new length L' (between 1 and 2′).

Strain, or *unit deformation*, is the change in length per unit of length, and it is denoted by ϵ, the Greek letter *epsilon*. From its definition, it is found by dividing the total deformation by the original length of the member. Thus,

(8) $$\epsilon = \frac{\delta}{L}$$

where δ is the total deformation in inches, L is the original length of the stressed member in inches, and ϵ is the strain in inches per inch. For example, if an iron rod 15 ft long acted upon by a tensile force of 5000 lb had a total deformation $\delta = 0.125$ in., the strain would be computed as follows:

$$\epsilon = \frac{\delta}{L} = \frac{0.125 \text{ in.}}{(15 \text{ ft})(12 \text{ in./ft})}$$

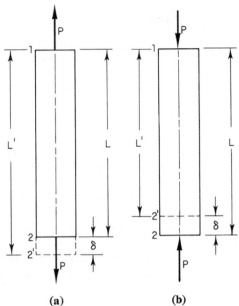
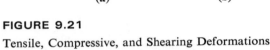
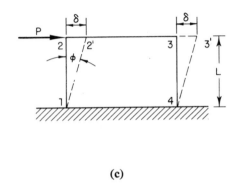

FIGURE 9.21

Tensile, Compressive, and Shearing Deformations

$$\epsilon = \frac{0.125 \text{ in.}}{180 \text{ in.}}$$

$$= 0.000695 \text{ in./in.}$$

For compression, as shown in Fig. 9.21b, the compressive deformation is also δ, which represents the total shortening of the member of original length L. Again, $\epsilon = \delta/L$. Shearing strain, the deformation caused by a shearing load, is a change of shape, not a change of length. In Fig. 9.21c, for example, the rectangular element 1-2-3-4 is changed to the rhomboid 1-2'-3'-4. The total deformation δ is measured as shown, and the shearing strain is

$$\epsilon_s = \frac{\delta}{L}$$

9.7 Hooke's Law: Modulus of Elasticity

Sir Robert Hooke discovered in 1678 that the deformation of a loaded spring or a straight wire is proportional to the load applied. He further established that stress is proportional to strain, a principle now known as *Hooke's law*.

In 1807, Thomas Young put Hooke's law into mathematical form, deriving the *constant of proportionality* between stress and strain. This constant, occasionally called *Young's modulus* or the *modulus of elasticity*, is denoted by the symbol E:

(9) $\text{modulus of elasticity} = E = \dfrac{\text{stress}}{\text{strain}} = \dfrac{s}{\epsilon}$

Since stress is in pounds per square inch and strain is in inches per inch, the units of the modulus of elasticity are pounds per square inch. If equation (9) is written as

(10) $s = E\epsilon$

and stress is plotted against strain, the resulting curve is a straight line of the algebraic form $y = Ax$, as shown in Fig. 9.22.

As mentioned in Chapter 8, the value of E for engineering materials is determined by laboratory experiments. A standard sample of the material (See Fig. 9.23.) is clamped into a universal testing machine, an extensometer is attached to the sample, and the sample is subjected to a steadily increasing load. As the load increases, the force

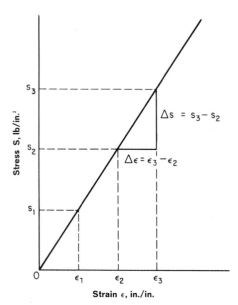

FIGURE 9.22

Graph of Hooke's Law

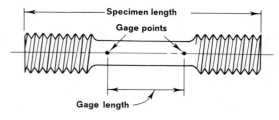

FIGURE 9.23

Tension-test Specimen

on the sample and the elongation of the sample are recorded. This process is continued until the sample fractures.

The recorded forces are then divided by the original cross-sectional area of the sample to give the *stress*. The corresponding elongations are divided by the sample's length to give the *strain*. The resulting data are plotted, as shown in Fig. 9.24.[1] As shown in the figure, which approximates the data obtained for a low-carbon steel, the first portion of the curve is linear, and the relation of

---

[1] Since the initial load is applied before the extensometer is attached, the stress at zero strain is slightly greater than zero.

stress to strain obeys Hooke's law; that is, stress is proportional to strain. At a certain point known as the *elastic limit*, the linear relation between stress and strain ends, and the specimen elongates with little or no increase in load. As the load continues to be increased, the sample reaches its *ultimate stress* (which is equivalent to the ultimate tensile strength) and finally the *rupture stress*, at which point the sample breaks. At a point just beyond the elastic limit there is permanent deformation of the material without a large increase in load. Since the permanent deformation at the *yield point* is sufficient to impair the usefulness of most machine and structural members, the *yield stress* is a good indication of the useful strength of a material.

Since E is the slope of the stress-strain curve, indicating the *rate* at which stress increases with strain, it is a measure of the stiffness of the material:

$$E = \frac{\Delta s}{\Delta \epsilon}$$

Physically, a stiff material such as steel shows a small strain under a given stress. A softer, more elastic material, such as bronze, deforms about twice as much as steel under the same stress. Copper and aluminum show strains three times as large as that for steel. Experimental values of E for various materials are listed in numerous engineering handbooks. E for steel, for example, is about 30,000,000 lb/in.²; E for bronze is 14,500,000 lb/in.²; and E for aluminum and copper is 10,000,000 lb/in.².

In this discussion, it has been said that the modulus of elasticity is the measure of the elasticity of a given material. It has also been said that the modulus of elasticity is a measure of the stiffness of a material. Elasticity is the property of a material that enables it to recover its shape after the deforming force is removed. The modulus of elasticity, then, is a measure of the stiffness of an elastic material. It is simply a measure of the resistance of a material to deformation under load.

Some materials, including nonferrous metals and high-strength steels, do not have a pronounced yield point. For these materials an arbitrary method for determining the yield point is used. Yield point is then defined as the stress that would cause a permanent set of 0.2 %. To locate

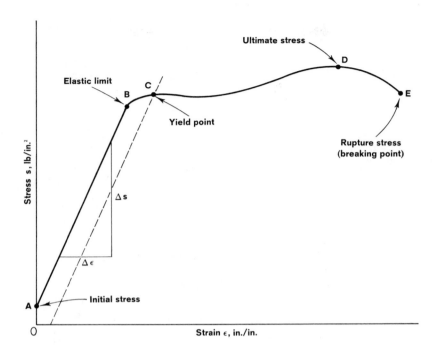

FIGURE 9.24

Stress-strain Diagram for Tensile Test of Steel

it on the stress-strain diagram, a line is drawn parallel to the linear portion of the curve from the point corresponding to 0.2% of the total deformation until it intersects the stress-strain curve. That intersection is taken as the yield point.

Beyond the yield point, the material seems to regain its ability to resist the applied load, which then increases with strain up to point *D*. At this point, the sample carries the largest tensile load. The ultimate strength of the material is the stress corresponding to this load. It is the stress obtained when the maximum load developed by the specimen is divided by its original cross-sectional area. Ultimate strength is also used as a basis for determining working stresses.

Beyond point *D*, the specimen elongates under a load less than that at the ultimate strength, "necks" down (the diameter decreases), and the specimen finally fractures at point *E*. No stress that occurs as the material necks down is more significant than the ultimate strength. In necking down or contracting laterally, the sample has begun to fail.

Shearing modulus of rigidity

For any given material, the value of the modulus of elasticity is not the same for all three basic stresses. For example, the modulus of elasticity of steel under tension and compression is approximately 30×10^6 lb/in.², but the shear modulus is approximately 12×10^6 lb/in.². The modulus of elasticity in shear is also called the *modulus of rigidity* and is designated by the symbol *G*. As for *E*, the units for *G* are lb/in.². *G* is a constant that depends on the mechanical properties of the material and, like *E*, is the ratio of shearing *stress* to shearing *strain*. The modulus *G* is related to the modulus of elasticity under tension by Poisson's ratio μ:

$$(10) \qquad G = \frac{E}{2(1 + \mu)}$$

where *E* is the modulus of elasticity in pounds per square inch, μ is Poisson's ratio (dimensionless), and *G* is the modulus of rigidity in pounds per square inch. The modulus of rigidity can be computed for a material if its modulus of elasticity E under tension and Poisson's ratio μ are known. For structural steel, $E = 30 \times 10^6$ lb/in.² and Poisson's ratio $\mu = 0.30$.

Therefore,

$$G = \frac{E}{2(1 + \mu)}$$

$$= \frac{30 \times 10^6 \text{ lb/in.}^2}{2(1 + 0.30)}$$

$$= \frac{30 \times 10^6 \text{ lb/in.}^2}{2.6}$$

$$= 11.5 \times 10^6 \text{ lb/in.}^2$$

The equation for the modulus of elasticity, $E = s/\epsilon$, can be written in another useful form when stress and strain are caused by axial loads on a member of uniform cross section.
Since

$$s = \frac{P}{A} \quad \text{and} \quad \epsilon = \frac{\delta}{L}$$

we may write

$$E = \frac{P/A}{\delta/L}$$

$$= \frac{PL}{A\delta}$$

from which we get

(11) $$\delta = \frac{PL}{AE}$$

where P is the total axial load in pounds, L is the length of the member in inches, A is the cross-sectional area of the member in square inches, E is the modulus of elasticity in pounds per square inch, and δ is the total deformation in inches. Equation (11) states that the elongation of a member is directly proportional to the tensile load and length of the member and inversely proportional to its cross-sectional area and modulus of elasticity.

EXAMPLE 9.10 _____

Given: A 2-ft steel bar subjected to a tensile stress of 20,000 lb/in.². The modulus of elasticity of the bar is 30×10^6 lb/in.².

Find: The total elongation of the bar.

Solution

Combine the equations for strain and stress as follows: since $\epsilon = \delta/L$, then $\delta = \epsilon L$; and since $s = E\epsilon$, then $\epsilon = s/E$. Therefore, $\delta/L = s/E$ and

$$\delta = \frac{sL}{E}$$

$$= \frac{(20{,}000 \text{ lb/in.}^2)(2 \text{ ft})(12 \text{ in./ft})}{30 \times 10^6 \text{ lb/in.}^2}$$

$$= \frac{(20 \times 10^3 \text{ lb/in.}^2)(24 \text{ in.})}{30 \times 10^6 \text{ lb/in.}^2}$$

$$= 16 \times 10^{-3} \text{ in.}$$

$$= 0.016 \text{ in.}$$

EXAMPLE 9.11 _____

Given: The strain on a steel bar in tension is 0.0005 in./in. The cross-sectional area of the bar is 1 in.², and $E = 30 \times 10^6$ lb/in.².

Find: The tensile load applied to the bar.

Solution

Since $P = sA$ and $s = E\epsilon$, write

$$P = E\epsilon A$$

$$= (30 \times 10^6 \text{ lb/in.}^2)(5 \times 10^{-4} \text{ in./in.})(1 \text{ in.}^2)$$

$$= 150 \times 10^2 \text{ lb}$$

$$= 15{,}000 \text{ lb}$$

EXAMPLE 9.12 _____

Given: A 1-in.-diameter aluminum rod 10 ft long loaded with a tension force of 10,000 lb. $E = 10 \times 10^6$ lb/in.²

Find: The total elongation.

Solution

$$\delta = \frac{PL}{AE}$$

$$A = \frac{\pi d^2}{4} = 0.7854(1 \text{ in.})^2$$

$$= 0.7854 \text{ in.}^2$$

$$\therefore \ \delta = \frac{(10 \times 10^3 \text{ lb})(10 \text{ ft})(12 \text{ in./ft})}{(0.7854 \text{ in.}^2)(10 \times 10^6 \text{ lb/in.}^2)}$$

$$= 15.3 \times 10^{-2} \text{ in.}$$

$$= 0.153 \text{ in.}$$

EXAMPLE 9.13 _____

Given: A tie rod made of wrought iron stretches 0.0643 in. when under a stress of 15,000 lb/in.². $E = 28 \times 10^6$ lb/in.².

Find: The original length of the tie rod.

Solution

From $s = E\epsilon$ and $\epsilon = \delta/L$, write $s = E\delta/L$ or

$$L = \frac{E\delta}{s}$$

Therefore,

$$L = \frac{(28 \times 10^6 \text{ lb/in.}^2)(0.0643 \text{ in.})}{(15 \times 10^3 \text{ lb/in.}^2)}$$

$$= 120 \text{ in., or } 10 \text{ ft}$$

EXAMPLE 9.14 _____

Given: A $\frac{1}{2}$-in.-diameter cable 200 ft. long supporting a suspended bin. When the bin and its contents total a load of 2000 lb, the cable is 0.815 in. longer than its 200-ft length.

Find: The modulus of elasticity of the cable material.

Solution

Solve

$$\delta = \frac{PL}{AE}$$

for E and compute:

$$E = \frac{PL}{A\delta}$$

$$= \frac{(2000 \text{ lb})(200 \text{ ft} \times 12 \text{ in./ft})}{[\pi(0.5 \text{ in.})^2/4](0.815 \text{ in.})}$$

$$= \frac{(2000 \text{ lb})(2400 \text{ in.})}{(0.1963 \text{ in.}^2)(0.815 \text{ in.})}$$

$$= 30 \times 10^6 \text{ lb/in.}^2$$

EXAMPLE 9.15 _____

Given: A steel bar with a uniform cross section of 0.5 in.² suspended vertically and loaded as shown in Fig. 9.25. The original length of the bar is 7 ft. $E = 30 \times 10^6$ lb/in.².

Find: The total elongation of the bar.

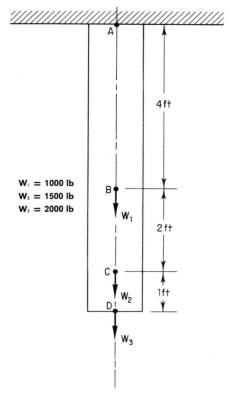

$W_1 = 1000$ lb
$W_2 = 1500$ lb
$W_3 = 2000$ lb

FIGURE 9.25

Solution

The bar is stretched by a combination of forces from three loads. To solve the problem, we find the elongation of each part of the bar.

Since the whole bar is in equilibrium, each part of it is also in equilibrium. If we separate each part from the rest, we can find the forces acting on it and the elongation caused in that part.

1. Starting at the bottom of the bar, draw the free-body diagram of the bar between points C and D, as shown in Fig. 9.26. At point D, $W_3 = 2000$ lb acts on the bar. Therefore, since P is the only force opposing the action of W_3 (from $\sum F_y = 0$), $W_3 = P = 2000$ lb; part CD is in 2000-lb tension. The length of CD is 1 ft and its cross-sectional area is $A = 0.5$ in.². Thus, the elongation of this part of the bar is

$$\delta_{CD} = \frac{PL}{AE}$$

$$= \frac{(2000 \text{ lb})(1 \text{ ft} \times 12 \text{ in./ft})}{(0.5 \text{ in.}^2)(30 \times 10^6 \text{ lb/in.}^2)}$$

$$= 0.0016 \text{ in.}$$

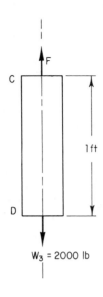

FIGURE 9.26

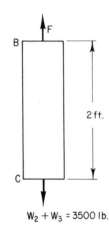

FIGURE 9.27

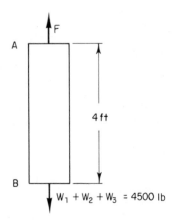

FIGURE 9.28

2. Draw the free-body diagram of part BC, as shown in Fig. 9.27. The total weight acting downward at point C is $W_2 + W_3 = 1500$ lb $+ 2000$ lb $= 3500$ lb. Therefore part BC is acted on by a total force $P = 3500$ lb. Since its length is 2 ft, its elongation is

$$\delta_{BC} = \frac{PL}{AE}$$

$$= \frac{(3500 \text{ lb})(2 \text{ ft} \times 12 \text{ in./ft})}{(0.5 \text{ in.}^2)(30 \times 10^6 \text{ lb/in.}^2)}$$

$$= 0.0056 \text{ in.}$$

3. Draw the free-body diagram of part AB, as shown in Fig. 9.28. The total weight P acting on part AB is $W_1 + W_2 + W_3 = 1000$ lb $+ 1500$ lb $+ 2000$ lb $= 4500$ lb. Therefore, the elongation of the 4-ft length AB is

$$\delta_{AB} = \frac{PL}{AE}$$

$$= \frac{(4500 \text{ lb})(4 \text{ ft} \times 12 \text{ in./ft})}{(0.5 \text{ in.}^2)(30 \times 10^6 \text{ lb/in.}^2)}$$

$$= 0.0144 \text{ in.}$$

4. The total elongation of bar AD is the sum of the elongations of the individual parts:

$$\delta_{AD} = \delta_{AB} + \delta_{BC} + \delta_{CD}$$

$$= 0.0144 \text{ in.} + 0.0056 \text{ in.} + 0.0016 \text{ in.}$$

$$= 0.0216 \text{ in.}$$

9.8 Bar Acted on by Its Own Weight

In the preceding discussions of stress and strain in a bar of uniform cross section, we assumed that the bar was weightless and that only the applied axial load P caused stress and strain. But if a bar is long, its own weight will also produce substantial stress. In practice, the weights of members must frequently be taken into account.

Consider the bar shown in Fig. 9.29a. If the cross-sectional area of the rod is A and its length is L, then its volume V is

$$V = AL$$

where A is the cross-sectional area in square inches, L is the length in inches, and V is the volume in cubic inches. The weight W of the rod,

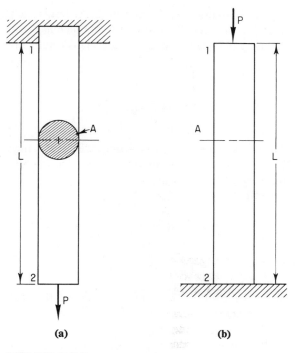

FIGURE 9.29

Stress in a Bar Due to a Load and Its own Weight

then, is the product of its volume and the density ρ (Greek *rho*) of the material:

$$W = \rho V$$

or

$$W = \rho AL$$

where ρ is measured in pounds per cubic inch. The maximum stress in the hanging bar would occur at point 1 in Fig. 9.27a. (If the bar were supported at its base, as in Fig. 9.29b, the maximum stress would occur at point 2.) Since $s = P/A$, where P is the total axial load,

$$s_{max} = \frac{P + W}{A}$$

or

$$s_{max} = \frac{P + \rho AL}{A}$$

$$= \frac{P}{A} + \frac{\rho AL}{A}$$

(12) $$\therefore \; s_{max} = \frac{P}{A} + \rho L$$

The first term on the right side of the equation is the stress produced by the axial load P. The

second term represents the stress produced by the weight of the bar.

In determining the elongation of a bar subjected to an axial load plus its own weight, we must consider that for each part of the bar the load due to its weight is different, and therefore the direct-stress equation $s = P/A$ cannot be used, since it assumes that axial load P is constant. We therefore analyze the elongation of a length of the bar small enough for us to assume that the tensile stress due to its weight is constant. In Fig. 9.30, this small length or element is shown as dy, where the symbol d means a "small piece of" or a "differential of"; dy means a differential of y, the distance from the free end of the bar.

The elongation of dy will be $d\delta$ (see Fig. 9.31). Therefore, if we can determine the elongation $d\delta$

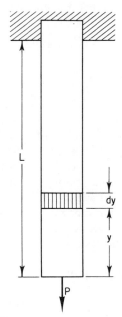

FIGURE 9.30

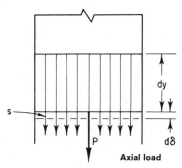

FIGURE 9.31

of element dy, we can mathematically add up the differential elongations of all the elements dy that make up the total length L and find the total elongation δ of the whole rod due to its own weight.

The fixed tensile load P acts on each element dy. Since $\delta = sL/E$, we write, for a small length dy whose elongation is $d\delta$,

$$d\delta = \frac{s\,dy}{E}$$

The stress s on any element dy a distance y from the free end of the bar is $s = P/A + \rho y$. Therefore, we write

$$d\delta = \frac{(P/A + \rho y)\,dy}{E}$$

Multiplying the numerator and the denominator by A, we obtain

$$d\delta = \frac{(P + \rho A y)\,dy}{AE}$$

$$= \frac{P\,dy}{AE} + \frac{\rho A y\,dy}{AE}$$

The first term on the right side of this equation ($P\,dy/AE$) is the elongation of element dy caused by fixed axial load P. The second term ($\rho A y\,dy/AE$) is the elongation of dy caused by a load equal to the weight of the bar below element dy, a length y above the end of the bar.

We find the total elongation by adding all the differential elongations $d\delta$, where the integral sign $\int$ indicates the "sum." Then

$$\delta_{\text{total}} = \int d\delta$$

and

$$\delta = \int d\delta$$

$$= \int \frac{P\,dy}{AE} + \int \frac{\rho A y\,dy}{AE}$$

Since the elements dy will be summed for the total length of the bar from the bottom where $y = 0$ to the top where $y = L$, the above equation is written as

$$\delta_{\text{total}} = \int_{y=0}^{y=L} d\delta = \int_0^L \frac{P\,dy}{AE} + \int_0^L \frac{\rho A y\,dy}{AE}$$

This can be simplified by canceling like terms such as A and moving all constant factors such as P, A, E, and ρ outside the integral signs. This results in

$$\delta = \int_0^L d\delta$$

$$= \frac{P}{AE} \int_0^L dy + \frac{\rho}{E} \int_0^L y\,dy$$

From the rules of integration, we know that $\int dy = y$ (the sum of all the elements equals the total length) and $\int y\,dy = y^2/2$. Therefore,

$$\delta = \frac{P}{AE} \int_0^L dy + \frac{\rho}{E} \int_0^L y\,dy$$

$$= \left(\frac{P}{AE}\right) y \Big|_0^L + \left(\frac{\rho}{E}\right) \frac{y^2}{2} \Big|_0^L$$

and substituting L and 0 for y, we find that the total elongation of the rod of length L is

(13) $$\delta = \frac{PL}{AE} + \frac{\rho L^2}{2E}$$

If the second term on the right-hand side of equation (13) is multiplied by A/A, we get

$$\frac{A\rho L^2}{A2E}$$

This can be factored and written as

$$\left(\frac{A\rho L}{2}\right)\left(\frac{L}{AE}\right)$$

Note that $(A\rho L) = (AL)\rho = $ volume $\times$ density and is actually the *weight* of the bar. Thus, $A\rho L/2$ is one half the weight of the bar. From this it can be seen that the elongation of a bar due to its own weight is the same as that caused by a load equal to one half the weight of the bar applied at its end.

EXAMPLE 9.16 _____

Given: A steel bar 200 ft long suspended by one end. The density $\rho = 490$ lb/ft^3, and $E = 30 \times 10^6$ lb/in.^{2}.

Find: The total elongation of the bar due to its own weight.

Solution

From equation (13), the elongation of a bar due to its own weight is

$$\delta = \frac{\rho L^2}{2E}$$

Therefore, the total elongation of the bar is

$$\delta = \frac{(490 \text{ lb/ft}^3)(1 \text{ ft}^3/1728 \text{ in.}^3)(200 \text{ ft} \times 12 \text{ in./ft})^2}{2(30 \times 10^6 \text{ lb/in.}^2)}$$

$$= \frac{(0.284 \text{ lb/in.}^3)(2400 \text{ in.})^2}{60 \times 10^6 \text{ lb/in.}^2}$$

$$= 0.0273 \text{ in.}$$

The elongation of a bar due to its own weight can also be found by using the general elongation formula. Since this elongation is the same as that caused by a load equal to half the weight of the bar at its end, the formula $\delta = PL/AE$ can be used, with P equal to half the weight of the bar.

In the example statement, the cross-sectional area A was not given. Nor was it needed in the formula $\delta = \rho L^2/2E$. And furthermore, it is not needed in the formula $\delta = PL/AE$. The weight of the bar is the product of its volume and density: $(AL)\rho$.

Therefore, half the weight of the bar is $P = \dfrac{(AL)\rho}{2}$.

Hence, we may write the equation for the total deflection as

$$\delta = \left[\frac{(AL)\rho}{2}\right]\frac{L}{AE}$$

$$= \frac{\rho L^2}{2E}$$

which is the same as the "special" formula, and which would yield the same result, $\delta = 0.0273$ in.

EXAMPLE 9.17 _____

Given: A reinforced concrete pier with two rectangular sections of equal length, as shown in Fig. 9.32. The pier supports a load of 500,000 lb. The material of which the pier is made weighs 150 lb/ft³, and the height of the pier is 100 ft.

Find: A. The volume of material required if the maximum allowable compressive stress is 500 lb/in.².
B. The volume of a single-section rectangular pier under the same load and stress.

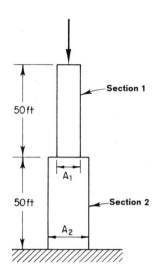

FIGURE 9.32

Solution

1. Find the volume of Section 1 of the pier: $V_1 = A_1 h_1$, where A_1 is the cross-sectional area of the section and h_1 is the height (50 ft). From equation (12)

$$s = \frac{P + A_1 h_1 \rho}{A_1}$$

we can find an expression for the area A_1:

$$A_1 s - A_1 h_1 \rho = P$$

$$A_1(s - h_1 \rho) = P$$

and finally,

$$A_1 = \frac{P}{s - h_1 \rho}$$

Since $h_1 = 50$ ft, $\rho = 150$ lb/ft³, $s = 500$ lb/in.², and $P = 500,000$ lb,

$$A_1 = \frac{500,000 \text{ lb}}{(500 \text{ lb/in.}^2) - (50 \text{ ft} \times 12 \text{ in./ft}) \times (150 \text{ lb/ft}^3)(1 \text{ ft}^3/1728 \text{ in.}^3)}$$

$$= \frac{500,000 \text{ lb}}{500 \text{ lb/in.}^2 - 52.1 \text{ lb/in.}^2}$$

$$= 1119 \text{ in.}^2$$

or, expressed in feet,

$$A_1 = \frac{1119 \text{ in.}^2}{144 \text{ in.}^2/\text{ft}^2}$$

$$= 7.76 \text{ ft}^2$$

Therefore, the volume of Section 1 is

$$V_1 = A_1 h_1$$
$$= (7.76 \text{ ft}^2)(50 \text{ ft})$$
$$= 388 \text{ ft}^3$$

2. Find the volume of Section 2. The load on Section 2 includes the load P and the weight of Section 1. Therefore, the total load on Section 2 is

$$P' = P + W_1$$
$$= P + V_1 \rho$$
$$= 500,000 \text{ lb} + (388 \text{ ft}^3)(150 \text{ lb/ft}^3)$$
$$= 500,000 \text{ lb} + 58,300 \text{ lb}$$
$$= 558,300 \text{ lb}$$

Again, from equation (12), we can write an expression for area A_2:

$$A_2 = \frac{P'}{s - h_2 \rho}$$

Since $P' = 558,300$ lb, $s = 500$ lb/in.^{2}, $h_2 = 50$ ft, and $\rho = 150$ lb/ft^3, the area of Section 2 is

$$A_2 = \frac{558,300 \text{ lb}}{(500 \text{ lb/in.}^2) - (50 \text{ ft} \times 12 \text{ in./ft})}$$
$$\times (150 \text{ lb/ft}^3)(1 \text{ ft}^3/1728 \text{ in.}^3)$$
$$= \frac{558,300 \text{ lb}}{500 \text{ lb/in.}^2 - 52.1 \text{ lb/in.}^2}$$
$$= 1245 \text{ in.}^2$$

or, in feet,

$$A_2 = \frac{1245 \text{ in.}^2}{144 \text{ in.}^2/\text{ft}^2}$$
$$= 8.65 \text{ ft}^2$$

The volume of Section 2 is therefore

$$V_2 = A_2 h_2$$
$$= (8.65 \text{ ft}^2)(50 \text{ ft})$$
$$= 432.5 \text{ ft}^3$$

3. The total volume of the pier is

$$V = V_1 + V_2$$
$$= 388 \text{ ft}^3 + 432.5 \text{ ft}^3$$
$$= 820.5 \text{ ft}^3$$

4. Find the volume of a single-section pier 100 ft long that could replace the given two-section pier. Since $P = 500,000$ lb, $s = 500$ lb/in.^{2}, $h = 100$ ft, and $\rho = 150$ lb/ft, we again use the modified equation (12):

$$A = \frac{P}{s - h\rho}$$
$$= \frac{500,000 \text{ lb}}{(500 \text{ lb/in.}^2) - (100 \text{ ft} \times 12 \text{ in./ft})}$$
$$\times (150 \text{ lb/ft}^3)(1 \text{ ft}^3/1728 \text{ in.}^3)$$
$$= \frac{500,000 \text{ lb}}{500 \text{ lb/in.}^2 - 104.2 \text{ lb/in.}^2}$$
$$= 1264 \text{ in.}^2$$

In feet,

$$A = \frac{1264 \text{ in.}^2}{144 \text{ in.}^2/\text{ft}^2}$$
$$= 8.80 \text{ ft}^3$$

The required volume of a single-section pier is therefore

$$V = Ah$$
$$= (8.80 \text{ ft}^2)(100 \text{ ft})$$
$$= 880 \text{ ft}^3$$

The volume of a two-part prismatic pier is 820 ft^3; for the one-part pier, it is 880 ft^3. Thus, a tapered pier with the same allowable stress as one with a uniform rectangular cross section requires a smaller volume to support the same load. From this it appears that a three-part prismatic pier would require less material than a two-part pier. In general, the most economical shape for a post or pier is one that tapers gradually toward the top and in which the stress on any cross section is the same. This is called a form of *equal strength*. A tree trunk is a natural example of this form: the trunk diameter increases from its top down to the roots in the ground to compensate for the increase in its own weight and to maintain a uniform stress.

9.9 Two-material Members; Statically Indeterminate Systems

Structural members or simple structures are often made of two different materials joined together to act as a single member. If a body consists of two or more axially loaded parts, the equations of equilibrium, $\sum F_x = 0$, $\sum F_y = 0$, and $\sum M = 0$, may not be sufficient to determine the force and stress in each part. In a case in which the forces *cannot* be found from the basic laws of statics because there are more unknown forces than there are equations of equilibrium, the system is called *statically indeterminate*. To solve problems of this nature, additional equations involving stresses in members must be used. Such equations can be obtained from the relations and geometry of the strains in the various members.

The strength-of-materials equations most commonly used to solve problems involving statically indeterminate structures are the equations for stress and strain: $s = P/A$ and $s = E\epsilon$. In using these equations, we assume that the material acts as if it were homogeneous; that is, we assume that all materials fastened together deform the same amount or that their deformations are related. Consider a simple structure made of two materials, a and b, so joined that they must both deform equally under external loading. The modulus of elasticity of a is E_a and the modulus of elasticity of b is E_b. Since the materials are of equal length and since they deform equally, we find that the strain in material a is equal to the strain in material b:

$$\epsilon_a = \frac{\delta_a}{L_a} \quad \text{and} \quad \epsilon_b = \frac{\delta_b}{L_b}$$

but since $\delta_a = \delta_b$ and $L_a = L_b$, $\epsilon_a = \epsilon_b$.

The strain in members a and b may also be written

$$\epsilon_a = \frac{s_a}{E_a} \quad \text{and} \quad \epsilon_b = \frac{s_b}{E_b}$$

But since $\epsilon_a = \epsilon_b$,

$$\frac{s_a}{E_a} = \frac{s_b}{E_b}$$

or

$$s_b = s_a \frac{E_b}{E_a}$$

If we let the ratio $E_b/E_a = n$, this equation may be written

(14) $s_b = ns_a$

Now consider the load P that is carried by this two-member structure. From $s = P/A$, we may write

$$P = sA$$

The load carried by material a is

$$P_a = s_a A_a$$

and the load carried by material b is

$$P_b = s_b A_b$$

The load carried by the two-material member is the sum of the loads carried by each:

(15) $P = s_a A_a + s_b A_b$

Substituting ns_a for s_b,

$$P = s_a A_a + ns_a A_b$$

or

(16) $P = s_a(A_a + nA_b)$

where s_a is the working stress of material a, A_a is the cross-sectional area of material a, s_b is the working stress of material b, $n = E_b/E_a$ (or s_b/s_a), A_b is the cross-sectional area of material b, and P is the total axial load carried by the composite member.

Another example of a statically indeterminate system is a bar of uniform cross section with ends held rigidly between supports and loaded axially at some point between the two supports, such as that in the following example.

EXAMPLE 9.18 _____

Given: A bar of uniform cross section rigidly fixed between two end supports and loaded with load P, as shown in Fig. 9.33. P, L, L_1, L_2, and A are known.

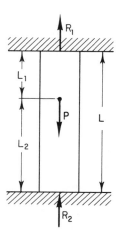

FIGURE 9.33

Find: The reaction forces R_1 and R_2 and the stress within the bar.

Solution

Draw the free-body diagram of the bar, as shown in Fig. 9.34. The bar is acted upon by axial load P and by the reactions of the supports R_1 and R_2. The equation of static equilibrium is $\Sigma F_y = 0$:

$$R_1 - P + R_2 = 0$$

$$P = R_1 + R_2$$

This equation contains two unknowns R_1 and R_2. Since we have only one equation and two unknowns, the problem cannot be solved using only the laws of statics. Another equation must be found to determine the forces R_1 and R_2. This other equation comes from considering the deformation of the bar.

Load P and reaction R_2 cause a compression, or shortening, of the lower part of the bar. Load P and reaction R_1 cause an elongation of the upper part of the bar. If the bar is not to break, the total shortening of the bottom part must equal the total elongation of the top part. Using $\delta = PL/AE$, we see that for the bottom part

$$\delta_2 = \frac{R_2 L_2}{AE}$$

and for the top part

$$\delta_1 = \frac{R_1 L_1}{AE}$$

Therefore, since $\delta_2 = \delta_1$,

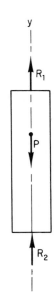

FIGURE 9.34

$$\frac{R_2 L_2}{AE} = \frac{R_1 L_1}{AE}$$

Then

$$R_2 L_2 = R_1 L_1$$

or

$$R_1 = \left(\frac{L_2}{L_1}\right) R_2$$

This equation enables us to solve for R_2 in the static-equilibrium equation $P = R_1 + R_2$. Substituting for R_1,

$$P = \left(\frac{L_2}{L_1}\right) R_2 + R_2$$

$$= R_2 \left(\frac{L_2}{L_1} + 1\right)$$

$$= R_2 \left(\frac{L_2 + L_1}{L_1}\right)$$

and therefore,

$$R_2 = \frac{PL_1}{L_1 + L_2}$$

Next, we find R_1:

$$R_1 = P - R_2$$

$$= P - \frac{PL_1}{L_1 + L_2}$$

$$= P \left(1 - \frac{L_1}{L_1 + L_2}\right)$$

$$= P \left(\frac{L_2 + L_1 - L_1}{L_1 + L_2}\right)$$

$$= \frac{PL_2}{L_1 + L_2}$$

The stress in the upper part of the bar is

$$s = \frac{R_1}{A}$$

$$= \frac{PL_2}{(L_1 + L_2)A}$$

For the lower part of the bar,

$$s = \frac{R_2}{A}$$

$$= \frac{PL_1}{(L_1 + L_2)A}$$

EXAMPLE 9.19 _____

Given: A square, steel-reinforced concrete column with four 1-in.-square steel reinforcing rods

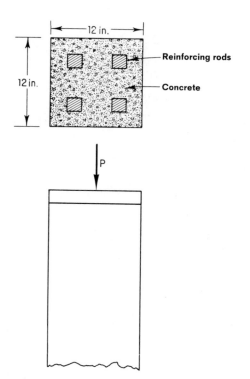

FIGURE 9.35

supporting an axial load of 192,000 lb, as shown in Fig. 9.35. The steel and the concrete will deform equally. E for concrete is $E_c = 2.5 \times 10^6$ lb/in.^{2}, and E for steel is $E_s = 30 \times 10^6$ lb/in.^{2}.

Find: The stress in the concrete and the stress in the steel.

Solution

Let s_s equal the stress in the steel and s_c equal the stress in the concrete. Then, from equation (15),

$$P = s_c A_c + s_s A_s$$

Since steel and concrete will deform equally in this column, the ratio of their stresses is the same as the ratio of their moduli of elasticity. That is,

$$\frac{s_s}{s_c} = \frac{E_s}{E_c}$$

or

$$s_s = \left(\frac{E_s}{E_c}\right) s_c$$

$$\therefore \ s_s = \left(\frac{30 \times 10^6 \text{ lb/in.}^2}{2.5 \times 10^6 \text{ lb/in.}^2}\right) s_c$$

$$= 12 s_c$$

Hence,

$$P = s_c A_c + 12 s_c A_s$$

$$= s_c (A_c + 12 A_s)$$

or

$$s_c = \frac{P}{A_c + 12 A_s}$$

Since there are four 1-in. steel rods in the column, $A_s = 4(1 \text{ in.}^2) = 4 \text{ in.}^2$. The cross-sectional area of the concrete is $A_c = A_{\text{total}} - A_s = (12 \text{ in.})^2 - 4 \text{ in.}^2 = 144 \text{ in.}^2 - 4 \text{ in.}^2 = 140 \text{ in.}^2$. Therefore, the stress in the concrete is

$$s_c = \frac{192,000 \text{ lb}}{140 \text{ in.}^2 + 12(4 \text{ in.}^2)}$$

$$= \frac{192,000 \text{ lb}}{188 \text{ in.}^2}$$

$$= 1020 \text{ lb/in.}^2$$

Since $s_s = 12 s_c$, the stress in the steel reinforcing rods is

$$s_s = 12(1020 \text{ lb/in.}^2)$$

$$= 12,240 \text{ lb/in.}^2$$

EXAMPLE 9.20

Given: A cylindrical cast-iron support 12 in. in diameter surrounded by a steel casing $1\frac{1}{2}$ in. thick compressed by an axial force applied to rigid cover plates, as shown in Fig. 9.36. The modulus of elasticity for cast iron is

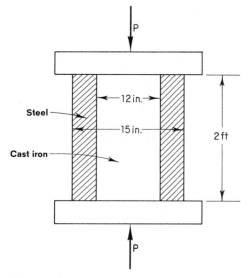

FIGURE 9.36

$E_{ci} = 15 \times 10^6$ lb/in.^{2} and that for steel is $E_s = 30 \times 10^6$ lb/in.^{2}.

Find: A. The stress in the cast-iron support.
B. The stress in the steel casing.
C. The deformation of the assembly.

Solution

Since the deformation of the steel and the deformation of the cast iron will be the same, the ratio of the stresses of the materials is equal to the ratio of their moduli of elasticity. Let s_s be the stress in the steel and s_{ci} be the stress in the cast iron. Then,

$$\frac{s_s}{s_{ci}} = \frac{E_s}{E_{ci}}$$

or

$$s_s = \left(\frac{E_s}{E_{ci}}\right) s_{ci}$$

$$= \left(\frac{30 \times 10^6 \text{ lb/in.}^2}{15 \times 10^6 \text{ lb/in.}^2}\right) s_{ci}$$

$$= 2s_{ci}$$

From equation (15),

$$P = s_{ci}A_{ci} + s_sA_s$$

$$= s_{ci}A_{ci} + 2s_{ci}A_s$$

$$= s_{ci}(A_{ci} + 2A_s)$$

where A_{ci} and A_s are the cross-sectional areas of the cast-iron and steel parts, respectively. Rearranging terms, we obtain an expression for s_{ci}:

$$s_{ci} = \frac{P}{A_{ci} + 2A_s}$$

The cross-sectional area of the cast iron is

$$A_{ci} = \frac{\pi d_{ci}^2}{4} = 0.7854(12 \text{ in.})^2$$

$$= 113 \text{ in.}^2$$

The cross-sectional area of the steel casing is the difference between the cross-sectional area of the complete support and that of the cast-iron post:

$$A_s = \frac{\pi d_s^2}{4} - A_{ci}$$

$$= 0.7854(15 \text{ in.})^2 - 113 \text{ in.}^2$$

$$= 177 \text{ in.}^2 - 113 \text{ in.}^2$$

$$= 64 \text{ in.}^2$$

Substituting these values into the equation for s_{ci} above, we find the stress in the cast-iron support:

$$s_{ci} = \frac{P}{A_{ci} + 2A_s}$$

$$= \frac{200,000 \text{ lb}}{113 \text{ in.}^2 + 2(64 \text{ in.}^2)}$$

$$= 830 \text{ lb/in.}^2$$

The stress in the steel casing is therefore

$$s_s = 2s_{ci}$$

$$= 2(830 \text{ lb/in.}^2)$$

$$= 1660 \text{ lb/in.}^2$$

Next, we find the deformation of the assembly. Since both materials will be deformed the same amount, we simply find the deformation of the cast-iron member:

$$\delta_{ci} = \epsilon_{ci}L$$

$$= \left(\frac{s_{ci}}{E_{ci}}\right) L$$

$$= \frac{(830 \text{ lb/in.}^2)(2 \text{ ft} \times 12 \text{ in./ft})}{15 \times 10^6 \text{ lb/in.}^2}$$

$$= 0.00133 \text{ in.}$$

EXAMPLE 9.21 _____

Given: An aluminum block and a wood block bolted together to form the compression member shown in Fig. 9.37. The dimensions of the blocks are identical: $4 \times 12 \times 12$ in. A load P applied to the cover plate causes both blocks to be deformed 0.01 in. The modulus of elasticity for aluminum is $E_a = 10 \times 10^6$ lb/in.^{2}, and for the wood it is $E_w = 2 \times 10^6$ lb/in.^{2}.

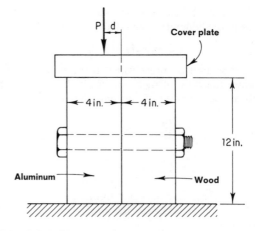

FIGURE 9.37

Find: A. The magnitude of load P.
  B. The distance d from the centerline of the assembly at which the load must be applied.

Solution

1. Find the load that can be supported by the two-material compression block. To do so, first note that the deformation of each material is $\delta_{al} = \delta_w = 0.01$ in. Therefore, since $\delta = PL/AE$,

$$\delta_{al} = 0.01 \text{ in.} = \frac{P_{al}L_{al}}{A_{al}E_{al}}$$

Therefore, the load that can be supported by the aluminum is

$$P_{al} = \frac{(0.01 \text{ in.})A_{al}E_{al}}{L_{al}}$$

Similarly, the load that can be supported by the wood is

$$P_w = \frac{(0.01 \text{ in.})A_wE_w}{L_w}$$

Since the total load that the member can support is the sum of P_{al} and P_w, the total load supported by this two-material member is

$$P = P_{al} + P_w = \frac{(0.01 \text{ in.})A_{al}E_{al}}{L_{al}} + \frac{(0.01 \text{ in.})A_wE_w}{L_w}$$

$$= \frac{(0.01 \text{ in.})(4 \text{ in.} \times 12 \text{ in.})(10 \times 10^6 \text{ lb/in.}^2)}{12 \text{ in.}}$$

$$+ \frac{(0.01 \text{ in.})(4 \text{ in.} \times 12 \text{ in.})(2 \times 10^6 \text{ lb/in.}^2)}{12 \text{ in.}}$$

$$= 400{,}000 \text{ lb} + 80{,}000 \text{ lb}$$

$$= 480{,}000 \text{ lb}$$

2. To find the distance d, draw the free-body diagram of the compression block, as shown in Fig. 9.38. The reactions of the two blocks act along their centerlines, and the load of $P = 480{,}000$ lb acts at a distance d from the centerline of the total support. Taking the sum of the moments about the centerline of the compression member, find d:

$$\sum M_c = 0$$

$$(480{,}000 \text{ lb})d - (400{,}000 \text{ lb})(2 \text{ in.})$$
$$+ (80{,}000 \text{ lb})(2 \text{ in.}) = 0$$

$$(480{,}000 \text{ lb})d = 800{,}000 \text{ lb-in.} - 160{,}000 \text{ lb-in.}$$

$$\therefore d = \frac{640{,}000 \text{ lb-in.}}{480{,}000 \text{ lb}}$$

$$= 1.33 \text{ in.}$$

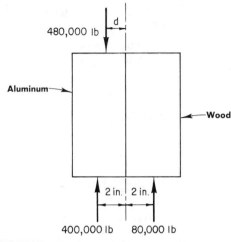

FIGURE 9.38

EXAMPLE 9.22 _____

Given: A short steel bar with a diameter of 1 in. held rigidly in place, as shown in Fig. 9.39, subjected to a horizontal axial load of 24,000 lb at a point 5 in. from the left support of the bar. $E = 30 \times 10^6$ lb/in.^{2}.

Find: A. The reaction R_1 of the left support and the reaction R_2 of the right support.
  B. The total deformation of the bar.

Solution

1. Draw the free-body diagram of the bar, as shown in Fig. 9.40. As shown in Example 9.18, since δ_1

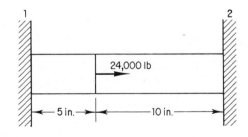

FIGURE 9.39

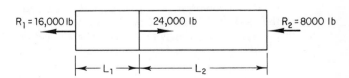

FIGURE 9.40

must equal δ_2, $R_1 = PL_2/(L_1 + L_2)$ and $R_2 = PL_1/(L_1 + L_2)$. Therefore,

$$R_1 = \frac{(24{,}000 \text{ lb})(10 \text{ in.})}{5 \text{ in.} + 10 \text{ in.}}$$

$$= \frac{240{,}000 \text{ lb-in.}}{15 \text{ in.}}$$

$$= 16{,}000 \text{ lb}$$

and

$$R_2 = \frac{(24{,}000 \text{ lb})(5 \text{ in.})}{5 \text{ in.} + 10 \text{ in.}}$$

$$= \frac{120{,}000 \text{ lb-in.}}{15 \text{ in.}}$$

$$= 8000 \text{ lb}$$

2. As shown in Example 9.18, the deformation is $\delta = PL_1L_2/(L_1 + L_2)AE$.

Therefore,

$$\delta = \frac{(24{,}000 \text{ lb})(5 \text{ in.})(10 \text{ in.})}{(5 \text{ in.} + 10 \text{ in.})[\pi(1 \text{ in.})^2/4](30 \times 10^6 \text{ lb/in.}^2)}$$

$$= \frac{1{,}200{,}000 \text{ lb-in.}^2}{(15 \text{ in.})(0.7854 \text{ in.}^2)(30 \times 10^6 \text{ lb/in.}^2)}$$

$$= 0.0034 \text{ in.}$$

EXAMPLE 9.23

Given: A $37\frac{1}{2}$-in. steel bolt with a pitch of $\frac{1}{20}$ in. and a rod cross section of 1 in.² extending through a cast-iron tube, as shown in Fig. 9.41.[2] The cross-sectional area of the cast-iron tube is 2 in.². $E_{ct} = 15 \times 10^6$ lb/in.² and $E_s = 30 \times 10^6$ lb/in.².

Find: A. The force on the steel and cast iron caused by one half turn of the nut to tighten it against the tube.
B. The stress in the steel and the cast iron after one half turn of the nut.

Solution

When the nut is tightened against the tube by half a turn, it moves closer to the head of the bolt. In so doing, it compresses the tube. At the same time, the tube exerts a compressive force against the underside of the head of the bolt and produces a tensile force in the bolt that causes it to stretch. The elongation of the bolt *plus* the shortening of the tube equals the

---

[2] The pitch of a thread is defined as the distance between a point on one thread and the corresponding point on an adjacent thread, measured parallel to the bolt's axis.

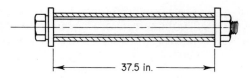

FIGURE 9.41

distance the nut has moved on the bolt.

Since the nut moves the pitch distance for each full turn, it will move half the pitch distance for half a turn. The displacement of the nut and therefore the total deformation is $\frac{1}{2}(\frac{1}{20} \text{ in.}) = \frac{1}{40}$ in. $= 0.025$ in.

Let P equal the unknown compressive force in the tube and the tensile force in the bolt. Then, the compressive deformation of the tube is

$$\delta_c = \frac{PL}{A_{ct}E_{ct}}$$

and the elongation, or tensile deformation, of the bolt is

$$\delta_t = \frac{PL}{A_s E_s}$$

Since the total deformation is the sum of the compressive and tensile deformations, the total deformation, 0.025 in., is

$$\frac{PL}{A_{ct}E_{ct}} + \frac{PL}{A_s E_s} = 0.025 \text{ in.}$$

Using this expression, we may derive an equation that gives the force P:

$$P\left(\frac{L}{A_{ct}E_{ct}} + \frac{L}{A_s E_s}\right) = 0.025 \text{ in.}$$

$$PL\left(\frac{1}{A_{ct}E_{ct}} + \frac{1}{A_s E_s}\right) = 0.025 \text{ in.}$$

$$P = \frac{0.025 \text{ in.}}{L\left(\dfrac{1}{A_{ct}E_{ct}} + \dfrac{1}{A_s E_s}\right)}$$

Incorporating the given values for L, A_{ct}, A_s, E_{ct}, and E_s we find that the force P is

$$P = \frac{0.025 \text{ in.}}{37.5 \text{ in.}}\left[\frac{1}{(2 \text{ in.}^2)(15 \times 10^6 \text{ lb/in.}^2)}\right.$$

$$\left. + \frac{1}{(1 \text{ in.}^2)(30 \times 10^6 \text{ lb/in.}^2)}\right]^{-1}$$

$$= \frac{0.025 \text{ in.}}{37.5 \text{ in.}}\left[\frac{2}{30 \times 10^6 \text{ lb}}\right]^{-1}$$

$$= \frac{(0.025 \text{ in.})(30 \times 10^6 \text{ lb})}{75 \text{ in.}}$$

$$= 10{,}000 \text{ lb}$$

The stress in the steel bolt and that in the cast-iron pipe are found directly from the stress equation $s = P/A$:

$$s_s = \frac{P}{A_s} = \frac{10,000 \text{ lb}}{1 \text{ in.}^2} = 10,000 \text{ lb/in.}^2$$

$$s_c = \frac{P}{A_{ci}} = \frac{10,000 \text{ lb}}{2 \text{ in.}^2} = 5000 \text{ lb/in.}^2$$

9.10 Lateral Deformation: Poisson's Ratio

Experiments show that when a bar undergoes an axial deformation in tension or compression, it also changes in width. When a bar is stretched, its width decreases; when it is compressed, its width increases, the bar becoming slightly barrel shaped. This change of dimension in a direction at right angles to the initial deformation is an interesting property of materials. Figure 9.42a illustrates the change in a dimension due to a tensile load, while Fig. 9.42b shows the change due to a compressive load.

The lateral deformations are directly related to axial deformations: the *ratio* of lateral deformation to axial deformation is *constant* for a given bar within the elastic limit. This ratio or constant, denoted by μ (Greek *mu*), is called *Poisson's ratio*, named for the French mathematician who determined this ratio mathematically using the molecular theory of material structure.

$$\text{Poisson's ratio} = \frac{\text{unit lateral contraction}}{\text{unit axial elongation}}$$

$$\text{Poisson's ratio} = \frac{\text{unit lateral expansion}}{\text{unit axial compression}}$$

(17)
$$\mu = \frac{\epsilon_{\text{lateral}}}{\epsilon_{\text{axial}}}$$

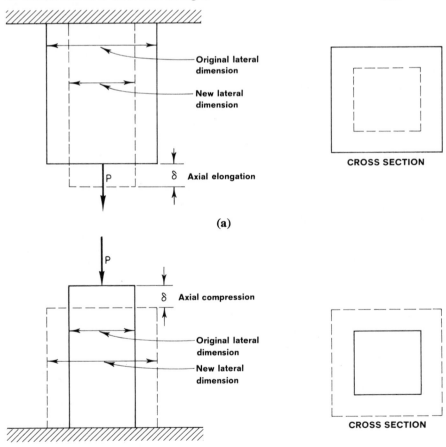

FIGURE 9.42

Poisson found that for materials with the same elastic properties in all directions (isotropic materials) $\mu = \frac{1}{4}$. Recent experimental studies show that μ for steel is approximately $\frac{1}{4}$. Values for various engineering materials are

Structural steel	0.30
Concrete	0.1–0.2
Copper	0.355
Glass	0.244
Wrought iron	0.278

The Poisson ratio of a material enables us to solve a number of practical problems. With it we can calculate the change in the volume of a strained bar. From the basic relationship $\epsilon_{lateral}/\epsilon_{axial} = \mu$, the change in the cross-sectional dimensions and area can be determined; and together with axial strain ϵ, the change in volume per unit volume can be computed. In tension, the unit change in volume is

$$(18) \qquad \Delta V = \epsilon(1 - 2\mu)$$

Poisson's ratio is also used in stress-strain relationships where stresses are applied in more than one direction. This occurs, for instance, in the case of tension or compression in two perpendicular directions. Poisson's ratio can also be used to relate shearing modulus (modulus of rigidity) to the modulus of elasticity (in tension):

$$(19) \qquad G = \frac{E}{2(1 + \mu)}$$

where E is the modulus of elasticity, μ is Poisson's ratio, and G is the modulus of rigidity.

EXAMPLE 9.24

Given: A structural steel bar for which $\mu = 0.30$ is under a tensile stress of 6000 lb/in.² $E = 30 \times 10^6$ lb/in.².

Find: The increase in unit volume of the steel bar.

Solution

From equation (18), the change in unit volume ΔV is

$$\Delta V = \epsilon(1 - 2\mu)$$

Since $\epsilon = s/E$, the change in unit volume may be calculated directly:

$$\Delta V = \left(\frac{6000 \text{ lb/in.}^2}{30 \times 10^6 \text{ lb/in.}^2}\right)[1 - (2)(0.30)] \text{ in.}^3/\text{in.}^3$$

$$= (2.0 \times 10^{-4})(0.40) \text{ in.}^3/\text{in.}^3$$

$$= 0.000080 \text{ in.}^3/\text{in.}^3$$

EXAMPLE 9.25

Given: A 2-in.-square structural steel bar for which $\mu = 0.30$ carries an axial load of 30,000 lb, as shown in Fig. 9.43. $E = 30 \times 10^6$ lb/in.².

Find: The axial stress, the axial strain, the lateral stress, and the lateral strain.

Solution

The axial stress and strain may be found directly:

$$s = \frac{P}{A}$$

$$= \frac{30,000 \text{ lb}}{(2 \text{ in.})^2}$$

$$= 7500 \text{ lb/in.}^2$$

$$\epsilon = \frac{s}{E}$$

$$= \frac{7500 \text{ lb/in.}^2}{30 \times 10^6 \text{ lb/in.}^2}$$

$$= 25 \times 10^{-5} \text{ in./in.}$$

Then, since $\mu = \epsilon_{lateral}/\epsilon_{axial}$

$$\epsilon_{lateral} = \mu \epsilon_{axial}$$

$$= (0.30)(25 \times 10^{-5} \text{ in./in.})$$

$$= 75 \times 10^{-6} \text{ in./in.}$$

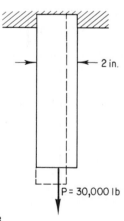

FIGURE 9.43

Since $s = E\epsilon$,

$$s_{\text{lateral}} = (30 \times 10^6 \text{ lb/in.}^2)(75 \times 10^{-6} \text{ in./in.})$$

$$= 2250 \text{ lb/in.}^2$$

EXAMPLE 9.26

Given: An aluminum bar 3 in. square and 20 in. long subjected to an axial load that causes an axial strain of 0.0002 in./in. $\mu = 0.33$.

Find: The volume of the loaded bar.

Solution

The unit volume expansion is

$$\frac{\text{change in volume}}{\text{original volume}} = \frac{V_2 - V_1}{V_1} = \epsilon(1 - 2\mu)$$

where V_2 is the volume of the loaded bar and V_1 is the volume of the unloaded bar.

From the given dimensions, calculate V_1:

$$V_1 = AL = (3 \text{ in.})^2(20 \text{ in.}) = 180 \text{ in.}^3$$

From this result and the equation for unit volume expansion, calculate V_2:

$$V_2 - V_1 = V_1\epsilon(1 - 2\mu)$$

$$V_2 = V_1 + V_1\epsilon(1 - 2\mu)$$

$$= 180 \text{ in.}^3 + (180 \text{ in.}^3)$$
$$\times (2.0 \times 10^{-4} \text{ in./in.})[1 - (2)(0.33)]$$

$$= 180 \text{ in.}^3 + 0.0122 \text{ in.}^3$$

$$= 180.0122 \text{ in.}^3$$

EXAMPLE 9.27

Given: A 2-in. diameter bar of wrought iron 10 in. long subjected to an axial force of 100,000 lb. $\mu = 0.278$ and $E = 30 \times 10^6 \text{ lb/in.}^2$.

Find: The change in the bar's diameter.

Solution

1. Find the axial stress:

$$s = \frac{P}{A}$$

$$= \frac{100,000 \text{ lb}}{\pi(2 \text{ in.})^2/4}$$

$$= 31,800 \text{ lb/in.}^2$$

2. The axial strain is

$$\epsilon_{\text{axial}} = \frac{s}{E}$$

$$= \frac{31,800 \text{ lb/in.}^2}{30 \times 10^6 \text{ lb/in.}^2}$$

$$= 106 \times 10^{-5} \text{ in./in.}$$

3. Since $\mu = \epsilon_{\text{lateral}}/\epsilon_{\text{axial}}$,

$$\epsilon_{\text{lateral}} = \mu\epsilon_{\text{axial}}$$

$$= 0.278(106 \times 10^{-5} \text{ in./in.})$$

$$= 0.000295 \text{ in./in.}$$

4. The change in the diameter of the bar is therefore

$$\delta_{\text{diameter}} = \epsilon_{\text{lateral}}d$$

$$= (0.000295 \text{ in./in.})(2 \text{ in.})$$

$$= 0.00059 \text{ in.}$$

9.11 Allowable Working Stress and Factor of Safety

The working stress, also called allowable stress or safe stress, is of great practical importance in the design of structures and machine parts. Working stress is the maximum stress that is considered safe in the material. Working stresses in structures and machines are generally kept below the elastic limit to prevent permanent set. Allowable working stresses have been determined from extensive tests of materials and from experience gained in the use of structures and machines under all kinds of service conditions.

Stress-strain diagrams resulting from the tensile tests of various materials provide valuable information in establishing allowable stresses. From the proportional limit (elastic limit), the yield point, and the ultimate strength, it is possible to determine safe stresses for many situations.

Because of the uncertainties surrounding design within strength of materials, we use a factor of safety (which is also referred to as a factor of ignorance because of the uncertainties). This is the ratio of the strength of a material to the maximum computed stress in the material. If N is the factor of safety, then

$$N = \frac{\text{yield point stress}}{\text{allowable stress}} \left(\text{or } \frac{\text{ultimate stress}}{\text{allowable stress}} \right)$$

(20) $N = \dfrac{s_{yp} \text{ (or } s_{us})}{S_{all}}$

from which

(21) $S_{all} = \dfrac{s_{yp} \text{ (or } s_{us})}{N} = \dfrac{P}{A}$ (maximum)

If the factor of safety N is too low, then S_{all}, the allowable stress, will be too high and the structure may be weak in actual use. If, on the other hand, N is taken too high and the allowable working stresses are too low, the structure becomes larger, heavier, and less economical. Broadly speaking, the uncertainties of establishing the factor of safety and allowable working stresses fall into three categories:

(1) variations in mechanical properties of the materials used,

(2) uncertainties in loading conditions, and

(3) the accuracy of the relationships for calculating stresses.

Some considerations in selecting factors of safety and working stresses are as follows:

1. Properties are measured indirectly from material samples believed to be similar but which may be slightly different because of their manufacture.

2. Nonuniformity of materials in which minute flaws might cause high local stresses or be starting points for progressive failure.

3. Inadequate information about the properties of materials under the action of variable stresses produced by dynamic causes such as vibration and impact.

4. Change in the properties of materials due to aging, decay, or corrosion.

5. Uncertainty of loading conditions: steady, impact, varying, repeated.

6. Size of estimated loads being reached.

7. Probability of the member being required to carry larger loads than those for which it was designed.

8. Temperature of the material in use may be substantially higher or lower than expected.

9. Questionable methods of analysis based on incorrect assumptions regarding the action of the material.

10. Difficulty involved in the calculations of stresses.

Other factors not related to properties, loading, or analysis include

11. The size of the loss involved in the event of failure—danger to life and property.

12. Durability of the structure—temporary or permanent.

13. Economy desired—capacity use of expensive, high-strength materials.

14. Degree of inspection, maintenance, and repair.

From the above, it is clear why allowable working stresses for ductile materials are usually based on the *yield points* (due to the possibility of permanent set), fracture under repeated loading, or creep at high temperatures under steady loading. A factor of safety of $N = 2$ is commonly used for the design of structures of ductile materials for static loads at normal room temperatures.

Brittle materials with no distinct yield points are used widely in compression, and their working stresses are based on their ultimate compressive strengths.

The factor of safety is also governed by the type of structure and the nature of its use. For a temporary structure designed to support only static loads and presenting no danger to life or property, a factor of safety of $N = 2$ might be adequate. But a factor of safety of $N = 10$ might be needed for a machine with unpredictable loads whose failure would endanger life and property. In aircraft design, sometimes two different factors of safety are used: one based on loading that would produce yielding and one based on loading that would cause complete collapse.

Allowable working stresses and factors of safety are established by numerous agencies. They may be set by building ordinances, design office regulations, or other agencies. Where the safety of the public is involved, building codes specify the maximum working stresses that may be used in structural and building materials. There is no comparable code for the design of machinery or equipment. However, recommendations are made by such recognized authorities as the American Society of Mechanical Engineers, the American Institute of Steel Construction, the American Railway Engineering Association, the American Concrete Institute, the U.S. Forest Service, and the National Lumber Manufacturing Association.

9.12 Temperature Stresses

When the temperature of a body is increased, its dimensions increase; when the temperature is decreased, the dimensions of the body decrease. If the temperature of a bar is increased and the bar is partially or fully prevented from expanding, compressive stresses will be produced in it. If the temperature is lowered and the bar is prevented from contracting, tensile stresses will be produced. The magnitude of these stresses and the forces they create can be determined by consideration of the amount of expansion δ the bar would undergo if it were free to expand or contract. The stresses set up are the same as those produced by a force sufficient to elongate it or compress it an amount equal to the free contraction or expansion.

The unit increase in length for a temperature rise of 1°F is called the *coefficient of linear expansion* α. Its units are in./in.-°F. Average values of α are shown in Table 9.2.

Deformation and stress

Under a temperature change Δt, each unit of length of a member will change an amount equal to

$$(22) \qquad \epsilon_t = \alpha \, \Delta t$$

where α is in inches per inch-degree-Fahrenheit, Δt is in degrees Fahrenheit, and ϵ_t is the thermal strain in inches per inch. The total deformation of the entire length L of the member will then be

$$(23) \qquad \delta_t = \epsilon_t L = \alpha L \, \Delta t$$

To find the stresses created in a fully restrained bar by an increase in temperature, we apply the basic equation

$$s = E\epsilon$$

Table 9.2

COEFFICIENTS OF LINEAR EXPANSION[a]

Material	Range of Values, $\times\ 10^{-6}$ *in./in.-°F*	Average Value, $\times\ 10^{-6}$ *in./in.-°F*
Porcelain	2.0	2.0
Wood (with the grain)	2.0–5.0	3.5
Glass	3.3–5.0	4.2
Concrete	5.5–8.0	6.0
Iron	5.5–6.7	6.1
Steel	5.6–7.3	6.5
Copper	9.2	9.2
Bronze, Brass	9.3–12.0	10.6
Aluminum	12.8	12.8
Lead	16.2	16.2
Ice	28	28
Rubber	43	43

[a] Adapted from Charles E. O'Rourke, *General Engineering Handbook*, 2nd. ed. (New York: McGraw-Hill, 1940), p. 837.

Since the deformation is δ_t and $\epsilon = \epsilon_t$,

$$s_t = E\epsilon_t$$

$$\epsilon_t = \alpha \, \Delta t$$

and therefore

(24) $\qquad\qquad s_t = E\alpha \, \Delta t$

From equation (24), we see that the temperature stress in a restrained bar is *independent* of its length.

EXAMPLE 9.28

Given: A steel cable that is 100 ft long on a hot day when the temperature is 100°F. $\alpha = 7.0 \times 10^{-6}$ in./in.-°F.

Find: The length of the cable if the temperature drops to 10°F. Assume that the stress in the cable remains constant.

Solution

The deformation follows directly from equation (23):

$\delta_t = \alpha L \, \Delta t$

$\qquad = (7.0 \times 10^{-6}\ \text{in./in.-°F})(100\ \text{ft} \times 12\ \text{in./ft})$
$\qquad\qquad\qquad\qquad\qquad \times (100°F - 10°F)$

$\qquad = (7.0 \times 10^{-6}\ \text{in./in.-°F})(1200\ \text{in.})(90°F)$

$\qquad = 0.756\ \text{in.}$

Since the temperature drops, the cable at 10°F will be 0.756 in. shorter than at 100°F. Therefore, its length will be

$$1200\ \text{in.} - 0.756\ \text{in.} = 1199.244\ \text{in.}$$

EXAMPLE 9.29

Given: A continuous, welded railroad rail is unstressed when at 60°F. $\alpha = 7.0 \times 10^{-6}$ in./in.-°F, and $E = 30 \times 10^6$ lb/in.²

Find: The stress created in the rail when the temperature rises to 90°F.

Solution

From equation (24),

$s_t = E\alpha \, \Delta t$

$\qquad = (30 \times 10^6\ \text{lb/in.}^2)(7.0 \times 10^{-6}\ \text{in./in.-°F})$
$\qquad\qquad\qquad\qquad\qquad \times (90°F - 60°F)$

$\qquad = 6300\ \text{lb/in.}^2$

EXAMPLE 9.30

Given: A 75-ft steel highway bridge located in a region in which the daily temperature extremes vary by 50°F. $\alpha = 7.0 \times 10^{-6}$ in./in.-°F, and $E = 30 \times 10^6$ lb/in.². The cross-sectional area of the side panel of the bridge is 10 in.².

Find: A. The stress in the side panel if it is fully restrained against expansion.

B. The force exerted by the panel against its support.

Solution

1. The stress may be found directly from equation (24):

$s_t = E\alpha \, \Delta t$

$\qquad = (30 \times 10^6\ \text{lb/in.}^2)(7.0 \times 10^{-6}\ \text{in./in.-°F})(50°F)$

$\qquad = 10{,}500\ \text{lb/in.}^2$

2. Since $s = P/A$,

$\qquad P = sA$

$\qquad\qquad = (10{,}500\ \text{lb/in.}^2)(10\ \text{in.}^2)$

$\qquad\qquad = 105{,}000\ \text{lb}$

EXAMPLE 9.31

Given: A steel tension rod with a turnbuckle to adjust the tension is rigidly fastened between fixed supports. The turnbuckle is adjusted when the temperature is 80°F to produce a stress of 1000 lb/in.². $E = 30 \times 10^6$ lb/in.² and $\alpha = 7.0 \times 10^{-6}$ in./in.-°F.

Find: The stress in the rod if the temperature drops to 0°F.

Solution

Thermal stresses act independently of other stresses in a material. The final stress in a material is therefore a combination of the thermal stress and the existing stress in a member. If there is an existing tensile stress and the thermal stress is also tensile, the two add up to produce the final stress. The addition of stresses also applies when there is an initial compressive stress and the thermal stress is likewise compressive, as in an expansion that is restrained. On the other hand, a thermal stress that is opposite in nature to an existing stress is subtracted from it.

The drop in temperature in this problem causes the rod to shrink, and since it is rigidly held, a tensile stress is created. This is then added to the existing tensile stress to find the resultant stress.

From equation (24),

$$s_t = E\alpha\,\Delta t$$

$$= (30 \times 10^6 \text{ lb/in.}^2)(7.0 \times 10^{-6} \text{ in./in.-}°F)$$
$$\times (80°F - 0°F)$$

$$= 16,800 \text{ lb/in.}^2$$

$$\therefore\ s = s_0 + s_t$$

$$= 1000 \text{ lb/in.}^2 + 16,800 \text{ lb/in.}^2$$

$$= 17,800 \text{ lb/in.}^2$$

EXAMPLE 9.32

Given: A 100-ft surveyor's steel measuring tape with a 0.0117-in.² cross-sectional area under a tension of 10 lb at 70°F. $E = 30 \times 10^6$ lb/in.² and $\alpha = 7.0 \times 10^{-6}$ in./in.-°F.

Find: A. The length of the tape at 50°F.

B. The force required to maintain the length of 100 ft at 50°F.

Solution

1. From equation (23),

$$\delta_t = \alpha L\,\Delta t$$

$$\delta_t = (7.0 \times 10^{-6} \text{ in./in.-}°F)$$
$$\times (100 \text{ ft} \times 12 \text{ in./ft})$$
$$\times (70°F - 50°F)$$

$$= (7.0 \times 10^{-6})(1200)(20) \text{ in.}$$

$$= 0.168 \text{ in. (contraction)}$$

$$\therefore\ \text{final length} = (100 \text{ ft} \times 12 \text{ in./ft}) - 0.168 \text{ in.}$$

$$= 1199.83 \text{ in.}$$

2. Since the change in temperature shortens the tape, which is under the original force of 10 lb, the force will have to be increased enough to stretch the tape an amount equal to the contraction it would experience if the ends were not restrained. The extra force to maintain the 100-ft length can be computed as follows. From

$$\delta_t = \frac{PL}{AE}$$

we have

$$P = \frac{\delta_t AE}{L}$$

$$= \frac{(0.168 \text{ in.})(0.0117 \text{ in.}^2)(30 \times 10^6 \text{ lb/in.}^2)}{1199.83 \text{ in.}}$$

$$= 49.2 \text{ lb}$$

Therefore, the total force is

$$P_{\text{total}} = 49.2 \text{ lb} + 10 \text{ lb}$$

$$= 59.2 \text{ lb}$$

PROBLEMS

9.1 What is the difference between a stress and a force?

9.2 A bar 1 in. in diameter is subjected to a pull of 5 tons at each end. What is the amount and type of stress?

9.3 A bar 1.0 in. square supports a load of 30 tons. What is the stress in the bar?

9.4 The plain concrete pier shown in Fig. 9.44 is 5 ft thick and supports a steel column resisting $P = 14,400$ lb. If the density of the concrete is 150 lb/ft³, what is the compressive stress at the bottom of the pier?

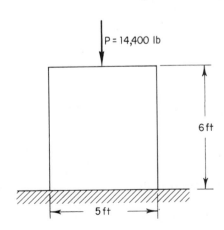

FIGURE 9.44

9.5 How is elongation related to the gage length of a specimen?

9.6 For the rod and yoke joint shown in Fig. 9.9, find the diameter of the rod if the tensile stress developed in it by an axial load is to be the same as the shearing stress in the pin.

9.7 A copper alloy has a modulus of elasticity of 16×10^6 lb/in.^{2}. How much stress is required to stretch a 5-ft bar of this alloy 0.03 in.?

9.8 A hole measuring 3 in. on each side is punched from a $\frac{1}{4}$-in.-thick structural steel plate by a force of 135,000 lb on a power press ram. What shear stress was developed in the metal?

9.9 An axial tensile load is applied to a bar of structural steel. The load is 45,000 lb, and the maximum allowable strain is 0.0003 in./in. What is the area of the bar? Assume $E = 30 \times 10^6$ lb/in.^{2}.

9.10 Sketch a stress-strain curve for a mild steel specimen, indicating the important points.

9.11 Tobin bronze has a shearing stress of 42,400 lb/in.^{2}. Will a power press capacity of 50 tons, 125 tons, or 250 tons be required to perforate (punch a hole in) a $\frac{1}{2}$-in.-thick plate of this material with 1-in. holes, as shown in Fig. 9.45?

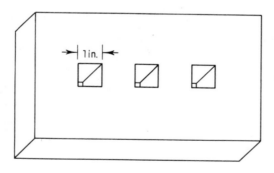

FIGURE 9.45

9.12 What is the difference between yield point and proportional limit?

9.13 What is modulus of elasticity?

9.14 What is the strain in a 1.0-in.-diameter bar when a load of 60,000 lb is applied. $E = 30 \times 10^6$ lb/in.^{2}.

9.15 Twenty people enter an elevator when the cable supporting it is 580 ft below the winding drum. The cross-sectional area of the cable is 1.0 in.^{2}, and its modulus of elasticity is 29×10^6 lb/in.^{2}. Assuming that the average weight per person is 150 lb and neglecting the weight of the cable, find how far the elevator settles.

9.16 A 2024T aluminum alloy bar is subjected to an axial tensile load that creates a stress of 12,000 lb/in.^{2}. If the bar is 1 ft long, what is the elongation of the bar? $E = 10 \times 10^6$ lb/in.^{2}.

9.17 A timber block 4×4 in. in cross section and 6 in. long supports a compressive load of 20,000 lb. If the block shortens 0.005 in., what is the modulus of elasticity of the wood?

9.18 A bar of steel 100 ft long has a cross-sectional area of 2 in.^{2}. Find the total elongation of this bar due to its own weight when it is supported at one end. Assume that the density of this steel is 450 lb/ft^3 and that $E = 30 \times 10^6$ lb/in.^{2}.

9.19 Why is an initial stress required in a conventional tensile test? Where does it appear in the stress-strain diagram?

9.20 A 10-in.-square concrete column contains four 1-in.-diameter round steel reinforcing bars and supports an axial load of 150,000 lb. The steel and concrete deform equally. Determine the stress in each material, assuming E_c for concrete is 2.5×10^6 lb/in.^{2} and E_s for steel is 30×10^6 lb/in.^{2}.

9.21 What is the difference between elastic limit and proportional limit.

9.22 A Lally column is a patented column made up of a cylindrical steel pipe shell filled with Portland cement concrete. The lightweight Lally column has an outside diameter of 4 in. and a shell thickness of 0.134 in. Assuming that $E_s = 30 \times 10^6$ lb/in.^{2}, $E_c = 2.5 \times 10^6$ lb/in.^{2}, and the allowable compressive stress for concrete is 1000 lb/in.^{2}, find the following:

A. Area of steel.
B. Area of concrete.
C. Safe load that the column can carry.

9.23 Find the change in the 1.5-in. diameter of a 12-in.-long steel bar subjected to an axial pull of 35,400 lb. Assume:

$$\mu = 0.30$$
$$E = 30 \times 10^6 \text{ lb/in.}^2.$$

9.24 What is the factor of safety?

9.25 A wire rope has a breaking strength of 10,000 lb and is used for a 5000-lb hoist. Can the factor of safety be definitely determined? Why?

9.26 What five considerations are related to the properties of materials when a factor of safety and a working stress are selected for a particular material?

9.27 A short, rectangular post of yellow pine is 4×5 in. in actual size. If its ultimate compressive strength is 8500 lb/in.² and its modulus of elasticity is 1.6×10^6 lb/in.², find the maximum axial load that can be carried using a factor of safety of 10.

9.28 Find the amount by which a 300-ft long steel bridge will lengthen when the temperature changes from 45°F to 75°F. $\alpha = 6.5 \times 10^{-6}$ and $E = 30 \times 10^6$ lb/in.².

9.29 A steel railroad rail was welded at a temperature of 90°F. If the temperature of the rail falls to 60°F, what tensile stress will be created? α for steel is 7.0×10^{-6} in./in.-°F.

9.30 A 1-in.-square tie rod of 99.97% iron 10 ft long is located between two rigid walls, and the nuts are tightened at 100°F. When the temperature drops to 10°F, what is the stress in the rod? $\alpha = 6.6 \times 10^{-6}$ in./in.-°F and $E = 29.7 \times 10^6$ lb/in.².

9.31 A surveyor's steel measuring tape has a cross-sectional area of 0.0117 in.² and is 100.000 ft long under a pull of 10 lb at 70°F.
   A. What is the actual length of this tape?
   B. At what temperature will the tape require no pull to be exactly 100.000 ft long?

Ten

STRAIN ENERGY

10.1 Axial Energy Loads

In the preceding chapters, the loads acting on members were assumed to be static, or steady, and applied gradually. Our concern was primarily with the ability of a member to resist the action of a force; the strength of a material was measured by its ability to withstand a load. In practical engineering problems, the ability of a member to absorb and store energy due to work done upon it may be more critical than its ability to resist force. The energy can come from an *energy load* that is delivered by a moving object, or it can come from a gradually applied static load.

Whenever a body is stressed by a force, there is, according to Hooke's law, a corresponding strain. When force and displacement in the direction of the force result, work is done. Therefore, during the elongation of a bar under an axial load that gradually increases to its final value P and produces an elongation δ, work is done on the bar. This work is transformed into *potential energy of strain*. If the strain remains within the elastic limit, the energy can be recovered as the strained bar is unloaded.

To determine the effect of an energy load on a member, we must (1) find the strain energy in terms of both external load and deformation, (2) find the strain energy per unit volume of the bar (modulus of resilience), and (3) find the stress in the bar caused by the energy load.

The bar in Fig. 10.1a is rigidly held at one end. (In this discussion, we assume that the weight of the bar causes no significant elongation.) In Fig. 10.1b, an external load has been applied gradually: its final value is P, and it produces a total elongation δ.

In Fig. 10.2, the load applied to the bar in Fig. 10.1 is plotted along the y axis, and the corresponding elongations are plotted along the x axis. P_1 is an intermediate value of the load, and δ_1 is the elongation caused by it. P_2 is another intermediate value of the load, larger than P_1, and δ_2 is the elongation caused by it. Therefore, $P_2 - P_1$ is the *increase* in load that causes an increase in elongation equal to $\delta_2 - \delta_1$. The work done by the increasing load during this elongation is equal to the force multiplied by the distance. The force is the *average* of P_1 and P_2; the distance is $\delta_2 - \delta_1$. Thus, the *work done* is equal to the area of the dark trapezoid in Fig. 10.2.

The *total work* done as the load goes from O (at the origin) to P is equal to the total of all similar

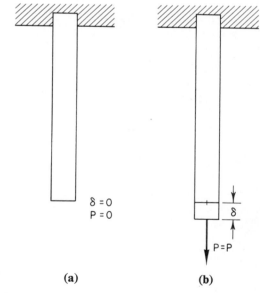

$\delta = 0$
$P = 0$

δ

$P = P$

(a)　　　　　　(b)

FIGURE 10.1

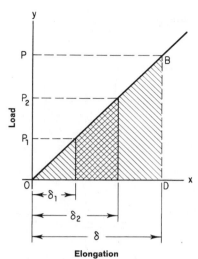

FIGURE 10.2

trapezoidal areas, which is the area of the large triangle OBD in Fig. 10.2. This area represents the *total energy* stored in the bar as it was strained. The symbol for this energy is U, and its value is

$$\text{area of triangle } OBD = \tfrac{1}{2}\text{base} \times \text{height}$$

Therefore,

$$\text{U} = \tfrac{1}{2}\delta P$$

$$(1) \qquad\qquad = \frac{P\delta}{2}$$

where P is the total load in pounds, δ is the total elongation in inches, and U is the strain energy in inch-pounds. From equation (1), we can find strain energy in terms of external load. Since stress s is within the proportional limit, and since $\delta = PL/AE$,

$$\text{U} = \left(\frac{P}{2}\right)\left(\frac{PL}{AE}\right)$$

$$(2) \qquad\qquad = \frac{P^2L}{2AE}$$

where L is the length of the bar in inches, A is the cross-sectional area of the bar in square inches, and E is the modulus of elasticity in pounds per square inch.

To find the strain energy per unit volume and thus the modulus of resilience, we introduce the symbol w for *energy per unit volume*. Then,

$$w = \frac{\text{U}}{\text{volume}}$$

Since the volume of the bar is its area times its length, or AL,

$$w = \frac{\text{U}}{AL}$$

Then, since $\text{U} = \dfrac{P\delta}{2}$,

$$w = \frac{P\delta}{2AL}$$

or

$$w = \frac{1}{2}\left(\frac{P}{A}\right)\left(\frac{\delta}{L}\right)$$

Then, since $\dfrac{P}{A} = s$ and $\dfrac{\delta}{L} = \epsilon$,

$$(3) \qquad\qquad w = \tfrac{1}{2}s\epsilon$$

Further, since $\epsilon = \dfrac{s}{E}$,

$$w = \frac{1}{2}s\left(\frac{s}{E}\right)$$

or

$$(4) \qquad\qquad w = \frac{s^2}{2E}$$

where s is the stress in pounds per square inch, E is the modulus of elasticity in pounds per square inch, and w is the strain energy per unit volume in inch-pounds per cubic inch.

Modulus of resilience was defined as the amount of energy that a cubic inch of material will absorb when stressed to the proportional limit. If we call the stress at the proportional limit s_{PL}, we can say that

$$(5) \qquad \text{modulus of resilience} = w_{PL} = \frac{s_{PL}^2}{2E}$$

This indicates that a material with the capacity to absorb energy without incurring permanent set should have a high value of w, which means it has a high proportional limit (s_{PL}) and a low modulus of elasticity (E).

Since strain energy per unit volume was expressed above as

$$w = \tfrac{1}{2}s\epsilon$$

where s and ϵ are ordinate (y axis) and abscissa (x axis), respectively, the *modulus of resilience* is represented on the stress-strain diagram for tension by the triangular area under the straight-line portion of the stress-strain curve.

Next, we wish to find the stress in a bar due to an energy load. Here, we have to relate stress s to energy U. We proceed as follows:

$$U = \frac{P\delta}{2}$$

Since $P = sA$ and $\delta = \epsilon L = \frac{sL}{E}$,

$$U = \frac{1}{2}(sA)\left(\frac{sL}{E}\right)$$

(6) $$= \frac{s^2 AL}{2E}$$

Therefore,

$$s^2 = \frac{2EU}{AL}$$

and

(7) $$s = \sqrt{\frac{2EU}{AL}}$$

where U is the energy load in inch-pounds causing axial stress.

The assumption made here is that the relationship between energy and stress is always the same, regardless of the way energy is transferred to the bar. It was mentioned at the beginning of this section that the energy can come from a gradually applied load or from a moving object that contains *kinetic* energy. In either case, s must not exceed the proportional limit of the material.

10.2 Special Cases

There are two special cases of axial energy loads that are of interest. The first is the tension produced by the impact of a falling body; the second is the effect of a suddenly applied load.

Tension produced by impact occurs when the energy load is delivered to a bar by a body falling before it comes in contact with the bar. For example, in Fig. 10.3, a weight W falls from a height h and stops at the flange, producing an elongation δ of the bar. It is assumed that there is no loss of energy during impact when the weight strikes the flange and that the weight continues its downward motion, causing elongation δ. When

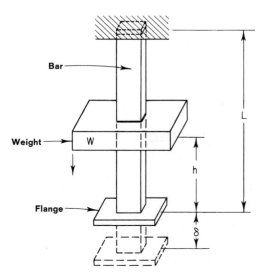

FIGURE 10.3

the bar can stretch no further, the weight is brought to a gradual stop. At this point, the deformation of the bar and the tensile forces in it are at a maximum.

The deformation of the bar and the tensile forces within it can be computed from the relationship between the work done by the weight in falling and the resulting strain energy in the bar. Since the work done by the weight is the product of its force (weight) and the distance through which it falls, we can write

$$\text{work} = \text{force} \times \text{distance}$$
$$= W(h + \delta)$$

From equation (6),

$$U = \frac{s^2 AL}{2E}$$

and from $\delta = \frac{sL}{E}$, from which we obtain $s = \frac{E\delta}{L}$, we can write the above equation as

$$U = \frac{E^2 \delta^2 AL}{2EL^2}$$

(8) $$U = \frac{AE\delta^2}{2L}$$

Then, since the work done by the weight falling a distance $h + \delta$ must be equal to the strain energy in the bar, strain energy = work

$$\frac{AE\delta^2}{2L} = W(h + \delta)$$

or

$$\delta^2 = \frac{2WL}{AE}(h + \delta)$$

If the weight were applied gradually to the flange, it would be considered a static load and would cause deformation

$$\delta_s = \frac{PL}{AE} = \frac{WL}{AE}$$

Substituting δ_s for $\frac{WL}{AE}$ in the expression for δ^2, we obtain

$$\delta^2 = 2\delta_s(h + \delta)$$
$$= 2\delta_s h + 2\delta_s\delta$$
$$\delta^2 - 2\delta_s\delta = 2\delta_s h$$

Completing the square by adding δ_s^2 to both sides,

$$\delta^2 - 2\delta_s\delta + \delta_s^2 = \delta_s^2 + 2\delta_s h$$
$$(\delta - \delta_s)^2 = \delta_s^2 + 2\delta_s h$$
$$\delta - \delta_s = \sqrt{\delta_s^2 + 2\delta_s h}$$

(9)
$$\delta = \delta_s + \sqrt{\delta_s^2 + 2\delta_s h}$$
$$= \delta_s + \sqrt{\delta_s^2 \left(1 + \frac{2h}{\delta_s}\right)}$$

(10)
$$\delta = \delta_s + \delta_s\sqrt{1 + \frac{2h}{\delta_s}}$$

This is the elongation (δ) of the bar due to the impact of the falling weight, where h is the height of the weight above the flange and δ_s is the elongation that would be caused if the same weight were gradually applied.

Strain energy can also be expressed in terms of elongation. From

$$\delta = \frac{PL}{AE}$$

we obtain

$$P = \frac{A\delta E}{L}$$

Then, since

$$U = \frac{P\delta}{2}$$

we find

$$U = \left(\frac{A\delta E}{L}\right)\left(\frac{\delta}{2}\right)$$

(11)
$$U = \frac{AE\delta^2}{2L}$$

A simpler version of equation (10) can be found by assuming that height h is very large compared with the static deformation δ_s. Then, the effect of δ_s and δ_s raised to exponents in equation (9) is insignificant, and the approximate deformation caused by a falling weight can be expressed as follows:

(12)
$$\delta_{\text{approx}} = \sqrt{2\delta_s h}$$

To find the stresses that result from the impact of the falling weight, we apply the relationship $s = \epsilon E = \delta E/L$ to $\delta = \delta_s + \delta_s\sqrt{1 + 2h/\delta_s}$:

$$\frac{\delta E}{L} = \frac{\delta_s E}{L} + \frac{\delta_s E}{L}\sqrt{1 + \frac{2h}{\delta_s}}$$

from which

(13)
$$s = s_s + s_s\sqrt{1 + \frac{2h}{\delta_s}}$$

where δ_s is the elongation due to weight W gradually applied to the bar, s_s is the stress due to weight W gradually applied to the bar, and s is the stress resulting from the impact of falling weight W.

To find an approximate value of s, we use the approximate value of δ:

$$s_{\text{approx}} = \delta_{\text{approx}}\frac{E}{L}$$
$$= \frac{E}{L}\sqrt{2\delta_s h}$$

Since $\delta_s = s_s \dfrac{L}{E}$,

$$s_{\text{approx}} = \sqrt{\left(\frac{E^2}{L^2}\right) 2 \left(s_s \frac{L}{E}\right) h}$$

(14)
$$s_{\text{approx}} = \sqrt{\left(\frac{2E}{L}\right) s_s h}$$

Equations (12) and (13) show that the stress caused by an impact energy load may be very much larger than that caused by the same weight applied gradually as a static load. From

$$s_{\text{approx}} = \sqrt{\left(\frac{2E}{L}\right)s_s h}$$

where $s_s = \dfrac{W}{A}$, we may write

$$s_{\text{approx}} = \sqrt{\left(\frac{2E}{L}\right)\left(\frac{W}{A}\right)h}$$

$$(15) \qquad = \sqrt{\left(\frac{2E}{AL}\right)(Wh)}$$

Using equation (7), where

$$s = \sqrt{\frac{2EU}{AL}}$$

and U is the energy load, we will arrive at the same result for s_{approx}. In the case of the falling weight, $U = W(h + \delta)$. If the deformation δ produced by the falling weight is considered small compared with h, it can be neglected, making $U = Wh$ and

$$s = \sqrt{\left(\frac{2E}{AL}\right)(Wh)}$$

which is the same as equation (15).

A great difference between impact stress and static stress is indicated by this equation. Impact stress in the above expression can be reduced by reducing the modulus of elasticity and by increasing the length and the cross-sectional area of the bar. To keep s_{approx} constant for a given material, the volume AL must increase if the energy Wh is increased. AL is the volume of a prismatic bar, a bar with similar bases and parallelogram-shaped sides. It follows, then, that the volume must be increased while the original shape of the bar is maintained; one obvious way of increasing the volume AL is to increase the length L. This has been proved in a number of practical cases where bolts were subjected to sharp blows. The bolts were subjected to extremely high energy loads and, as a result, broke in service. The solution to the problem was a redesigned holding arrangement that required the use of longer bolts.

The second special case of energy loads is the effect of a suddenly applied load. A sudden load remains constant throughout the elongation of the member. It is not applied gradually, as is the static, or steady, load. The problem is different from that of the static loading of a bar. And unlike impact loading, the kinetic energy of the load is not a factor.

In a sudden application of an axial load, the load falls because of its own weight (refer to Fig. 10.3). In this case, the placement of the weight W on the flange of the bar creates the sudden load. The weight elongates the rod until the resisting force in the rod equals the weight W. At this point, the elongation δ is just equal to that produced by the weight as a static load. In a static-loading situation, the load would stop at this point; but in this case, the load has gained energy in moving the small distance δ_s and therefore continues to move downward until it is stopped by the resisting force in the bar. The problem now is to determine the maximum elongation δ and the maximum stress s produced by this condition of loading. To make the method of approach to this problem clear to the student, it will be solved in two ways.

In the first approach, we use equation (7):

$$s = \sqrt{\frac{2EU}{AL}}$$

Since the sudden axial load acting on the bar is W and its total elongation is δ, the work done by the load on the bar is equal to $W\delta = U$, the energy load. Thus,

$$s = \sqrt{\frac{2EW\delta}{AL}}$$

But $\dfrac{\delta}{L} = \epsilon$. Therefore,

$$s = \sqrt{\frac{2EW\epsilon}{A}}$$

and since $E\epsilon = s$, we may write

$$s = \sqrt{\frac{2Ws}{A}}$$

$$s^2 = \frac{2Ws}{A}$$

Thus,

$$(16) \qquad s = \frac{2W}{A}$$

where W/A equals the stress caused by static loading. From this we see that within the proportional limit the stress caused by a sudden load is *twice as large* as that caused by the same load gradually applied.

The deformation under a sudden load can be determined as follows. Since $s = E\delta/L$,

$$\delta = \frac{Es}{L}$$

The static deformation is

$$\delta_s = \frac{Es_s}{L}$$

and the sudden deformation is

$$\delta = \frac{Es}{L}$$

But $s = 2s_s$. Therefore,

$$\delta = \frac{E2s_s}{L}$$

and since $\frac{Es_s}{L} = \delta_s$,

$$\delta = 2\delta_s$$

The deflection caused by an axial sudden load is *twice as large* as that caused by the same load gradually applied.

These results can be verified by the second [method of] approach, which uses the relationship

$$\delta = \delta_s + \delta_s \sqrt{1 + \frac{2h}{\delta_s}}$$

Unlike the impact-load condition, the weight is not dropped from a height h. Instead, it is placed directly on the flange of the bar, thereby making $h = 0$.

Substituting $h = 0$ in the above equations,

$$\delta = \delta_s + \delta_s \sqrt{1 + \frac{0}{\delta_s}}$$

$$= \delta_s + \delta_s$$

$$= 2\delta_s$$

which verifies the previous result: the deformation caused by a sudden load is twice that produced by the same load gradually applied. Similarly,

(17) $$s = s_s + s_s \sqrt{1 + \frac{2h}{\delta_s}}$$

When $h = 0$,

$$s = s_s + s_s \sqrt{1 + \frac{0}{\delta_s}}$$

$$= s_s + s_s$$

$$= 2s_s$$

which also verifies the previous result that the stress caused by a sudden load is twice as large as that caused by the same load gradually applied.

EXAMPLE 10.1 _____

Given: A uniform steel bar 12 in. long with a cross-sectional area of 3 in.^{2} is compressed by a force of 2000 lb. $E = 30 \times 10^6$ lb/in.^{2}.

Find: The strain energy in the bar.

Solution

From equation (2),

$$U = \frac{P^2L}{2AE}$$

$$= \frac{(2000 \text{ lb})^2(12 \text{ in.})}{2(3 \text{ in.}^2)(30 \times 10^6 \text{ lb/in.}^2)}$$

$$= 0.267 \text{ in.-lb}$$

EXAMPLE 10.2 _____

Given: A steel bar 60 in. long and $\frac{3}{4}$ in. in diameter stretched 0.06 in. $E = 30 \times 10^6$ lb/in.^{2}.

Find: The strain energy stored in the bar.

Solution

From equation (8),

$$U = \frac{AE\delta^2}{2L}$$

$$= \frac{[\pi(0.75 \text{ in.})^2/4](30 \times 10^6 \text{ lb/in.}^2)(0.06 \text{ in.})^2}{2(60 \text{ in.})}$$

$$= \frac{(0.442 \text{ in.}^2)(30 \times 10^6 \text{ lb/in.}^2)(0.0036 \text{ in.}^2)}{120 \text{ in.}}$$

$$= 398 \text{ in.-lb}$$

EXAMPLE 10.3 _____

Given: The steel bar in Example 10.2, deformed as described, for which 0.06 in. is the deformation at the proportional limit.

Find: The modulus of resilience.

Solution

Modulus of resilience is the greatest amount of strain energy per unit volume that can be stored in a bar without permanent set. It is therefore the strain energy stored by the application of the stress at the *proportional limit*.

$$\text{modulus of resilience} = \frac{U}{AL} = \frac{s^2}{2E}$$

Since $U = 398$ in.-lb, $A = 0.442$ in.^{2}, and $L = 60$ in.,

$$\text{modulus of resilience} = \frac{398 \text{ in.-lb}}{(0.442 \text{ in.}^2)(60 \text{ in.})}$$

$$= 15 \text{ in.-lb/in.}^3$$

EXAMPLE 10.4

Given: A prismatic steel bar mounted vertically is strained by an axial load of 2000 lb applied at its free end and by its own weight. The bar is 50 ft long and has a cross-sectional area of 1 in.^{2}. The weight of steel is 490 lb/ft^3. $E = 30 \times 10^6$ lb/in.^{2}.

Find: The strain energy in the bar.

Solution

The deformation δ is caused by the axial load and by the weight W of the bar:

$$\delta = \delta_P + \delta_W$$

The deformation caused by the axial load is $\delta_P = \dfrac{PL}{AE}$:

$$\delta_P = \frac{(2000 \text{ lb})(50 \text{ ft} \times 12 \text{ in./ft})}{(1 \text{ in.}^2)(30 \times 10^6 \text{ lb/in.}^2)}$$

$$= \frac{1.2 \times 10^6 \text{ lb-in.}}{30 \times 10^6 \text{ lb}}$$

$$= 0.04 \text{ in.}$$

The deformation caused by the weight of the bar is the same as that produced by an axial load of *half* its weight applied at its free end:

$$\delta_W = \frac{PL}{AE}$$

$$= \frac{\left(\dfrac{W}{2}\right)L}{AE}$$

Since the weight is equal to the density times the volume,

$$W = \frac{490 \text{ lb/ft}^3}{1728 \text{ in.}^3/\text{ft}^3} (1 \text{ in.}^2)(50 \text{ ft} \times 12 \text{ in./ft})$$

$$= 170 \text{ lb}$$

Therefore, the deformation caused by the weight is

$$\delta_W = \frac{(170 \text{ lb}/2)(50 \text{ ft} \times 12 \text{ in./ft})}{(1 \text{ in.}^2)(30 \times 10^6 \text{ lb/in.}^2)}$$

$$= 0.000170 \text{ in.}$$

and the total deformation is

$$\delta = \delta_P + \delta_W$$

$$= 0.040 \text{ in.} + 0.000170 \text{ in.}$$

$$= 0.04017 \text{ in.}$$

Thus, from equation (8), the strain energy is

$$U = \frac{AE\delta^2}{2L}$$

$$= \frac{(1 \text{ in.}^2)(30 \times 10^6 \text{ lb/in.}^2)(0.04017 \text{ in.})^2}{2(50 \text{ ft} \times 12 \text{ in./ft})}$$

$$= 40.5 \text{ in.-lb}$$

EXAMPLE 10.5

Given: A 15-lb weight with a hole in its center is free to travel up and down a long, threaded, circular rod rigidly held at its threaded end, as shown in Fig. 10.4. The rod is 5 ft long and is made of steel, with a proportional limit of 30,000 lb/in.^{2}. The weight falls from a height of 2ft $2\frac{1}{2}$ in. and strikes the square head of the rod. $E = 30 \times 10^6$ lb/in.^{2}.

Find: The cross-sectional area of the rod required to prevent the stress created in the rod from exceeding the proportional limit. Neglect the effect of the threaded portion of the rod.

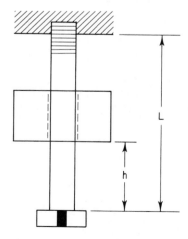

FIGURE 10.4

Solution

Use the formula for the approximate value of stress caused by an impact load. From equation (15), where

$$s_{approx} = \sqrt{\left(\frac{2E}{AL}\right)Wh}$$

the required area is

$$A = \frac{2EWh}{s^2L}$$

Substituting given data,

$$A = \frac{2(30 \times 10^6 \text{ lb/in.}^2)(15 \text{ lb})(26.5 \text{ in.})}{(30,000 \text{ lb/in.}^2)^2(5 \text{ ft} \times 12 \text{ in./ft})}$$

$$= 0.442 \text{ in.}^2$$

EXAMPLE 10.6 —————————————

Given: The two cylindrical bars shown in Fig. 10.5 are subjected to equal loads P, which produce uniformly distributed stress in the bars.

Find: A. The *ratio* of the resistance to energy loads of the bar in Fig. 10.5b to that of the bar in Fig. 10.5a.

B. The ratio of the resistance of the bars to static loads.

Solution

A. Resistance to energy loads is the capacity of each bar to absorb strain energy. For bar a,

$$U_a = \frac{P^2L}{2AE} \quad \text{and} \quad L_a = 2L$$

Therefore,

$$U_a = \frac{P^2(2L)}{2AE}$$

$$= \frac{P^2L}{AE}$$

For bar b, the strain energy must be found separately for the top and bottom parts. For the bottom part of the bar,

$$U_{bottom} = \frac{P^2L}{2AE}$$

For the top part of the bar, P, L, and E are the same as for the bottom. The value of area A for the top part, however, is four times as large as for the bottom, since the diameter is twice as large as the bottom diameter and area is proportional to the square of its linear dimensions. Then,

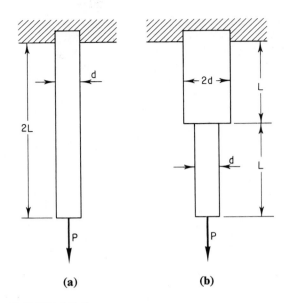

(a)   **(b)**

FIGURE 10.5

$$U_{top} = \frac{P^2L}{2(4A)E}$$

and

$$U_b = \frac{P^2L}{2AE} + \frac{P^2L}{8AE}$$

$$= \frac{5}{8}\left(\frac{P^2L}{AE}\right)$$

Therefore,

$$\frac{U_b}{U_a} = \frac{5P^2L/8AE}{P^2L/AE} = \frac{5}{8}$$

This result indicates that for a given maximum stress the amount of energy that can be absorbed by a bar of nonuniform cross section is less than that absorbed by a bar of uniform shape. Bar a, then, of constant cross section has a greater resistance to energy loads than bar b, even though bar b has a greater volume. The reduction in the diameter of the top part of bar b, to produce bar a, has increased its capacity to absorb energy.

A bar's ability to absorb an energy load U and store it as strain energy depends not only on the maximum stress, but also on the *distribution of stress* in the bar and on the volume of the bar. Energy absorbed by a unit volume of the bar is $s^2/2E$, and the energy absorbed by a given part with stress s is $(s^2/2E)(AL)$. In bar b, while its top part has a four-fold increase in volume, its stress is reduced to one quarter of that in the bottom, and the s^2 factor has become $\frac{1}{16}$. The s^2 factor has decreased at a faster rate than the volume has increased, resulting in a *net decrease* in energy.

B. The resistance offered by a member to a static load P depends only on the maximum stress developed. The maximum stress occurs on the smallest cross section, and $P = sA$. Resistance to static loads is measured by $s = P/A$. For bar a,

$$s_a = \frac{P}{A}$$

where A is the smallest cross section. For bar b,

$$s_b = \frac{P}{A}$$

Here the smallest cross section occurs in the bottom part of the bar; it is the same as that for bar a. Therefore,

$$s_a = s_b$$
$$= \frac{P}{A}$$

and the two bars have the same resistance to static loads.

The static strengths of the two bars in Fig. 10.5 are equal, since the smallest cross-sectional areas are equal and the loads required to produce a given stress are equal.

EXAMPLE 10.7

Given: A weight of 1000 lb falls from a height of 2 ft 6 in. onto the top of a 10 × 10-in. wood post 8 ft 4 in. long. $E = 1.5 \times 10^6$ lb/in.²

Find: A. The maximum compressive stress in the post, neglecting its mass and deflection.
B. The compressive stress in the post caused by the same weight gradually applied.

Solution

A. Since δ_s may be neglected, we use equation (15) to find the maximum compressive stress:

$$s = \sqrt{\frac{2EWh}{AL}}$$
$$= \sqrt{\frac{2(1.5 \times 10^6 \text{ lb/in.}^2)(1000 \text{ lb})(30 \text{ in.})}{(10 \text{ in.} \times 10 \text{ in.})(100 \text{ in.})}}$$
$$= \sqrt{\frac{9.0 \times 10^{10} \text{ lb}^2}{10^4 \text{ in.}^4}}$$
$$= 3000 \text{ lb/in.}^2$$

B. The compressive stress caused by a static load of 1000 lb is

$$s = \frac{P}{A}$$
$$= \frac{1000 \text{ lb}}{10 \text{ in.} \times 10 \text{ in.}}$$
$$= 10 \text{ lb/in.}^2$$

Comparing the two answers, we see that an energy load, particularly an impact load, causes a severe increase in stress.

EXAMPLE 10.8

Given: An aluminum bar 4 ft long with a cross-sectional area of 1 in.² supports a static load of 4000 lb. $E = 10 \times 10^6$ lb/in.²

Find: The stress produced by the same load dropped on its end from a height of 0.0288 in.

Solution

We solve this problem by using equation (17),

$$s = s_s + s_s \sqrt{1 + \frac{2h}{\delta_s}}$$

First, we solve the equation $s_s = P/A$:

$$s_s = \frac{4000 \text{ lb}}{1 \text{ in.}^2}$$
$$= 4000 \text{ lb/in.}^2$$

Next, we solve $\delta_s = PL/AE$:

$$\delta_s = \frac{(4000 \text{ lb})(4 \text{ ft} \times 12 \text{ in./ft})}{(1 \text{ in.}^2)(10 \times 10^6 \text{ lb/in.}^2)}$$
$$= 0.0192 \text{ in.}$$

Since $\delta_s = 0.0192$ in. is not negligible compared to $h = 0.0288$ in., we cannot use the approximate formula. Hence,

$$s = s_s + s_s \sqrt{1 + \frac{2h}{\delta_s}}$$
$$= 4000 \text{ lb/in.}^2 + (4000 \text{ lb/in.}^2)\sqrt{1 + \frac{2(0.0288 \text{ in.})}{0.0192 \text{ in.}}}$$
$$= 4000 \text{ lb/in.}^2 + (4000 \text{ lb/in.}^2)\sqrt{1 + 3}$$
$$= (4000 + 8000) \text{ lb/in.}^2$$
$$= 12,000 \text{ lb/in.}^2$$

Note that dropping the static load on the bar from a distance $1\frac{1}{2}$ times its static deflection triples the stress in the bar.

10.1 Define strain energy. Give a few examples of its application in strength of materials.

10.2 A steel bar is 18 in. long and has a cross-sectional area of 2 in.². It is subjected to an axial energy load of 240 in.-lb. Find the maximum axial stress developed in the bar. $E = 30 \times 10^6$ lb/in.².

10.3 What is the available strain energy in 2024T aluminum alloy if its elastic limit is one half its ultimate strength? $E = 10 \times 10^6$ lb/in.².

10.4 What is the total energy required to strain a steel bar 1 in. in diameter and 12 in. long to its elastic limit of 40,000 lb/in.²? $E = 30 \times 10$ lb/in.².

10.5 Assuming that the part referred to in Prob. 10.4 is designed to absorb only one half of its elastic energy capacity, find the maximum stress that can be induced by an impact load.

10.6 If the part referred to in Prob. 10.4 is to be designed with a factor of safety of 2 applied to the stress at its elastic limit, find the maximum elastic energy in inch-pounds that it may withstand.

10.7 What is meant by recoverable energy from an elastically strained material?

10.8 An impact force transmits 44 in.-lb of energy to a bar with a 4.5-in.² cross-sectional area. If the bar is 3.0 ft long and its modulus of elasticity is 30×10^6 lb/in.², what stress does this energy load induce in the bar?

10.9 For half of its length, a 36-in.-long bar has a cross-sectional area of 1 in.², and for the remaining half a cross-sectional area of 2 in.². The bar supports an axial tensile load of 20,000 lb, and its modulus of elasticity is 30×10^6 lb/in.². Find the recoverable unit strain energy in each part.

10.10 A steel bar with a length of 10 in. and a cross section of 1.0 in.² is struck axially by a moving body. The work done on the bar when the body is brought to rest is 5 ft-lb. What is the maximum stress developed in the bar? $E = 30 \times 10^6$ lb/in.².

10.11 What is modulus of resilience?

10.12 A weight of 300 lb falls 2 in. onto a flange at the end of a vertical steel rod 10 ft long and 1 in.² in cross-sectional area. Find
A. The static deflection of the rod.
B. The elongation produced in the rod by the impact load. The approximate formula may be used.

10.13 For the rod in Prob. 10.12, compute
A. The stress that would be produced by the gradual application of the load.
B. The stress produced in the rod by the 300-lb impact load. The approximate formula may be used.

10.14 If the allowable stress of the rod in Prob. 10.12 is not to exceed 30,000 lb/in.², find the greatest height from which the weight can be dropped.

10.15 A bar 3 ft long and 1 in.² in cross-sectional area is made of medium carbon steel and is stressed to its proportional limit by an axial energy load U. If the diameter of the bar is reduced to one half its original dimension over one quarter of its length, what energy load U will stress the bar to its proportional limit?

10.16 A 2000-lb weight falls on the top of a 10-in.-square wood post 8 ft 4 in. long from a height of 15 in. Find the maximum compressive stress developed in the post, neglecting its mass and deflection. $E = 1.5 \times 10^6$ lb/in.².

10.17 What is the difference between endurance limit and toughness?

10.18 The static strengths of the two members of Fig. 10.6 are equal. Which member has the greater energy-absorbing capacity? By what factor?

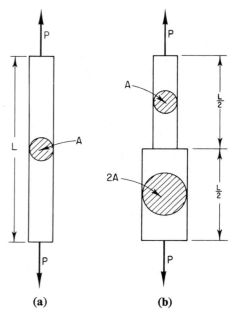

(a)   **(b)**

FIGURE 10.6

10.19 A 200-lb weight falls a distance of 3 ft and is then caught on the end of a steel wire cable, 0.785 in.² in cross section. If the cable is 100 ft long and $E = 15 \times 10^6$ lb/in.², what is the maximum stress developed in it? Neglect the weight of the cable.

10.20 A 100-lb weight drops 10 in. axially onto the top of a cast-iron block 5 in. square. What is the compressive stress induced in the material if the block is 3 in. high? $E = 15 \times 10^6$ lb/in.².

10.21 A 1-in.-diameter steel rod has to absorb the impact load of a 100-lb weight falling 3 ft. If the maximum allowable tensile stress is 25,000 lb/in.², how long must the rod be?

10.22 Explain why adding material at certain cross sections of a member may reduce rather than increase its resistance to impact loads.

10.23 Why does a reduction in the shank of the threaded bolt in Fig. 10.7a have a higher energy resistance than the bolt in Fig. 10.7b?

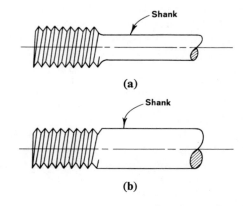

FIGURE 10.7

Eleven

SIMPLE BEAMS: LOADING, ANALYSIS, AND STRESSES

11.1 Introduction

In Chapters 9 and 10, we considered structural members subjected to axial forces. These forces created internal resisting tensile and compressive stresses. Members acted upon by forces creating shearing stresses were also analyzed. In this chapter, we will discuss structural members that resist loads perpendicular to their long axes. This type of load, called a *transverse* load, also lies in a plane containing a long axis of the member, or beam. A beam is defined as a bar that carries transverse loads. Thus, a beam rests on supports, spans a distance, and carries transverse loads or forces that tend to bend it. Most beams are used in a horizontal position. The downward loads on beams result from weights or forces that are usually, but not always, vertical. The reaction forces that resist the loads are exerted by the beam supports, and they are usually vertical. Transverse loads on a beam tend to bend it.

Any structural member that resists bending caused by transverse loads or forces acts as a beam.

11.2 Types of Beams

1. A *simple beam* is a horizontal bar that rests on a support at each end of the beam (see Fig. 11.1). Every part of the beam between supports is free to move vertically when subjected to vertical loads.

2. A *fixed beam* or *restrained beam* is a bar that is rigidly held at both ends, as shown in Fig. 11.2a, or fixed at one end and simply supported at the other, as shown in Fig. 11.2b. A fixed end is one that is restrained against rotation.

3. An *overhanging beam* is a beam that has one or both ends projecting somewhat beyond the beam supports, as shown in Fig. 11.3.

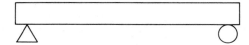

FIGURE 11.1

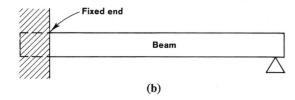

(a)

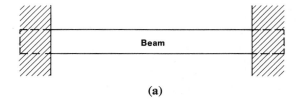

(b)

FIGURE 11.2

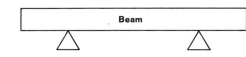

FIGURE 11.3

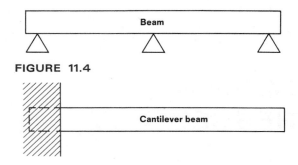

FIGURE 11.4

FIGURE 11.5

4. A *continuous beam* (see Fig. 11.4) is a beam that rests on more than two supports.

5. A *cantilever beam* is a structural member that has one fixed end (Fig. 11.5). The loading of cantilever beams is on the projecting part.

Of the five types of beams described above, only three are *statically determinate*. That is, in only three of them is the number of unknown forces equal to the number of equations available to solve them. The statically determinate beams, which we will examine in this chapter, are the simple beam, the overhanging beam, and the cantilever beam. Fixed beams and continuous beams are *statically indeterminate* and are not discussed in this book.

11.3 Statically Determinate Beams

The two supports of a simple beam exert only vertical reactions and do not prevent the beam

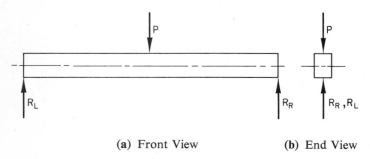

(a) Front View   (b) End View

FIGURE 11.6

Simple Beam

from bending. They exert no moment, and therefore the ends can rotate slightly when the beam is bent by a load. Such a beam is said to be freely supported.

The conventional representation of a simple beam is shown in Fig. 11.6. P is the applied load; R_L and R_R are the supporting reactions.

Since, in a simple beam, at least one of the supports must be free to move horizontally so that under bending action no force will be exerted in the direction of the long axis of the beam, a frictionless roller is often used as one support (see Fig. 11.7). If both ends were restrained and no horizontal motion were possible, an axial force would be created in the beam as it was deformed. This would add two horizontal unknown reactions to the two vertical reactions, creating four unknowns to be solved by three equations. A fully restrained beam, then, is not statically determinate and is not considered a simple beam.

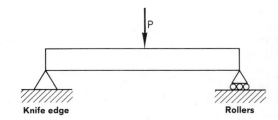

Knife edge   Rollers

FIGURE 11.7

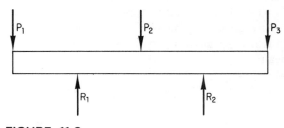

FIGURE 11.8

Overhanging Beam

The overhanging beam (Fig. 11.8) is freely supported and has one or both ends extending beyond the supports. Both end supports exert reaction forces only, *not moments*.

The cantilever beam is fixed at one end and loaded at the other. Any transverse force, such as

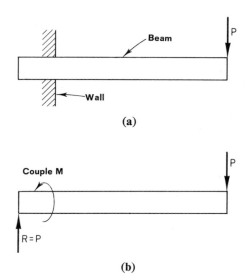

(a)

(b)

FIGURE 11.9

P in Fig. 11.9a, will make the beam tend to rotate, since *P* creates a moment about the fixed end. Rotation is prevented, however, by a system of forces at the fixed end, which creates a *resultant couple* opposing the load moment (Fig. 11.9b). The beam is also prevented from translating, or moving down, by a resultant force *R*, which is equal to *P*.

11.4 Beam Loading

Loads on beams may be either *concentrated* or *distributed*. A concentrated load is applied on a very small area of the beam and for convenience is assumed to act at a single point. Concentrated loads are expressed in pounds or kips, which is shorthand for kilopounds, or thousands of pounds. Examples of concentrated loads include the forces exerted by a tripod on a floor, a cable sling over a beam, the wheels of a gantry crane on a girder, and a column resting on a beam (see Figs. 11.10 and 11.11). While each of these concentrated loads actually extends over a relatively small area of the beam, each is considered to act at a point on the beam. A concentrated load is also exerted by the connecting rod on a crankshaft in an internal-combustion engine.

A distributed load is spread over a large area. It acts over a substantial length of a beam; it may be either uniform or nonuniform. A uniformly

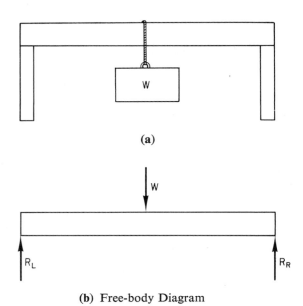

(a)

(b) Free-body Diagram

FIGURE 11.10

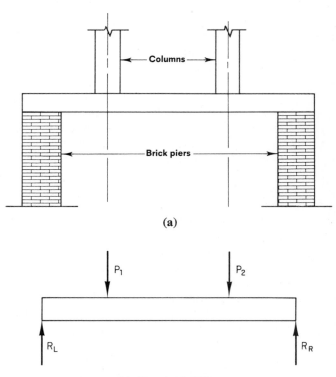

(a)

(b) Free-body Diagram

FIGURE 11.11

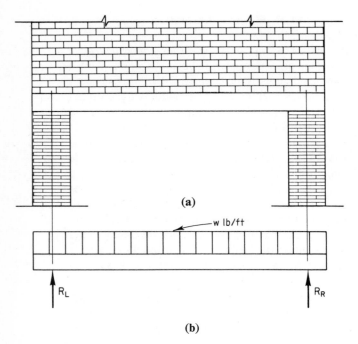

FIGURE 11.12

distributed load is spread out *evenly* over the length of the beam. It exerts an *equal* downward force for *each linear unit* of beam length and is usually expressed in pounds per linear foot or kips per linear foot. Normally, the small letter *w* is used to represent a uniform load. A brick wall of a given height built on a beam exerts a uniformly distributed load on the beam (see Fig. 11.12). In fact, the weight of the beam itself is a uniform load. A beam supporting a row of closely spaced floor joists, which in turn supports a floor and its load, is another example of a structure subjected to a uniform load. Loads distributed over a relatively large area are expressed in pounds per square inch or pounds per square foot. Steam pressure applied to a piston in a cylinder is an example of a uniformly distributed load expressed in pounds per square inch.

A nonuniform distributed load is similar to a uniform load except that its magnitude varies from one point to another. One example of such a load is materials stored at random on a warehouse floor. A nonuniform load that has a linear variation in magnitude can be treated in a simple mathematical way. If the load varies in a uniform manner from zero at one specific point to a certain value at another point, it is called a *triangular load* (see Fig. 11.13). If the load has a certain value at one point along the length of a beam or girder and a steady increase to some other value w_2 at a different point along the beam, it is called a *trapezoidal load* (see Fig. 11.14). In some instances, two triangular loads may meet at a zero load point and rise in opposite directions along a supporting member. This is sometimes called a "butterfly load," since its outline resembles the outstretched wings of a butterfly (see Fig. 11.15).

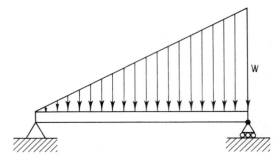

FIGURE 11.13

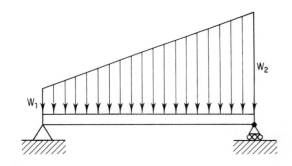

FIGURE 11.14

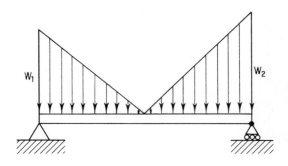

FIGURE 11.15

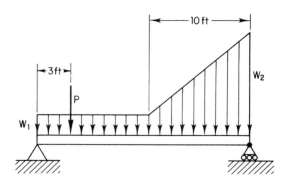

FIGURE 11.16

In actual practice, beam loading in both structural and machine components consists of a variety of loads. When it is too large to be neglected, the weight of the member can be assumed to be a uniform load. For short, simple timber beams carrying uniformly distributed loads, an estimated beam weight of 5% of the imposed load is usually considered. The simple beam in Fig. 11.16 carries three distinctly different loads. One is a uniform load that extends over the entire length of the beam. Another is a concentrated load P exerted 3 ft from the left support. The third load is the triangular pattern superimposed on the uniform load and extending 10 ft from the right support.

11.5 Beam Design

A beam must be designed to resist the *maximum stresses* caused by the loads it will carry. The allowable stress of the material, the length of the span, and the maximum bending moment to which the beam will be subjected are quantities known from the problem specifications. To design a beam, therefore, the designer must determine its size and shape. The designer first determines whether bending or shear stress is critical and attempts to meet this requirement. When the dimensions of the beam are established for the critical stress, the designer analyzes the beam to determine the *maximum value* of the other stress. If the noncritical stress is less than the allowable value, the design is complete. If it exceeds the

allowable value, a set of different dimensions or a different material must be chosen.

Bending stresses are important in long beams, while shearing stresses are the controlling factor in short beams. In general, a beam is designed to resist bending stresses, and then its ability to resist shearing stresses is checked. In structural applications where appearance is important, the *deflection* of the center of the beam under load is a critical factor.

When the strength requirements have been met, the *economy* of the final beam is considered. The beam that has the *lowest weight per linear foot* (or smallest cross-sectional area) is considered the most economical. A deep beam is more economical than a shallower beam of the same strength.

A load on a simply supported beam causes the beam to bend. If the load is between the two supports, bending occurs at all points in the beam, and the beam curves downward between the supports. When loaded, the rectangular cross-section beam in Fig. 11.17a is curved, as shown in Fig. 11.17b. The top of the beam *AB* is shortened, and the bottom *DC* is stretched. Such shortening and stretching creates internal resisting stresses of *compression* in the *upper part* of the beam and *tension* in the *lower part*. Since stress is proportional to deformation and since the deformation is greatest at the top and bottom of the beam, it follows that the compressive stress is greatest at the top, the tensile stress is greatest at the bottom,

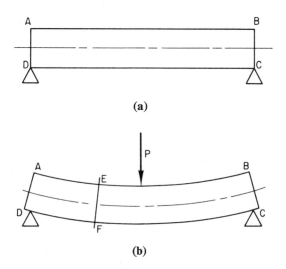

FIGURE 11.17

and the stress at the center of the beam is zero. The point of zero stress and zero deformation within the beam occurs on the *neutral axis*, an imaginary horizontal plane that coincides with the centroid or center of gravity of the section. In Fig. 11.17, the neutral axis is shown by the center-line symbol. In Fig. 11.18, which is the cross section at *EF*, the neutral axis is labeled *N.A.*

If the beam were cut at section *EF*, the left end of the beam would appear as shown in Fig. 11.19. The maximum compressive and tensile stresses caused by the bending of the beam occur at the extreme top and bottom fibers. If the triangular pattern of compressive stress is replaced by its resultant F_c and if the tensile stress pattern is replaced by its resultant F_t, the result is the free-body diagram in Fig. 11.20. Since the centroid of a triangle is located on a line one third of the distance between its side and the opposite vertex and since this distance for the right-triangle stress pattern is C, F_c and F_t are located a distance $\frac{2}{3}C$ from the neutral axis.

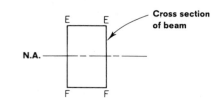

FIGURE 11.18

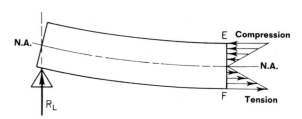

FIGURE 11.19

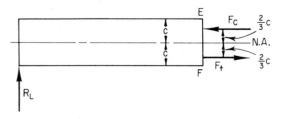

FIGURE 11.20

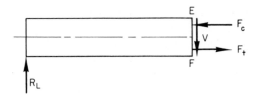

FIGURE 11.21

The beam deflection shown in Fig. 11.19 is exaggerated for purposes of illustration. In practice, deflections are so small that tensile and compressive stresses can be considered horizontal. For this reason, forces on beam sections are shown horizontal and vertical.

For equilibrium, the sum of the horizontal forces must be zero; therefore, $-F_c + F_t = 0$, or $F_c = F_t$. The forces are equal, opposite, and parallel and create a couple. The couple produces a counterclockwise resisting moment opposite in direction to the clockwise moment caused by the external force R_L acting with a lever arm equal to the distance from R_L to section *EF*. Thus, we have two of the three conditions for static equilibrium. $\sum F_x = 0$ and $\sum M = 0$. Since a vertical force acts on the beam, the third condition of static equilibrium must be satisfied. $\sum F_y = 0$. The only external vertical force acting on the left part of the beam is R_L, which acts upward. It can be opposed only by an internal vertical force acting downward at section *EF*. This internal force we label V (see Fig. 11.21). The vertical force V is called vertical *shear*, since it resists the tendency of the end part of the beam to slip with respect to the adjacent section. Were it not for the shear force in the fibers of the beam in section *EF*, the left end of the beam would be forced up relative to the center part of the beam. Shearing stress results when two opposite but parallel forces act on a body, creating a tendency in one part to slide past an adjacent part.

11.6 Bending Stresses in Beams

Experimentation in stress analysis indicates that the tensile and compressive *strains* are proportional to their distances from the neutral surface, or plane of zero stress. Since stress is proportional to strain, stress in a section is proportional to its distance from the neutral axis. Figure 11.22 shows a beam with a rectangular cross section that is bent by the load P. In Fig. 11.23, a side view of the beam showing section EF as an edge is seen with its stress distribution. Maximum compressive stress s_c is at the top of the beam, and maximum tensile stress s_t is at the bottom of the beam. The stress at a height y above the neutral axis is labeled s_y.

Let us find the formula for the stress in this beam due to bending. Although we use a rectangular section for *convenience*, the results and the procedure apply to any cross-sectional shape. Let Δa in Fig. 11.23a be a small strip of area at a distance y from the neutral axis. Since stress is proportional to distance from the neutral axis,

$$\frac{s_y}{y} = \frac{s_c}{c}$$

where c is the distance to the top fiber. Therefore, the stress on a fiber at a distance y from the neutral axis is

$$s_y = \frac{s_c y}{c}$$

Since $s = P/A$, the force F_y on the elemental area Δa is

$$F_y = s_y \Delta a$$
$$= \left(\frac{s_c y}{c}\right) \Delta a$$

Therefore, the moment of the force F_y about the neutral axis is

$$M_{N.A.,y} = F_y y = \left(\frac{s_c y \Delta a}{c}\right) y$$
$$= \left(\frac{s_c}{c}\right) y^2 \Delta a$$

Since the total resisting moment is the sum of the elemental resisting moments F_y, the total resisting moment is

$$M_{N.A.} = \sum \left(\frac{s_c}{c}\right) y^2 \Delta a$$

The ratio s_c/c is a constant for any beam, and we may write this equation as

$$M_{N.A.} = \frac{s_c}{c} \sum y^2 \Delta a$$

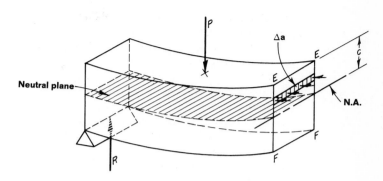

FIGURE 11.22

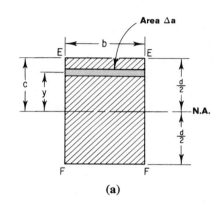

(a)

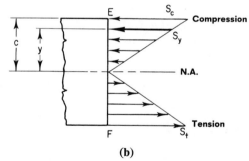

(b)

FIGURE 11.23

The expression $\sum y^2 \Delta a$ is, by definition, the expression for the *moment of inertia* of an area about the neutral axis. Therefore, letting the moment of inertia be $I = \sum y^2 \Delta a$, we have

$$M_{N.A.} = \frac{s_c I}{c}$$

For static equilibrium of the left portion of the beam (see Fig. 11.20), the moment of the internal resisting forces F_y about the neutral axis must equal the external moment caused by the force R_L acting with lever arm equal to the distance from the left support to the section EF. Therefore

$$M = M_{N.A.} = \frac{s_c I}{c}$$

Further, letting s be the maximum fiber stress, and rearranging terms, we write the *flexure formula*.

$$s = \frac{Mc}{I} \qquad (1)$$

Moment of inertia

Let us return for a moment to consider the *moment of inertia*. A mathematical expression in the form of $\sum y^2 \Delta a$ or $\sum x^2 \Delta a$ (where Δa is a small element of area a and x and y are distances from the coordinate axes) occurs in many formulas in engineering mechanics. Above, for example, $\sum y^2 \Delta a$ appears in the formula for the bending stress in a beam. Similar expressions occur in formulas for analysis of strength of columns. Since it appears so often, this type of expression has been given a name: the *moment of inertia*. Its symbol is I, and its units are the product of the square of a linear value, x^2 or y^2, and an area, which is also the square of a linear value, x^2 or y^2. Thus, if the length is measured in inches, the units of moment of inertia are inches^4.

As a *mathematical* definition, the moment of inertia of an area with units of inches^4 has no physical meaning. When viewed in the following manner, however, it does. The general expression for moment of inertia $y^2 \Delta a$ can be written in the form $(y \Delta a)y$. The expression $y \Delta a$ is the product of each element of area Δa and its moment arm y and is thus the moment of an area. Multiplying by the moment arm y, we obtain the moment of inertia, or the *second moment of an area*. Thus, moment of inertia can be considered the second moment of an area.

Moment of inertia is defined with respect to an axis. For an area, especially where the flexure formula is involved, the axis is that about which the area may rotate, and it generally lies in the same plane as the area. For rotation about the x axis, I is defined as $\sum y^2 \Delta a$; about the y axis, $I = \sum x^2 \Delta a$.

Moment of inertia is a mathematical property of an *area*, and therefore different geometric shapes have different moments. From the basic expression $I = \sum y^2 \Delta a$, values have been calculated for a large number of geometric figures and are available in a number of engineering handbooks. For convenience, expressions for the moment of inertia for simple shapes about the axis through the centroid (I_c) and about the base of the shape (I_b) are given in Table 11.1.

The basic formula for the moment of inertia gives I about the centroid of the area. To find I for a section about an axis other than that through its centroid, but parallel to it, we use a *transfer formula* (or parallel axis theorem). *The moment of inertia of any area about any axis in the plane of the area is equal to the moment of inertia of the area about its own centroidal axis parallel to the given axis plus the product of the area and the square of the distance between the two axes.* In symbols,

$$I_x = I_c + Ad^2$$

where I_c is the moment of inertia of the area about its centroid, A is the area of the shape (see Fig. 11.24), d is the distance from the new axis to the centroidal axis of the area, and I_x is the moment of inertia of the area about the new axis. It is evident that the least moment of inertia for an area is that about an axis through its centroid, or its centroidal moment of inertia.

Section modulus

Since, for a given beam, I and c are constant factors that depend only on the geometry of the beam's cross section, we may substitute for convenience the term $Z = I/c$ into the flexure formula, equation (1). Like I and c, the *section modulus Z*

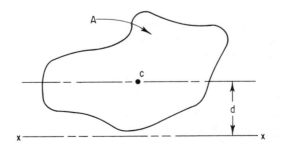

FIGURE 11.24

Table 11.1

		I_c	I_b
Rectangle		$\dfrac{bd^3}{12}$	$\dfrac{bd^3}{3}$
Square		$\dfrac{b^4}{12}$	$\dfrac{b^4}{3}$
Triangle		$\dfrac{bh^3}{36}$	$\dfrac{bh^3}{12}$
Circle		$\dfrac{\pi r^4}{4}$	$\dfrac{5\pi r^4}{4}$
Semicircle		$0.11r^4$	$\dfrac{\pi r^4}{8}$

depends only on the geometry of the cross section of the beam. The alternative form of the flexure formula may then be written as

$$s = \frac{M}{Z} \qquad (2)$$

Values for I and Z are listed in the tables of properties of sections in engineering handbooks. The symbol S is sometimes used in place of Z for section modulus.

The flexure formula is the basic tool a designer uses in analyzing bending stresses in beams. Knowing the external bending moment and the allowable stress of the material, the designer simply determines an economical size for the beam. He uses the flexure formula:

$$Z = \frac{M}{s} \quad \text{or} \quad S = \frac{M}{s}$$

Then, from the section modulus Z (or S), he selects the proper beam dimensions by referring to appropriate tables; for example, see Table 11.2.

EXAMPLE 11.1 ───────────

Given: A rectangle 6 in. deep and 2 in. wide, as shown in Fig. 11.25.

Find: The moment of inertia of the rectangle about its horizontal centroidal axis.

Solution

From Table 11.1, $I = bd^3/12$. For this section, $b = 2$ in. and $d = 6$ in. Therefore,

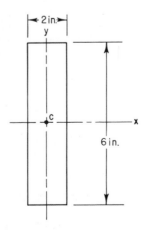

FIGURE 11.25

$$I = \frac{bd^3}{12} = \frac{(2 \text{ in.})(6 \text{ in.})^3}{12}$$

$$= \frac{(2 \text{ in.})(216 \text{ in.}^3)}{12}$$

$$= 36 \text{ in.}^4$$

EXAMPLE 11.2 ───────────

Given: The rectangle in Example 11.1.

Find: The moment of inertia of the rectangle about its vertical centroidal axis.

Solution

Viewed this way, the base $b = 6$ in. and the depth $d = 2$ in. Therefore, the moment of inertia is

$$I = \frac{bd^3}{12} = \frac{(6 \text{ in.})(2 \text{ in.})^3}{12}$$

$$= \frac{(6 \text{ in.})(8 \text{ in.}^3)}{12}$$

$$= 4 \text{ in.}^4$$

EXAMPLE 11.3 ───────────

Given: A circle with a radius of 3 in.

Find: The moment of inertia of the circle about its diameter.

Solution

From Table 11.1, $I = \pi r^4/4$. Therefore,

$$I = \frac{\pi r^4}{4} = \frac{\pi(3 \text{ in.})^4}{4}$$

$$= \frac{\pi(81 \text{ in.}^4)}{4}$$

$$= 63.6 \text{ in.}^4$$

EXAMPLE 11.4 ───────────

Given: A rectangle 6 in. wide and 2 in. deep.

Find: The moment of inertia of the rectangle about the axis shown in Fig. 11.26.

Solution

First, compute the moment of inertia of the rectangle about its centroidal axis:

Table 11.2

ROLLED STEEL SHAPES

WF SHAPES
Properties for designing

Nominal Size	Weight per Foot	Area	Depth	Flange		Web Thick-ness	$\dfrac{d}{A_f}$	AXIS X - X			AXIS Y - Y		
				Width	Thick-ness			I	S	r	I	S	r
In.	Lb.	In.²	In.	In.	In.	In.		In.⁴	In.³	In.	In.⁴	In.³	In.
27×14	177	52.10	27.31	14.090	1.190	.725	1.63	6728.6	492.8	11.36	518.9	73.7	3.16
	160	47.04	27.08	14.023	1.075	.658	1.80	6018.6	444.5	11.31	458.0	65.3	3.12
	145	42.68	26.88	13.965	.975	.600	1.97	5414.3	402.9	11.26	406.9	58.3	3.09
27×10	114	33.53	27.28	10.070	.932	.570	2.91	4080.5	299.2	11.03	149.6	29.7	2.11
	102	30.01	27.07	10.018	.827	.518	3.27	3604.1	266.3	10.96	129.5	25.9	2.08
	94	27.65	26.91	9.990	.747	.490	3.61	3266.7	242.8	10.87	115.1	23.0	2.04
	‡ 84	24.71	26.69	9.963	.636	.463	4.21	2824.8	211.7	10.69	95.7	19.2	1.97
24×14	160	47.04	24.72	14.091	1.135	.656	1.55	5110.3	413.5	10.42	492.6	69.9	3.23
	145	42.62	24.49	14.043	1.020	.608	1.71	4561.0	372.5	10.34	434.3	61.8	3.19
	‡130	38.21	24.25	14.000	.900	.565	1.93	4009.5	330.7	10.24	375.2	53.6	3.13
24×12	120	35.29	24.31	12.088	.930	.556	2.16	3635.3	299.1	10.15	254.0	42.0	2.68
	110	32.36	24.16	12.042	.855	.510	2.34	3315.0	274.4	10.12	229.1	38.0	2.66
	‡100	29.43	24.00	12.000	.775	.468	2.58	2987.3	248.9	10.08	203.5	33.9	2.63
24×9	94	27.63	24.29	9.061	.872	.516	3.07	2683.0	220.9	9.85	102.2	22.6	1.92
	84	24.71	24.09	9.015	.772	.470	3.47	2364.3	196.3	9.78	88.3	19.6	1.89
	76	22.37	23.91	8.985	.682	.440	3.90	2096.4	175.4	9.68	76.5	17.0	1.85
	‡ 68	20.00	23.71	8.961	.582	.416	4.55	1814.5	153.1	9.53	63.8	14.2	1.79
21×13	142	41.76	21.46	13.132	1.095	.659	1.49	3403.1	317.2	9.03	385.9	58.8	3.04
	127	37.34	21.24	13.061	.985	.588	1.65	3017.2	284.1	8.99	338.6	51.8	3.01
	‡112	32.93	21.00	13.000	.865	.527	1.87	2620.6	249.6	8.92	289.7	44.6	2.96
21×9	96	28.21	21.14	9.038	.935	.575	2.50	2088.9	197.6	8.60	109.3	24.2	1.97
	82	24.10	20.86	8.962	.795	.499	2.93	1752.4	168.0	8.53	89.6	20.0	1.93
21×8¼	73	21.46	21.24	8.295	.740	.455	3.46	1600.3	150.7	8.64	66.2	16.0	1.76
	68	20.02	21.13	8.270	.685	.430	3.73	1478.3	139.9	8.59	60.4	14.6	1.74
	62	18.23	20.99	8.240	.615	.400	4.15	1326.8	126.4	8.53	53.1	12.9	1.71
	‡ 55	16.18	20.80	8.215	.522	.375	4.85	1140.7	109.7	8.40	44.0	10.7	1.65

‡ Non-compact shape in A242, A440 and A441.

Adapted from *Manual of Steel Construction*, 6th ed. (New York: American Institute of Steel Construction, Inc., 1967), pp. 1–8 and 1–9.

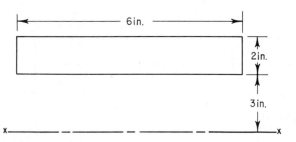

FIGURE 11.26

$$I_c = \frac{bd^3}{12} = \frac{(6 \text{ in.})(2 \text{ in.})^3}{12}$$

$$= 4 \text{ in.}^4$$

Then, since $I_{xx} = I_c + Ad^2$,

$$I_{xx} = 4 \text{ in.}^4 + (6 \text{ in.})(2 \text{ in.})(3 \text{ in.} + 1 \text{ in.})^2$$

$$= 4 \text{ in.}^4 + (12 \text{ in.}^2)(16 \text{ in.}^2)$$

$$= 196 \text{ in.}^4$$

EXAMPLE 11.5 _____

Given: The simple beam in Fig. 11.27 with a rectangular cross section is 15 ft long. The beam supports a single concentrated load of 6000 lb at its midpoint, and the cross-sectional dimensions of the beam are 10 in. wide and 12 in. deep.

Find: The maximum tensile and compressive stress in the beam.

Solution

1. Draw the free-body diagram of the beam, as shown in Fig. 11.28a. For static equilibrium, $\sum F_y = 0$. Therefore,

$$R_L + R_R - P = 0$$

Since $R_L = R_R$, we write

$$R_R + R_R - 6000 \text{ lb} = 0$$

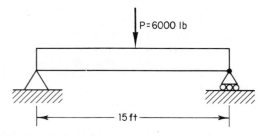

FIGURE 11.27

or

$$2R_R = 6000 \text{ lb}$$

and thus

$$R_R = 3000 \text{ lb} = R_L$$

2. Draw the free-body diagram of the left half of the beam, as shown in Fig. 11.28b. The external moment caused by reaction force R_L is

$$M = R_L \left(\frac{L}{2}\right)$$

$$= (3000 \text{ lb}) \frac{15 \text{ ft} \times 12 \text{ in./ft}}{2}$$

$$= (3000 \text{ lb})(90 \text{ in.})$$

$$= 270,000 \text{ lb-in.}$$

The distance from the fiber in maximum compression to the neutral axis is one half the depth of the cross section:

$$c = \frac{d}{2} = \frac{12 \text{ in.}}{2} = 6 \text{ in.}$$

Finally, from the equation for the moment of inertia of a rectangular section about the neutral axis,

$$I = \frac{1}{12} bd^3$$

$$= \frac{1}{12} (10 \text{ in.})(12 \text{ in.})^3$$

$$= \frac{17,280 \text{ in.}^4}{12}$$

$$= 1440 \text{ in.}^4$$

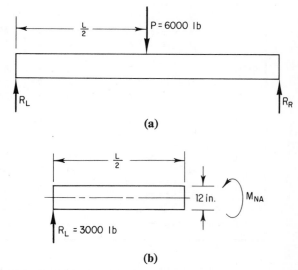

FIGURE 11.28

Substituting these values into the flexure formula, equation (1), we find the maximum stress in the beam:

$$s = \frac{Mc}{I}$$

$$= \frac{(270{,}000 \text{ lb-in.})(6 \text{ in.})}{1440 \text{ in.}^4}$$

$$= 1125 \text{ lb/in.}^2$$

EXAMPLE 11.6

Given: A wooden beam 4 in. wide, 12 in. deep, and 12 ft long, loaded as shown in Fig. 11.29. The uniformly distributed load $w = 100$ lb/ft.

Find: The maximum flexural stress in the beam.

Solution

1. Find the total load on the beam:

$$F = (12 \text{ ft})(100 \text{ lb/ft.})$$

$$= 1200 \text{ lb}$$

2. Let the load $F = 1200$ lb be applied at the mid-point of the beam span, as shown in Fig. 11.30, and find the reactions of the support R_A and R_B. Since $\sum F_y = 0$.

$$R_A + R_B = F = 1200 \text{ lb}$$

Also, since w is uniformly distributed between supports A and B, $R_A = R_B$. Therefore,

$$R_A = R_B = 600 \text{ lb}$$

3. Draw the free-body diagram of the left half of the beam (Fig. 11.31), and find the maximum moment in the beam:

$$M = (600 \text{ lb})(6 \text{ ft} \times 12 \text{ in./ft})$$
$$- (600 \text{ lb})(3 \text{ ft} \times 12 \text{ in./ft})$$

$$= 43{,}200 \text{ lb-in.} - 21{,}600 \text{ lb-in.}$$

$$= 21{,}600 \text{ lb-in.}$$

4. Then, from the flexure formula, $s = Mc/I$, we may find the maximum stress. Since $b = 4$ in. and $d = 12$ in.,

$$I = \frac{bd^3}{12} = \frac{(4 \text{ in.})(12 \text{ in.})^3}{12}$$

$$= \frac{(4 \text{ in.})(1728 \text{ in.}^3)}{12}$$

$$= 576 \text{ in.}^4$$

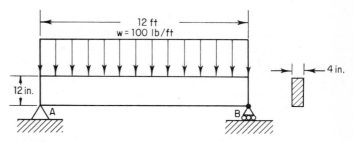

FIGURE 11.29

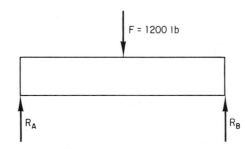

FIGURE 11.30

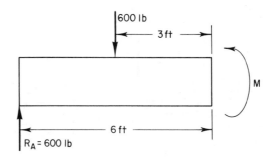

FIGURE 11.31

Finally, since $c = \frac{1}{2}d = \frac{1}{2}(12 \text{ in.}) = 6$ in.,

$$s_{\max} = \frac{Mc}{I} = \frac{(21{,}600 \text{ lb-in.})(6 \text{ in.})}{576 \text{ in.}^4}$$

$$= 225 \text{ lb/in.}^2$$

11.7 Shearing Stresses in Beams

Shear is the tendency of two adjacent parts of a body to slide past each other. Less apparent than vertical shear, which was described in Sec. 11.5, but equally important is the tendency for shear to occur in a *horizontal plane* within a beam.

Consider the stack of flat boards shown in Fig. 11.32a. Before load P is applied, the ends line up. When a vertical load P is placed on the center of the stack of lumber, the boards bend like a beam. As the stack bends, each board tends to slide past the boards above and below it, as shown in Fig. 11.32b. This sliding, or horizontal motion of one plank over another, is *horizontal shear*.

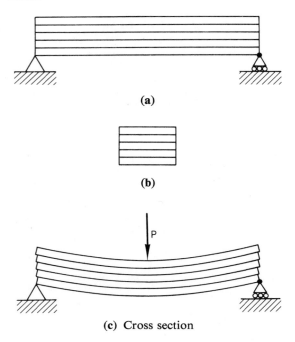

(a)

(b)

(c) Cross section

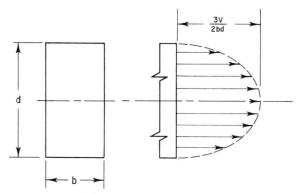

(d) Parabolic distribution of horizontal shear stress

FIGURE 11.32

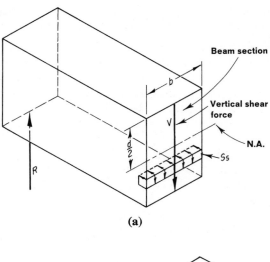

(a)

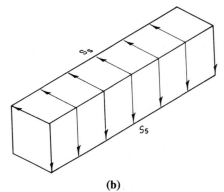

(b)

FIGURE 11.33

This same tendency for horizontal planes to slip past one another occurs in solid beams. The tendency is always present, and it is resisted by internal stresses in the beam. Fibrous materials have a greater tendency to fail in horizontal shear than materials with no internal cleavage planes. Wood, which naturally has a low shearing stress parallel to the grain, fails readily in horizontal shear. Horizontal shearing forces are also a factor on the design of built-up beams and those made of different kinds of material fastened together.

The action of horizontal shearing stresses can be easily visualized if we draw a free-body diagram of a rectangular portion of the inside of a beam carrying a transverse load, as shown in Fig. 11.33. Since the beam is in equilibrium, the small block is in equilibrium. Therefore, $\sum F_x = 0$, $\sum F_y = 0$, and $\sum M_0 = 0$—which occurs only when the shear stresses on the four faces of the block are equal, as shown in Fig. 11.33b. At any point in the beam, therefore, the horizontal shearing stress $s_{s,h}$ must equal the vertical shearing stress $s_{s,v}$. (See Fig. 11.34.) In other words, in a member subjected to shearing forces, shearing stresses of equal magnitudes act in planes at right angles to each other. However, the horizontal shearing stresses are not distributed uniformly over the beam cross section, as we will now prove.

The formula for the horizontal shear stress at any point in a beam is

$$s_s = \frac{VA\bar{y}}{Ib}$$

where s_s is the horizontal shearing stress in pounds per square inch, V is the total vertical shear force in the beam at the chosen section in pounds (as shown in Fig. 11.35), A is the area of the beam cross section above the horizontal plane in square inches, $\bar{y}$ is the distance from the neutral axis to the centroid of the area in inches, I is the moment of inertia of the entire beam cross section about the neutral axis in inches[4], and b is the width of the beam at the neutral axis in inches.

To find the distribution of the horizontal shearing stresses in a rectangular beam, we apply the shear-stress equation to the beam section shown in Fig. 11.36:

$$s_s = \frac{VA\bar{y}}{Ib}$$

Since

$$A = b\left(\frac{d}{2} - y\right)$$

and

$$\bar{y} = y + \frac{1}{2}\left(\frac{d}{2} - y\right)$$

$$s_s = \frac{V}{Ib}\left[b\left(\frac{d}{2} - y\right)\right]\left[y + \frac{1}{2}\left(\frac{d}{2} - y\right)\right]$$

$$= \frac{V}{I}\left(\frac{d}{2} - y\right)\left(\frac{y}{2} + \frac{d}{4}\right)$$

which may be written as

$$s_s = \frac{V}{2I}\left(\frac{d^2}{4} - y^2\right)$$

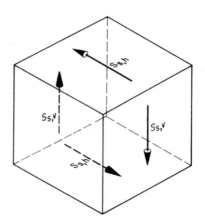

FIGURE 11.34

Shearing Stresses on an Element of a Beam

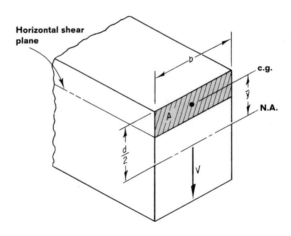

FIGURE 11.35

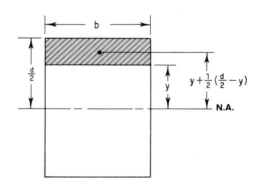

FIGURE 11.36

This is a quadratic equation that represents a parabola. Thus, the shearing-stress distribution along the depth of the beam has a parabolic profile, as shown in Fig. 11.32d.

At the top and bottom of the beam, where $y = d/2$, the shear stress is

$$s_s = \frac{V}{2I}\left[\frac{d^2}{4} - \left(\frac{d}{2}\right)^2\right]$$

$$= \frac{V}{2I}\left(\frac{d^2}{4} - \frac{d^2}{4}\right)$$

$$= 0$$

Conversely, the shear stress is maximum when $y = 0$, which coincides with the neutral axis.

Shearing stresses in rolled beams

Studies of shear-stress distribution in steel I beams, channels, T beams, and W sections show that the flanges do not resist a significant portion of vertical shear. The web alone may carry over 90% of the shearing force. Usually, we may assume that the total vertical shear is carried by the web alone. The average shearing stress using this assumption is very close to the value of the maximum shearing stress in the web obtained by the horizontal shearing-stress formula.

In this case, the web is considered to extend the full height of the beam, as shown in Figure 11.37. Thus,

$$\text{average } s_s = \frac{V}{A_{\text{web}}} = \frac{V}{td} = s_s$$

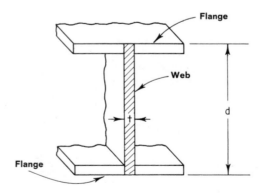

FIGURE 11.37

where t is the thickness of the web in inches, d is the full height of the beam in inches, and V is the total vertical shear force in pounds.

EXAMPLE 11.7 _____

Given: A rectangular beam of width b and depth d.

Find: The horizontal maximum shear stress in the beam.

Solution

From the parabolic distribution of the shear stress, we know that the maximum horizontal shear stress occurs at $y = 0$. From Table 11.1, $I = \frac{1}{12}bd^3$. Then, since $A = bd/2$, and $\bar{y} = d/4$,

$$s_s = \frac{VA\bar{y}}{Ib}$$

$$= \frac{V(bd/2)(d/4)}{(bd^3/12)b}$$

$$= \frac{3V}{2bd}$$

Since V is the shearing force in the beam cross section and bd is the area of the beam cross section, V/bd is the average vertical shear stress. The maximum horizontal shear stress is therefore $\frac{3}{2}$ of the average vertical shear stress in a beam of rectangular cross section.

EXAMPLE 11.8 _____

Given: A beam with a circular cross section having a diameter of 1 in. subjected to a vertical shearing force of 1000 lb.

Find: The shearing stress at the neutral axis of the beam.

Solution

1. Draw the cross-sectional area, as shown in Fig. 11.38.
2. The neutral axis coincides with the diameter of the circle. The area above the neutral axis is

$$A = \frac{1}{2}\pi r^2$$

and its centroid is

$$y = \frac{4r}{3\pi}$$

3. From Table 11.1,

$$I = \frac{\pi r^4}{4}$$

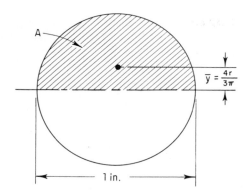

$$\bar{y} = \frac{4r}{3\pi}$$

1 in.

FIGURE 11.38

4. Finally, since $b = 2r$,

$$s_s = \frac{VA\bar{y}}{Ib}$$

$$= \frac{V(\pi r^2/2)(4r/3\pi)}{(\pi r^4/4)(2r)}$$

$$s_s = \frac{4V}{3\pi r^2}$$

$$= \frac{4(1000\ \text{lb})}{3\pi(\tfrac{1}{2}\ \text{in.})^2}$$

$$= \frac{4(1000\ \text{lb})}{3\pi(\tfrac{1}{4}\ \text{in.}^2)}$$

$$= \frac{16(1000\ \text{lb})}{3\pi\ \text{in.}^2}$$

$$= 1700\ \text{lb/in.}^2$$

Note that πr^2 in the expression for shearing stress in this section,

$$s_s = \frac{4V}{3\pi r^2}$$

is the area of the section. Further, $V/\pi r^2$ is the *average vertical shear stress.* Thus, the *maximum horizontal shear stress* in a circular beam,

$$s_s = \frac{4V}{3\pi r^2}$$

is $\tfrac{4}{3}$ of the average vertical shear stress.

PROBLEMS

11.1 Give several examples of common structures that are classified as cantilever beams.

11.2 A simply supported beam 21 ft long carries a triangular load that varies uniformly from zero at the left of the beam to 10,000 lb/ft at the right end. Find the right and left reactions.

11.3 Find the moment of inertia of a right triangle with 6-in. legs about its centroidal axis.

11.4 If the moment of inertia of a semicircle about its centroidal axis is $(\pi/8 - 8/9\pi)r^4$ and $\bar{y} = 4r/3\pi$, show that the moment of inertia about its diameter is $\pi r^4/8$. Use the transfer formula.

11.5 What is the section modulus of a beam?

11.6 A simple beam with a rectangular cross section is 10 ft long and supports a single concentrated load of 10,000 lb at its midpoint. The beam dimensions are 8 in. wide and 10 in. deep. Find

A. The support reactions.

B. The maximum bending moment.

C. The moment of inertia of the beam section.

11.7 For the beam in Prob. 11.3, compute the maximum tensile and compressive stresses.

11.8 If the depth of the beam in Prob. 11.6 were doubled, what would be

A. The moment of inertia.

B. The maximum tensile and compressive stress.

C. The section modulus.

11.9 A. Define a nonuniform distributed load, and give a practical illustration.

B. What is a "butterfly load"?

11.10 A cantilever beam 10 ft long supported at its left end carries a uniform load of 3000 lb/ft for its entire length. What is the restraining moment at the support?

11.11 If the cantilever beam in Prob. 11.10 supported a single concentrated load of 10,000 lb at its midpoint, find

  A. The moment at the support.

  B. The section modulus required for this beam if the allowable bending stress of structural steel is 22,000 lb/in.^{2}.

11.12 What is the neutral axis of a beam?

11.13 The beam in Example 11.6 has a maximum allowable flexural stress of 1200 lb/in.^{2}. Find the maximum concentrated load that the beam can support.

11.14 A simple beam with a span length of 20 ft must support a uniformly distributed load of 40,000 lb, including the weight of the beam. Using an allowable fiber stress of 25,000 lb/in.^{2}, find the required section modulus.

11.15 A simple timber beam 14 ft long and 12 in. deep is used to carry a single concentrated load of 6000 lb at a point 5 ft from its left end. Find the minimum required width of this beam, assuming that the allowable stress of the material is 1200 lb/in.^{2}.

11.16 A simply supported 12W-27 steel beam must support a uniform load. If the span is 12 ft and the allowable stress is 22,000 lb/in.^{2}, what is the maximum allowable load in pounds per lineal foot of beam? [*Note*: This is a wide flanged rolled shape approximately 12 in. deep weighing 27 lb per linear foot. $I_c = 204.1$ in.^{4}, and $Z = 34.1$ in.^{3}.]

11.17 A 6 × 10-in. timber beam 12 ft long supports a concentrated load of 4000 lb at its center. If the beam is supported at its ends, find

  A. The total vertical shear.

  B. The maximum horizontal shearing stress in the beam.

11.18 For the beam in Prob. 11.17, find the average vertical stress.

11.19 For the circular beam shown in Example 11.8, find the minimum required diameter if the allowable horizontal shearing stress is not to exceed 100 lb/in.^{2}.

11.20 What is a statically indeterminate beam?

11.21 Draw the stress distribution profile for a rectangular beam 4 in. wide and 8 in. deep with a vertical shearing force of 34,100 lb. Use layers 1 in. apart from top to bottom.

11.22 A laminated wood beam is built of 6 planks, each 2 in. × 4 in. (full size) glued together to form a cross section 4 in. wide by 12 in. high. The allowable strength of the glue is 62.5 lb/in.^{2}. Find

  A. The maximum vertical shear force that the section can withstand.

  B. The maximum flexure stress developed when a concentrated load is simply supported on a 16-ft span.

  C. The uniform load in pounds per linear foot that may be carried without exceeding the flexure stress found in *B*.

11.23 A 12W-31 cantilever beam 5 ft long supports a uniform load of 5000 lb/ft. The web thickness is 0.265 in. and the depth is 12 in. Find the shear stress in the web.

Part Three

SUPPLEMENTARY TOPICS

Topic A

INTRODUCTION TO VECTOR ALGEBRA

A.1 Vector Addition

Vector algebra, a "shorthand" method of symbolically manipulating vectors can be conveniently used to add and subtract vector quantities and to multiply vectors by scalars or other vectors. This system is especially advantageous in analyzing noncoplanar vector systems, since with it we can describe concisely the spatial or geometrical conditions of a given vector system.

Vector equations were introduced in Chapter 2 in the form

$$\vec{F_1} + \vec{F_2} = \vec{R}$$

where the geometric representation of this vector equation indicating addition is as shown in Fig. A.1. In Fig. A.1, the vector $\overrightarrow{OP}$ is represented by $\vec{F_1}$, $\overrightarrow{PQ}$ is represented by $\vec{F_2}$, and $\overrightarrow{OQ}$ is represented by $\vec{R}$.

The vectors in the above equation can also be indicated by boldface capital letters, as follows:

$$\mathbf{A} + \mathbf{B} = \mathbf{C}$$

where vectors $\overrightarrow{OP}$, $\overrightarrow{PQ}$, and $\overrightarrow{OQ}$ are represented by $\mathbf{A}$, $\mathbf{B}$, and $\mathbf{C}$, respectively (see Fig. A.2). We shall use the latter notation to develop the discussion that follows.

It was indicated in Chapter 2 that vector addition follows the *commutative law* of algebra, which means that the resultant of the vectors of any given system is independent of the order in which the vectors are added (see, for example, Fig. A.3).

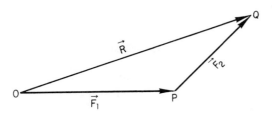

FIGURE A.1

$\vec{F_1} + \vec{F_2} = \vec{R}$

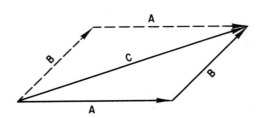

(a) A + B = C; B + A = C

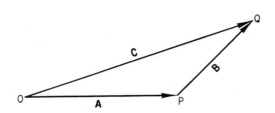

FIGURE A.2

A + B = C

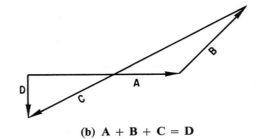

(b) A + B + C = D

FIGURE A.3

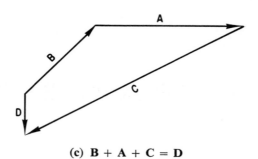

(c) **B** + **A** + **C** = **D**

FIGURE A.3

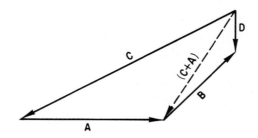

FIGURE A.6

(**C** + **A**) + **B** = **D**

Vector addition also follows the *associative law*, which means that the vectors in a given vector system can be added in any grouping or order without changing the sum or resultant. For example, consider the vector diagram in Fig. A.4, which is represented by the equation

A + **B** + **C** = **D**

The same resultant **D** is obtained when the resultant of **A** + **B** is added to **C** (see Fig. A.5). Similarly, the same resultant **D** is obtained if the resultant of **C** + **A** is added to **B** (see Fig. A.6).

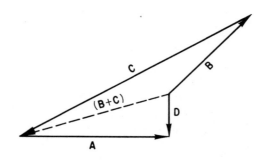

FIGURE A.7

(**B** + **C**) + **A** = **D**

Finally, the same resultant is obtained for (**B** + **C**) + **A** (see Fig. A.7).

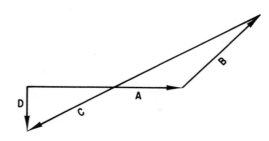

FIGURE A.4

A + **B** + **C** = **D**

A.2 Vector Subtraction

To subtract vector quantities, we must first consider their directions. For example, let us assume that vectors **A** and **B** are given as follows:

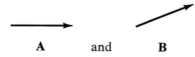

A   and   **B**

To subtract **B** from **A**, we would write the vector equation

A − **B** = **E**

which is equivalent to writing

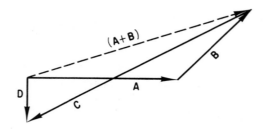

FIGURE A.5

(**A** + **B**) + **C** = **D**

A +   (−**B**) = **E**

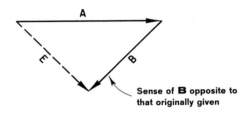

FIGURE A.8

$A + (-B) = E$

where the *minus sign* in front of **B** indicates that the original direction of **B** is to be reversed. The graphical interpretation of this vector equation is shown in Fig. A.8.

A.3 Multiplication of Vectors by Scalars

If two *equal vectors* are added, the magnitude of their vector sum is equal to twice their individual magnitudes.

Assume that there are two equal vectors **A**, which means that both vectors have equal magnitudes and act in the same direction (see Fig. A.9). The sum of the two vectors **A** is

$$A + A = 2A$$

This means that 2**A** is a new vector that has twice the magnitude of the original vectors and acts in the same direction as the two given vectors (see Fig. A.10).

This principle is true for the addition of any number of equal vectors:

$$A + A + A = 3A$$

$$A + A + A + A = 4A$$

$$\underbrace{A + A + A + A + \cdots + A}_{n \text{ terms}} = nA$$

The product of a scalar and a vector, such as n**A**, is a new vector that is n times as long as the original vector **A** (or n times the magnitude of the original vector).

If the vector **A** is multiplied by two different scalars, then the result is the sum of the two products:

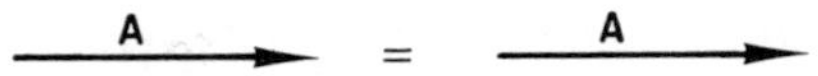

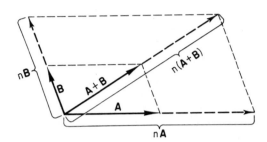

FIGURE A.9

FIGURE A.10

FIGURE A.11

or

$$2A + 4A = 6A$$

$$(2 + 4)A = 6A$$

which means that the multiplication of vectors by scalars follows the *distributive* law of algebra. Written in general terms, this law is

$$nA + mA = (n + m)A$$

or (see Fig. A.11)

$$nA + nB = n(A + B)$$

If the *sign* of the scalar multiplier of a vector is negative, then the *direction* of the resulting vector is opposite to that of the original vector. Thus,

$$-n(A) = n(-A) = -nA$$

A.4 Division of Vectors by Scalars

Vectors are divided by scalars by *multiplying* the vector by the *reciprocal* of the scalar. For example, to divide vector **A** by scalar n, we write

$$\frac{1}{n}(A) = \frac{A}{n}$$

The sign of n affects the direction of **A**.

A.5 Unit Vectors

In Chapters 2 and 3, it was shown that vectors can be resolved into rectangular components. In two-dimensional systems, the components are usually related to the x-y coordinate axis system. In a three-dimensional spatial system, the three co-ordinate axes x, y, and z are necessary to define the components of a particular vector or system of vectors.

Consider three vectors $\mathbf{i}$, $\mathbf{j}$, and $\mathbf{k}$ acting parallel to the x, y, and z coordinate axes, respectively, in *positive directions* (see Fig. A.12). Each vector ($\mathbf{i}$, $\mathbf{j}$, and $\mathbf{k}$) has a magnitude of *unity*; we call these vectors *unit vectors*. If the unit vectors are multiplied by scalars, then they define (or describe) any vector quantity that has the same line of action as they do. For example, consider a vector $\mathbf{A}$ that has a line of action along the x axis and a magnitude of 40 lb, as shown in Fig. A.13. The magni-

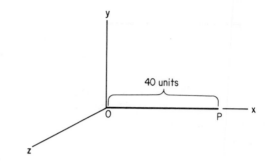

FIGURE A.14

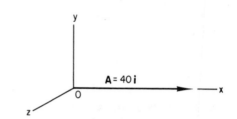

FIGURE A.15

tude of $\mathbf{A}$ is represented by the distance OP laid off to a suitable scale 40 units along the x axis, as shown in Fig. A.14. We know that the *distance* OP alone on the x axis does not completely fulfill the definition of a vector. The magnitude and the line of action are known, but the *sense* is not defined in Fig. A.14.

Since the *unit vector* $\mathbf{i}$ has been defined as being parallel to the x axis, we can *superimpose* this unit vector on the x axis and *multiply* it by the scalar units represented by OP. This results in a vector $\mathbf{i}$ that is 40 units long and that now describes the original vector $\mathbf{A}$ (since we now have all the specifications of a vector) as $\mathbf{A} = 40\mathbf{i}$ (see Fig. A.15). From this, we can again see that vector equations include both scalar and vector quantities (the number 40 and the sense and direction of the unit vector $\mathbf{i}$ in the above case).

Extending this system of vector notation, we can fully describe any vector by *unit vector components*. Consider vector $\mathbf{B}$, as shown in Fig. A.16, which makes a given angle θ with the x axis. To describe this vector $\mathbf{B}$ by its unit vector components, we first determine the *projections* of the *magnitude* (OM) of $\mathbf{B}$ on the x and y axes; we call these projections B_x and B_y, respectively.

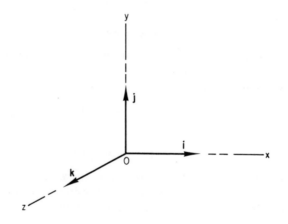

FIGURE A.12

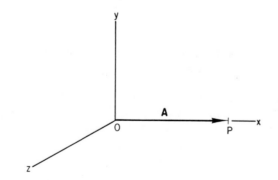

FIGURE A.13

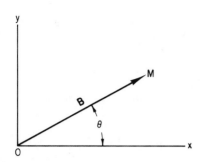

FIGURE A.16

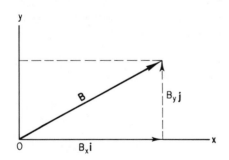

FIGURE A.17

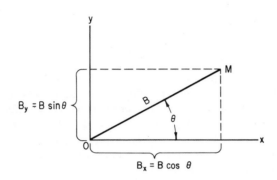

FIGURE A.18

These projections define specific *magnitudes* along the x and y axes (see Fig. A.17):

$$B_x = B \cos \theta \quad \text{and} \quad B_y = B \sin \theta$$

where B is the magnitude of **B**, that is, $B = |\mathbf{B}|$. Since B_x and B_y are scalars, we *multiply* the unit vectors **i** and **j** (unit vector **j** is parallel to the y axis and superimposed upon it) by B_x and B_y, respectively, to get $B_x\mathbf{i}$ and $B_y\mathbf{j}$. These two quan-

tities now are *unit vector components* of vector **B** having scalar magnitudes (as defined by $B \cos \theta$ and $B \sin \theta$) and directions (as defined by unit vectors **i** and **j**). Adding these components vectorially, we get

$$B_x\mathbf{i} + B_y\mathbf{j} = \mathbf{B}$$

which is a complete description of vector **B** in terms of its unit vector components (see Fig. A.18).

If we let $\mathbf{B} = 40$ lb and $\theta = 30°$, the unit vector component description of **B** would be as follows (refer to Fig. A.19):

$$\mathbf{B} = B_x\mathbf{i} + B_y\mathbf{j}$$
$$= (B \cos 30°)\mathbf{i} + (B \sin 30°)\mathbf{j}$$
$$= (40)\left(\frac{\sqrt{3}}{2}\right)\mathbf{i} + (40)\left(\frac{1}{2}\right)\mathbf{j}$$
$$= 20\sqrt{3}\,\mathbf{i} + 20\mathbf{j}$$

If a length of $20\sqrt{3}$ units is laid off in the positive **i** direction along the x axis and a length of 20 units is laid off in the positive **j** direction along the y axis, the vector **B** will be fully defined as the resultant of these two unit vector components (see Fig. A.20).

To determine the magnitude of vector **B** from the unit vector equation $\mathbf{B} = B_x\mathbf{i} + B_y\mathbf{j}$, use the *scalars* $20\sqrt{3}$ and 20 by applying the Pythagorean theorem:

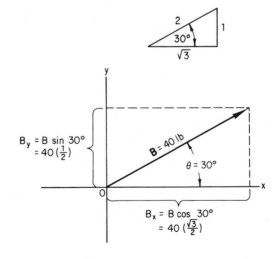

FIGURE A.19

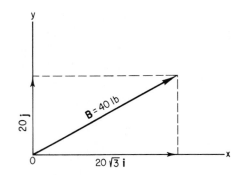

FIGURE A.20

$$B^2 = B_x^2 + B_y^2$$

$$= (20\sqrt{3})^2 + 20^2$$

$$= 400(3) + 400$$

$$= 1200 + 400$$

$$= 1600$$

$$\therefore\ B = \sqrt{1600\ \text{lb}^2} = 40\ \text{lb}$$

(which is the given value of B)

This same result can be attained by taking advantage of the geometric concept of the proportionality of similar triangles. Triangles OPM and OQR in Fig. A.21 are similar; therefore by direct proportion,

$$\frac{OP}{OQ} = \frac{PM}{QR} = \frac{OM}{OR}$$

Also, $OP = B\cos 30°$, $PM = B\sin 30°$, and $OM = B$. From the relative lengths of the sides of a $30°$–$60°$ right triangle, we can write

$$OQ = \sqrt{3}; \qquad QR = 1; \quad \text{and} \quad OR = 2$$

We can now rewrite the original ratio, substituting $B\cos 30°$ for OP, $B\sin 30°$ for PM, etc.:

$$\frac{OP}{OQ} = \frac{PM}{QR} = \frac{OM}{OR}$$

$$\frac{B\cos 30°}{\sqrt{3}} = \frac{B\sin 30°}{1} = \frac{B}{2}$$

Substituting the values $\cos 30° = \sqrt{3}/2$ and $\sin 30° = \frac{1}{2}$ in the above relationship, we get

$$\frac{B(\sqrt{3}/2)}{\sqrt{3}} = \frac{B(\frac{1}{2})}{1} = \frac{B}{2}$$

Therefore,

$$\frac{B}{2} = \frac{B}{2} = \frac{B}{2}$$

indicating that $B/2$ is the *proportionality constant* (P.C.), a ratio that usually can be read directly from the geometry of the given system. In other words, the hypotenuse $OM = B = 40$ of the triangle OMP is directly proportional to the hypotenuse $OR\ (=2)$ of triangle ORQ (which, in this case, is a $30°$–$60°$ triangle).

Using the proportionality constant (P.C.), in this case $40/2$, we can now write the vector equation for our given vector **B** in terms of its unit vector components *without* having to resort to trigonometric expressions directly (see Fig. A.22).

$$\mathbf{B} = (\sqrt{3}\,\mathbf{i} + 1\mathbf{j})\frac{40}{2}$$

$$= \left(\frac{40}{2}\right)\sqrt{3}\,\mathbf{i} + \left(\frac{40}{2}\right)\mathbf{j}$$

$$= 20\sqrt{3}\,\mathbf{i} + 20\mathbf{j}$$

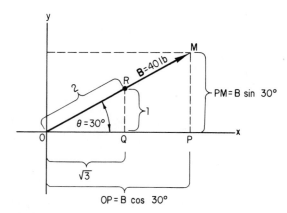

FIGURE A.21

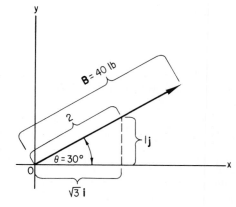

FIGURE A.22

which is identical to the equation previously developed for describing vector **B**. We shall use the proportionality factor to advantage in subsequent problems.

EXAMPLE A.1

The determination of the resultant of a coplanar, concurrent force system by unit vector components.

Given: Coplanar, concurrent forces **A** = 100 lb and **B** = 200 lb, as shown in Fig. A.23. Forces **A** and **B** act through point O and make angles α and β (as defined by the geometry of the angles).

Find: In vector notation the magnitude and the sense of the resultant **C** of **A** and **B**.

Vector Analysis

1. Describe force **A** in terms of its unit vector components (see Fig. A.24). (The proportionality constant (100 lb)/2 is proportional to the hypotenuse of the defining angle α.)

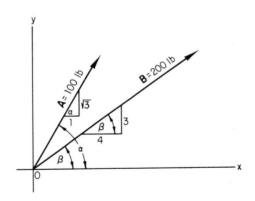

FIGURE A.23

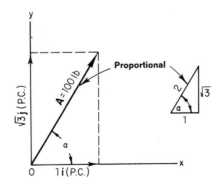

FIGURE A.24

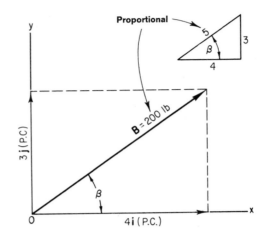

FIGURE A.25

$$\mathbf{A} = (1\mathbf{i} + \sqrt{3}\,\mathbf{j})\left(\frac{100}{2}\right)$$

where 100/2 is the proportionality constant: magnitude of **A** ($=100$) is proportional to the hypotenuse of triangle defining angle α.

$$\therefore \ \mathbf{A} = \left(\frac{100}{2}\right)\mathbf{i} + \left(\frac{100}{2}\right)\sqrt{3}\,\mathbf{j}$$

$$= 50\mathbf{i} + 50\sqrt{3}\,\mathbf{j}$$

2. Describe force **B** in terms of its unit vector components (see Fig. A.25). (The proportionality constant (200/5) is proportional to the hypotenuse of the defining angle β.)

$$\mathbf{B} = (4\mathbf{i} + 3\mathbf{j})\left(\frac{200}{5}\right)$$

where 200/5 is the proportionality constant: magnitude of **B** ($=200$) is proportional to the hypotenuse of triangle defining angle β.

$$\therefore \ \mathbf{B} = \left(\frac{200}{5}\right)4\mathbf{i} + \left(\frac{200}{5}\right)3\mathbf{j}$$

$$= 160\mathbf{i} + 120\mathbf{j}$$

3. Algebraically add the unit vector components of **A** and **B**.

$$\mathbf{A} = 50\mathbf{i} + 50\sqrt{3}\,\mathbf{j}$$

$$\mathbf{B} = 160\mathbf{i} + 120\mathbf{j}$$

$$\therefore \ \mathbf{A} + \mathbf{B} = (50\mathbf{i} + 160\mathbf{i}) + (50\sqrt{3}\,\mathbf{j} + 120\mathbf{j})$$

$$= \mathbf{C}$$

$$\therefore \ \mathbf{C} = 210\mathbf{i} + 207\mathbf{j}$$

which is the description of resultant **C** in vector notation.

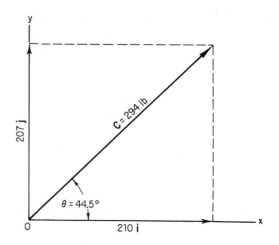

FIGURE A.26

4. Sketch the unit vector components of resultant **C** on the *x-y* axis system (see Fig. A.26).

5. Determine the magnitude of resultant **C** (refer to Fig. A.26).

$$C^2 = 210^2 + 207^2$$

$$= 44,000 + 42,800$$

$$= 86,800$$

$$\therefore \ C = \sqrt{86,800}$$

$$= 294 \text{ lb}$$

6. Determine the angle θ that resultant **C** makes with the *x* axis (refer to Fig. A.26).

$$\tan \theta = \frac{207}{210}$$

$$= 0.987$$

$$\therefore \ \theta = 44.5°$$

The sense of the resultant **C** is determined by the combined sense of the unit vector components that describe vectors **A** and **B**. In this example, both **i** and **j** have positive senses.

EXAMPLE A.2 _____

The determination of the resultant of a coplanar, concurrent force system by unit vector components.

Given: Coplanar, concurrent forces **A** = 50 lb, **B** = 100 lb, and **C** = 250 lb, as shown in Fig. A.27. Forces **A**, **B**, and **C** act through point *O* and make angles α, β, and γ,

respectively (as defined by the geometry of the angles), with the *x* axis.

Find: In vector notation, the magnitude and the sense of the resultant **D** of **A**, **B**, and **C**.

Vector Analysis

1. Describe force **A** in terms of its unit vector components (see Fig. A.28).

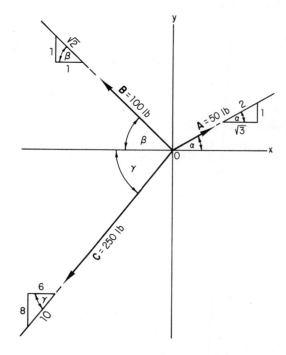

FIGURE A.27

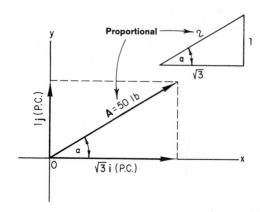

FIGURE A.28

$$A = (\sqrt{3}\,i + 1j)\frac{50}{2}$$

$$= \left(\frac{50}{2}\right)\sqrt{3}\,i + \left(\frac{50}{2}\right)j$$

$$= 25\sqrt{3}\,i + 25j$$

$$= 43.3i + 25j$$

2. Describe force **B** in terms of its unit vector components (see Fig. A.29).

$$B = (-1i + 1j)\left(\frac{100}{\sqrt{2}}\right)$$

$$= -\left(\frac{100}{\sqrt{2}}\right)i + \left(\frac{100}{\sqrt{2}}\right)j$$

$$= -70.8i + 70.8j$$

3. Describe force **C** in terms of its unit vector components (see Fig. A.30).

$$C = (-6i - 8j)\frac{250}{10}$$

$$= -\left(\frac{250}{10}\right)6i - \left(\frac{250}{10}\right)8j$$

$$= -150i - 200j$$

4. Algebraically add the unit vector components of **A**, **B**, and **C**.

$$A = \quad 43.3i + 25j$$

$$B = -70.8i + 70.8j$$

$$C = -150i - 200j$$

$$A + B + C = (43.3 - 70.8 - 150)i$$
$$+ (25 + 70.8 - 200)j$$

$$= D$$

$$\therefore\ D = -177.5i - 104.2j$$

5. Sketch the unit vector components of resultant **D** on the *x-y* axis system (see Fig. A.31).
6. Determine the magnitude of resultant **D** (see Fig. A.31).

$$D^2 = (-177.5)^2 + (-104.2)^2$$

$$= 31,500 + 10,850$$

$$= 42,350$$

$$D = \sqrt{42,350}$$

$$= 206\ \text{lb}$$

7. Determine the angle θ that resultant **D** makes with the *x* axis (see Fig. A.31).

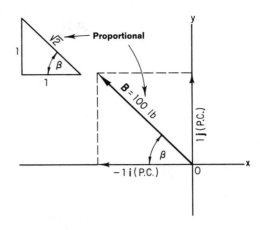

FIGURE A.29

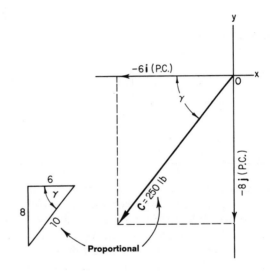

FIGURE A.30

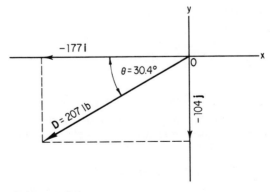

FIGURE A.31

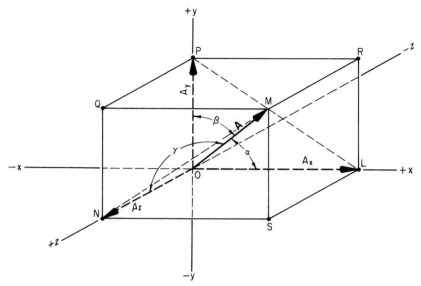

FIGURE A.32

$$\tan \theta = \frac{104.2}{177.5}$$

$$= 0.588$$

$$\therefore \ \theta = 30.50°$$

To expand the use of unit vectors to three-dimensional systems, we need only to introduce the unit vector **k**. Let us take a general case of a vector **A** that is oriented to the *x-y-z* coordinate axis system in such a manner that it makes angles α, β, and γ with the *x*, *y*, and *z* axes, respectively, and therefore has projections on all three axes (see Fig. A.32).

The projections of the *magnitude* of vector **A** (as represented by *OM*) are

$$A_x = OL$$

$$A_y = OP$$

$$A_z = ON$$

The projections *OL*, *OP*, and *ON* are the rectangular components of *OM*, and therefore they can be expressed in terms of the angles α, β, and γ (see Fig. A.33):

$$A_x = OL = OM \cos \alpha = A \cos \alpha$$

$$A_y = OP = OM \cos \beta = A \cos \beta$$

$$A_z = ON = OM \cos \gamma = A \cos \gamma$$

From the above relationships, the cosines of α, β, and γ can be expressed as

$$\cos \alpha = \frac{A_x}{A}$$

$$\cos \beta = \frac{A_y}{A}$$

$$\cos \gamma = \frac{A_z}{A}$$

where $\cos \alpha$, $\cos \beta$, and $\cos \gamma$ are defined as the *direction cosines* of the vector **A**.

Applying the Pythagorean theorem, we can write the following relationship, which defines the magnitude of *OM* in terms of its components (see Fig. A.34):

(1) $(OM)^2 = (MS)^2 + (OS)^2$

From Fig. A.34, we see that

$$(OS)^2 = (NS)^2 + (ON)^2$$

Substituting this expression for $(OS)^2$ in equation (1), we get

(2) $(OM)^2 = (MS)^2 + (NS)^2 + (ON)^2$

From Fig. A.34, we also see that $NS = OL$ and $MS = OP$. We can make these substitutions in equation (2) and rearrange the terms to get the following expression for $(OM)^2$:

(3) $(OM)^2 = (OP)^2 + (OL)^2 + (ON)^2$

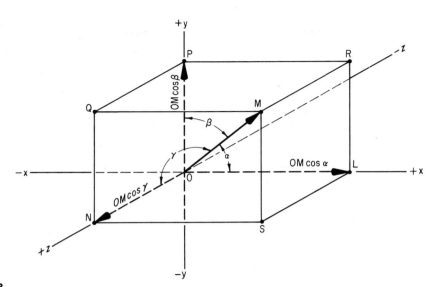

FIGURE A.33

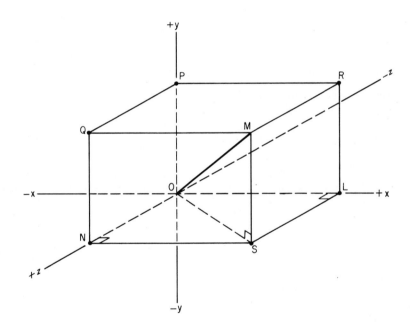

FIGURE A.34

Since $OM = A$, $OL = A_x$, $OP = A_y$, and $ON = A_z$, we can write equation (3) as

(4) $$A^2 = A_x{}^2 + A_y{}^2 + A_z{}^2$$

(5) $$\therefore \ A = \sqrt{A_x{}^2 + A_y{}^2 + A_z{}^2}$$

= the magnitude of vector **A**

If we write A_x, A_y, and A_z in terms of the direction cosines, we can make these substitutions in equation (4) and write

(6) $$A^2 = (A \cos \alpha)^2 + (A \cos \beta)^2 + (A \cos \gamma)^2$$

Dividing both sides of equation (6) by A^2, we get the following familiar relationship involving the direction cosines:

(7) $$1 = \cos^2 \alpha + \cos^2 \beta + \cos^2 \gamma$$

Since A_x, A_y, and A_z define the *magnitudes* of the components of the given vector **A**, we can multiply the unit vectors **i**, **j**, and **k** by these scalar magnitudes and establish complete speci-

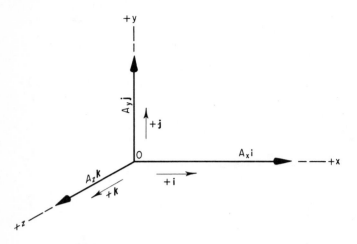

FIGURE A.35

fications for the *three* unit vector components necessary to define vector **A** (see Fig. A.35). Adding the unit vector components vectorially, we get

$$\mathbf{A} = A_x\mathbf{i} + A_y\mathbf{j} + A_z\mathbf{k}$$

which is the description of vector **A** in terms of its unit vector components (see Fig. A.36).

It has been shown that we can add vector quantities in terms of unit vector components in coplanar systems. This is also true for non-coplanar systems. Consider two vector quantities **A** and **B** in a three-dimensional system that, in terms of their unit vector components (refer to Fig. A.37), are described by

$$\mathbf{A} = A_x\mathbf{i} + A_y\mathbf{j} + A_z\mathbf{k}$$

$$\mathbf{B} = B_x\mathbf{i} + B_y\mathbf{j} + B_z\mathbf{k}$$

Let the resultant of **A** and **B** be **C**; then **A** + **B** = **C**. By adding the unit vector expressions for **A** and **B**, we get (see Fig. A.38)

$$\mathbf{A} = A_x\mathbf{i} + A_y\mathbf{j} + A_z\mathbf{k}$$

$$\mathbf{B} = B_x\mathbf{i} + B_y\mathbf{j} + B_z\mathbf{k}$$

$$\mathbf{A} + \mathbf{B} = (A_x\mathbf{i} + B_x\mathbf{i}) + (A_y\mathbf{j} + B_y\mathbf{j}) + (A_z\mathbf{k} + B_z\mathbf{k})$$

$$= \mathbf{C}$$

(8) $$\therefore\ \mathbf{C} = (A_x + B_x)\mathbf{i} + (A_y + B_y)\mathbf{j} + (A_z + B_z)\mathbf{k}$$

Since **A** + **B** = **C**, we can write

(9) $$\mathbf{C} = C_x\mathbf{i} + C_y\mathbf{j} + C_z\mathbf{k}$$

This approach can be used to add any number of vectors in any given system.

EXAMPLE A.3 ——————————

The determination of the resultant of a noncoplanar, concurrent force system by unit vector components.

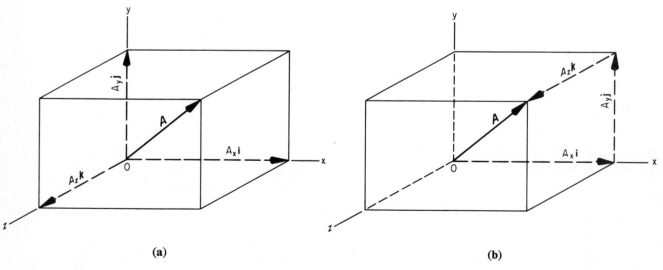

(a)   (b)

FIGURE A.36

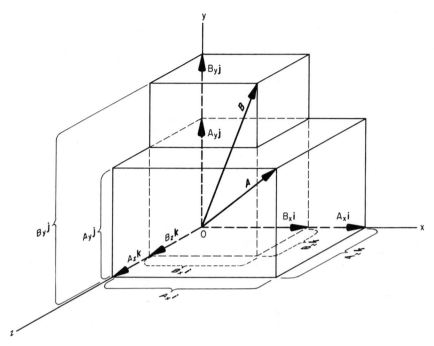

FIGURE A.37

Given: Noncoplanar, concurrent forces $A = 100\,\text{lb}$, $B = 50\,\text{lb}$, and $C = 80\,\text{lb}$, as shown in Figs. A.39 and A.40. The forces act through point O, and the angles their lines of action make with the x, y, and z axes are defined by the geometry of each angle.

Find: In unit vector notation, the magnitude and the sense of the resultant **R** of **A**, **B**, and **C**.

Vector Analysis

1. Describe the vectors **A**, **B**, and **C** in terms of their unit vector components, as shown in Fig. A.41 (pages 306–307), and add these components algebraically.

$$\mathbf{A} = (4\mathbf{i} + 2\mathbf{j} - 4\mathbf{k})\frac{100}{6}$$

$$= \left(\frac{100}{6}\right)4\mathbf{i} + \left(\frac{100}{6}\right)2\mathbf{j} - \left(\frac{100}{6}\right)4\mathbf{k}$$

$$= 66.7\mathbf{i} + 33.3\mathbf{j} - 66.7\mathbf{k}$$

$$\mathbf{B} = (0\mathbf{i} - 3\mathbf{j} + 2\mathbf{k})\frac{50}{\sqrt{13}}$$

$$= \left(\frac{50}{\sqrt{13}}\right)0\mathbf{i} - \left(\frac{50}{\sqrt{13}}\right)3\mathbf{j} + \left(\frac{50}{\sqrt{13}}\right)2\mathbf{k}$$

$$= 0\mathbf{i} - 41.6\mathbf{j} + 27.8\mathbf{k}$$

$$\mathbf{C} = (-3\mathbf{i} + 4\mathbf{j} - 2\mathbf{k})\frac{80}{\sqrt{29}}$$

$$= -\left(\frac{80}{\sqrt{29}}\right)3\mathbf{i} + \left(\frac{80}{\sqrt{29}}\right)4\mathbf{j} - \left(\frac{80}{\sqrt{29}}\right)2\mathbf{k}$$

$$= -44.6\mathbf{i} + 59.0\mathbf{j} - 29.7\mathbf{k}$$

$$\mathbf{A} + \mathbf{B} + \mathbf{C} = \mathbf{R}$$

$$= 22.1\mathbf{i} + 50.7\mathbf{j} - 68.6\mathbf{k}$$

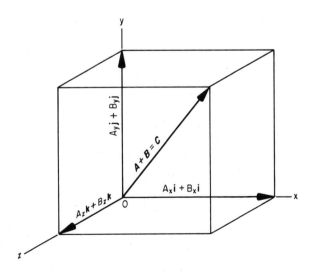

FIGURE A.38

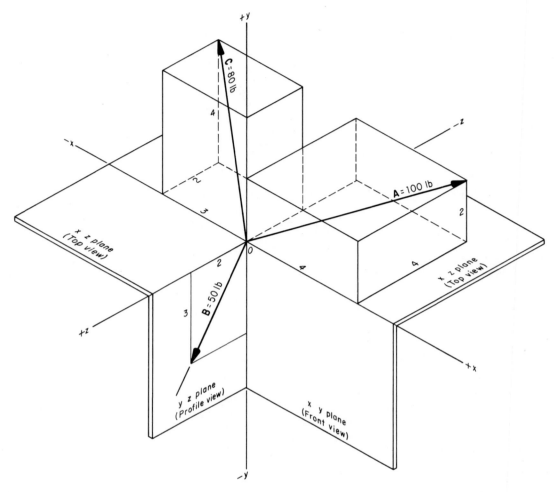

FIGURE A.39

2. Sketch the unit vector components of resultant **R** on the x-y-z axis system (see Fig. A.42, page 308).

3. Determine the magnitude of resultant **R** (refer to Fig. A.42).

$$R^2 = 22.1^2 + 50.7^2 + (-68.6)^2$$

$$= 490 + 2570 + 4700$$

$$= 7760$$

$$R = \sqrt{7760}$$

$$= 88.0 \text{ lb}$$

4. Determine the angles α, β, and γ that resultant **R** makes with the x, y, and z axes, respectively (see Fig. A.42).

$$\cos \alpha = \frac{R_x}{R} = \frac{22.1}{88.0}$$

$$= 0.251$$

$$\therefore \ \alpha = 75.5°$$

$$\cos \beta = \frac{R_y}{R} = \frac{50.7}{88.0}$$

$$= 0.576$$

$$\therefore \ \beta = 54.8°$$

$$\cos \gamma = \frac{R_z}{R} = \frac{68.6}{88.0}$$

$$= 0.780$$

$$\therefore \ \gamma = 38.7°$$

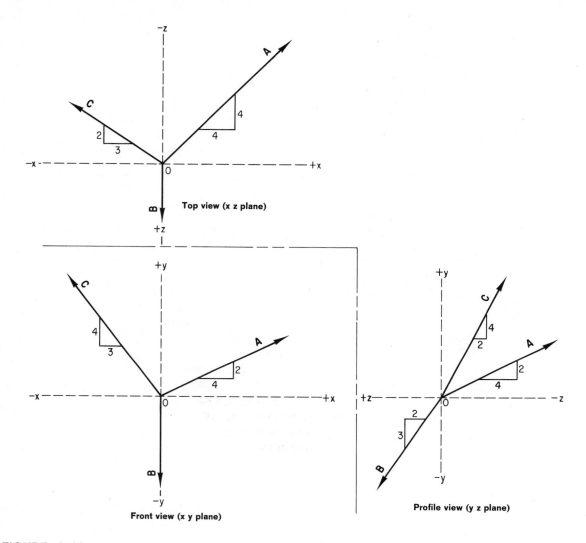

Top view (x z plane)

Front view (x y plane)

Profile view (y z plane)

FIGURE A.40

A.6 Vector Products

We have seen that the product of a vector and a scalar is another vector having the same line of action as the original vector but having a possible change in its magnitude and sense, depending on the numerical value and sign of the scalar. By special definitions, the concept of "multiplication" can be enlarged to include the products of vectors and *other vectors*. The special definitions that are presented in this chapter are based on geometrical relationships and include the concepts of *work* and the *moment of a force*.

A.7 The Scalar or Dot Product

Work can be defined as the product of a *force of constant magnitude* and the *displacement distance* of the point of application of the force along the line of action of the force (see Fig. A.43, page 308). If the *displacement* of the point of application of the force does *not* occur along the line of action of the force, then the work done by the force is equal to the product of the *magnitude of the force* and the *projection of the displacement distance* on the line of action of the force (see Fig. A.44).

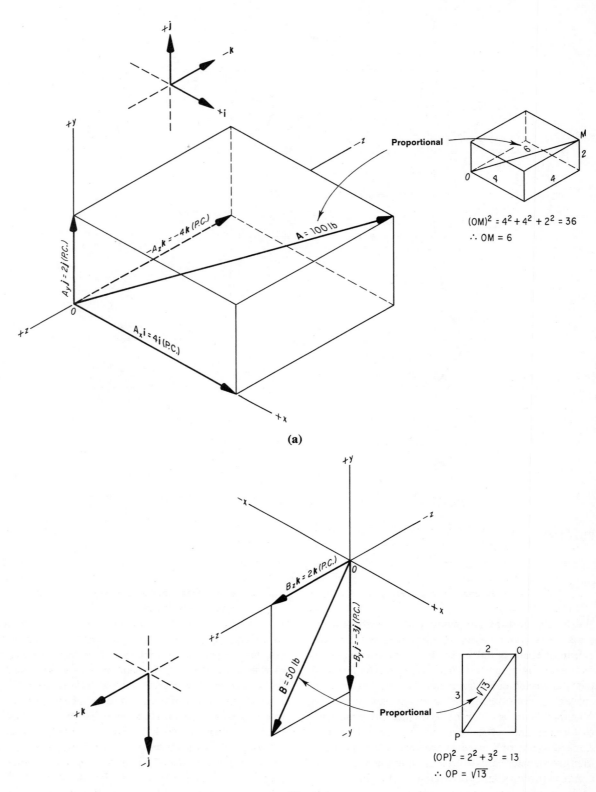

$(OM)^2 = 4^2 + 4^2 + 2^2 = 36$

$\therefore OM = 6$

(a)

$(OP)^2 = 2^2 + 3^2 = 13$

$\therefore OP = \sqrt{13}$

(b)

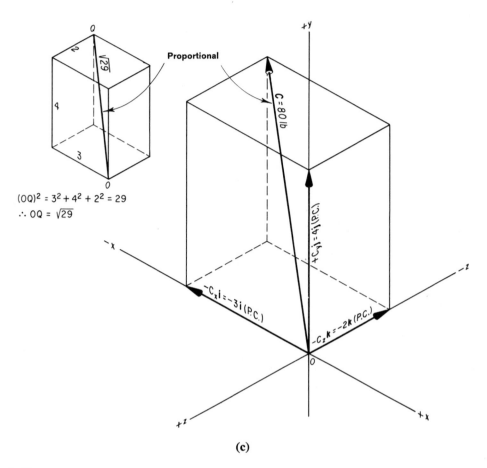

$(OQ)^2 = 3^2 + 4^2 + 2^2 = 29$

$\therefore OQ = \sqrt{29}$

(c)

FIGURE A.41

From Fig. A.44, we see that work $W = A(d \cos \alpha)$. Examining this relationship, we see that we can rewrite it as $W = d(A \cos \alpha)$, where $A \cos \alpha$ is the *projection* of the force A on the displacement line of action s_1 to s_2. Thus, *work* can also be defined as the product of the *displacement distance* and the *projection of the force* along the displacement line of action of the point of application of the force. Therefore, $W = A(d \cos \alpha) = d(A \cos \alpha)$. (See Fig. A.45.) It should be emphasized at this point that *work* is a *scalar* quantity and that in the discussion above, we were dealing with *two vector quantities—a force vector* and a *displacement vector.*

We can now introduce the concept of the *scalar or dot product* of two vectors. The *dot product* is a *scalar* quantity and is designated in a special way, where the *dot product operation* between two vectors such as **A** and **B** is indicated as **A·B**. The *dot* between **A** and **B** identifies the dot product operation. The *magnitude* of the dot product **A·B** is defined as $AB \cos \alpha$, where α is the enclosed angle between the two vectors, as shown in Fig. A.46.

From this definition, we see that the dot product **A·B** is the product of the *projection of vector* **B** on vector **A** and vector **A** (see Fig. A.47).

Similarly, since $A(B \cos \alpha) = B(A \cos \alpha)$, we conclude that **A·B** = **B·A**, which shows that the dot product **A·B** can also be defined as the product of the *projection of vector* **A** on vector **B** and vector **B**, as shown in Fig. A.48. Thus, the dot product is a *commutative process*, since the product of the *projection of vector* **B** *on vector* **A** *and vector* **A** is equal to the product of the *projection of vector* **A** *on vector* **B** *and vector* **B**.

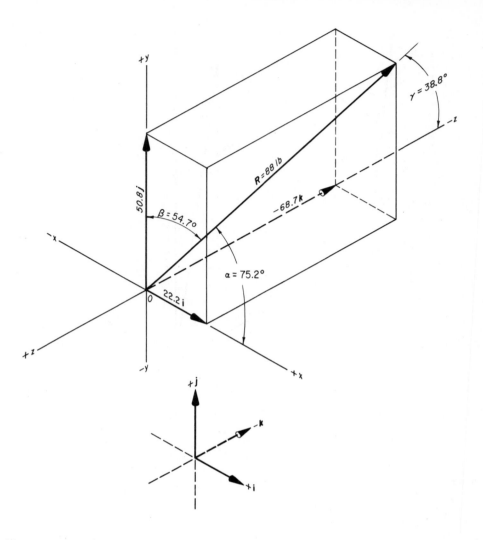

FIGURE A.42

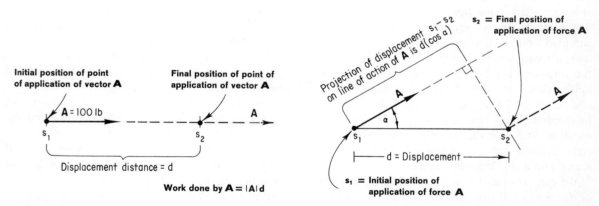

Initial position of point
of application of vector **A**

Final position of point of
application of vector **A**

A = 100 lb   **A**

s_1 s_2

Displacement distance = d

Work done by **A** = |**A**| d

FIGURE A.43

s_2 = Final position of
application of force **A**

Projection of displacement $s_1 - s_2$
on line of action of **A** is d(cos α)

A   **A**

α

s_1 s_2

d = Displacement

s_1 = Initial position of
application of force **A**

FIGURE A.44

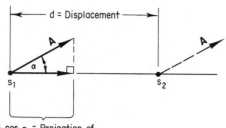

A cos α = Projection of
force vector **A** on line
of displacement

FIGURE A.45

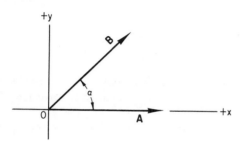

FIGURE A.46

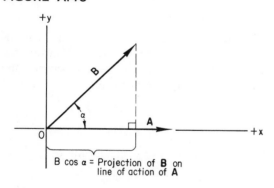

B cos α = Projection of **B** on
line of action of **A**

FIGURE A.47
Dot Product $\mathbf{A} \cdot \mathbf{B} = A(B \cos \alpha)$

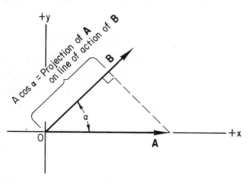

FIGURE A.48
Dot Product $\mathbf{B} \cdot \mathbf{A} = B(A \cos \alpha)$

EXAMPLE A.4 _____

The dot product of two vectors.

Given: Vector **A** = 50 ft   [displacement vector]
Vector **B** = 100 lb [force vector]
$\cos \alpha = \frac{4}{5}$
(see Fig. A.49.)

Find: The dot products $\mathbf{A} \cdot \mathbf{B}$ and $\mathbf{B} \cdot \mathbf{A}$.

Vector Analysis

1. See Fig. A.50: by definition,

$$\mathbf{A} \cdot \mathbf{B} = A(B \cos \alpha)$$

$$= (50 \text{ ft})(100 \text{ lb})(\tfrac{4}{5})$$

$$= 4000 \text{ ft-lb}$$

2. See Fig. A.51: geometrically,

$$\mathbf{B} \cdot \mathbf{A} = B(A \cos \alpha)$$

$$= (100 \text{ lb})(50 \text{ ft})(\tfrac{4}{5})$$

$$= 4000 \text{ ft-lb}$$

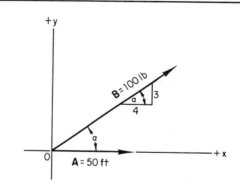

FIGURE A.49

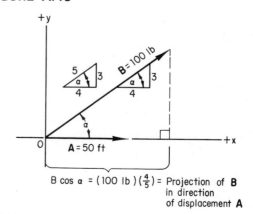

B cos α = (100 lb)($\frac{4}{5}$) = Projection of **B**
in direction
of displacement **A**

FIGURE A.50

The *sign* of the dot product of two vectors depends upon the size of the angle α between the vectors. If, as in Fig. A.52, the angle α is *less than* 90°, then the dot product is *positive*. (This is equivalent to positive work.) If, as in Fig. A.53, the angle α is *greater than* 90° *but less than* 270°, then the dot product is negative. (This would be

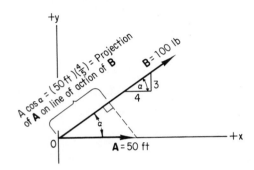

FIGURE A.51

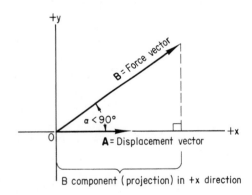

FIGURE A.52

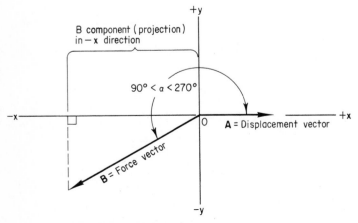

FIGURE A.53

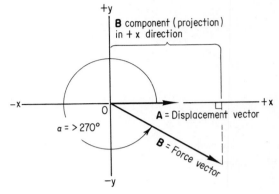

FIGURE A.54

equivalent to negative work.) If α is *greater than* 270°, then the dot product is positive (see Fig. A.54).

If we examine the numerical values and signs of

$$\cos 0° = +1; \qquad \cos 90° = 0;$$

$$\cos 270° = 0; \qquad \cos 360° = +1$$

we uncover some interesting and useful relationships of dot products of *unit vectors*. Consider the dot product $\mathbf{i} \cdot \mathbf{i}$: the *enclosed angle* between the two unit vectors $\mathbf{i}$ is zero. Since $\cos 0° = 1$,

$$\mathbf{i} \cdot \mathbf{i} = |\mathbf{i}|\,|\mathbf{i}|\,(\cos 0°)$$

$$= |\mathbf{i}|\,|\mathbf{i}|\,(1)$$

Since unit vectors have a magnitude of unity,

$$\mathbf{i} \cdot \mathbf{i} = (1)(1)(1)$$

$$= 1$$

Using the same approach for unit vectors $\mathbf{j}$ and $\mathbf{k}$, we find that

$$(10) \qquad \mathbf{i} \cdot \mathbf{i} = \mathbf{j} \cdot \mathbf{j} = \mathbf{k} \cdot \mathbf{k} = 1$$

Next, let us consider the dot products of $\mathbf{i} \cdot \mathbf{j}$, $\mathbf{j} \cdot \mathbf{k}$, and $\mathbf{k} \cdot \mathbf{i}$, where the angle enclosed by each pair of unit vectors is 90° (see Fig. A.55). From the definition of the dot product, we can write

$$\mathbf{i} \cdot \mathbf{j} = |\mathbf{i}|\,|\mathbf{j}|\,(\cos 90°)$$

$$= |\mathbf{i}|\,|\mathbf{j}|\,(0)$$

$$= 0$$

The same result is found for $\mathbf{j} \cdot \mathbf{k}$ and $\mathbf{k} \cdot \mathbf{i}$. Therefore,

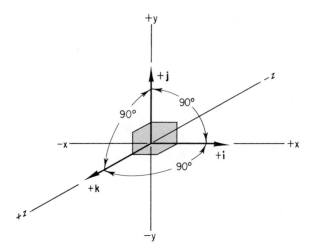

FIGURE A.55

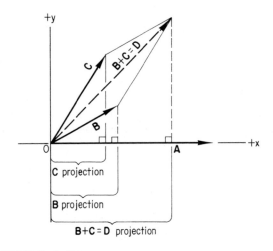

FIGURE A.56

$$(11) \qquad \mathbf{i}\cdot\mathbf{j} = \mathbf{j}\cdot\mathbf{k} = \mathbf{k}\cdot\mathbf{i} = 0$$

Thus, if the dot product of two vectors is zero, the vectors are at *right angles* to each other. This is analogous to the work done by a force vector that is *perpendicular* to a displacement vector. Since the force vector *has no component* in the direction of the displacement vector, no work is done (according to the definition of work).

To show that the dot product of two vectors follows the distributive law of multiplication [where $\mathbf{A}\cdot(\mathbf{B} + \mathbf{C}) = \mathbf{A}\cdot\mathbf{B} + \mathbf{A}\cdot\mathbf{C}$], let us consider the three vectors $\mathbf{A}$, $\mathbf{B}$, and $\mathbf{C}$, as shown in Fig. A.56. According to the principle of pro-

jections, the projection of the resultant $\mathbf{D}$ (of $\mathbf{B} + \mathbf{C}$) is equal to the sum of the projections of $\mathbf{B}$ and $\mathbf{C}$. Therefore, we can write

$$\mathbf{A}\cdot\mathbf{D} = \mathbf{A}\cdot(\mathbf{B} + \mathbf{C}) = \mathbf{A}\cdot\mathbf{B} + \mathbf{A}\cdot\mathbf{C}$$

If two vectors $\mathbf{A}$ and $\mathbf{B}$ are expressed in terms of their unit vector components, $\mathbf{A} = A_x\mathbf{i} + A_y\mathbf{j} + A_z\mathbf{k}$ and $\mathbf{B} = B_x\mathbf{i} + B_y\mathbf{j} + B_z\mathbf{k}$, the dot product of the two vectors results in the following:

$$\begin{aligned}
\mathbf{A}\cdot\mathbf{B} &= (A_x\mathbf{i} + A_y\mathbf{j} + A_z\mathbf{k})(B_x\mathbf{i} + B_y\mathbf{j} + B_z\mathbf{k}) \\
&= A_x\mathbf{i}(B_x\mathbf{i} + B_y\mathbf{j} + B_z\mathbf{k}) \\
&\quad + A_y\mathbf{j}(B_x\mathbf{i} + B_y\mathbf{j} + B_z\mathbf{k}) \\
&\quad + A_z\mathbf{k}(B_x\mathbf{i} + B_y\mathbf{j} + B_z\mathbf{k}) \\
&= A_xB_x\mathbf{i}\cdot\mathbf{i} + A_xB_y\mathbf{i}\cdot\mathbf{j} + A_xB_z\mathbf{i}\cdot\mathbf{k} \\
&\quad + A_yB_x\mathbf{j}\cdot\mathbf{i} + A_yB_y\mathbf{j}\cdot\mathbf{j} + A_yB_z\mathbf{j}\cdot\mathbf{k} \\
&\quad + A_zB_x\mathbf{k}\cdot\mathbf{i} + A_zB_y\mathbf{k}\cdot\mathbf{j} + A_zB_z\mathbf{k}\cdot\mathbf{k}
\end{aligned}$$

Since $\mathbf{i}\cdot\mathbf{i} = \mathbf{j}\cdot\mathbf{j} = \mathbf{k}\cdot\mathbf{k} = 1$, $\mathbf{i}\cdot\mathbf{j} = \mathbf{j}\cdot\mathbf{k} = \mathbf{k}\cdot\mathbf{i} = 0$, and $\mathbf{j}\cdot\mathbf{i} = \mathbf{k}\cdot\mathbf{j} = \mathbf{i}\cdot\mathbf{k} = 0$, this equation reduces to

$$(12) \qquad \mathbf{A}\cdot\mathbf{B} = A_xB_x + A_yB_y + A_zB_z$$

This equation says that the dot product of two vectors in terms of their unit vectors is equal to the sum of the products (A_xB_x, A_yB_y, and A_zB_z) of the *projections* of these vectors on the x, y, and z axes.

If we refer back to the definition of the dot product, we can develop an expression for the cosine of the angle between two vectors. Since $\mathbf{A}\cdot\mathbf{B} = A(B \cos \alpha)$, we can rearrange the terms and write

$$\cos \alpha = \frac{\mathbf{A}\cdot\mathbf{B}}{|A|\,|B|}$$

Substituting $A_xB_x + A_yB_y + A_zB_z$ for $\mathbf{A}\cdot\mathbf{B}$,

$$\sqrt{A_x{}^2 + A_y{}^2 + A_z{}^2} \qquad \text{for } |\mathbf{A}|,$$

and

$$\sqrt{B_x{}^2 + B_y{}^2 + B_z{}^2} \qquad \text{for } |\mathbf{B}|,$$

we get

$$(13)$$

$$\cos \alpha = \frac{A_xB_x + A_yB_y + A_zB_z}{\sqrt{A_x{}^2 + A_y{}^2 + A_z{}^2}\,\sqrt{B_x{}^2 + B_y{}^2 + B_z{}^2}}$$

The following examples illustrate a few applications of the dot product of two vectors.

314

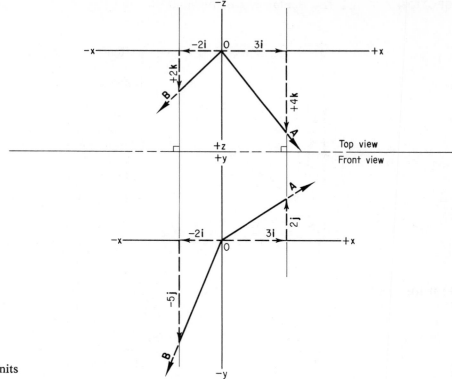

FIGURE A.57

Space Scale: 1 in. = 3 units

EXAMPLE A.5

The angle between two vectors in a coplanar system.

Given: Vectors **A** and **B**:

$$A = -25i + 25\sqrt{3}\,j$$
$$B = 50\sqrt{3}\,i + 50j$$

Find: The enclosed angle α between **A** and **B**.

Vector Analysis

1. Determine the dot product **A·B**

$$A\cdot B = (-25i + 25\sqrt{3}\,j)(50\sqrt{3}\,i + 50j)$$

$$= -25(50\sqrt{3})i\cdot i - 25(50)i\cdot j$$
$$+ 25\sqrt{3}(50\sqrt{3})j\cdot i + 25\sqrt{3}(50)j\cdot j$$

2. Since $i\cdot i = j\cdot j = 1$ and $i\cdot j = j\cdot i = 0$,

$$A\cdot B = -25(50\sqrt{3}) + 25\sqrt{3}(50)$$

$$= 0$$

3. Since $A\cdot B = 0$, the enclosed angle α between **A** and **B** is 90°.

EXAMPLE A.6

The angle between two vectors **A** and **B** in a non-coplanar system.

Given: $A = 3i + 2j + 4k$
$\qquad\quad B = -2i - 5j + 2k$

Find: The enclosed angle α between vectors **A** and **B**.

Vector Analysis

1. Determine the dot product **A·B**

$$A\cdot B = (3i + 2j + 4k)(-2i - 5j + 2k)$$

2. Using the approach taken in equation (12), we get

$$A\cdot B = 3(-2)i\cdot i + 2(-5)j\cdot j + 4(2)k\cdot k$$

$$= -6 - 10 + 8$$

$$= -8$$

3. Since $|A| = \sqrt{A_x^2 + A_y^2 + A_z^2}$ and $|B| = \sqrt{B_x^2 + B_y^2 + B_z^2}$, we can determine the scalar values for **A** and **B**:

$$A = \sqrt{3^2 + 2^2 + 4^2}$$

$$= \sqrt{29}$$

$$B = \sqrt{(-2)^2 + (-5)^2 + 2^2}$$

$$= \sqrt{33}$$

4. Substituting $A\cdot B = -8$, $A = \sqrt{29}$, and $B = \sqrt{33}$ in $\cos\alpha = A\cdot B/AB$, we get

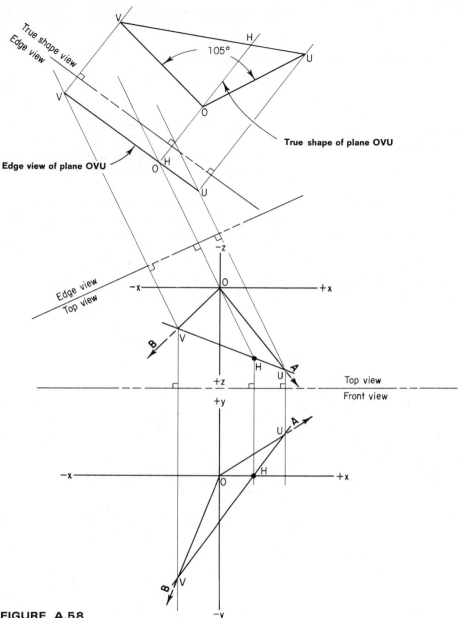

FIGURE A.58

$$\cos \alpha = \frac{-8}{\sqrt{29}\ \sqrt{33}}$$

$$= -\frac{8}{30.9} = -0.258$$

Since $-\cos \alpha = \cos (180° - \alpha)$,

$$\alpha = 105°$$

Graphical Analysis

1. To a convenient space scale, lay out the top and front views of the given vector system, as shown in Fig. A.57.

2. Using the principles of descriptive geometry,[1] determine the *edge view* of the *plane* formed by the lines of action (OU and OV, respectively) of **A** and **B**. (Line OH in this plane is seen as a point in the edge view.) (See Fig. A.58.)

3. Determine the *true shape* of the plane formed by OU and OV looking *perpendicular* to the *edge view* of the plane. The true shape is seen in the true shape

[1] See, for example, Steve M. Slaby, *Fundamentals of Three-Dimensional Descriptive Geometry* (New York: Harcourt, Brace & World, 1966).

view in Fig. A.58. In the true shape view, the angle α can be measured: $\alpha = 105°$.

EXAMPLE A.7 ─────────

The work done by a force whose line of action is oblique to a straight-line displacement path in a noncoplanar system.

Given: A. Force vector $\mathbf{A} = 2\mathbf{i} - 8\mathbf{j} + 6\mathbf{k}$.
   B. The initial point on the straight-line displacement path is a point P having its coordinates in feet $(5, 6, -3)$.
   C. The *final* point on the straight-line displacement path is a point Q having its coordinates in feet $(-3, 3, 4)$.

Find: The work done by force $\mathbf{A}$ along the displacement path from point P to point Q.

Vector Analysis

1. Sketch the given conditions on a three-dimensional, rectangular coordinate axis system, as shown in Fig. A.59.

2. We can consider the *distances* from origin O to point P and from origin O to point Q to be *position vectors* ($\overrightarrow{OP}$ and $\overrightarrow{OQ}$, respectively) that locate P and Q relative to the origin O of the coordinate axes (see Fig. A.60).

3. From Fig. A.60, we can see that the displacement path from point P to point Q (which is a straight line) can be considered a vector $\overrightarrow{PQ}$ that is the *vector difference* between the *position vectors* $\overrightarrow{OP}$ and $\overrightarrow{OQ}$. For convenience, let $\overrightarrow{OP} = \mathbf{C}$, $\overrightarrow{OQ} = \mathbf{B}$, and $\overrightarrow{PQ} = \mathbf{D}$. We can then express this vector difference as the vector subtraction $\mathbf{B} - \mathbf{C} = \mathbf{D}$.

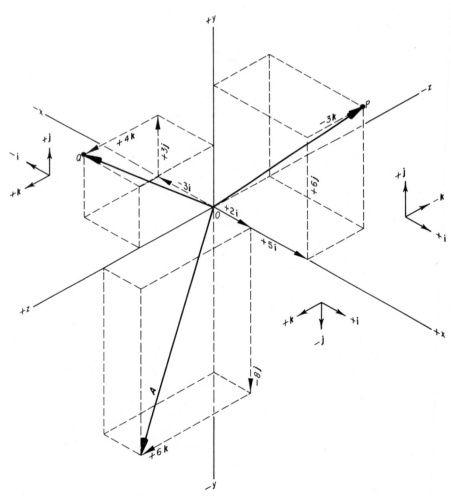

FIGURE A.59

4. Write **C** and **B** in terms of their unit vector components, which are defined by the coordinates for points P and Q:

$$\mathbf{B} = -3\mathbf{i} + 3\mathbf{j} + 4\mathbf{k}$$

$$\mathbf{C} = 5\mathbf{i} + 6\mathbf{j} - 3\mathbf{k}$$

5. Determine the unit vector description of the *displacement vector* **D** by the subtraction **B** − **C**:

$$\mathbf{B} = -3\mathbf{i} + 3\mathbf{j} + 4\mathbf{k} \quad = -3\mathbf{i} + 3\mathbf{j} + 4\mathbf{k}$$

$$-\mathbf{C} = -(5\mathbf{i} + 6\mathbf{j} - 3\mathbf{k}) = -5\mathbf{i} - 6\mathbf{j} + 3\mathbf{k}$$

$$\therefore \ \mathbf{B} - \mathbf{C} = \mathbf{D} = -8\mathbf{i} - 3\mathbf{j} + 7\mathbf{k}$$

6. The unit vector equation for **D** defines the position of the displacement vector as starting from the origin O of the given coordinate axes and as being *parallel* to the given displacement path from point

P to point Q. Since the unit vector description of force **A** defines the position of **A** as starting from the same origin O, we now have a typical arrangement for performing a dot product operation to determine the work done by force **A** in terms of the given displacement (see Fig. A.61).

7. Perform the dot product operation **A·D**:

$$\mathbf{A \cdot D} = (2\mathbf{i} - 8\mathbf{j} + 6\mathbf{k})(-8\mathbf{i} - 3\mathbf{j} + 7\mathbf{k})$$

$$= -16 + 24 + 42$$

$$= 50 \text{ ft-lb}$$

Graphical Analysis

1. To a convenient space scale, lay out the top and front views of vector **A** and points P and Q (assuming the rectangular coordinate axes x-y-z, as shown in Fig. A.62).

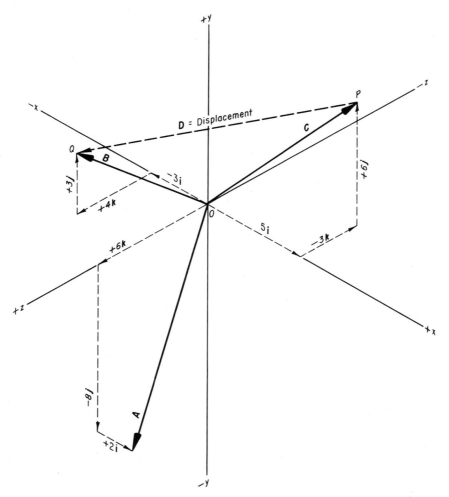

FIGURE A.60

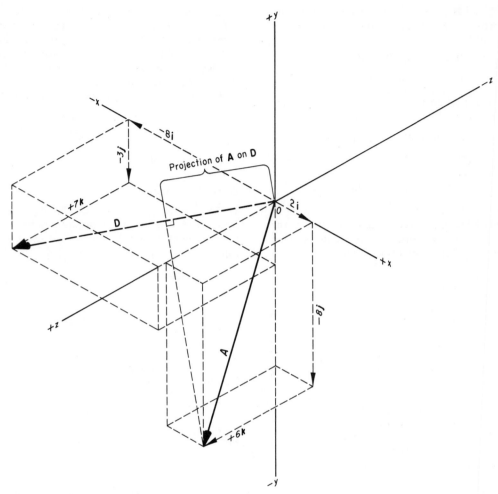

FIGURE A.61

2. Considering distances from origin O to points P and Q as *position vectors* $\overrightarrow{OP}$ and $\overrightarrow{OQ}$ (equal to $\mathbf{C}$ and $\mathbf{B}$, respectively), graphically perform the vector subtraction $\mathbf{B} - \mathbf{C}$ to determine $\mathbf{D}$ $(=\overrightarrow{PQ})$. (See Fig. A.63, top and front views.)

3. Draw vector $\mathbf{D}$ (indicated in parallel position as $\overrightarrow{OU}$) parallel to $\overrightarrow{PQ}$ and originating from the origin O in both the top and front views (see Fig. A.64).

4. Form a plane from line of action vector $\mathbf{D}$ (which is $\overrightarrow{OU}$) and vector $\mathbf{A}$ (which is indicated as $\overrightarrow{OV}$) by connecting points U and V with a straight line (see top and front views of Fig. A.64).

5. Using the principles of descriptive geometry, determine the edge view of the plane formed by $\overrightarrow{OU}$

and $\overrightarrow{OV}$ (line OH in the plane is seen as a point in the edge view).

6. Determine the *true shape* of the plane formed by $\overrightarrow{OU}$ and $\overrightarrow{OV}$ looking *perpendicular* to the *edge view* of the plane. In this true shape view, all lines in the plane appear as *true length*. (See Fig. A.64.)

7. According to the space scale, 1 in. = 5 ft; the vector scale is 1 in. = 5 lb. The magnitude of vector $\mathbf{A} = 10.2$ lb (length of line OV), and the displacement vector $\mathbf{D} = 11.1$ ft (length of line OU). *Project OV perpendicular* to the displacement line OU. This is the projection of vector $\mathbf{A}$ on the displacement line of action. Measure this projection ($=4.5$ lb).

8. To determine the work done by force $\mathbf{A}$, multiply:

$$(4.5 \text{ lb})(11.1 \text{ ft}) = 49.9 \text{ ft-lb}$$

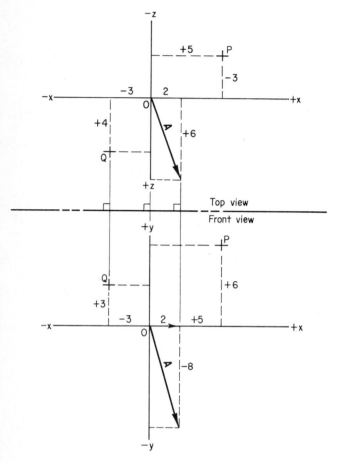

FIGURE A.62

Space Scale: 1 in. = 5 ft

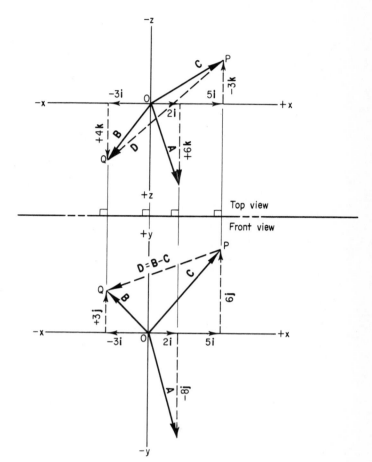

FIGURE A.63

A.8 The Cross Product

In earlier parts of this book, it was shown how the moment of a force can be *represented* by a moment vector that is *perpendicular* to the plane formed by the vector (representing a force) and its moment arm relative to a moment center. The moment vector has a *sense* (positive or negative) that depends on the sense of the force (or forces, as in a couple) that creates the moment (see Figs. 1.13–1.17) and the sign convention adopted see Figs. 3.37–3.40). From the concepts and definitions of the moment of a force, we can define another type of vector product, one that is analogous to the physical concept of moment.

Let us consider the moment of force **A** about a point P located by position vector **B**, which is perpendicular to **A**, as shown in Fig. A.65. The moment of **A** about P can be written as the product $AB = M_A$, which is equal to the *area* of the rectangle $OLQP$. This moment of **A** can be represented by a *moment vector* $\mathbf{M}_A$ *perpendicular* to the plane $OLQP$ (formed by vectors **A** and **B**) and having a sense determined by the right-hand screw rule adopted in Chapter 3. (See Fig. A.66.) Note that the *product operation* proceeded from **A** to **B** (see Fig. A.66). If the product operation proceeded from **B** to **A**, the result would be $BA = -\mathbf{M}_A$. The minus sign follows the sign convention adopted in Chapter 3. (Also see Fig. A.67.)

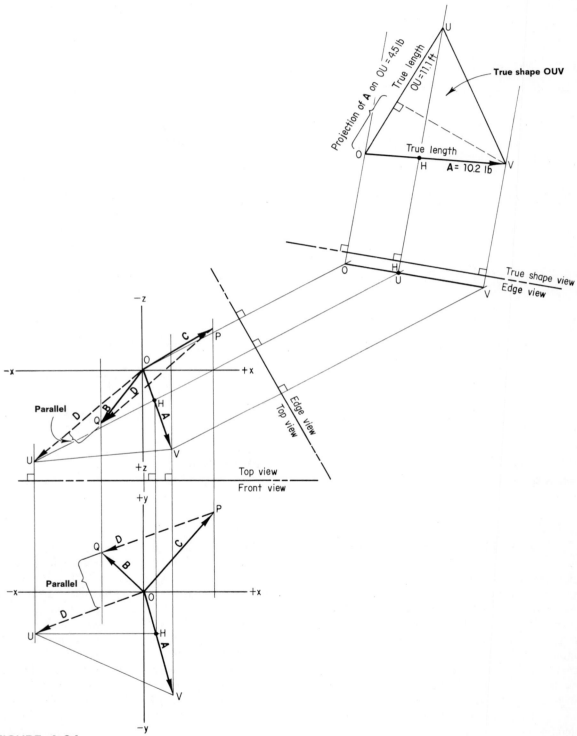

FIGURE A.64

Space Scale: 1 in. = 5 ft
Vector Scale: 1 in. = 5 lb

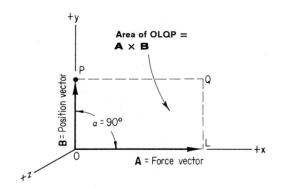

FIGURE A.65

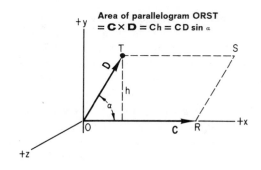

FIGURE A.68

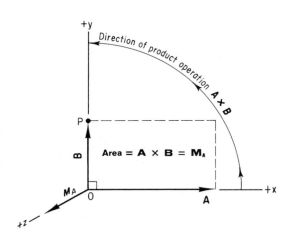

FIGURE A.66

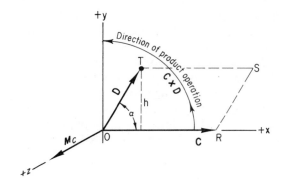

FIGURE A.69

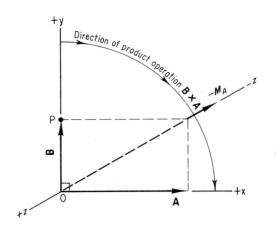

FIGURE A.67

Let us now consider a condition where a force vector **C** and a position vector **D** (which locates a moment center T) are *not* at right angles to each other, as shown in Fig. A.68. If we express the moment of force **C** about T in terms of a product operation (as we did for **A** and **B** in Fig. A.66), then it can be seen that M_C does not equal CD, since **D** in this case is *not* the perpendicular distance from force **C** to moment center T. The moment of **C** about T in this case is $M_C = Ch$, where h is the perpendicular distance from **C** to T. We can define h in terms of D and the enclosed angle between **C** and **D**, since $\sin \alpha = h/D$ and therefore $h = D \sin \alpha$. With this relationship, we can write $M_C = CD \sin \alpha$, which is equal to the area of the parallelogram $ORST$ and represented by a moment vector $\mathbf{M}_C$ perpendicular to the plane of $ORST$ (formed by **C** and **D**). (See Fig. A.69.)

In Fig. A.66, where vectors **A** and **B** are at right angles with each other, we can also express the moment of **A** about P as $M_A = AB \sin \alpha$, since $\sin 90° = 1$ so that (as we saw before) $M_A = AB$ = area of the parallelogram $OLQP$.

Analogous to the moment of a force about a moment center and its representation as a vector quantity is the *cross product* of two vectors. The *cross product* is defined as a *vector quantity* and is designated in a special way, where the *cross product operation* between two vectors such as **C** and **D** is indicated as **C ✕ D**. The *cross* between **C** and **D** *identifies* the cross product operation. The magnitude of the vector representing the cross product **C ✕ D** is *defined* as $CD \sin \alpha$, where α is the enclosed angle between the two vectors. The cross product vector is perpendicular to the plane formed by **C** and **D** (see Fig. A.70).

If the cross product operation between **C** and **D** proceeds from **D** to **C** ($=$ **D ✕ C**), the sign (or sense) of the resulting moment vector as determined by the right-hand rule is **D ✕ C** $= -\mathbf{M}_C$ (see Fig. A.71). Thus, the cross product is *not* commutative, since **C ✕ D** $\neq$ **D ✕ C**.

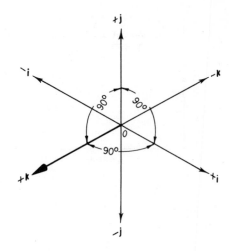

FIGURE A.72

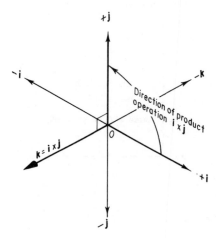

FIGURE A.73

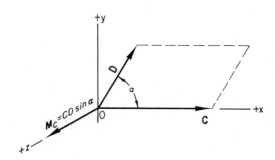

FIGURE A.70

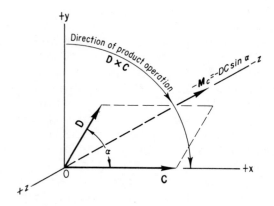

FIGURE A.71

If we consider the numerical values of $\sin 0° = 0$, $\sin 90° = 1$, $\sin 180° = 0$, and $\sin 270° = -1$ (which can all be the sines of the enclosed angles α between two vectors), we can develop some interesting and useful relationships of the cross products of *unit vectors*. Consider the cross product **i ✕ i**, which means that the enclosed angle α between the two unit vectors **i** is zero. Since $\sin 0° = 0$,

$$\mathbf{i} \times \mathbf{i} = |\mathbf{i}|\,|\mathbf{i}|\,(\sin 0°)$$

$$= |\mathbf{i}|\,|\mathbf{i}|(0)$$

$$= 0$$

In a similar way, we can find

$$(14) \qquad \mathbf{i} \times \mathbf{i} = \mathbf{j} \times \mathbf{j} = \mathbf{k} \times \mathbf{k} = 0$$

Next, let us consider the cross products of $\mathbf{i} \times \mathbf{j}$, $\mathbf{j} \times \mathbf{k}$, and $\mathbf{k} \times \mathbf{i}$, where the angle α enclosed by each pair of unit vectors is 90° (see Fig. A.72). According to the definition of the cross product,

$$\mathbf{i} \times \mathbf{j} = |\mathbf{i}|\,|\mathbf{j}|(\sin 90°)$$
$$= |\mathbf{i}|\,|\mathbf{j}|(1)$$
$$= 1$$

The result is a vector having a magnitude of *unity* that is *perpendicular* to the plane formed by $\mathbf{i}$ and $\mathbf{j}$ and that, according to our adopted sign convention, must therefore be equal to the unit vector $\mathbf{k}$ (see Fig. A.73).

Expanding this approach to all combinations of the unit vectors that are at right angles to each other (see Fig. A.74) and remembering that cross products are *not* commutative, we can write the following:

$$\mathbf{i} \times \mathbf{j} = \mathbf{j} \times -\mathbf{i} = -\mathbf{i} \times -\mathbf{j} = -\mathbf{j} \times \mathbf{i} = +\mathbf{k}$$
$$\mathbf{j} \times \mathbf{i} = \mathbf{i} \times -\mathbf{j} = -\mathbf{j} \times -\mathbf{i} = -\mathbf{i} \times -\mathbf{j} = -\mathbf{k}$$
$$\mathbf{i} \times -\mathbf{k} = -\mathbf{k} \times -\mathbf{i} = -\mathbf{i} \times \mathbf{k} = \mathbf{k} \times \mathbf{i} = +\mathbf{j}$$
$$-\mathbf{k} \times \mathbf{i} = \mathbf{i} \times \mathbf{k} = \mathbf{k} \times -\mathbf{i} = -\mathbf{i} \times -\mathbf{k} = -\mathbf{j}$$
$$\mathbf{j} \times \mathbf{k} = \mathbf{k} \times -\mathbf{j} = -\mathbf{j} \times -\mathbf{k} = -\mathbf{k} \times \mathbf{j} = +\mathbf{i}$$
$$\mathbf{k} \times \mathbf{j} = \mathbf{j} \times -\mathbf{k} = -\mathbf{k} \times -\mathbf{j} = -\mathbf{j} \times \mathbf{k} = -\mathbf{i}$$

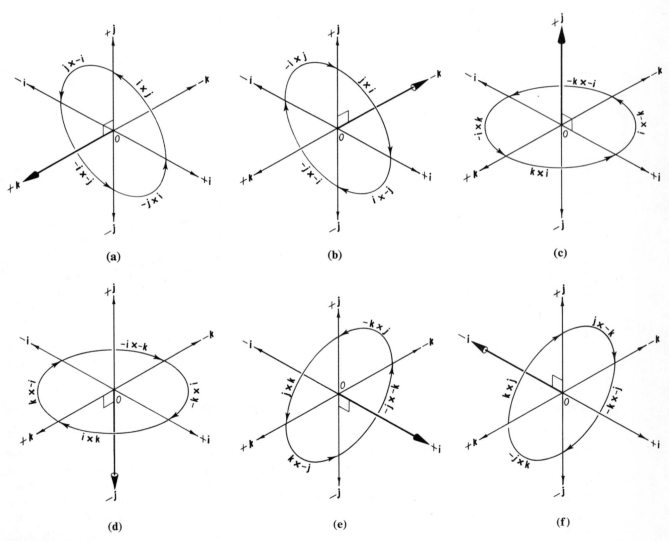

(a)   (b)   (c)

(d)   (e)   (f)

FIGURE A.74

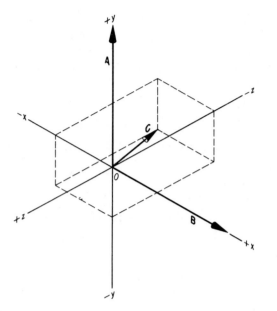

FIGURE A.75

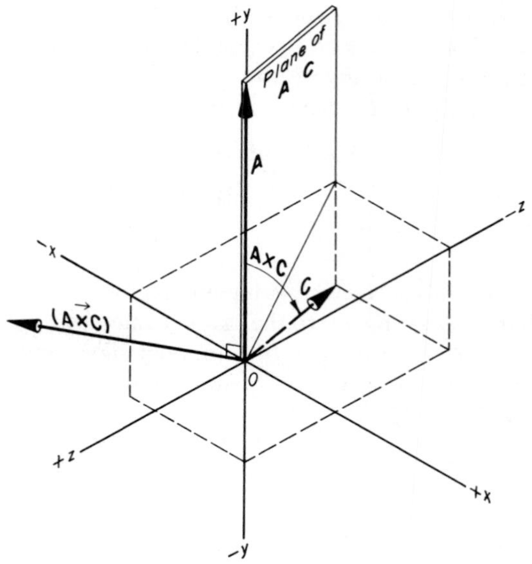

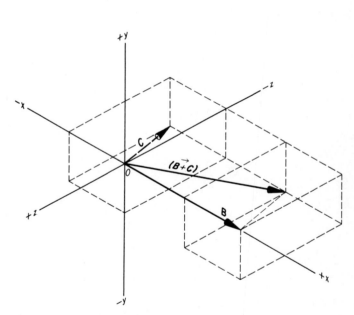

FIGURE A.77

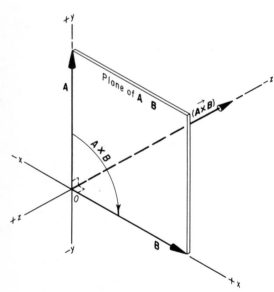

FIGURE A.76

FIGURE A.78

To show that the cross product follows the distributive law of multiplication, let us consider three vectors **A**, **B**, and **C**, as shown in Fig. A.75. The cross product **A ✕ B** results in a moment vector $[\overrightarrow{\mathbf{A} \times \mathbf{B}}]$ perpendicular to the plane formed by **A** and **B**, as shown in Fig. A.76. The cross

product **A ✕ C** results in a moment vector $[\overrightarrow{\mathbf{A} \times \mathbf{C}}]$ perpendicular to the plane formed by **A** and **C**, as shown in Fig. A.77. If we vectorially add **B** and **C**, the vector representing this sum is $[\overrightarrow{\mathbf{B} + \mathbf{C}}]$, as shown in Fig. A.78. Performing the cross product operation between **A** and $[\overrightarrow{\mathbf{B} + \mathbf{C}}]$,

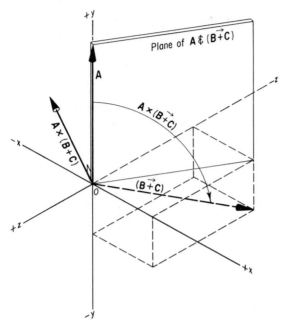

FIGURE A.79

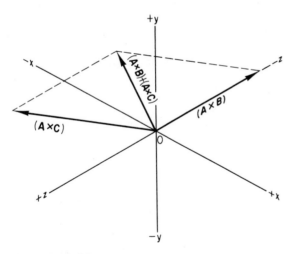

FIGURE A.80

Since all the cross product vectors $[\overrightarrow{A \times B}]$, $[\overrightarrow{A \times C}]$, and $[\overrightarrow{A \times (B + C)}]$ are *perpendicular* to their respective planes formed by **A** and **B**, **A** and **C**, and **A** and $[\overrightarrow{B + C}]$, *all lines* in these planes that pass through the common point of intersection (origin *O*) of the respective cross product vectors are perpendicular to the lines of action of the moment vectors (see Fig. A.81). This being the case, then $[\overrightarrow{B + C}]$ in the vector diagram (triangle) showing the vectorial addition of **B** + **C** can be projected as $[\overrightarrow{B + C}]'$ onto the *x-z* plane, as shown in Fig. A.82. Thus, the entire vector triangle of **B** + **C** is projected onto the *x-z* plane.

If we superimpose the vector triangle of the cross product vectors and the vector triangle of the given vectors **B** and **C** on the same coordinate axes, we see that side $[\overrightarrow{A \times B}]$ of the moment vector triangle is perpendicular to side **B** of the vector triangle of the given vectors **B** and **C**. We also see that $[\overrightarrow{A \times C}]$ is perpendicular to **C**′ and that $[\overrightarrow{A \times (B + C)}]$ is perpendicular to $[\overrightarrow{B + C}]'$ (see Fig. A.83). From this geometry, we

we get the moment vector $[\overrightarrow{A \times (B + C)}]$, as shown in Fig. A.79. Vectorially adding $[A \times B]$ and $[A \times C]$, we get the resulting vector $[(A \times B) + (A \times C)]$ (see Fig. A.80). Note that all the cross product vectors in this illustration are located in the *x-z* plane because vector **A** is perpendicular to the *x-y* plane.

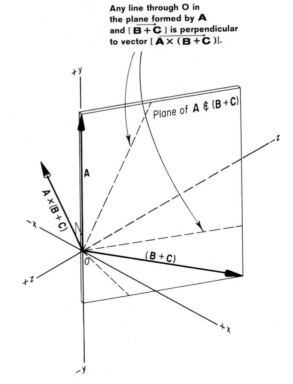

FIGURE A.81

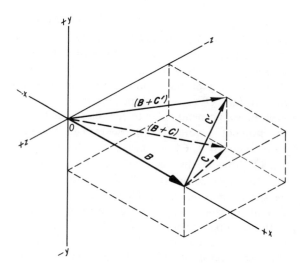

FIGURE A.82

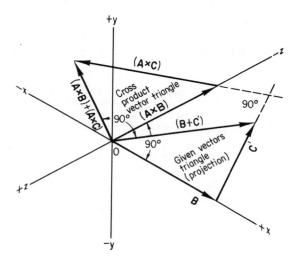

FIGURE A.83

see that the vector triangles are *similar*, and their sides are therefore proportional to each other. This proportionality can be expressed as follows:

$$\frac{\overrightarrow{[B + C]'}}{[(A \times B) + (A \times C)]} : \frac{B}{[A \times \overrightarrow{B}]} : \frac{C'}{[A \times \overrightarrow{C}]}$$

If we form a cross product of **A** with each numerator in the above expression, we get

$$\frac{A \times \overrightarrow{[B + C]'}}{[(A \times B) + (A \times C)]} : \frac{A \times B}{[A \times \overrightarrow{B}]} : \frac{A \times C'}{[A \times \overrightarrow{C}]}$$

From this,

$$A \times (B + C)' = (A \times B) + (A \times C')$$

It can also be shown by graphical analysis that the cross product follows the distributive law of multiplication. Example A.8 illustrates this as well as illustrating the way cross product vectors can be handled through the use of basic descriptive geometry principles.

EXAMPLE A.8

Graphical analysis of the cross product and its adherence to the distributive law of multiplication.

Given: Vectors **A** = 5 lb, **B** = 8 ft, and **C** = 10 ft, as shown in Fig. A.84.

Find: Graphically show that **A** × (**B** + **C**) = (**A** × **B**) + (**A** × **C**)

Graphical Analysis

1. Draw the top and front views, starting at point *O'* of the top view of Fig. A.85, of the vector diagram showing the addition of **B** + **C**. Determine the *true length* of $\overrightarrow{[B + C]}$, using descriptive geometry principles; measure this length to the given vector scale: $\overrightarrow{[B + C]}$ = 9.4 ft.

2. Applying the descriptive geometry principles

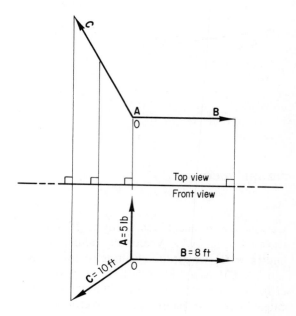

FIGURE A.84

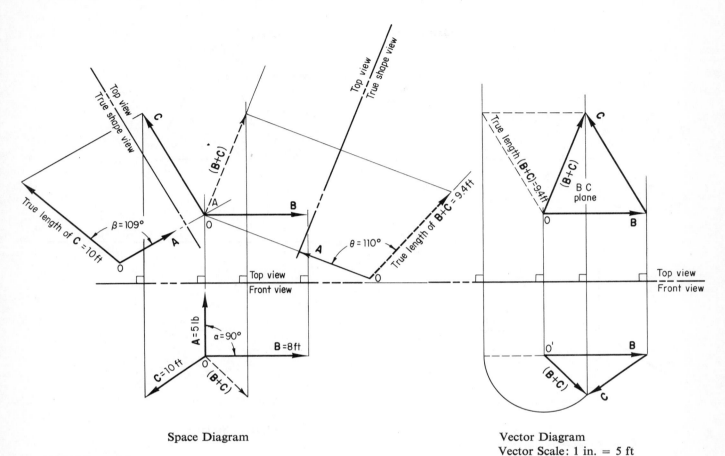

Space Diagram

Vector Diagram
Vector Scale: 1 in. = 5 ft

FIGURE A.85

dealing with the true shape of planes, determine the angles α, β, and θ that vector **A** makes with vectors **B**, **C**, and $[\overrightarrow{\mathbf{B} + \mathbf{C}}]$, respectively (see Fig. A.85). Measuring these angles in the front view and in the two true shape views, where the true shape of the planes formed by **A** and **B**, **A** and **C**, and **A** and $[\overrightarrow{\mathbf{B} + \mathbf{C}}]$ appear, we find $\alpha = 90°$, $\beta = 109°$, and $\theta = 110°$.

3. Evaluating the following cross products, we get:

$$\mathbf{A} \times \mathbf{B} = AB(\sin \alpha) = 5 \cdot 8 \cdot (\sin 90°)$$

$$= 5 \cdot 8 \cdot (1) = 40 \text{ ft-lb}$$

$$\mathbf{A} \times \mathbf{B} = AC(\sin \beta) = 5 \cdot 10 \cdot (\sin 109°)$$

$$= 5 \cdot 10 \cdot (0.94) = 47.0 \text{ ft-lb}$$

$$\mathbf{A} \times (\mathbf{B} + \mathbf{C}) = A(B + C)(\sin \theta)$$

$$= 5 \cdot 9.4 \cdot (\sin 110°)$$

$$= 5 \cdot 9.4 \cdot (0.93) = 41.7 \text{ ft-lb}$$

4. Draw the vectors (to the given moment vector

scale) representing the cross products $[\overrightarrow{\mathbf{A} \times \mathbf{B}}]$, $[\overrightarrow{\mathbf{A} \times \mathbf{C}}]$, and $[\overrightarrow{\mathbf{A} \times (\mathbf{B} + \mathbf{C})}]$ *perpendicular* to their respective planes formed by the vectors in each cross product. (See top view in Fig. A.86.)

5. Draw a *vector diagram* in the top view, showing the addition of the cross product vectors $[\overrightarrow{\mathbf{A} \times \mathbf{B}}]$ and $[\overrightarrow{\mathbf{A} \times \mathbf{C}}]$. (In the top view in Fig. A.86, this vector diagram was started at point O'.)

6. Vector $[\overrightarrow{\mathbf{A} \times (\mathbf{B} + \mathbf{C})}]$ closes this diagram showing that

$$\mathbf{A} \times (\mathbf{B} + \mathbf{C}) = (\mathbf{A} \times \mathbf{B}) + (\mathbf{A} \times \mathbf{C})$$

7. In comparing the directions of the vectors in the two vector diagrams, we see that $[\overrightarrow{\mathbf{A} \times \mathbf{B}}]$ is perpendicular to **B**, $[\overrightarrow{\mathbf{A} \times \mathbf{C}}]$ is perpendicular to **C**, and $[\overrightarrow{\mathbf{A} \times (\mathbf{B} + \mathbf{C})}]$ is perpendicular to $[\overrightarrow{\mathbf{B} + \mathbf{C}}]$, making both diagrams similar and proportional, with the cross product vector diagram rotated 90° from the **B** + **C** vector diagram.

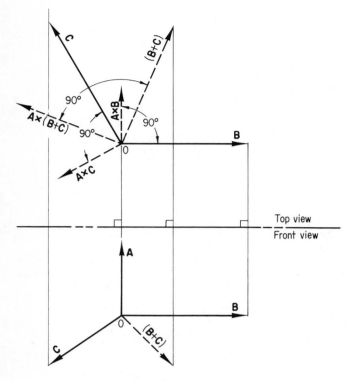

Space Diagram

FIGURE A.86

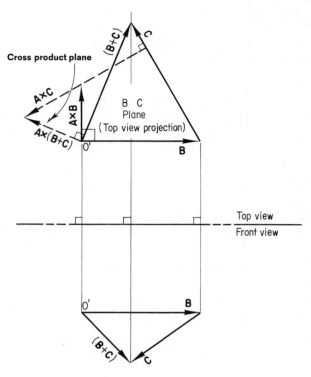

Vector Diagram
Vector Scale: 1 in. = 5 ft
Moment Scale: 1 in. = 5 ft-lb

The cross product operation can be applied to vectors that are defined in terms of their unit vector components. Let us consider the cross product of $\mathbf{A} \times \mathbf{B}$, where

$$\mathbf{A} = A_x\mathbf{i} + A_y\mathbf{j} + A_z\mathbf{k}$$

and

$$\mathbf{B} = B_x\mathbf{i} + B_y\mathbf{j} + B_z\mathbf{k}$$

Therefore,

$$\mathbf{A} \times \mathbf{B} = (A_x\mathbf{i} + A_y\mathbf{j} + A_z\mathbf{k})$$
$$\times (B_x\mathbf{i} + B_y\mathbf{j} + B_z\mathbf{k})$$

Expanding the right side of this relationship and keeping in mind that the order of the cross product operation is from $\mathbf{A}$ to $\mathbf{B}$, we get

$$\mathbf{A} \times \mathbf{B} = A_x\mathbf{i}(B_x\mathbf{i} + B_y\mathbf{j} + B_z\mathbf{k})$$
$$+ A_y\mathbf{j}(B_x\mathbf{i} + B_y\mathbf{j} + B_z\mathbf{k})$$
$$+ A_z\mathbf{k}(B_x\mathbf{i} + B_y\mathbf{j} + B_z\mathbf{k})$$

$$= A_xB_x\mathbf{i} \times \mathbf{i} + A_xB_y\mathbf{i} \times \mathbf{j} + A_xB_z\mathbf{i} \times \mathbf{k}$$
$$+ A_yB_x\mathbf{j} \times \mathbf{i} + A_yB_y\mathbf{j} \times \mathbf{j} + A_yB_z\mathbf{j} \times \mathbf{k}$$
$$+ A_zB_x\mathbf{k} \times \mathbf{i} + A_zB_y\mathbf{k} \times \mathbf{j} + A_zB_z\mathbf{k} \times \mathbf{k}$$

Since

$$\mathbf{i} \times \mathbf{i} = \mathbf{j} \times \mathbf{j} = \mathbf{k} \times \mathbf{k} = 0$$

and

$$\mathbf{i} \times \mathbf{j} = \mathbf{k} \qquad \mathbf{j} \times \mathbf{k} = \mathbf{i}$$
$$\mathbf{i} \times \mathbf{k} = -\mathbf{j} \qquad \mathbf{k} \times \mathbf{i} = +\mathbf{j}$$
$$\mathbf{j} \times \mathbf{i} = -\mathbf{k} \qquad \mathbf{k} \times \mathbf{j} = -\mathbf{i}$$

we get

$$\mathbf{A} \times \mathbf{B} = A_xB_y\mathbf{k} - A_xB_z\mathbf{j} - A_yB_x\mathbf{k} + A_yB_z\mathbf{i}$$
$$+ A_zB_x\mathbf{j} - A_zB_y\mathbf{i}$$

Grouping terms,

$$(15) \quad \mathbf{A} \times \mathbf{B} = (A_yB_z - A_zB_y)\mathbf{i}$$
$$+ (A_zB_x - A_xB_z)\mathbf{j} + (A_xB_y - A_yB_x)\mathbf{k}$$

EXAMPLE A.9 ─────────────────

The cross product of two vectors in terms of their unit vector components.

Given: Vectors $A = 3i + 2j + 4k$

$B = -2i - 5j + 2k$

as shown in Fig. A.87.

Find: The cross product $A \times B$.

Vector Analysis

1. Perform the cross product operation $A \times B$:

$A \times B = (3i + 2j + 4k) \times (-2i - 5j + 2k)$

$= 3i(-2i - 5j + 2k) + 2j(-2i - 5j + 2k)$
$+ 4k(-2i - 5j + 2k)$

$= -6i \times i - 15i \times j + 6i \times k$
$- 4j \times i - 10j \times j + 4j \times k$
$- 8k \times i - 20k \times j + 8k \times k$

2. Since $i \times i = j \times j = k \times k = 0$, we can write

$A \times B = -15i \times j + 6i \times k - 4j \times i + 4j \times k$
$- 8k \times i - 20k \times j$

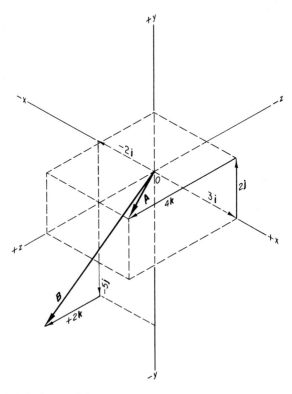

FIGURE A.87

3. Since $i \times j = +k$, $i \times k = -j$, $j \times i = -k$, $j \times k = i$, $k \times i = +j$, and $k \times j = -i$, we get

$A \times B = -15k - 6j + 4k + 4i - 8j + 20i$

$= 24i - 14j - 11k$

4. The magnitude of $A \times B$ is

$|A \times B| = \sqrt{24^2 + (-14)^2 + (-11)^2}$

$= \sqrt{576 + 196 + 121}$

$= \sqrt{893}$

$= 29.8$ ft-lb

Graphical Analysis

1. Draw the top and front views of the given vectors, as shown in Fig. A.88.
2. Draw the *edge view* of the plane formed by A and B as shown in Fig. A.88.
3. Draw the *true shape* view of the plane formed by A and B, as shown in Fig. A.88.
4. In the true shape view, construct a *perpendicular* line from the end of B to the line of action of A. Measuring this perpendicular, we get 5.5 ft, according to the given *space scale*.
5. Measure the true length of A (in the true shape view) to the given vector scale. A = 5.4 lb.
6. Perform the multiplication

$AB \sin \alpha = (5.4\text{ lb})(5.5\text{ ft})(1) = 29.7$ ft-lb

EXAMPLE A.10 ───────────────

Deriving the moment of a force about a point by using the cross product concept.

Given: Vector $A = 10$ lb whose line of action passes through points $P(5, 2, -5)$ and $Q(-5, 4, -2)$ and has a sense from P to Q, as shown in Fig. A.89.

Find: Determine the moment of A relative to the origin O of the assumed rectangular co-ordinate axis system that locates P and Q in space.

Vector Analysis

1. Regard the distances from O to P and from O to Q as *position vectors* that locate P and Q. Express these position vectors in terms of their unit vector components:

$$\overrightarrow{OP} = 5i + 2j - 5k$$

(The coefficients 5, 2, and -5 are the coordinates of P.)

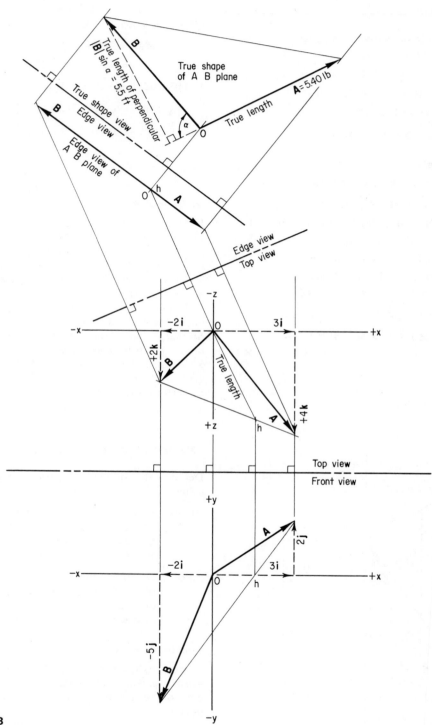

FIGURE A.88

Distance Scale: 1 in. = 3 ft
Vector Scale: 1 in. = 3 lb

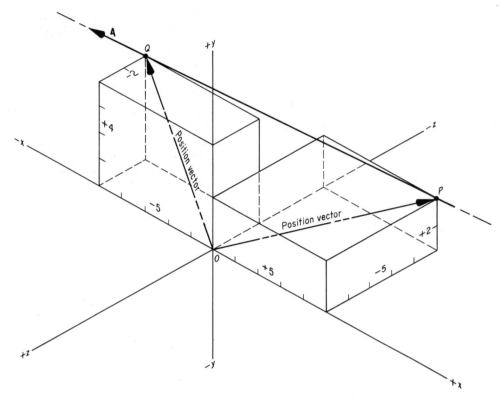

FIGURE A.89

$$\overrightarrow{OQ} = -5\mathbf{i} + 4\mathbf{j} - 2\mathbf{k}$$

(The coefficients -5, 4, and -2 are the coordinates of Q.)

2. The distance from P to Q can be regarded as a *vector* $\overrightarrow{PQ}$ which represents $\mathbf{A}$ (which must be multiplied by the proper proportionality constant) and which therefore is equal to the vector difference between $\overrightarrow{OQ}$ and $\overrightarrow{OP}$. This vector difference is represented by

$$\overrightarrow{OQ} - \overrightarrow{OP}$$

and in terms of unit vectors it is written as

$$\overrightarrow{OQ} = -5\mathbf{i} + 4\mathbf{j} - 2\mathbf{k} \quad = -5\mathbf{i} + 4\mathbf{j} - 2\mathbf{k}$$

$$-\overrightarrow{OP} = -(5\mathbf{i} + 2\mathbf{j} - 5\mathbf{k}) = -5\mathbf{i} - 2\mathbf{j} + 5\mathbf{k}$$

$$\therefore \ \overrightarrow{OQ} - \overrightarrow{OP} = \overrightarrow{PQ} = -10\mathbf{i} + 2\mathbf{j} + 3\mathbf{k}$$

3. To determine the *moment* of $\overrightarrow{PQ}$ ($=\mathbf{A}$) about O, perform the cross product operation between *one* of the position vectors (such as $\overrightarrow{OP}$) and $\overrightarrow{PQ}$.

$\mathbf{M}_A = \overrightarrow{OP} \times \overrightarrow{PQ}$ (proportionality constant)

$$= (5\mathbf{i} + 2\mathbf{j} - 5\mathbf{k}) \times (-10\mathbf{i} + 2\mathbf{j} + 3\mathbf{k})(\text{P.C.})$$

$$= [5\mathbf{i}(-10\mathbf{i} + 2\mathbf{j} + 3\mathbf{k}) + 2\mathbf{j}(-10\mathbf{i} + 2\mathbf{j} + 3\mathbf{k})$$
$$- 5\mathbf{k}(-10\mathbf{i} + 2\mathbf{j} + 3\mathbf{k})](\text{P.C.})$$

$$= (-50\mathbf{i} \times \mathbf{i} + 10\mathbf{i} \times \mathbf{j} + 15\mathbf{i} \times \mathbf{k} - 20\mathbf{j} \times \mathbf{i}$$
$$+ 4\mathbf{j} \times \mathbf{j} + 6\mathbf{j} \times \mathbf{k} + 50\mathbf{k} \times \mathbf{i} - 10\mathbf{k} \times \mathbf{j}$$
$$- 15\mathbf{k} \times \mathbf{k})(\text{P.C.})$$

$$= (10\mathbf{k} - 15\mathbf{j} + 20\mathbf{k}$$
$$+ 6\mathbf{i} + 50\mathbf{j} + 10\mathbf{i})(\text{P.C.})$$

$$= (16\mathbf{i} + 35\mathbf{j} + 30\mathbf{k})(\text{P.C.})$$

4. Determine the value of the proportionality constant (P.C.) by determining the magnitude of the distance from P to Q and forming a ratio between this distance and the given value for force $\mathbf{A}$ ($=10$ lb). From the unit vector expression for PQ,

$$|\overrightarrow{PQ}| = \sqrt{(-10)^2 + 2^2 + 3^2}$$

$$= \sqrt{100 + 4 + 9}$$

$$= \sqrt{113}$$

Therefore, the proportionality constant is equal to $10/\sqrt{113}$.

5. Determine the magnitude of the moment of **A** about O ($=\mathbf{M}_A$) from the unit vector expression for $\mathbf{M}_A$.

$$\therefore \ |\mathbf{M}_A| = \left(\sqrt{16^2 + 35^2 + 30^2}\right)\left(\frac{10}{\sqrt{113}}\right)$$

$$= \left(\sqrt{256 + 1225 + 900}\right)\left(\frac{10}{\sqrt{113}}\right)$$

$$|\mathbf{M}_A| = \left(\sqrt{2381}\right)\left(\frac{10}{\sqrt{113}}\right)$$

$$= 45.8 \text{ lb-ft}$$

Graphical Analysis

1. Using a convenient space scale, lay out the top and front views of the given points P and Q.

2. Connect P and Q with a straight line in the top and front views. This is the direction of vector **A** having a given sense toward Q. (See the drawing shown in Fig. A.91.)

3. Draw the *position vectors* $\overrightarrow{OP}$ and $\overrightarrow{OQ}$ forming the plane OPQ.

4. Draw the *edge view* of plane OPQ.

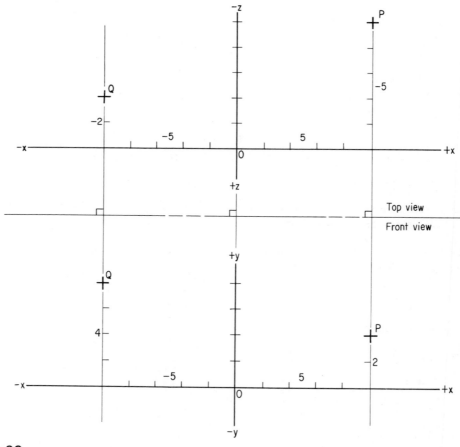

FIGURE A.90

Space Scale: 1 in. = 3 ft

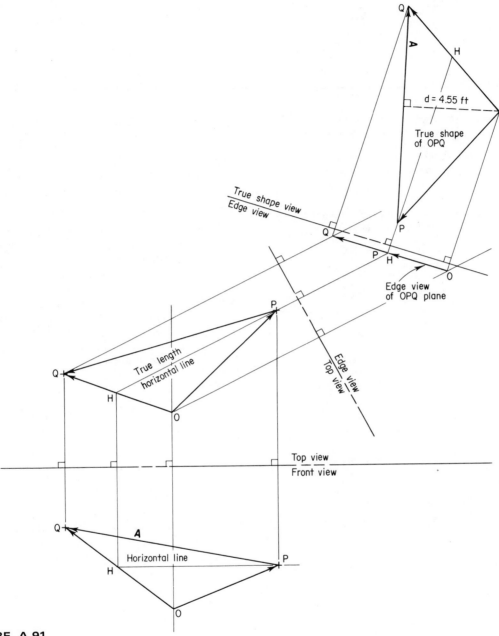

FIGURE A.91

Space Scale: 1 in. = 3 ft

5. Draw the *true shape* of the plane *OPQ*.

6. In the true shape view, construct a *perpendicular* line from *O* to the line of action of **A**. (This perpendicular line is the moment arm *d* that measures 4.55 ft to the given space scale.) (See Fig. A.91.)

7. Since **A** = 10 lb, multiply *dA* to get the required moment M_A.

$$\therefore\ M_A = (4.55\ \text{ft})(10\ \text{lb})$$

$$= 45.5\ \text{lb-ft}$$

PROBLEMS _____

A.1 **Given:** Coplanar, concurrent vectors **A** = 5**i**,
B = 4**i** + 3**j**, and **C** = 12**i** + 5**j**.

Find: A, B, and C and the angle θ that each
vector makes with the x axis.

A.2 **Given:** Coplanar, concurrent vectors **A** = 5**i**,
B = 4**i** + 3**j**, and **C** = 12**i** + 5**j**.

Find: **A** + **B**, **B** − **C**, and $3A − (B + C)$.

A.3 **Given:** The coplanar force system **A** = 50 lb,
B = 15 lb, and **C** = 65 lb, as shown
in Fig. A.92.

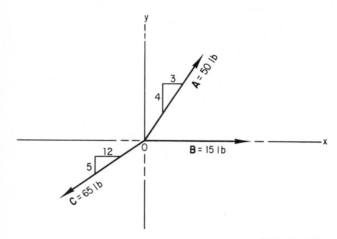

FIGURE A.92

Find: The magnitude of the resultant force
of the given system and the angle it
makes with the x axis, using vector
notation and trigonometric analyses.

A.4 **Given:** Concurrent, noncoplanar vectors **A** =
4**i** + 2**j** + 4**k**, **B** = −3**i** + 5**j**, and
C = 5**i** − 5**j** − 3**k**.

Find: The magnitude and direction angles
of each vector.

A.5 **Given:** Vector **F** = 4**i** + 2**j** + 3**k**, which
passes through a point whose coordinates are (3, 2, −1).

Find: The dot and cross products, relative
to the origin of the x-y axis system, of
the given vector **F**.

A.6 **Given:** Vectors **A** and **B** are components of
the force **R**, as shown in Fig. A.93.
P is the location vector from any
point to the point of concurrency of
the forces.

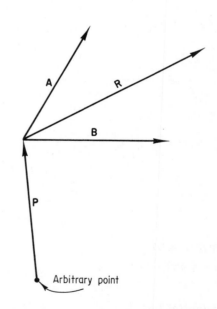

FIGURE A.93

Find: Prove Varignon's theorem, using
vector notation analysis. (Suggestion:

334

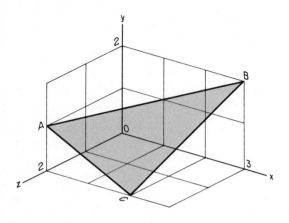

FIGURE A.94

Let $\mathbf{A} = A_x\mathbf{i} + A_y\mathbf{j} + A_z\mathbf{k}$, $\mathbf{B} = B_x\mathbf{i} + B_y\mathbf{j} + B_z\mathbf{k}$, $\mathbf{P} = P_x\mathbf{i} + P_y\mathbf{j} + P_z\mathbf{k}$, and $\mathbf{R} = \mathbf{A} + \mathbf{B}$. Prove that $\mathbf{P} \times \mathbf{R} = (\mathbf{P} \times \mathbf{A}) + (\mathbf{P} \times \mathbf{B})$. Do not use the distributive law in this solution.)

A.7 **Given**: Triangle *ABC*, as shown in Fig. A.94.

  Find: The area of triangle *ABC*, using vector notation analysis.

A.8 Solve Prob. 6.8, using vector notation.

A.9 Solve Prob. 5.9, using vector notation.

A.10 Solve Prob. 5.10, using vector notation.

Topic B

VIRTUAL WORK

B.1 The Definition of Work

In Sec. A.7, *work* was defined as the product of a force of constant magnitude and the *projection* of the displacement distance of the force on the line of action of the force (see Fig. B.1). A force does *positive work* if the *projection* of its displacement distance (from an initial point to a final point) *follows the sense* of the force, as shown in Fig. B.1. A force does *negative work* if the projection of its displacement distance (from an initial point to a final point) is opposite in sense to the force, as shown in Fig. B.2. If, as shown in Fig. B.3, the displacement of a force is at 90° to the line of action of the force, then the force does *zero work* (since cos 90° = 0 and therefore the projection of the displacement distance on the line of action of the force is zero).

The amount of work performed by a force of constant magnitude whose point of application is displaced from an initial position to a final position is always the *same*, no matter what *path* the point of application follows during its transi-

tion from the initial to the final position. For example, the force F in Fig. B.4a is displaced from point s_1 to point s_3. Path I of displacement is a straight line displacement from s_1 to some intermediate point s_2 and then from s_2 to the final point s_3 on a straight line. Displacement path II is directly from s_1 to s_3 on a straight line. The work performed by the force F following path I from s_1 to s_2 is *negative work* equal to $-Fa$, as shown in Fig. B.4b. The work performed by the force F during its displacement from s_2 to s_3 is positive work equal to Fb. The work performed by the force F following path II directly from s_1 to s_3 is positive work equal to Fc.

From Fig. B.4b, we see that $b = a + c$. Therefore, the total work performed by the force F following path I from s_1 to s_2 to s_3 is

$$W = -Fa + Fb$$
$$= -Fa + F(a + c)$$
$$= -\cancel{Fa} + \cancel{Fa} + Fc$$
$$= Fc$$

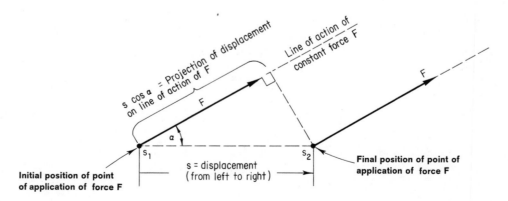

FIGURE B.1

EXAMPLE B.2 _____

The static equilibrium analysis of a rigid structure.

Given: Structure $ABCD$ in equilibrium, supporting a vertical load $F_2 = 5000$ lb applied at point D, as shown in Fig. B.11a. All joints in the structure are frictionless, and all bars are weightless.

Find: The magnitude and type of load carried by bar BC, using the principle of virtual work.

Virtual Work Analysis

1. Imagine, as shown in Fig. B.11b, that bar BC is removed and replaced by a force F_1 that maintains the given equilibrium conditions. This makes it possible to give the structure an angular virtual displacement of $\delta\theta$, since F_1 can be given a linear virtual displacement of δs_1.

2. Since F_1 received a virtual displacement δs_1, force F_2 must receive a virtual displacement of $\delta s_2 = l\,\delta\theta\cos 30°$, in order to maintain geometric

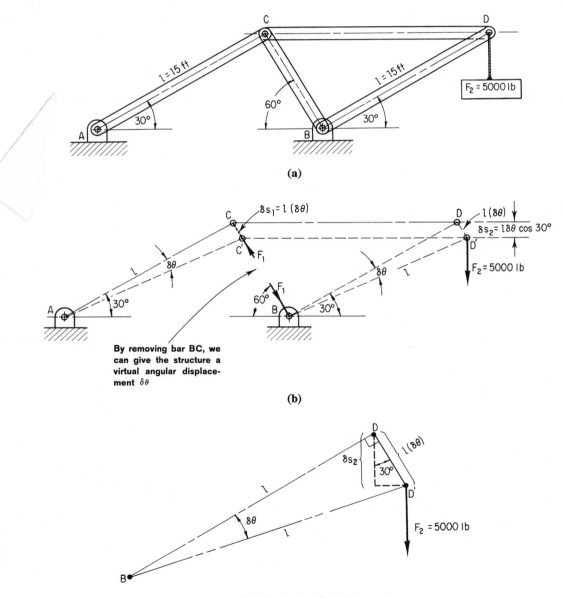

(a)

(b)

By removing bar BC, we can give the structure a virtual angular displacement $\delta\theta$

(c) Geometry Detail

FIGURE B.11

compatibility (l = distances AC and BD). (See Fig. B.11c.)

3. Support points A and B are *workless* supports, and therefore, *no* virtual displacement takes place at these points.

4. Write the virtual work static equilibrium equation for the given system:

$$\delta W = -F_1\,\delta s_1 + F_2\,\delta s_2 = 0$$

$$\therefore\ F_1 = \frac{F_2\,\delta s_2}{\delta s_1}$$

Substitute $s_1 = l\,\delta\theta$ and $\delta s_2 = l\,\delta\theta \cos 30°$ in the above expression for F_1:

$$F_1 = \frac{F_2 l\,\delta\theta \cos 30°}{l\,\delta\theta} = F_2 \cos 30°$$

$$= (5000\ \text{lb})\left(\frac{\sqrt{3}}{2}\right) = +4340\ \text{lb}$$

The positive sign indicates that our assumed virtual displacement direction is correct; therefore, the force in bar DC = 4340 lb compression.

NOTE: The principle of virtual work allowed us to solve directly for the load in bar BC. This approach is very useful, providing the geometry of the problem remains relatively simple; otherwise, the method of joints or sections (in the case of a structure) would be more direct.

PROBLEMS

B.1 Given: A beam pin connected at point A on its left end and resting on a roller at its right end, as shown in Fig. B.12. A load P acts on the beam one third of the distance from A to B.

Find: Using the method of virtual work, determine the magnitude of the reaction force that acts at point B to keep beam AB in equilibrium.

Ans. $F_B = P/3$

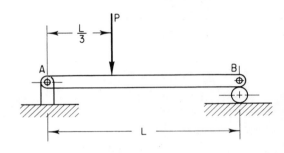

FIGURE B.12

B.2 Given: Two beams AC and BD loaded and supported, as shown in Fig. B.13.

Find: Using the method of virtual work, determine the magnitude of the force acting at support point C.

Ans. $F_C = 200$ lb

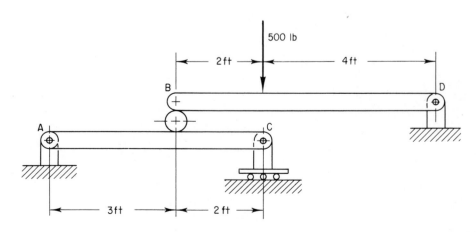

FIGURE B.13

B.3 Given: A pin-connected truss externally loaded with a 10,000 lb load, as shown in Fig. B.14.

Find: Using the method of virtual work, determine the magnitude and type of load in member *DE*. Check your results, using graphical analysis.

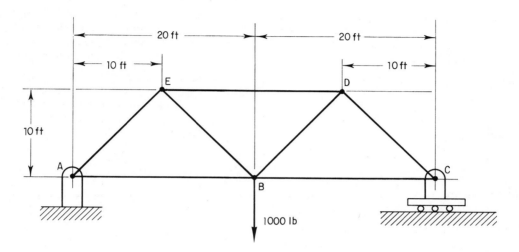

FIGURE B.14

B.4 Given: A tripod with vertex *O* and legs *OA*, *OB*, and *OC* loaded vertically with 1000 lb, as shown in Fig. B.15.

Find: Using the method of virtual work, determine the magnitude of the load carried by leg *OA*. Check your answer by using vector notation analysis or graphical analysis.

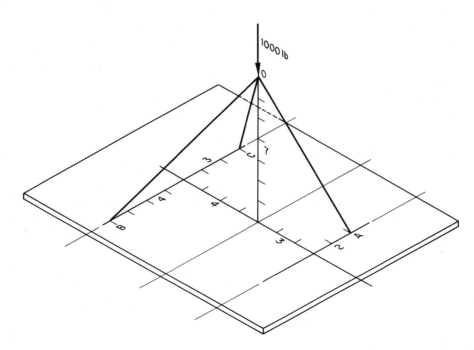

FIGURE B.15

B.5 Given: A ladder rests against a frictionless wall and floor, as shown in Fig. B.16. A man of weight W stands on the ladder at the indicated position C.

Find: Using the method of virtual work, determine the magnitude of the force P necessary to hold the ladder in equilibrium.

Ans. $P = \frac{3}{8}W$

B.6 Given: Two 1000-lb weights connected by a weightless, perfectly flexible cable that passes over a frictionless pulley, as shown in Fig. B.17.

Find: Using the method of virtual work, determine the coefficient of friction between the plane and the weight that rests on it when motion is impending.

Ans. $\mu = 0.414$

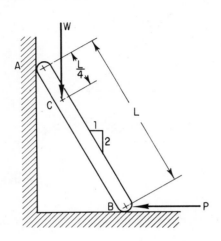

FIGURE B.16

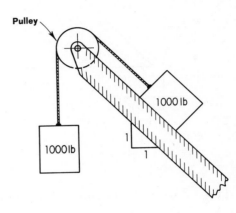

FIGURE B.17

Topic C

CASE STUDIES IN STATICS

Introduction

This section contains two solved problems where basic design data dealing with the static equilibrium conditions of a particular statically loaded structure or system must be determined.[1]

The requirements and assumptions for each problem are presented in a general form and are followed by a detailed solution. These problems and solutions "pull together" a number of the basic principles of statics under approximately real conditions; they illustrate a systematic method of "attack" of solving problems.

PROBLEM C.1 _____

A tubular fuselage structure of an experimental aircraft must be designed to withstand the externally applied loads shown in Fig. C.1 Experiments have shown that at the normal flying speed of the craft, the lift and drag forces that act upon the structure, as shown in Fig. C.1, are as follows:

The force L_3 is 30 lb and is inclined, as shown.

The main lifting surface, the wing, is attached to the fuselage at A and B. Pressure measurements on this experimental wing gave the distributed load shown in Fig. C.2. The distributed load acts in *each* of the two *vertical planes* that contain A and B (see pictorial view in Fig. C.1). The loads L_1 and L_2 are exerted upon the fuselage by the wing at the points of attachment A and B. The drag force of the wing ($D_R = 15$ lb) is exerted upon the fuselage at *each* point B.

----

[1] The basic problems in this section were designed by Robert W. Bosma.

The pilot, whose weight is $W_P = 160$ lb, lies upon a platform that is supported at A and C. This platform is designed in such a manner that it does *not* contribute to the structural strength of the fuselage. The pilot's weight results in the forces W_1 and W_2, which the platform transmits to the fuselage.

The load T is the thrust applied to the fuselage by a pusher-type propeller.

The members of the fuselage structure are assumed to be weightless, and all joints are assumed to be frictionless pin connected.

All of the calculations in the solution below are based upon static equilibrium considerations. That is, the aircraft is assumed to be in a straight-line level flight at a constant velocity.

Required Design Data

1. Determine the thrust T necessary to maintain the aircraft speed at the design value.
2. Determine the maximum permissible weight for the entire aircraft, based on the given information.
3. Assuming that the combined weight of the aircraft structure and the pilot has a single line of action, determine the location of this line of action relative to O such that the aircraft will be in rotational equilibrium.
4. Using the line of action of the combined weight, determine W_1 and W_2 due to the pilot's weight.
5. Determine the magnitude and type of load acting in members BD due to the loading shown in Fig. C.1.

Solution Analysis

Part 1. To determine the thrust T, we can apply the principle of summation of forces in the horizontal direction, as shown in Fig. C.3 ($\sum F_x = 0$ for equilibrium), as follows:

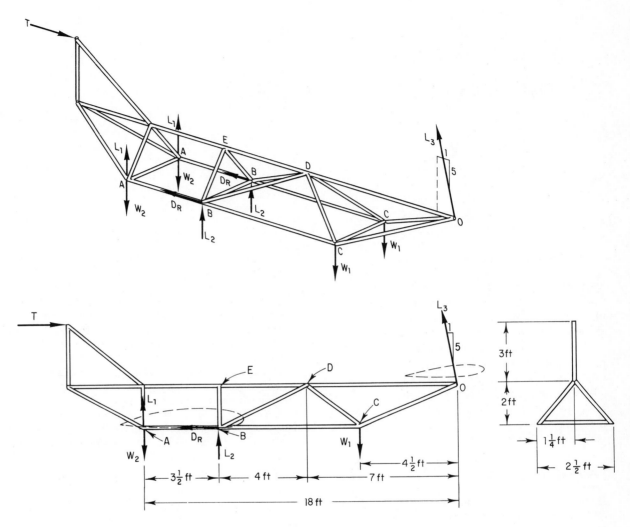

FIGURE C.1

$$T = 2D_R + L_3 \cos \theta$$

$$= 2(15 \text{ lb}) + (30 \text{ lb})\left(\frac{1}{\sqrt{26}}\right)$$

$$= 30 \text{ lb} + 5.88 \text{ lb} = 35.88 \text{ lb}$$

Part 2. To determine the maximum permissible weight of the entire aircraft, it is first necessary to determine the magnitude and line of action of the *resultant* of the lifting forces of the wing (due to the distributed lifting forces over the wing surface; see Fig. C.2). This requires the application of the concepts of the load diagram and the centroid of a plane area (the center of parallel forces).

With the above information, we will be able to determine the forces that act at A and B, where the

wing is attached to the fuselage. (Remember that there are *two* points A and *two* points B—left side and right side of the fuselage—and that the lifting forces of the wing act with equal magnitude on both sides.)

When all of the above information is obtained, we can consider the total vertical equilibrium conditions of the aircraft to determine its maximum permissible weight.

a. The resultant lifting force. The area of the load diagram (Fig. C.2) represents the magnitude of the resultant lifting force. The centroid of this area is the point through which the resultant force acts. In this example, the area of the load diagram can be divided into subareas Q, R, S, and T, as shown in Fig. C.4. We will locate the centroid of the load

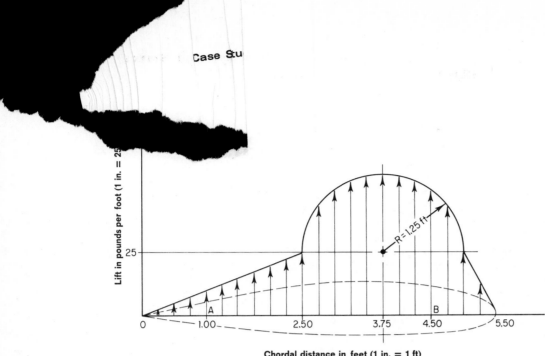

FIGURE C.2

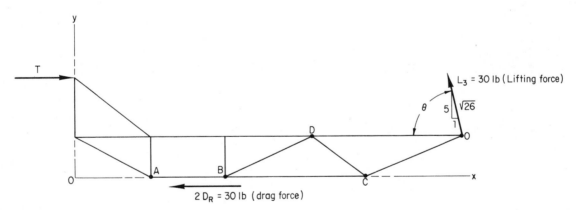

FIGURE C.3

diagram relative to the vertical centerline of sub-area T, using the following scale.

$$1 \text{ in.}^2 = (25 \text{ lb/ft})(1 \text{ ft}) = 25 \text{ lb}$$

As shown in Fig. C.5a,

$$\text{area } Q = \frac{(2.50 \text{ in.})(1 \text{ in.})}{2} = 1.25 \text{ in.}^2$$

Therefore, the force represented by area Q is

$$F_Q = (1.25 \text{ in.}^2)(25 \text{ lb/in.}^2) = 31.20 \text{ lb}$$

As illustrated in Fig. C.5b,

$$\text{area } R = (2.50 \text{ in.})(1 \text{ in.}) = 2.50 \text{ in.}^2$$

Therefore, the force represented by area R is

$$F_R = (2.50 \text{ in.}^2)(25 \text{ lb/in.}^2) = 62.50 \text{ lb}$$

From Fig. C.5c,

$$\text{area } S = \frac{(0.50 \text{ in.})(1 \text{ in.})}{2} = 0.25 \text{ in.}^2$$

Therefore, the force represented by area S is

$$F_S = (0.25 \text{ in.}^2)(25 \text{ lb/in.}^2) = 6.25 \text{ lb}$$

Finally, for area T in Fig. C.5d,

$$\text{area } T = \frac{\pi(1.25 \text{ in.})^2}{2} = 2.45 \text{ in.}^2$$

and the force represented by area T is

$$F_T = (2.45 \text{ in.}^2)(25 \text{ lb/in.}^2) = 61.30 \text{ lb}$$

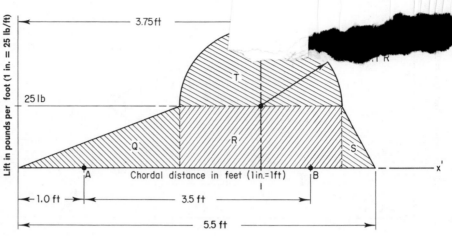

FIGURE C.4

The total lifting force (resultant) acting at the centroid of the load diagram is

$$L_T = 31.20 \text{ lb} + 62.50 \text{ lb} + 6.25 \text{ lb} + 61.30 \text{ lb}$$

$$= 161.25 \text{ lb}$$

b. *The centroid of the load diagram.* The centroid of the load diagram will be located relative to the vertical centerline of area T by applying

$$x_c = \frac{\sum x\,\Delta A}{\sum \Delta A}$$

Referring to Fig. C.6, we see that

$$x_c = \frac{-[1.25 + \frac{1}{3}(2.50)](\text{area } Q)}{(\text{area } Q) + (\text{area } R)} \rightarrow$$

$$\leftarrow \frac{+ [1.25 + \frac{1}{3}(0.50)](\text{area } S)}{+ (\text{area } S) + (\text{area } T)}$$

$$= \frac{-2.08(31.20) + 1.42(6.25)}{161.25}$$

$$= \frac{-64.89 + 8.87}{161.25} = \frac{-56.02}{161.25}$$

$$= -0.35 \text{ ft}$$

(see Fig. C.7.)

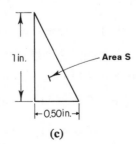

Area Q

2.50 in.

(a)

Area R

1 in.

2.50 in.

(b)

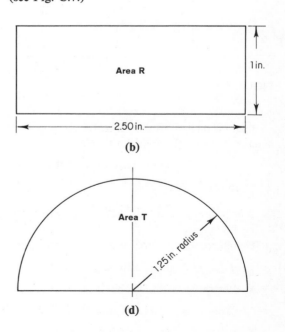

1 in.

Area S

0.50 in.

(c)

Area T

1.25 in. radius

(d)

FIGURE C.5

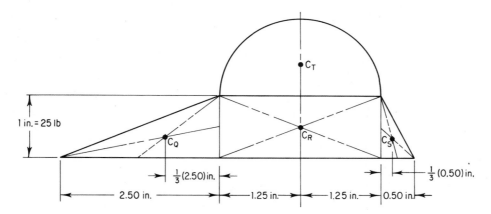

FIGURE C.6

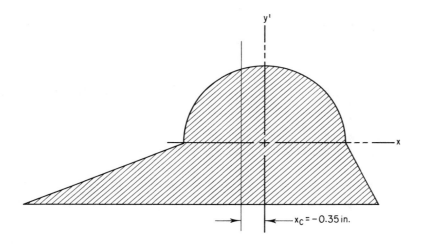

FIGURE C.7

When many numbers are used to determine a particular value, it is useful to apply a graphical analysis as a check on the numerical calculation. In Fig. C.8, the centroid distance x_c of the load diagram is determined graphically through the use of the ray and funicular polygons. From this, we see that the result of our numerical calculation is valid.

c. *Forces acting at A and B due to lifting force L_T.* By considering the equilibrium conditions necessary to balance the lifting force L_T, we can apply $\sum M_A = 0$ and $\sum F_y = 0$ to determine the forces acting at A and B, respectively, due to the total lifting force L_T (see Fig. C.9).

$$\sum M_A = 0$$

$$\therefore (3.50 \text{ ft})F_B = (2.40 \text{ ft})L_T$$

$$\therefore F_B = \frac{(2.40 \text{ ft})L_T}{3.50 \text{ ft}}$$

$$= \frac{(2.40 \text{ ft})(161.2 \text{ lb})}{3.50 \text{ ft}}$$

$$= 110 \text{ lb}$$

Since we are interested in the *lifting force L_2* acting at B, we make the substitution $L_2 = -F_B$ (see Fig. C.1).

$$\sum F_y = 0$$

$$\therefore L_T = F_A + F_B$$

$$\therefore F_A = L_T - F_B$$

$$= 161.2 \text{ lb} - 110 \text{ lb}$$

$$= 51.2 \text{ lb}$$

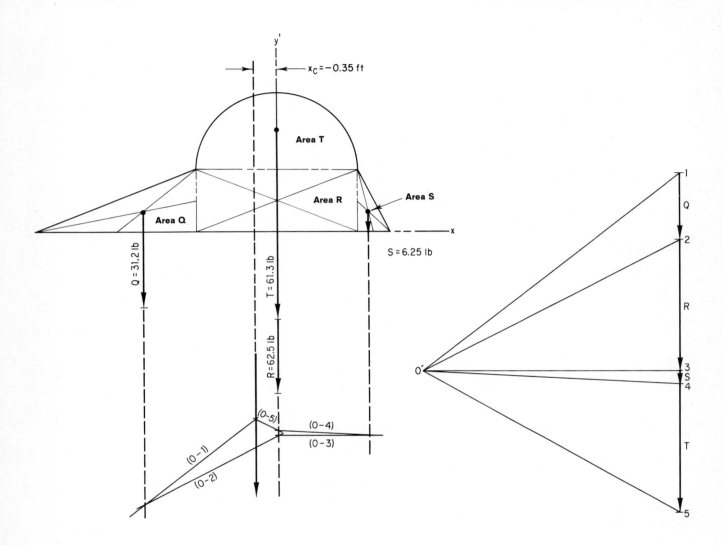

(a) Space Scale: 1 in. = 1 ft
     Vector Scale: 1 in. = 20 lb

(b) Vector Diagram
     Vector Scale: 1 in. = 20 lb

FIGURE C.8

Referring to Fig. C.1, we see that the *lifting force L_1 acting at A is equal to* $-F_A$.

d. *Maximum permissible weight of entire aircraft structure.* With the above data ($L_1 = 51.2$ lb and $L_2 = 110$ lb), we can easily determine the maximum permissible weight W_S of the entire aircraft structure by summing the vertical forces ($\sum F_y = 0$) acting on the structure (refer to Fig. C.10).

$$\sum F_y = 0$$

$$\therefore \ W_S + W_P = 2L_1 + 2L_2 + L_3 \sin \theta$$

$$\therefore \ W_S = 2L_1 + 2L_2 + L_3 \sin \theta - W_P$$

$$= 2(51.2 \text{ lb}) + 2(110 \text{ lb}) + \frac{5}{\sqrt{26}}(30 \text{ lb})$$

$$- 160 \text{ lb}$$

$$= 191.8 \text{ lb}$$

Part 3 To determine the line of action of the combined weight of the aircraft structure and the pilot such that the aircraft will be in rotational equilibrium about point O, we apply the principle of moments, using given and previously calculated data (refer to Fig. C.11).

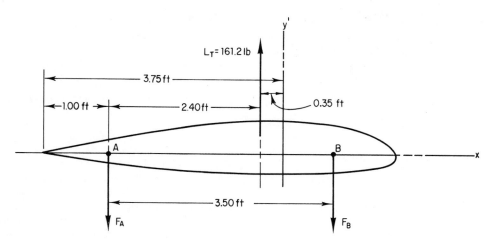

FIGURE C.9

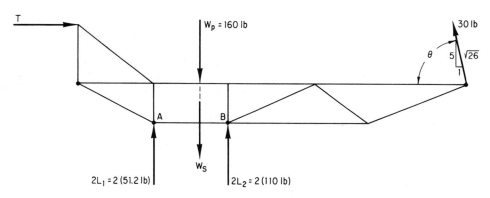

FIGURE C.10

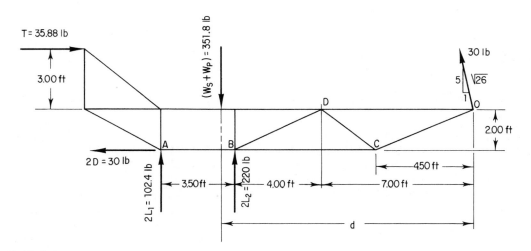

FIGURE C.11

Assuming that the weight of the aircraft structure and the weight of the pilot have the same line of action and keeping in mind that there are two points A, B, C, and D *each* on the aircraft structure, we can take moments about point O and write

$$(W_S + W_P)d = 3T + 2(2D) + 14.5(2L_1) + 11(2L_2)$$

Substituting known values for W_S, W_P, T, D, L_1, and L_2, we get

$$(191.8 + 160)d = 3.00(35.88) + 2.00(30)$$
$$+ 14.50(102.40) + 11(220)$$
$$\therefore\ 351.8d = 107.6 + 60.0 + 1484.8 + 2420$$
$$= 4072$$
$$\therefore\ d = \frac{4072}{351.8}$$
$$= 11.58 \text{ ft}$$

Part 4   To determine the loads W_1 and W_2 (due to the pilot's weight alone) acting at A and C, we can regard the weight of the pilot as being the resultant of the four parallel forces, $2W_1$ and $2W_2$. The magnitudes of W_1 and W_2 can then be determined by the application of Varignon's theorem. (Refer to Fig. C.12.)

Taking moments about C, we get

$$\sum M_C = 7.08 W_P = 10(2W_2)$$
$$\therefore\ W_2 = \frac{(7.08 \text{ ft})(W_P)}{20 \text{ ft}}$$
$$= \frac{(7.08 \text{ ft})(160 \text{ lb})}{20 \text{ ft}}$$
$$= 56.6 \text{ lb}$$

Taking moments about A, we get

$$\sum M_A = -2.92 W_P = -10(2W_1)$$
$$\therefore\ W_1 = \frac{(2.92 \text{ ft})(W_P)}{20 \text{ ft}}$$
$$= \frac{(2.92 \text{ ft})(160 \text{ lb})}{20 \text{ ft}}$$
$$= 23.4 \text{ lb}$$

Part 5   With the data obtained from previous calculations, we can now determine the magnitude and type of load that acts in members BD due to the external loading shown in Fig. C.1. (Actually, the loads in all the members of the aircraft structure can be determined at this stage if this were desired.)

Using the method of sections to solve this problem, we cut the aircraft structure by a plane, as shown in Fig. C.13; members BC, BD, and BE are assumed to be in tension. (NOTE: There are two BC members and two BD members.)

Using vector notation analysis, we may write vector equations using **i**, **j**, and **k** unit vector notation for the forces acting in the members BC, BD, and BE, remembering to include the proportionality constant (P.C.) based on the geometry of the aircraft structure and the spatial positions of the external loads:

$$30 \text{ lb} = (-\mathbf{i} + 5\mathbf{j} + 0\mathbf{k})\frac{30}{\sqrt{26}}$$
$$= \frac{30}{\sqrt{26}}\mathbf{i} + \frac{150}{\sqrt{26}}\mathbf{j} + 0\mathbf{k}$$
$$2F_{BC} = (-\mathbf{i} + 0\mathbf{j} + 0\mathbf{k})2F_{BC}$$
$$= -2F_{BC}\mathbf{i} + 0\mathbf{j} + 0\mathbf{k}$$

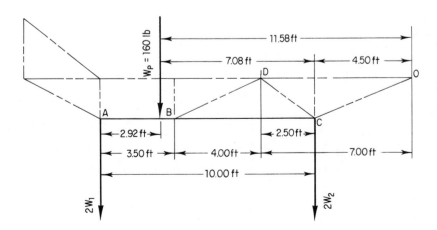

FIGURE C.12

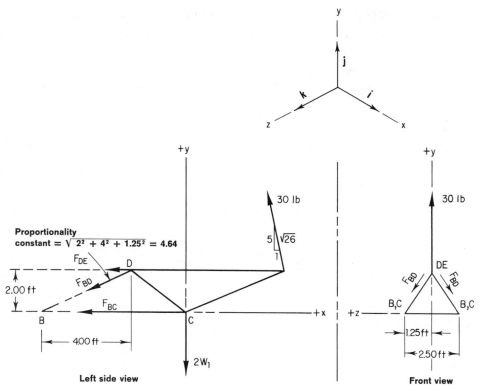

FIGURE C.13

F_{BD} (left side) $= (-4\mathbf{i} - 2\mathbf{j} + 1.25\mathbf{k}) \dfrac{F_{BD}}{4.64}$

$\qquad = \dfrac{-4F_{BD}}{4.64}\mathbf{i} - \dfrac{2F_{BD}}{4.64}\mathbf{j} + \dfrac{1.25F_{BD}}{4.64}\mathbf{k}$

F_{BD} (right side) $= (-4\mathbf{i} - 2\mathbf{j} - 1.25\mathbf{k}) \dfrac{F_{BD}}{4.64}$

$\qquad = \dfrac{-4F_{BD}}{4.64}\mathbf{i} - \dfrac{2F_{BD}}{4.64}\mathbf{j} - \dfrac{1.25F_{BD}}{4.64}\mathbf{k}$

$2W_1 = 46.8 = (0\mathbf{i} - \mathbf{j} + 0\mathbf{k})46.8$

$\qquad = 0\mathbf{i} - 46.8\mathbf{j} + 0\mathbf{k}$

If we examine the **j** *components* of all the vectors, we see that they involve only one unknown, F_{BD}. Summing these **j** components, we get for equilibrium conditions

$$\sum \mathbf{j} = \sum F_y = \left[\dfrac{150}{\sqrt{26}} - \dfrac{4F_{BD}}{4.64} - 46.8 \right]\mathbf{j} = 0$$

Solving for F_{BD}, we get

$$-\dfrac{4F_{BD}}{4.64} = 46.8 - \dfrac{150}{\sqrt{26}}$$

$$= 46.8 - 29.4 = 17.4$$

$$\therefore \ F_{BD} = -\dfrac{17.4(4.64)}{4}$$

$$= -20.1 \text{ lb compression}$$

(The minus sign indicates that the sense of the force is opposite to that assumed.)

(NOTE: This part of the problem obviously can be solved by using the direct algebraic approach to determine $\sum F_y = 0$.)

We could also apply direct graphical analysis, as in Fig. C.14, where the front and left side views are shown. Applying Bow's notation, as shown in the space diagram, we draw vectors representing the known external forces (30 lb and $2W_1$) to a vector scale followed in consecutive order by the directions of the unknown forces in the members in this section of the aircraft structure (see Vector Diagram in Fig. C.14).

The true length of the vector $[\overrightarrow{7\text{–}8}]$ representing the force in member BD is determined by revolution ($F_{BD} = 20$ lb compression).

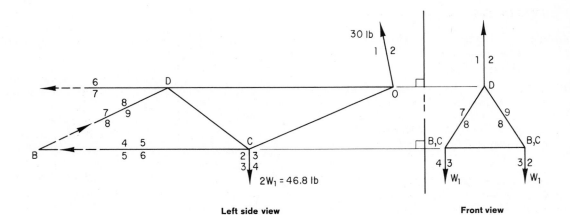

Space Diagram
Space Scale: 1 in. = 2 ft

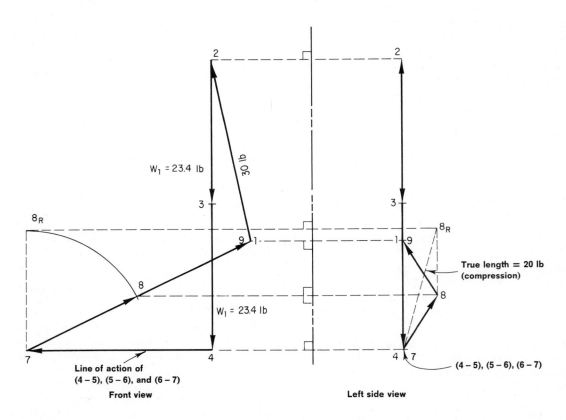

Vector Diagram
Vector Scale: 1 in. = 10 lb

FIGURE C.14

PROBLEM C.2 —————————————————

Given: A proposed mechanism for a weather rocket elevating and launching platform, as shown in Fig. C.15.

Find: The magnitude of the forces that act on each member of the mechanism and the force that the hydraulic cylinder must exert if body (1) of the platform is to be held in equilibrium in the position shown in Fig. C.15.

NOTE: The platform body (1) is supported by two lifting mechanisms, one on the left side of the platform and the other on the right side. The pins at *D* and *G* extend across the width of the platform body (1) and are common to both lifting mechanisms. There is a *single* hydraulic cylinder in this whole mechanism; it is attached to the pins *D* and *G* at their midspans. The load *L* acts through the center of gravity of the platform body (1) so that it is carried equally by the two lifting mechanisms that support the platform body (1). All of the pin joints are frictionless, and the weights of the individual members are small enough to be safely neglected in the analysis of this problem.

Solution Analysis

Part 1 Draw the free-body diagrams of all the members of the elevating and launching platform mechanism.

a. Free-body diagram of platform body (1). Since the load *L* is shared equally by the two lifting mechanisms (right and left sides) that support the platform body (1), the coplanar mechanism, as it appears in Fig. C.15, "feels" like one half of the applied load *L*. The portion of the platform body (1) supported by one of the lifting mechanisms is in equilibrium because of *three* forces that act upon it, and therefore, these forces must be *concurrent*. The line of action of the force at *B* is known, since member *BC* is a two-force member. Since the line of action of the load component is also known, the point of concurrency can be established. The force at *H* must pass through this point. (See Fig. C.16.)

It is important to note that there is only one force acting on the platform body at *H*, even though Fig. C.15 shows two other members that have one end common to that point. What must be remembered here is that these three parts of the mechanism are *not* interconnected directly,

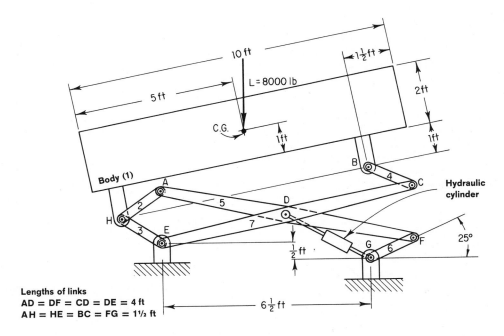

FIGURE C.15

Space Scale: $\frac{1}{2}$ in. = 1 ft

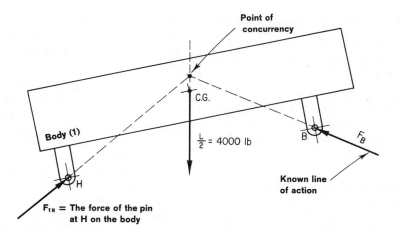

FIGURE C.16

but instead are indirectly connected through the existence of the pin at *H*. In isolating the platform body (1) to draw a free-body diagram of it, only the pin at *H* was removed, and therefore, only the *force of the pin on the body* has to be shown.

It is necessary to make this pin analysis only when *more than* two members are connected by a pin common to all. For example, at *B*, only two members are connected. The pin at *B* is therefore a two-force member, which means that the forces acting at *B* must be equal, opposite, and collinear for equilibrium. This being the case, the members connected by the pin at *B* must "feel" forces that are equal in magnitude and that have the same line of action.

b. *Free-body diagram of the pin at H*. The line of action of the force F_{1H} of the platform body (1) on the pin at *H* is known from the free-body diagram of the platform body (1). The line of action of the forces of members 2 and 3 on the pin at *H* (F_{2H} and F_{3H}, respectively) are known, since these members are two-force members. (See Fig. C.17.)

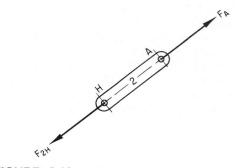

FIGURE C.18
Link 2 (*AH*)

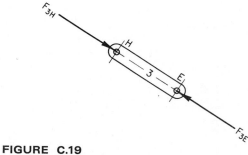

FIGURE C.19
Link 3 (*HE*)

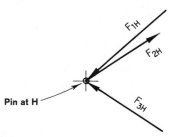

FIGURE C.17

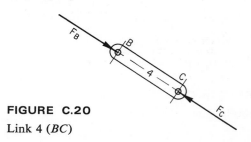

FIGURE C.20
Link 4 (*BC*)

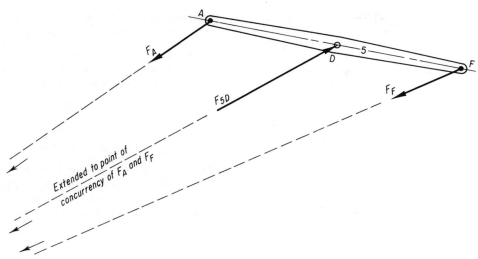

FIGURE C.21
Link 5 (*AF*)

c. *Free-body diagram of member 2 (AH)*. Refer to Fig. C.18.

d. *Free-body diagram of member 3 (HE)*. Refer to Fig. C.19. Note that the force at point *E* (F_{3E}) is due to the pin at *E* and is *not* due to link 4. This is because *three* different members are interconnected at *E* through the pin at *E*. (See Fig. C.15.)

e. *Free-body diagram of member 4 (BC)*. Refer to Fig. C.20.

f. *Free-body diagram of member 5 (AF)*. Refer to Fig. C.21. Point *D* is another example of a pin connecting three members: namely, members 5, 7, and the hydraulic cylinder (see Fig. C.15).

g. *Free-body diagram of the pin at D*. Refer to Fig. C.22. The hydraulic cylinder force (*F*) must be shared equally by the two lifting mechanisms (right and left sides), since it was specified as acting at the midspan of the pin at *D*. Therefore, the notation *F*/2 is used to record this fact. The line of action of the force of member 7 upon the pin at *D* is unknown; therefore, this force is represented by its *x* and *y* components. (See Fig. C.22.)

h. *Free-body diagram of member 6 (FG)*. Refer to Fig. C.23.

i. *Free-body diagram of member 7 (CE)*. Refer to Fig. C.24.

j. *Free-body diagram of entire mechanism*. Refer to Fig. C.25.

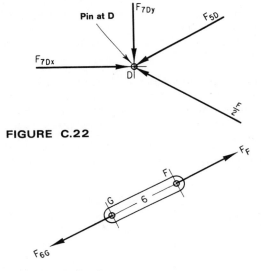

FIGURE C.22

FIGURE C.23
Link 6 (*FG*)

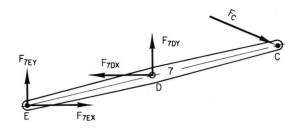

FIGURE C.24
Link 7 (*CE*)

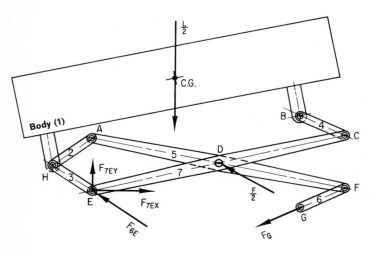

FIGURE C.25

Free-body Diagram of Entire Mechanism

Part 2   Using the free-body diagrams developed in Part I, specify the forces that act on each member of the given mechanism. Graphical analysis will be emphasized for convenience and for brevity of description.

a. Vector diagram for platform body (1). Inspection of the free-body diagram of the platform body (1) shows that the vector diagram in Fig. C.26 can be constructed to evaluate the unknown forces.

b. Vector diagram for the pin at H. Inspection of the freebody diagram of the pin at H shows that the

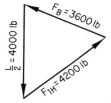

FIGURE C.26

Vector Diagram of Platform Body (1)
Vector Scale: 1 in. = 4000 lb

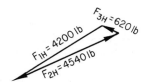

FIGURE C.27

Vector Diagram of Pin H
Vector Scale: 1 in. = 4000 lb

vector diagram in Fig. C.27 can be constructed to evaluate the unknowns at this point.

c. Inspection of the free-body diagram of members 2, 3, and 4 and the *vector diagrams* of the platform body (1) and the pin at H reveal that

$$F_{2H} = F_A = 4540 \text{ lb}$$

$$F_{3H} = F_{3E} = 620 \text{ lb}$$

$$F_B = F_C = 3600 \text{ lb}$$

d. Vector diagram for member 5. With the information obtained from the vector diagrams in Part II, above, it is now possible to draw the vector diagram of the forces acting on member 5, as shown in Fig. C.28.

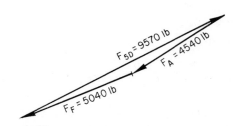

FIGURE C.28

Vector Diagram for Member 5
Vector Scale: 1 in. = 4000 lb

e. By inspection of the free-body diagram of member 6 and the vector diagram of member 5,

$$F_F = F_{6G} = 5040 \text{ lb}$$

f. Vector diagram for the entire mechanism. Vector diagrams cannot as yet be constructed from the free-body diagram of the pin at D or of member 7, since each of these diagrams contains too many unknowns. However, the free-body diagram of the *entire* mechanism (Fig. C.25) offers possibilities for the solution of its unknowns.

At this stage, the free-body diagram of the entire mechanism involves three unknown magnitudes: $F/2$, F_{7Ex}, and F_{7Ey}. Since three unknowns may be solved in the usual coplanar, nonconcurrent case, a solution can be obtained in this case in the following manner.

First, the resultant of *all* the known forces must be determined. (See Fig. C.29.) The system of forces that now acts on the entire mechanism consists of the resultant just obtained, the force $F/2$, and the *total* force of the pin at E acting on member 7 (F_{7E}). Since these three forces are in equilibrium, they must be concurrent. By ex-

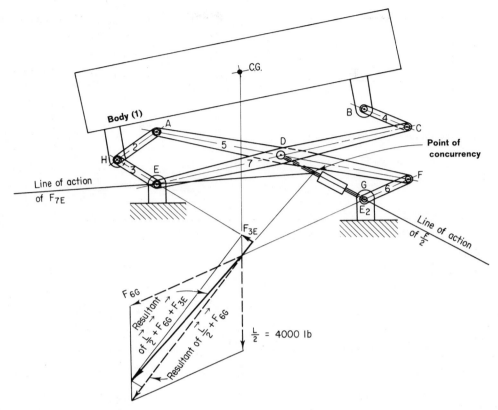

FIGURE C.29

Vector Diagram of All Known Forces
Vector Scale: 1 in. = 4000 lb

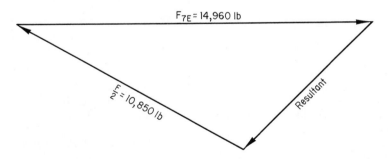

FIGURE C.30

Vector Diagram of Entire Mechanism
Vector Scale: 1 in. = 4000 lb

tending the line of action of the resultant force until it intersects the line of action of force $F/2$, we can determine the point of concurrency. (See Fig. C.29.) The line of action of force F_{7E} is now determined, and the vector diagram of the entire mechanism can be drawn, as shown in Fig. C.30.

g. *Vector diagram for the pin at D.* The last force to be determined is the force of the pin at D acting upon member 7 (F_{7D}). The free-body diagram of member 7 can be redrawn by incorporating the now known information about the force F_{7E}. (See Fig. C.31.)

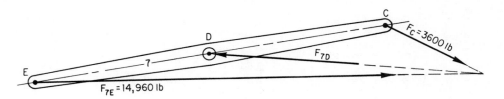

FIGURE C.31

Redrawn Free-body Diagram of Member 7

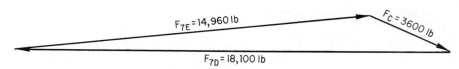

FIGURE C.32

Vector Diagram of Member 7
Vector Scale: 1 in. = 4000 lb

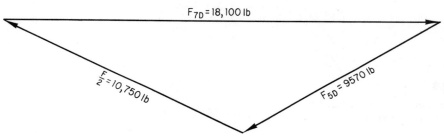

FIGURE C.33

Check Vector Diagram for Pin at D
Vector Scale: 1 in. = 4000 lb

Construct the vector diagram for the pin at D on the basis of the free-body diagram shown in Fig. C.31, as shown in Fig. C.32.

As a check, draw a vector diagram based on the the free-body diagram of the pin at D, as shown in Fig. C.33. The forces F_{7D} and F_{5D}, as determined in Fig. C.33, are added. The vector $F/2$ that is necessary to close the vector polygon is then drawn and compared with the answer previously obtained. If the line of action and magnitude agree closely with the previous values,

then it can be confidently assumed that no gross error has occurred during the construction of the graphical solution.

There are other methods of attacking this problem, both mathematical and graphical. It is recommended that the student carefully study the free-body diagrams developed above and attempt to devise alternative means of solving the given problem in order to verify, to himself, the magnitudes of the forces determined by the method used in this solution analysis.

APPENDIXES

BIBLIOGRAPHY

Statics

Beer, F. P., and E. R. Johnston, Jr. *Mechanics for Engineers*, 2nd ed., 2 vols. New York: McGraw-Hill, 1962.

Brown, Frank L. *Engineering Mechanics*, 2nd ed. New York: John Wiley & Sons, 1942.

Cox, G. N., and W. G. Plumtree. *Engineering Mechanics*, 2nd ed. Princeton, N. J.: D. Van Nostrand, 1954.

Den Hartog, J. P. *Mechanics*. New York: McGraw-Hill, 1948 (also, Dover, 1948).

Grinter, L. E. *Engineering Mechanics*. New York: Macmillan, 1953.

Higdon, A., and W. B. Stiles. *Engineering Mechanics*, 2nd ed., 2 vols. Englewood Cliffs, N. J.: Prentice-Hall, 1955.

Housner, G. W., and D. E. Hudson, *Applied Mechanics: Statics*, 2nd ed. Princeton, N. J.: D. Van Nostrand, 1961.

Jensen, A. *Applied Engineering Mechanics*, 2nd ed., 3 vols. New York: McGraw-Hill, 1960.

Langhaar, H. L., and A. P. Boresi. *Engineering Mechanics*, 2 vols. New York: McGraw-Hill, 1959.

Meriam, J. L. *Mechanics*, 2nd ed., 2 vols. New York: John Wiley & Sons, 1959.

Singer, F. L. *Engineering Mechanics*, 2 vols. New York: Harper & Row, 1954.

Timoshenko, S., and D. H. Young. *Engineering Mechanics*, 4th ed., 2 vols. New York: McGraw-Hill, 1956.

Strength of Materials

Alcoa Structural Handbook. Aluminum Company of America, 200 Park Avenue, Pittsburgh, Pa., 1960.

Alexander, J. M., and R. C. Brewer. *Manufacturing Properties of Materials*. Princeton, N. J.: D. Van Nostrand, 1963.

Bassin, Milton G., and Stanley M. Brodsky. *Statics and Strength of Materials*. New York: McGraw-Hill, 1960.

Begeman, Myron L., and B. H. Amstead. *Manufacturing Processes*, 4th ed. New York: John Wiley & Sons, 1960.

Brady, G. S. *Materials Handbook*, 9th ed. New York: McGraw-Hill, 1963.

Breneman, John W. *Strength of Materials*, 3rd ed. New York: McGraw-Hill, 1965.

Building Code Requirements for Reinforced Concrete. American Concrete Institute, Redford Station, Detroit, Mich., 1963.

Cernica, John H. *Strength of Materials*. New York: Holt, Rinehart, and Winston, 1966.

Degarmo, E. P., *Materials and Processes in Manufacturing*. New York: Macmillan, 1957.

Doyle, L. M., *et al. Manufacturing Processes and Materials for Engineers*. Englewood Cliffs, N. J.: Prentice-Hall, 1961.

Edelglass, S. M. *Engineering Materials Science*. New York: Ronald Press, 1966.

Edgar, Carroll. *Fundamentals of Manufacturing Processes and Materials*. Reading, Mass.: Addison-Wesley, 1965.

Fitzgerald, Robert W. *Strength of Materials*. Reading, Mass.: Addison-Wesley, 1967.

Kinney, G. F. *Engineering Properties and Applications of Plastics*. New York: John Wiley & Sons, 1957.

Lyman, Taylor (Ed.). *Metals Handbook*. American Society for Metals, Metals Park, Ohio, 1964.

Mahin, W. E., and H. W. Lownie, Jr. *The Engineering Properties of Cast Iron*. American Foundrymen's Society, Golf and Wolf Roads, Des Plaines, Iowa, 1950.

McGannon, H. E. (Ed.). *The Making, Shaping and Treating of Steel*, 8th ed. United States Steel Corporation, 525 William Penn Place, Pittsburgh, Pa., 1964.

Modern Steels and Their Properties. Bethlehem Steel Corporation, Bethlehem, Pa., 1960.

Moore, H. F. *Textbook of the Materials of Engineering*. New York: McGraw-Hill, 1953.

Murphy, Glenn. *Properties of Engineering Materials*. Scranton, Pa.: International Textbook Company, 1939.

Olsen, Gerner A. *Elements of Mechanics of Materials*. Englewood Cliffs, N.J.: Prentice-Hall, 1958.

Samons, Carl H. *Engineering Metals and Their Alloys*. New York: Macmillan, 1949.

Sinnott, Maurice J. *The Solid State for Engineers*. New York: John Wiley & Sons, 1958.

Van Vlack, Lawrence H. *Elements of Materials Science*. Reading, Mass.: Addison-Wesley, 1959.

Woldman, N. E. *Engineering Alloys*, 4th ed. New York: Reinhold, 1962.

Wood Handbook. United States Department of Agriculture, Washington, D.C., 1955.

ORGANIZATIONS CONCERNED WITH STRENGTH OF MATERIALS

Aluminum Association
420 Lexington Avenue
New York, New York   10017

American Concrete Institute
P.O. Box 4754
Redford Station
Detroit, Michigan   48219

American Institute of Steel Construction (AISC)
101 Park Avenue
New York, New York   10017

American Iron and Steel Institute (AISI)
150 East 42 Street
New York, New York   10017

American Railway Engineering Association (AREA)
59 East Van Buren Street
Chicago, Illinois   60605

American Society for Testing and Materials (ASTM)
1916 Race Street
Philadelphia, Pennsylvania   19103

American Society of Civil Engineers (ASCE)
345 East 47 Street
New York, New York   10017

American Society of Mechanical Engineers (ASME)
345 East 47 Street
New York, New York   10017

American Welding Society (AWS)
345 East 47 Street
New York, New York   10017

National Bureau of Standards
U.S. Department of Commerce

1700 K Street, N.W.
Washington, D.C.   20234

Concrete Reinforcing Steel Institute
228 North LaSalle Street
Chicago, Illinois   60601

Construction Specifications Institute, Inc.
1717 Massachusetts Avenue, N.W.
Washington, D.C.   20036

Forest Products Research Society
417 North Walnut Street
Madison, Wisconsin   53705

National Forest Products Association
1619 Massachusetts Avenue, N.W.
Washington, D.C.   20036

Portland Cement Association
33 West Grand Avenue
Chicago, Illinois   60610

Society for Experimental Stress Analysis (SESA)
21 Bridge Square
Westport, Connecticut   06880

Society for Non-Destructive Testing
914 Chicago Avenue
Evanston, Illinois   60202

Society of Automotive Engineers (SAE)
485 Lexington Avenue
New York, New York   10017

Steel Founder's Society of America
Westview Towers
21010 Center Ridge Road
Rocky River, Ohio   44116

INDEX